Mikhail J. Atallah   Nicholas J. Hopper (Eds.)

Privacy Enhancing Technologies

10th International Symposium, PETS 2010
Berlin, Germany, July 21-23, 2010
Proceedings

 Springer

Volume Editors

Mikhail J. Atallah
Purdue University
Department of Computer Science
West Lafayette, IN 47907-2107, USA
E-mail: mja@cs.purdue.edu

Nicholas J. Hopper
University of Minnesota
Department of Computer Science & Engineering
Minneapolis, MN 55455, USA
E-mail: hopper@cs.umn.edu

Library of Congress Control Number: 2010930652

CR Subject Classification (1998): K.6.5, E.3, C.2, D.4.6, H.5, E.4

LNCS Sublibrary: SL 4 – Security and Cryptology

ISSN   0302-9743
ISBN-10   3-642-14526-4 Springer Berlin Heidelberg New York
ISBN-13   978-3-642-14526-1 Springer Berlin Heidelberg New York

springer.com

Printed in Germany

Typesetting: Camera-ready by author, data conversion by Scientific Publishing Services, Chennai, India
Printed on acid-free paper   06/3180

Lecture Notes in Computer Science   6205

Commenced Publication in 1973
Founding and Former Series Editors:
Gerhard Goos, Juris Hartmanis, and Jan van Leeuwen

The original version of the book frontmatter was revised:
The copyright line was incorrect. The Erratum
to the book frontmatter is available at
DOI: 10.1007/978-3-642-14527-8_17

Message from the Program Chairs

The 2010 Privacy-Enhancing Technologies Symposium was held at the Hotel Berlin in Berlin during July 21-23, 2010. It was the 10th in this series of meetings, and the third after the transition from workshop to symposium. PETS remains a premier forum for publishing research on both the theory and the practice of privacy-enhancing technologies, and has a broad scope that includes all facets of the field.

The PETS program this year included a diverse set of 16 peer-reviewed papers, selected from 57 submissions. Each submission was reviewed by at least three members of the Program Committee. This was the third year of the popular HotPETs session, designed as a venue to present exciting but still preliminary and evolving ideas, rather than formal and rigorous completed research results. HotPETs this year included a program of 11 presentations of 10–20 minutes each; as was the case in each of the last two years, there were no published proceedings for HotPETs. PETS also included the traditional "rump session," with brief presentations on a variety of topics.

We are grateful to all of the authors who submitted, to the PETS and Hot-PETs speakers who presented their work selected for the program, and to the rump session participants. We are also grateful to the Program Committee members, and to the external reviewers who assisted them, for their thorough reviews and participation in discussions – they were central to the resulting high-quality program. The following subset of these reviewers gracefully volunteered to continue their work as shepherds helping the authors improve their papers and address the reviewer comments and suggestions: Nikita Borisov, Rachel Greenstadt, Aaron Johnson, and Meredith Patterson. It is a also a pleasure to acknowledge the contribution of our General Chair, Hannes Federrath, and our webmaster since 2007, Jeremy Clark, who did his usual outstanding job at evolving and maintaining the symposium's website. Our gratitude also goes to the HotPETs Chairs, Carmela Troncoso and Andrei Serjantov, who put together an outstanding HotPETs program. Finally, we are particularly grateful to Microsoft for its continued sponsorship and support.

May 2010   Mikhail Atallah
                                                               Nicholas Hopper

Organization

External Reviewers

Elli Androulaki
Stefan Berthold
Scott Coull
Dana Dachman-Soled
Roger Dingledine
Elizabeth Durham
Seung Geol Choi
Xun Gong
Hans Hedbom
Man Ho Allen Au
Sonia Jahid
Meredith L. Patterson
Michael Locasto

Grigorios Loukides
Damon McCoy
Prateek Mittal
David Molnar
Mariana Raykova
Alfredo Rial
Sherman S. M. Chow
Stefan Schiffner
Eugene Vasserman
Qiyan Wang
Matthew Wright
Ge Zhang

Table of Contents

2010 Privacy Enhancing Technologies Symposium

How Unique Is Your Web Browser?

Peter Eckersley[*]

Electronic Frontier Foundation
pde@eff.org

Abstract. We investigate the degree to which modern web browsers are subject to "device fingerprinting" via the version and configuration information that they will transmit to websites upon request. We implemented one possible fingerprinting algorithm, and collected these fingerprints from a large sample of browsers that visited our test side, panopticlick.eff.org. We observe that the distribution of our fingerprint contains at least 18.1 bits of entropy, meaning that if we pick a browser at random, at best we expect that only one in 286,777 other browsers will share its fingerprint. Among browsers that support Flash or Java, the situation is worse, with the average browser carrying at least 18.8 bits of identifying information. 94.2% of browsers with Flash or Java were unique in our sample.

By observing returning visitors, we estimate how rapidly browser fingerprints might change over time. In our sample, fingerprints changed quite rapidly, but even a simple heuristic was usually able to guess when a fingerprint was an "upgraded" version of a previously observed browser's fingerprint, with 99.1% of guesses correct and a false positive rate of only 0.86%.

We discuss what privacy threat browser fingerprinting poses in practice, and what countermeasures may be appropriate to prevent it. There is a tradeoff between protection against fingerprintability and certain kinds of debuggability, which in current browsers is weighted heavily against privacy. Paradoxically, anti-fingerprinting privacy technologies can be self-defeating if they are not used by a sufficient number of people; we show that some privacy measures currently fall victim to this paradox, but others do not.

1 Introduction

It has long been known that many kinds of technological devices possess subtle but measurable variations which allow them to be "fingerprinted". Cameras [1,2], typewriters [3], and quartz crystal clocks [4,5] are among the devices that can be

---

[*] Thanks to my colleagues at EFF for their help with many aspects of this project, especially Seth Schoen, Tim Jones, Hugh D'Andrade, Chris Controllini, Stu Matthews, Rebecca Jeschke and Cindy Cohn; to Jered Wierzbicki, John Buckman and Igor Serebryany for MySQL advice; and to Andrew Clausen, Arvind Narayanan and Jonathan Mayer for helpful discussions about the data. Thanks to Chris Soghoian for suggesting backoff as a defence to font enumeration.

M.J. Atallah and N. Hopper (Eds.): PETS 2010, LNCS 6205, pp. 1–18, 2010.

entirely or substantially identified by a remote attacker possessing only outputs or communications from the device.

There are several companies that sell products which purport to fingerprint web browsers in some manner [6,7], and there are anecdotal reports that these prints are being used both for analytics and second-layer authentication purposes. But, aside from limited results from one recent experiment [8], there is to our knowledge no information in the public domain to quantify how much of a privacy problem fingerprinting may pose.

In this paper we investigate the real-world effectiveness of browser fingerprinting algorithms. We defined one candidate fingerprinting algorithm, and collected these fingerprints from a sample of 470,161 browsers operated by informed participants who visited the website https://panopticlick.eff.org. The details of the algorithm, and our collection methodology, are discussed in Section 3. While our sample of browsers is quite biased, it is likely to be representative of the population of Internet users who pay enough attention to privacy to be aware of the minimal steps, such as limiting cookies or perhaps using proxy servers for sensitive browsing, that are generally agreed to be necessary to avoid having most of one's browsing activities tracked and collated by various parties.

In this sample of privacy-conscious users, 83.6% of the browsers seen had an instantaneously unique fingerprint, and a further 5.3% had an anonymity set of size 2. Among visiting browsers that had either Adobe Flash or a Java Virtual Machine enabled, 94.2% exhibited instantaneously unique fingerprints and a further 4.8% had fingerprints that were seen exactly twice. Only 1.0% of browsers with Flash or Java had anonymity sets larger than two. Overall, we were able to place a lower bound on the fingerprint distribution entropy of 18.1 bits, meaning that if we pick a browser at random, at best only one in 286,777 other browsers will share its fingerprint. Our results are presented in further detail in Section 4.

In our data, fingerprints changed quite rapidly. Among the subset of 8,833 users who accepted cookies and visited panopticlick.eff.org several times over a period of more than 24 hours, 37.4% exhibited at least one fingerprint change. This large percentage may in part be attributable to the interactive nature of the site, which immediately reported the uniqueness or otherwise of fingerprints and thereby encouraged users to find ways to alter them, particularly to try to make them less unique. Even if 37.4% is an overestimate, this level of fingerprint instability was at least momentary grounds for privacy optimism.

Unfortunately, we found that a simple algorithm was able to guess and follow many of these fingerprint changes. If asked about all newly appearing fingerprints in the dataset, the algorithm was able to correctly pick a "progenitor" fingerprint in 99.1% of cases, with a false positive rate of only 0.87%. The analysis of changing fingerprints is presented in Section 5.

2   Fingerprints as Threats to Web Privacy

The most common way to track web browsers (by "track" we mean associate the browser's activities at different times and with different websites) is via HTTP cookies, often set by with 3rd party analytics and advertising domains [9].

There is growing awareness among web users that HTTP cookies are a serious threat to privacy, and many people now block, limit or periodically delete them. Awareness of supercookies is lower, but political and PR pressures may eventually force firms like Adobe to make their supercookies comply with the browser's normal HTTP cookie privacy settings.

In the mean time, a user seeking to avoid being followed around the Web must pass three tests. The first is tricky: find appropriate settings that allow sites to use cookies for necessary user interface features, but prevent other less welcome kinds of tracking. The second is harder: learn about all the kinds of supercookies, perhaps including some quite obscure types [10,11], and find ways to disable them. Only a tiny minority of people will pass the first two tests, but those who do will be confronted by a third challenge: fingerprinting.

As a tracking mechanism for use against people who limit cookies, fingerprinting also has the insidious property that it may be much harder for investigators to detect than supercookie methods, since it leaves no persistent evidence of tagging on the user's computer.

2.1 Fingerprints as Global Identifiers

If there is enough entropy in the distribution of a given fingerprinting algorithm to make a recognisable subset of users unique, that fingerprint may essentially be usable as a 'Global Identifier' for those users. Such a global identifier can be thought of as akin to a cookie that cannot be deleted except by a browser configuration change that is large enough to break the fingerprint.

Global identifier fingerprints are a worst case for privacy. But even users who are not globally identified by a particular fingerprint may be vulnerable to more context-specific kinds of tracking by the same fingerprint algorithm, if the print is used in combination with other data.

2.2 Fingerprint + IP Address as Cookie Regenerators

Some websites use Adobe's Flash LSO supercookies as a way to 'regenerate' normal cookies that the user has deleted, or more discretely, to link the user's previous cookie ID with a newly assigned cookie ID [12].

Fingerprints may pose a similar 'cookie regeneration' threat, even if those fingerprints are not globally identifying. In particular, a fingerprint that carries no more than 15-20 bits of identifying information will in almost all cases be sufficient to uniquely identify a particular browser, given its IP address, its subnet, or even just its Autonomous System Number.[1] If the user deletes their cookies

---

[1] One possible exception is that workplaces which synchronize their desktop software installations completely may provide anonymity sets against this type of attack. We were able to detect installations like this because of the appearance of interleaved cookies (A then B then A) with the same fingerprint and IP. Fingerprints that use hardware measurements such as clock skew [5] (see also note 4) would often be able to distinguish amongst these sorts of "cloned" systems.

while continuing to use an IP address, subnet or ASN that they have used previously, the cookie-setter could, with high probability, link their new cookie to the old one.

2.3   Fingerprint + IP Address in the Absence of Cookies

A final use for fingerprints is as a means of distinguishing machines behind a single IP address, even if those machines block cookies entirely. It is very likely that fingerprinting will work for this purpose in all but a tiny number of cases.

3   Methodology

3.1   A Browser Fingerprinting Algorithm

We implemented a browser fingerprinting algorithm by collecting a number of commonly and less-commonly known characteristics that browsers make available to websites. Some of these can be inferred from the content of simple, static HTTP requests; others were collected by AJAX[2]. We grouped the measurements into eight separate strings, though some of these strings comprise multiple, related details. The fingerprint is essentially the concatenation of these strings. The source of each measurement and is indicated in Table 1.

In some cases the informational content of the strings is straightforward, while in others the measurement can capture more subtle facts. For instance, a browser with JavaScript disabled will record default values for `video`, `plugins`, `fonts` and `supercookies`, so the presence of these measurements indicates that JavaScript is active. More subtly, browsers with a Flash blocking add-on installed show Flash in the `plugins` list, but fail to obtain a list of system fonts via Flash, thereby creating a distinctive fingerprint, even though neither measurement (`plugins`, `fonts`) explicitly detects the Flash blocker. Similarly many browsers with forged User Agent strings are distinguished because the other measurements do not comport with the User Agent.[3]

An example of the fingerprint measurements is shown in Table 3. In fact, Table 3 shows the modal fingerprint among browsers that included Flash or Java plugins; it was observed 16 times from 16 distinct IP addresses.

There are many other measurements which could conceivably have been included in a fingerprint. Generally, these were omitted for one of three reasons:

1. We were unaware of the measurement, or lacked the time to implement it correctly — including the full use of Microsoft's ActiveX and Silverlight APIs

---

[2] AJAX is JavaScript that runs inside the browser and sends information back to the server.

[3] We did not set out to systematically study the prevalence of forged User Agents in our data, but in passing we noticed 378 browsers sending iPhone User Agents but with Flash player plugins installed (the iPhone does not currently support Flash), and 72 browsers that identified themselves as Firefox but supported Internet Explorer userData supercookies.

Table 1. Browser measurements included in Panopticlick Fingerprints

Variable	Source	Remarks
User Agent	Transmitted by HTTP, logged by server	Contains Browser micro-version, OS version, language, toolbars and sometimes other info.
HTTP ACCEPT headers	Transmitted by HTTP, logged by server	
Cookies enabled?	Inferred in HTTP, logged by server	
Screen resolution	JavaScript AJAX post	
Timezone	JavaScript AJAX post	
Browser plugins, plugin versions and MIME types	JavaScript AJAX post	Sorted before collection. Microsoft Internet Explorer offers no way to enumerate plugins; we used the PluginDetect JavaScript library to check for 8 common plugins on that platform, plus extra code to estimate the Adobe Acrobat Reader version.
System fonts	Flash applet or Java applet, collected by JavaScript/AJAX	Not sorted; see Section 6.4.
Partial supercookie test	JavaScript AJAX post	We did not implement tests for Flash LSO cookies, Silverlight cookies, HTML 5 databases, or DOM globalStorage.

to collect fingerprintable measures (which include CPU type and many other details); detection of more plugins in Internet Explorer; tests for other kinds of supercookies; detection of system fonts by CSS introspection, even when Flash and Java are absent [13]; the order in which browsers send HTTP headers; variation in HTTP Accept headers across requests for different content types; clock skew measurements; TCP stack fingerprinting [14]; and a wide range of subtle JavaScript behavioural tests that may indicate both browser add-ons and true browser versions [15].

2. We did not believe that the measurement would be sufficiently stable within a given browser — including geolocation, IP addresses (either yours or your gateway's) as detected using Flash or Java, and the CSS history detection hack [16].

3. The measurement requires consent from the user before being collectable — for instance, Google Gears supercookie support or the wireless router–based geolocation features included in recent browsers [17] (which are also non-constant).

In general, it should be assumed that commercial browser fingerprinting services would not have omitted measurements for reason 1 above, and that as a result, commercial fingerprinting methods would be more powerful than the one studied here.[4]

3.2   Mathematical Treatment

Suppose that we have a browser fingerprinting algorithm $F(\cdot)$, such that when new browser installations x come into being, the outputs of $F(x)$ upon them follow a discrete probability density function $P(f_n)$, $n \in [0, 1, .., N]$.[5] Recall that the "self-information" or " surprisal" of a particular output from the algorithm is given by:

$$I\big(F(x) = f_n\big) = -\log_2\big(P(f_n)\big), \tag{1}$$

The surprisal I is measured here in units of bits, as a result of the choice of 2 as the logarithm base. The *entropy* of the distribution $P(f_n)$ is the expected value of the surprisal over all browsers, given by:

$$H(F) = -\sum_{n=0}^{N} P(f_n) \log_2\big(P(f_n)\big) \tag{2}$$

Surprisal can be thought of as an amount of information about the identity of the object that is being fingerprinted, where each bit of information cuts the number of possibilities in half. If a website is regularly visited with equal probability by a set of X different browsers, we would intuitively estimate that a particular browser $x \in X$ would be uniquely recognisable if $I\big(F(x)\big) \gtrless log_2|X|$. The binomial distribution could be applied to replace this intuition with proper confidence intervals, but it turns out that with real fingerprints, much bigger uncertainties arise with our estimates of $P(f_n)$, at least when trying to answer questions about which browsers are uniquely recognisable. This topic will be reprised in Section 4.1, after more details on our methodology and results.

In the case of a fingerprint formed by combining several different measurements $F_s(\cdot), s \in S$, it is meaningful to talk about the surprisal of any particular

---

[4] While this paper was under review, we were sent a quote from a Gartner report on fingerprinting services that stated,

> Arcot... claims it is able to ascertain PC clock processor speed, along with more-common browser factors to help identify a device. 41st Parameter looks at more than 100 parameters, and at the core of its algorithm is a time differential parameter that measures the time difference between a user's PC (down to the millisecond) and a server's PC. ThreatMetrix claims that it can detect irregularities in the TCP/IP stack and can pierce through proxy servers... Iovation provides device tagging (through LSOs) and clientless [fingerprinting], and is best distinguished by its reputation database, which has data on millions of PCs.

[5] Real browser fingerprints are the result of decentralised decisions by software developers, software users, and occasionally, technical accident. It is not obvious what the set of possible values is, or even how large that set is. Although it is finite, the set is large and sparse, with all of the attendant problems for privacy that that poses [18].

measurement, and to define entropy for that component of the fingerprint accordingly:

$$I_s(f_{n,s}) = -\log_2\left(P(f_{n,s})\right) \tag{3}$$

$$H_s(F_s) = -\sum_{n=0}^{N} P(f_{s,n})\log_2\left(P(f_{s,n})\right) \tag{4}$$

Note that the surprisal of two fingerprint components F_s and F_t can only be added linearly if the two variables are statistically independent, which tends not to be the case. Instead, conditional self-information must be used:

$$I_{s+t}(f_{n,s}, f_{n,t}) = -\log_2\left(P(f_{n,s} \mid f_{n,t})\right) \tag{5}$$

Cases like the identification of a Flash blocker by combination of separate plugin and font measurements (see Section 3.1) are predicted accordingly, because $P(\texttt{fonts} = \text{"not detected"} \mid \text{"Flash"} \in \texttt{plugins})$ is very small.

3.3   Data Collection and Preprocessing

We deployed code to collect our fingerprints and report them — along with simple self-information measurements calculated from live fingerprint tallies — at `panopticlick.eff.org`. A large number of people heard about the site through websites like Slashdot, BoingBoing, Lifehacker, Ars Technica, io9, and through social media channels like Twitter, Facebook, Digg and Reddit. The data for this paper was collected between the 27th of January and the 15th of February, 2010.

For each HTTP client that followed the "test me" link at `panopticlick.eff.org`, we recorded the fingerprint, as well as a 3-month persistent HTTP cookie ID (if the browser accepted cookies), an HMAC of the IP address (using a key that we later discarded), and an HMAC of the IP address with the least significant octet erased.

We kept live tallies of each fingerprint, but in order to reduce double-counting, we did not increment the live tally if we had previously seen that precise fingerprint with that precise cookie ID. Before computing the statistics reported throughout this paper, we undertook several further offline preprocessing steps.

Firstly, we excluded a number of our early data points, which had been collected before the diagnosis and correction of some minor bugs in our client side JavaScript and database types. We excluded the records that had been directly affected by these bugs, and (in order to reduce biasing) other records collected while the bugs were present.

Next, we undertook some preprocessing to correct for the fact that some users who blocked, deleted or limited the duration of cookies had been multi-counted in the live data, while those whose browsers accepted our persistent cookie would not be. We assumed that all browsers with identical fingerprints and identical IP addresses were the same.

There was one exception to the (fingerprint, IP) rule. If a (fingerprint, IP) tuple exhibited "interleaved" cookies, all distinct cookies at that IP were counted as separate instances of that fingerprint. "Interleaved" meant that the same fingerprint was seen from the same IP address first with cookie A, then cookie B, then cookie A again, which would likely indicate that multiple identical systems were operating behind a single firewall. We saw interleaved cookies from 2,585 IP addresses, which was 3.5% of the total number of IP addresses that exhibited either multiple signatures or multiple cookies.

Starting with 1,043,426 hits at the test website, the successive steps described above produced a population of 470,161 fingerprint-instances, with minimal multi-counting, for statistical analysis.

Lastly we considered whether over-counting might occur because of hosts changing IP addresses. We were able to detect such IP changes among cookie-accepting browsers; 14,849 users changed IPs, with their subsequent destinations making up 4.6% of the 321,155 IP addresses from which users accepted cookies. This percentage was small enough to accept it as an error rate; had it been large, we could have reduced the weight of every non-cookie fingerprint by this percentage, in order to counteract the over-counting of non-cookie users who were visiting the site from multiple IPs.

4   Results

The frequency distribution of fingerprints we observed is shown in Figure 1. Were the x axis not logarithmic, it would be a strongly "L"-shaped distribution, with 83.6% in an extremely long tail of unique fingerprints at the bottom right, 8.1% having fingerprints that were fairly "non rare", with anonymity set sizes in our

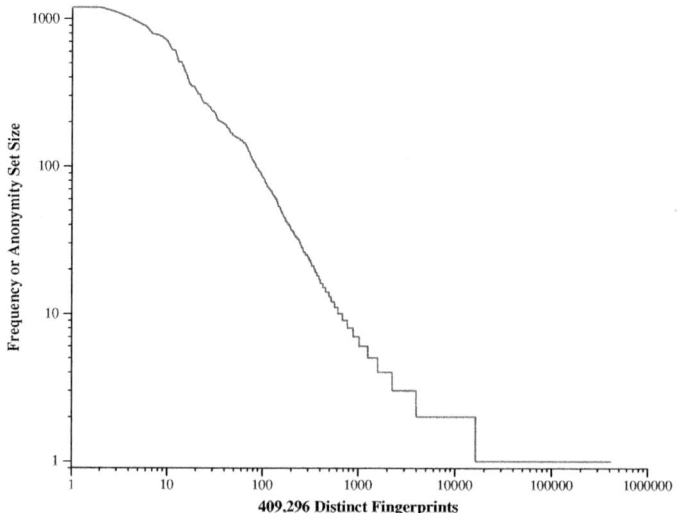

Fig. 1. The observed distribution of fingerprints is extremely skewed, with 83.6% of fingerprints lying in the tail on the right

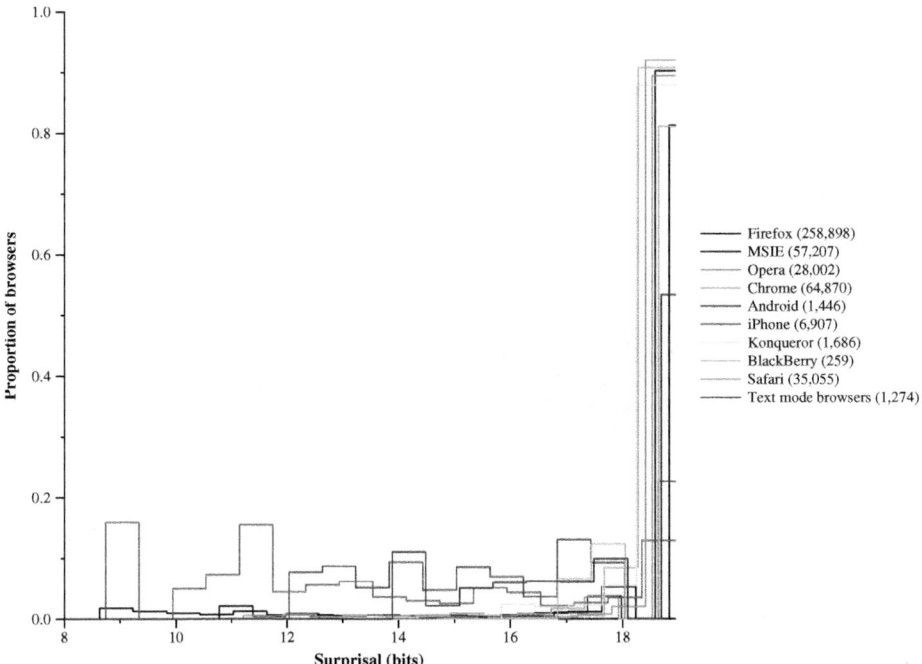

Fig. 2. Surprisal distributions for different categories of browser
(believing the User Agent naively; see note 3)

sample of 10, and 8.2% in the joint of the L-curve, with fingerprints that were
seen between 2 and 9 times.

Figure 2 shows the distribution of surprisal for different browsers. In general, modern desktop browsers fare very poorly, and around 90% of these are
unique. The least unique desktop browsers often have JavaScript disabled (perhaps via NoScript). iPhone and Android browsers are significantly more uniform and harder to fingerprint than desktop browsers; for the time being, these
smartphones do not have the variety of plugins seen on desktop systems.[6] Sadly,
iPhones and Androids lack good cookie control options like session-cookies-only
or blacklists, so their users are eminently trackable by non-fingerprint means.

Figure 3 shows the sizes of the anonymity sets that would be induced if each
of our eight measurements were used as a fingerprint on its own. In general,
plugins and fonts are the most identifying metrics, followed by User Agent,
HTTP Accept, and screen resolution, though all of the metrics are uniquely
identifying in some cases.

---

[6] Android and iPhone fonts are also hard to detect for the time being, so these are
also less fingerprintable.

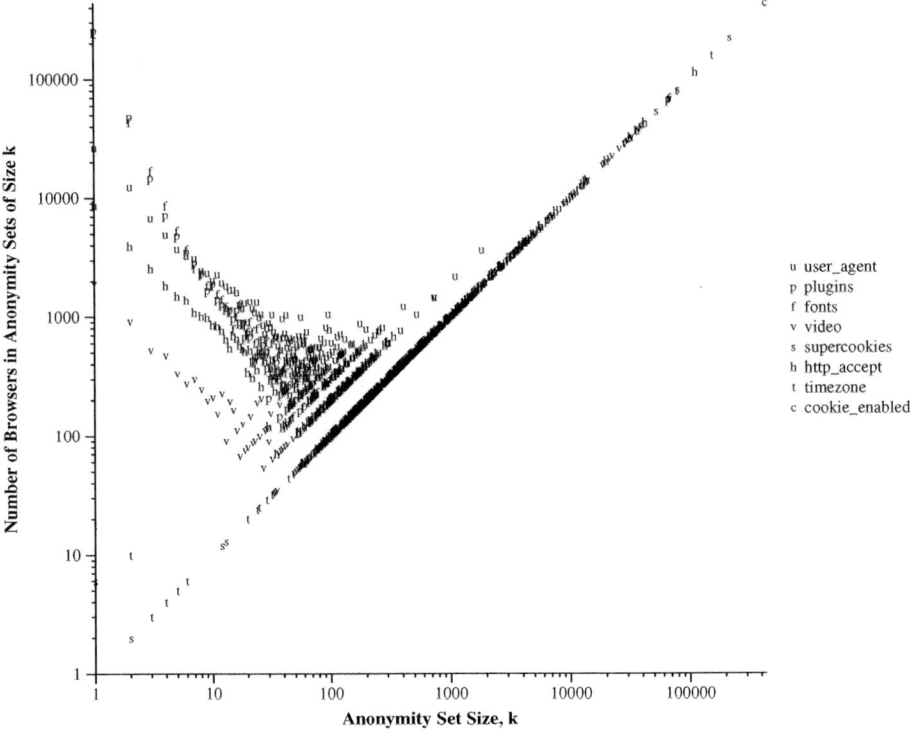

Fig. 3. Number of users in anonymity sets of different sizes, considering each variable separately

4.1   Global Uniqueness

We know that in the particular sample of browsers observed by Panopticlick, 83.6% had unique fingerprints. But we might be interested in the question of what percentage of browsers in existence are unique, regardless of whether they visited our test website.

Mayer has argued [8] that it is almost impossible to reach any conclusions about the *global* uniqueness of a browser fingerprint, because the multinominal theorem indicates that the maximum likelihood for the probability of any fingerprint that was unique in a sample of size N is:

$$P(f_i) = \frac{1}{N} \qquad (6)$$

A fingerprint with this probability would be *far* from unique in the global set of browsers G, because $G \gg N$. This may indeed be the maximum subjective likelihood for any single fingerprint that we observe, but in fact, this conclusion is wildly over-optimistic for privacy. If the probability of each unique fingerprint in the sample N had been $\frac{1}{N}$, the applying the multinomial expansion for those 392,938 events of probabilty $\frac{1}{N}$, it would have been inordinately unlikely that we would have seen each of these events precisely once. Essentially, the maximum likelihood approach has assigned a probability of zero for all fingerprints that were not seen in the sample N, when in fact many new fingerprints would appear in a larger sample G.

What we could attempt to meaningfully infer is the global *proportion* of uniqueness. The best way to do that would be to fit a very-long-tailed probability density function so that it reasonably predicts Figure 1. Then, we could employ Monte Carlo simulations to estimate levels of uniqueness and fingerprint entropy in a global population of any given size G. Furthermore, this method could offer confidence intervals for the proposition that a fingerprint unique in N would remain unique in G.

We did not prioritise conducting that analysis for a fairly prosaic reason: the dataset collected at `panopticlick.eff.org` is so biased towards technically educated and privacy-conscious users that it is somewhat meaningless to extrapolate it out to a global population size. If other fingerprint datasets are collected that do not suffer from this level of bias, it may be interesting to extrapolate from those.

5   How Stable Are Browser Fingerprints?

Many events can cause a browser fingerprint to change. In the case of the algorithm we deployed, those events include upgrades to the browser, upgrading a plugin, disabling cookies, installing a new font or an external application which includes fonts, or connecting an external monitor which alters the screen resolution.

By collecting other tracking information alongside fingerprints, we were able to observe how constant or changeable fingerprints were among Panopticlick users. In particular, we used cookies to recognise browsers that were returning visitors, and checked to see whether their fingerprints had changed.

Our observations probably overstate the rate at which fingerprints change in the real world, because the interactive nature of the Panopticlick website encourages to experiment with alterations to their browser configuration.

5.1   Changing Fingerprints as a Function of Time

Among our userbase, rates of fingerprint change for returning cookie-accepting users were very high, with 37.4% of users who visited the site more than once[7] exhibiting more than one fingerprint over time.

The time-dependence of fingerprint changes is illustrated in Figure 4, which plots the proportion of fingerprints that was constant among cookies that were seen by Panopticlick exactly twice, with a substantial time interval in between. The population with precisely two time-separated hits was selected because this

---

[7] Our measure of returning visitors was based on cookies, and did not count reloads within 1–2 hours of the first visit.

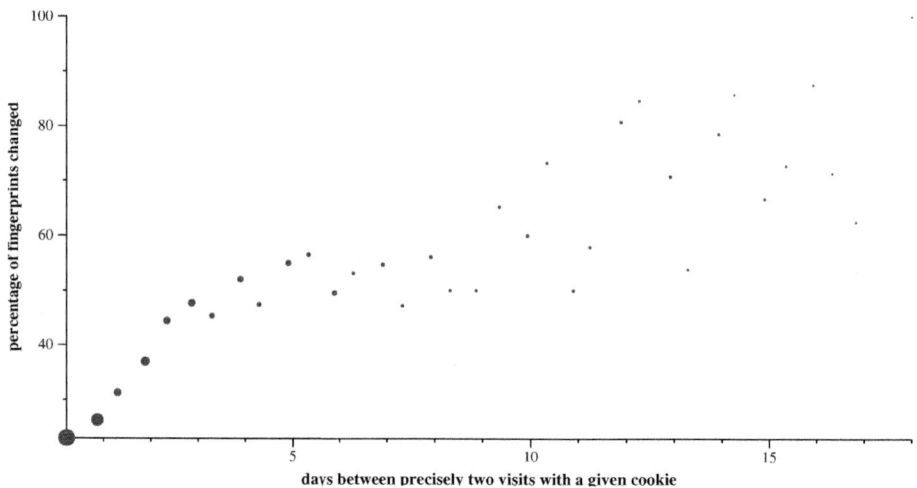

Fig. 4. Proportion of fingerprints that change over given intervals
(area of datapoints indicates number of observations encompassed, $N = 4{,}638$)

group is significantly less likely to be actively *trying* to alter their browser fingerprints (we assume that most people experimenting in order to make their browsers unique will reload the page promptly at some point).

Upon first examination, the high rate of change for fingerprints — even if it overstates the rate of change in the wider Internet population — appears to constitute a powerful protection against fingerprinting attacks.

5.2   Following Changing Fingerprints

We performed a simple test to see whether a connection can be inferred between the old and new values of fingerprints that change over time.

We implemented a very simple algorithm to heuristically estimate whether a given fingerprint might be an evolved version of a fingerprint seen previously.

The algorithm (set out below) operated on an input fingerprint q, where $F_i(g), i \in \{1..8\}$ are the 8 fingerprint components illustrated in Table 1, and G is the set of all browsers observed in our dataset. The algorithm did not attempt to guess a preceding fingerprint if q indicated that the browser did not have Flash or Java installed.

We ran our algorithm over the set of users whose cookies indicated that they were returning to the site 1–2 hours or more after their first visit, and who now had a different fingerprint. Excluding users whose fingerprints changed because they disabled javascript (a common case in response to visiting panopticlick.eff.org, but perhaps not so common in the real world), our heuristic made a correct guess in 65% of cases, an incorrect guess in 0.56% of cases, and no guess in 35% of cases. 99.1% of guesses were correct, while the false

Algorithm 1. guesses which other fingerprint might have changed into q

```
candidates ← [ ]
for all g ∈ G do
  for i ∈ {1..8} do
    if for all j ∈ {1..8}, j ≠ i : Fⱼ(g) = Fⱼ(q) then
      candidates ← candidates + (g, j)
    end if
  end for
end for
if length(candidates) = 1 then
  g, j ← candidates[0]
  if j ∈ {cookies?, video, timezone, supercookies} then
    return g
  else
    # j ∈ {user_agent, http_accept, plugins, fonts}
    if SequenceMatcher(Fⱼ(g), Fⱼ(q)).ratio() < 0.85 then
      return g
    end if
  end if
end if
return NULL
```

`difflib.SequenceMatcher().ratio()` is a Python standard library function for estimating the similarity of strings. We used Python 2.5.4.

positive rate was 0.86%. Our algorithm was clearly very crude, and no doubt could be significantly improved with effort.

6   Defending against Fingerprinting

6.1   The Paradox of Fingerprintable Privacy Enhancing Technologies

Sometimes, technologies intended to enhance user privacy turn out to make fingerprinting easier. Extreme examples include many forms of User Agent spoofing (see note 3) and Flash blocking browser extensions, as discussed in Section 3.1. The paradox, essentially, is that many kinds of measures to make a device harder to fingerprint are themselves distinctive unless a lot of other people also take them.

Examples of measures that might be intended to improve privacy but which appear to be ineffective or even potentially counterproductive in the face of fingerprinting include Flash blocking (the mean surprisal of browsers with Flash blockers is 18.7), and User Agent alteration (see note 3). A small group of users had "Privoxy" in their User Agent strings; those User Agents alone averaged 15.5 bits of surprisal. All 7 users of the purportedly privacy-enhancing "Browzar" browser were unique in our dataset.

There are some commendable exceptions to this paradox. TorButton has evolved to give considerable thought to fingerprint resistance [19] and may be receiving the levels of scrutiny necessary to succeed in that project [15]. NoScript is a useful privacy enhancing technology that seems to reduce fingerprintability.[8]

6.2   Enumeratable Characteristics vs Testable Characteristics

One significant API choice that several plugin and browser vendors made, which strengthens fingerprints tremendously, is offering function calls that enumerate large amounts of system information. The `navigator.plugins` object is one example, as are the font lists returned by Flash and Java. Microsoft Internet Explorer deserves an honourable mention for not allowing plugin enumeration, and even though we collected version numbers for $8\frac{1}{2}$ plugins,[9] the plugin entropy on IE was 16.5 bits, somewhat lower than the 17.7 seen in non-IE browsers.

The benefits of allowing Java and Flash to read exhaustive system font lists is questionable. Any website that cares whether someone has the "False Positive BRK" font installed[10] could surely test for it explicitly.

There are probably stronger ease-of-development arguments for making plugins enumeratable, but the example of IE shows that it is not strictly necessary. We recommend that browsers switch to confirm-only testing for fonts and plugins, with an exponential backoff to prevent exhaustive searches by malicious javascript.

6.3   Fingerprintability ∝ Debuggability

Much of the entropy we observe in browsers comes from the precise micro-version numbers of all of their plugins. This is somewhat true even in IE, where we were limited to testing the version numbers of $8\frac{1}{2}$ common plugins using PluginDetect and custom JavaScript. A similar, though less severe, problem comes from precise micro-version numbers in User Agent strings.

The obvious solution to this problem would be to make the version numbers less precise. Why report `Java 1.6.0_17` rather than just `Java 1.6`, or `DivX Web Player 1.4.0.233` rather than just `DivX Web Player 1.4`? The motivation for these precise version numbers appears to be debuggability. Plugin and browser developers want the *option* of occasionally excavating the micro-version numbers of clients when trying to retrospectively diagnose some error that may be present in a particular micro-version of their code. This is an understandable desire, but it should now be clear that this decision trades off the user's privacy against the developer's convenience.

There is a spectrum between extreme debuggability and extreme defense against fingerprinting, and current browsers choose a point in that spectrum close to the debuggability extreme. Perhaps this should change, especially when users enter "private browsing" modes.

---

[8] We did not try to devise a detection method for NoScript, though they probably exist if users allow scripts from certain important domains.

[9] Our version numbers for Acrobat were approximate and limited to the major version number.

[10] We noticed that font while grepping through the output of one of our analysis scripts.

6.4   Font Orders as an Unnecessary Source of Entropy

When implementing our fingerprinting code, we observed that Adobe Flash and Sun's Java VM not only report complete lists of fonts installed on a system, but return them in non-sorted order, perhaps due to a filesystem inode walk.

We tested the hypothesis that font orders are informative, by checking to see if any returning, cookie-accepting users had font lists whose order had changed. We found that only 30 returning browsers had font lists that were different solely with respect to order. Interestingly, these font lists only varied in the ordering of certain fonts from the "Lucida" family, and there was a related population of about 200 browsers where the same fonts varied in ordering and surrounding whitespace. All of these browsers had Mac OS X User Agent strings, so we concluded that some application on OS X overwrites these font files, either during upgrades or at other times. Aside from this group, our hypothesis that font list orderings were stable turned out to be correct.

Next, we investigated whether a substantial reduction in font list entropy could be achieved if plugins like Flash and Java began sorting these lists before returning them via their APIs. Among browsers where the fonts were detectable, the entropy of the `fonts` variable was 17.1 bits. We recalculated this quantity after sorting to be 16.0, a decrease of only 1.1 bits. Confounding this calculation slightly is the fact that the maximum possible entropy we could detect for either of these numbers, given our dataset, was only 18.4. It is possible that sorting the font lists would have made a much larger difference if the sample size had been large enough for the font entropy and its conceivable ceiling to diverge further.

In contrast to the font case, our pre-launch testing seemed to indicate that the ordering of `navigator.plugins` was not stable in all browsers, so, as noted in Table 1, we sorted the plugin list before recording it. We subsequently read Jonathan Mayer's claims that Mozilla actually exposes two different plugin orderings based on *different* inode timestamps [8]. Unfortunately, having sorted our plugin dataset, we cannot test his claims.

7   Conclusions

We implemented and tested one particular browser fingerprinting method. It appeared, in general, to be very effective, though as noted in Section 3.1 there are many measurements that could be added to strengthn it.

Browser fingerprinting is a powerful technique, and fingerprints must be considered alongside cookies, IP addresses and supercookies when we discuss web privacy and user trackability. Although fingerprints turn out not to be particularly stable, browsers reveal so much version and configuration information that they remain overwhelmingly trackable. There are implications both for privacy policy and technical design.

Policymakers should start treating fingerprintable records as potentially personally identifiable, and set limits on the durations for which they can be associated with identities and sensitive logs like clickstreams and search terms.

The Tor project is noteworthy for already considering and designing against fingerprintability. Other software that purports to protect web surfers' privacy should do likewise, and we hope that the test site at `panopticlick.eff.org` may prove useful for this purpose. Browser developers should also consider what they can do to reduce fingerprintability, particularly at the JavaScript API level.

We identified only three groups of browser with comparatively good resistance to fingerprinting: those that block JavaScript, those that use TorButton, and certain types of smartphone. It is possible that other such categories exist in our data. Cloned machines behind firewalls are fairly resistant to our algorithm, but would not be resistant to fingerprints that measure clock skew or other hardware characteristics.

References

1. Lukáš, J., Fridrich, J., Goljan, M.: Digital camera identification from sensor pattern noise. IEEE Transactions on Information Forensics and Security 1(2), 205–214 (2006)
2. Kai San Choi, E.Y.L., Wong, K.K.: Source Camera Identification Using Footprints from Lens Aberration. In: Proc. of SPIE-IS&T Electronic Imaging, vol. 6069. SPIE (2006)
3. Hilton, O.: The Complexities of Identifying the Modern Typewriter. Journal of Forensic Sciences 17(2) (1972)
4. Kohno, T., Broido, A., Claffy, K.: Remote Physical Device Fingerprinting. IEEE Transactions on Dependable and Secure Computing 2(2), 108 (2005)
5. Murdoch, S.: Hot or not: Revealing hidden services by their clock skew. In: Proc. 13th ACM conference on Computer and Communications Security, p. 36. ACM, New York (2006)
6. The 41st Parameter: PCPrint^{TM} (2008),
   `http://www.the41st.com/land/DeviceID.asp`
7. Mills, E.: Device identification in online banking is privacy threat, expert says. CNET News (April 2009)
8. Mayer, J.: Any person... a pamphleteer: Internet Anonymity in the Age of Web 2.0. Undergraduate Senior Thesis, Princeton University (2009)
9. Krishnamurthy, B., Wills, C.: Generating a privacy footprint on the Internet. In: Proc. ACM SIGCOMM Internet Measurement Conference. ACM, New York (2006)
10. McKinkley, K.: Cleaning Up After Cookies. iSec Partners White Paper (2008)
11. Pool, M.B.: Meantime: non-consensual HTTP user tracking using caches (2000),
    `http://sourcefroge.net/projects/meantime/`
12. Soltani, A., Canty, S., Mayo, Q., Thomas, L., Hoofnagle, C.: Flash Cookies and Privacy. SSRN preprint (August 2009),
    `http://papers.ssrn.com/sol3/papers.cfm?abstract_id=1446862`
13. Robinson, S.: Flipping Typical, demonstration of CSS font detection (2009),
    `http://flippingtypical.com/`
14. TCP/IP stack fingerprinting,
    `http://en.wikipedia.org/wiki/TCP/IP_stack_fingerprinting`

15. Fleischer, G.: Attacking Tor at the Application Layer. Presentation at DEFCON 17 (2009),
    http://pseudo-flaw.net/content/defcon/
16. CSS history hack demonstration,
    http://www.whattheinternetknowsaboutyou.com/
17. W3C: Geolocation API, http://en.wikipedia.org/wiki/W3C_Geolocation_API
18. Narayanan, A., Shmatikov, V.: Robust De-anonymization of Large Sparse Datasets 2(2), 108 (2008)
19. Perry, M.: Torbutton Design Doccumentation (2009),
    https://www.torproject.org/torbutton/design

A   Appendix : Some Dataset Queries of Interest

Table 2. Mean surprisal for each variable in isolation

Variable	Entropy (bits)
user_agent	10.0
plugins	15.4
fonts	13.9
video	4.83
supercookies	2.12
http_accept	6.09
timezone	3.04
cookies_enabled	0.353

Table 3. A typical Panopticlick fingerprint

Variable	Value
User Agent	Mozilla/5.0 (X11; U; Linux i686; en-US; rv:1.9.1.7) Gecko/20100106 Ubuntu/9.10 (karmic) Firefox/3.5.7
HTTP ACCEPT headers	text/html, */* ISO-8859-1,utf-8;q=0.7,*;q=0.7 gzip,deflate en-us,en;q=0.5
Cookies enabled?	Yes
Screen resolution	1280x800x24
Timezone	300
Browser plugins	Plugin 0: DivX Web Player; DivX Web Player version 1.4.0.233; libtotem-mully-plugin.so; (AVI video; video/divx; divx). Plugin 1: QuickTime Plug-in 7.2.0; The <a href="http://www.gnome.org/projects/totem/">Totem</a> 2.28.2 plugin handles video and audio streams.; libtotem-narrowspace-plugin.so; (QuickTime video; video/quicktime; mov) (MPEG-4 video; video/mp4; mp4) (MacPaint Bitmap image; image/x-macpaint; pntg) (Macintosh Quickdraw/PICT drawing; image/x-quicktime; pict, pict1, pict2) (MPEG-4 video; video/x-m4v; m4v). Plugin 2: Shockwave Flash; Shockwave Flash 10.0 r42; libflashplayer.so; (Shockwave Flash; application/x-shockwave-flash; swf) (FutureSplash Player; application/futuresplash; spl). Plugin 3: VLC Multimedia Plugin (compatible Totem 2.28.2); The <a href="http://www.gnome.org/projects/totem/">Totem</a> 2.28.2 plugin handles video and audio streams.; libtotem-cone-plugin.so; (VLC Multimedia Plugin; application/x-vlc-plugin;) (VLC Multimedia Plugin; application/vlc;) (VLC Multimedia Plugin; video/x-google-vlc-plugin;) (Ogg multimedia file; application/x-ogg; ogg) (Ogg multimedia file; application/ogg; ogg) (Ogg Audio; audio/ogg; oga) (Ogg Audio; audio/x-ogg; ogg) (Ogg Video; video/ogg; ogv) (Ogg Video; video/x-ogg; ogg) (Annodex exchange format; application/annodex; anx) (Annodex Audio; audio/annodex; axa) (Annodex Video; video/annodex; axv) (MPEG video; video/mpeg; mpg, mpeg, mpe) (WAV audio; audio/wav; wav) (WAV audio; audio/x-wav; wav) (MP3 audio; audio/mpeg; mp3) (NullSoft video; application/x-nsv-vp3-mp3; nsv) (Flash video; video/flv; flv) (Totem Multimedia plugin; application/x-totem-plugin;). Plugin 4: Windows Media Player Plug-in 10 (compatible; Totem); The <a href="http://www.gnome.org/projects/totem/">Totem</a> 2.28.2 plugin handles video and audio streams.; libtotem-gmp-plugin.so; (AVI video; application/x-mplayer2; avi, wma, wmv) (ASF video; video/x-ms-asf-plugin; asf, wmv) (AVI video; video/x-msvideo; asf, wmv) (ASF video; video/x-ms-asf; asf) (Windows Media video; video/x-ms-wmv; wmv) (Windows Media video; video/x-wmv; wmv) (Windows Media video; video/x-ms-wvx; wmv) (Windows Media video; video/x-ms-wm; wmv) (Windows Media video; video/x-ms-wmp; wmv) (Windows Media video; application/x-ms-wms; wms) (Windows Media video; application/x-ms-wmp; wmp) (Microsoft ASX playlist; application/asx; asx) (Windows Media audio; audio/x-ms-wma; wma).
System fonts	wasy10, UnDotum, Century Schoolbook L, OpenSymbol, msam10, Mukti Narrow, Vemana2000, KacstQurn, Umpush, DejaVu Sans Mono, Purisa, msbm10, KacstBook, KacstLetter, cmr10, Norasi, Loma, KacstDigital, KacstTitleL, mry_KacstQurn, URW Palladio L, Phetsarath OT, Sawasdee, Tlwg Typist, URW Gothic L, Dingbats, URW Chancery L, FreeSerif, ori1Uni, KacstOffice, DejaVu Sans, VL Gothic, Kinnari, KacstArt, TlwgMono, Lohit Punjabi, Symbol, Bitstream Charter, KacstOne, Courier 10 Pitch, cmmi10, WenQuanYi Zen Hei Mono, Nimbus Sans L, TlwgTypewriter, VL PGothic, Rachana, Standard Symbols L, Lohit Gujarati, kacstPen, KacstDecorative, Nimbus Mono L, Mallige, Nimbus Roman No9 L, KacstPoster, Mukti Narrow, WenQuanYi Zen Hei, FreeSans, cmex10, KacstNaskh, Lohit Tamil, Tlwg Typo, UnBatang, KacstFarsi, Waree, KacstTitle, Lohit Hindi, DejaVu Serif, Garuda, KacstScreen, FreeMono, URW Bookman L, cmsy10 (via Flash)
(Partial) supercookie tests	DOM localStorage: Yes, DOM sessionStorage: Yes, IE userData: No

On the Privacy of Web Search Based on Query Obfuscation: A Case Study of TrackMeNot

Sai Teja Peddinti and Nitesh Saxena

Computer Science and Engineering
Polytechnic Institute of New York University
psaiteja@cis.poly.edu, nsaxena@poly.edu

Abstract. Web Search is one of the most rapidly growing applications on the internet today. However, the current practice followed by most search engines – of logging and analyzing users' queries – raises serious privacy concerns. One viable solution to search privacy is *query obfuscation*, whereby a client-side software attempts to mask real user queries via injection of certain noisy queries. In contrast to other privacy-preserving search mechanisms, query obfuscation does not require server-side modifications or a third party infrastructure, thus allowing for ready deployment at the discretion of privacy-conscious users. In this paper, our higher level goal is to analyze whether query obfuscation can preserve users' privacy in practice against an adversarial search engine. We focus on TrackMeNot (TMN) [10,20], a popular search privacy tool based on the principle of query obfuscation. We demonstrate that a search engine, equipped with only a short-term history of a user's search queries, can break the privacy guarantees of TMN by only utilizing off-the-shelf machine learning classifiers.

Keywords: Web Search Privacy, Query Obfuscation, Noisy Queries.

1 Introduction

With an enormous amount and wide variety of data available on the web today, web search has emerged as one of the most important services. In the recent past, the prevalent practice followed by search engines – of logging and analyzing users' web search queries – has received considerable attention from media and public as well as researchers all over the world. The issue was first brought into limelight in August 2005 in the wake of US Department of Justice's subpoena to Google for a week's worth of search query records [15]. This was followed by publishing of AOL's three month (pseudonymized) search query logs, from which identities of certain users had been extracted based on personal information embedded in their queries [9,2]. Right after, other media reports shed more light on how several major search engines (Yahoo!, AOL, MSN and Google) log, store and analyze individual search query logs.

Archiving search queries, from search engine's perspective, is inherently useful for improving the efficiency of search and quality of search results, and for revenue generation through sponsored search advertising. However, it has serious

M.J. Atallah and N. Hopper (Eds.): PETS 2010, LNCS 6205, pp. 19–37, 2010.

privacy implications for the users of the search services. Some common examples of search behavior that can have an *explicit* adverse effect on a user's privacy, when queries are logged, include – searching for information on a particular disease the user or a family member might be suffering from, searching for one's social security number or phone number just to verify if it exists on the web, locating directions, subscribing to news items, and "ego-surfing[1]." Additionally, and perhaps more seriously, query logs can also be used for *implicit* privacy violations. By implicit, we mean that the sensitive information can not be learned directly, but has to be extracted from a user's queries via profiling and aggregation methods or data mining techniques. For instance, it is possible to infer a user's income level from the brands of products he or she often searches for [21].

A number of techniques have been proposed to address the problem of search privacy. One class of these techniques involves third-party infrastructure such as a proxy, e.g., Scroogle [18] or an anonymizing network [17], e.g. Tor [19]. These approaches, however, require the user to impose (unwanted) trust onto third-party servers and usually have performance penalties. Another body of work applicable to web search privacy is on private information retrieval (PIR) protocols [14]. Current PIR protocols, unfortunately, are not feasible to be deployed in practice due to high computation and communication overheads.

A third class of solutions, which is the focus of this paper, is based on the principle of *query obfuscation*. Basically, the idea is that a client-side software injects *noisy* queries into the stream of queries transmitted to the search engine; if the engine is unable to distinguish between noisy queries and real user queries, user profiling may not be possible, thereby preventing implicit privacy violations. A query obfuscation technique does not require any server-side modifications and allows for ready deployment at the discretion of privacy-conscious users.

Our Contributions: A higher level goal of this work is to analyze how effective query obfuscation can be – in preserving users' privacy in practice – against an adversarial search engine. To this end, we focus on TrackMeNot (TMN) [10,20], a real-world search privacy tool based on query obfuscation (the only one we are aware of). TMN is implemented as Mozilla Firefox plugin that attempts to hide user queries in a stream of programmatically generated search queries, which mimic or simulate the user's search behavior.

As we discuss in the following section, TMN has taken necessary measures to simulate user's search behavior and generate noisy queries as similar as possible to user's queries. TMN has also evolved considerably over time shaping into a potentially robust and popular query obfuscation tool.[2,3] We set out to investigate whether it is still possible (and to what extent) for an adversarial search engine – equipped with users' search histories – to filter out TMN queries

---

[1] It is the prevalent practice of searching for one's own name, on a popular search engine, to see what results appear.

[2] Currently, TMN's plugin version 0.6.719 has been downloaded 390,909 times.

[3] We refer the reader to Bruce Schneier's criticism of TMN and subsequent discussion, following TMN's introduction back in 2006 [3].

using off-the-shelf machine learning classifiers and thus undermine the privacy guarantees provided by TMN.

We answer the above question affirmatively. We selected 60 users from the publicly-available AOL search logs and treated them as users of the TMN software. For each of these users, we measured the efficiency of some known machine learning classifiers with respect to two metrics: (1) percentage of *correctly identified user queries*, and (2) percentage of *TMN queries incorrectly identified* as user queries. If there are u user queries and t TMN queries, recorded by the search engine, and a classifier predicted $u' + t'$ queries as user queries, where u' corresponds to correctly identified user queries and t' corresponds to incorrectly identified TMN queries, then our two metrics are given by u'/u and t'/t, respectively. The classifier is said to be doing a good job if u'/u is close to 1 and t'/t is close to 0, i.e, percentage of correctly classified user queries is close to 100% and percentage of incorrectly classified TMN queries is close to 0%. Through our current experiments, we are able to achieve an average accuracy of 48.88% for identifying user queries, while the percentage of incorrectly classified TMN queries is only 0.02%. We also observed that queries corresponding to some of the users could be identified with 100% and greater than 80% accuracies, whereas for others, the identification rate was less than 10%. Based on our results, we can conclude that most users are susceptible to privacy violations even while using TMN, some of them being significantly more vulnerable than others.

In terms of related work, we find that theoretical models have previously been developed to bring insights into the effectiveness of query obfuscation for search privacy [24]. We are also recently made aware of a short paper [4], which presents a brief analysis of TMN using search logs from a single user (see Section 2.1 of [4]). Current paper represents the first step, to the best of authors' knowledge, towards a larger scale analysis of TMN using existing classifiers.

We also note that the problem considered in this paper is different from the problem of identifying queries from an anonymized search log (see, e.g., [12,11]). First, an adversary in our application is the search engine itself and not a third party attempting to de-anonymize a search log. Second, unlike a third party, the search engine is already in possession of users' search history using which it can effectively train a classifier. Moreover, the goals of our study are also different; we are interested in evaluating known classifiers to study our problem so as to keep our attacks simple and easy enough for an unsophisticated adversary.

The rest of this paper is organized as follows. In Section 2, we discuss TMN's query generation. In Section 3, we present our experimentation methodology and set-up, user selection criteria and query logging methods. This is followed by Section 4, where we put forward our query classification results, and finally, some discussion based on our results in Section 5.

2   Background: TMN Query Generation

In this section, we discuss TMN query generation process. We first try to understand this process based on what was reported in [10], and then, for deeper insights, inspect TMN's source code [20].

2.1   Understanding TMN from the Literature

As mentioned earlier, TMN hides the user queries in a stream of programmatically generated search queries, which mimic or simulate the user's search behavior. TMN maintains a dynamic query list, which is instantiated with an initial seed list of queries obtained from popular RSS feeds and publicly available recent searches. Later, individual queries from this list are randomly selected and substituted with query-like words from HTTP response messages returned by the search engine for actual user queries. Over time, each TMN instance develops a unique set of queries and adapts itself to the user's search behavior and mimics the user more closely.

TMN employs a "Selective Click-Through" mechanism, which simulates the user behavior of clicking on the query results returned and listed by the search engine. It uses regular expressions to avoid clicking on revenue generating advertisements, and thus claims to leave the web business model unharmed. It keeps track of the user searches by monitoring all outgoing HTTP requests from the browser using the "Real Time Search Awareness" mechanism. The "Live Header Maps" feature enables TMN to adapt dynamically to the specific client browser data, such as browser version and operating system details, helping TMN to use the exact set of headers that the browser uses. TMN also implements "Burst Mode" queries in order to incorporate the common user behavior of firing related queries in immediate succession as part of a query session.

With all these features, TMN is believed to be a good simulator of user's searching behavior. However, it has certain drawbacks as mentioned in [10]. TMN can not mask a user's private information (e.g., names or phone numbers) included in the search queries themselves, and it can not prevent user identification based on the IP address or cookies typically used by search engines. In order to hide one's IP address while searching, TMN developers [10] recommend the use of anonymizing networks, such as Tor [19]. Bruce Schneier, in his blog [3], also commented about the weaknesses of TMN. Though most of the raised objections have already been addressed in the latest version of TMN, some of them are noteworthy, such as the problem of "hot-button issue" searches. This problem may occur when TMN itself generates sensitive search queries, e.g., those involving "HIV", "drug-use" and "bombings", and which might be problematic for TMN users. The TMN authors claim that this problem can be prevented by configuring the initial RSS input feeds and thus controlling the type of queries sent by TMN. Based on these discussions, we can say that TMN (potentially) only provides protection against aggregation and profiling of individual search queries by adversarial search engines. With and without the use of TMN, user's area of interest would be exposed to the adversary, but when using TMN, the actual search queries would be masked in a stream of related queries. The better the simulated queries resemble the actual user queries, the better are the chances for TMN to hide the actual user queries.

2.2   Understanding TMN from the Source Code

In order to obtain a deeper understanding of TMN, we analyzed the supporting code of TMN's Firefox extension. Mozilla extensions which are written in XUL and JavaScript, provide an easy way to develop new applications on top of the basic Firefox browser platform. The XUL language extends the GUI of the browser while the JavaScript helps in defining the functionality.

When TMN is installed on the Firefox browser, it creates a default query seed file along with a query list. This query list is initialized with some queries extracted from the default or supplied RSS feeds and this list is padded with some queries from the default seed file if the queries extracted are less in number. Once the query list is generated, a search is scheduled immediately without any delay (delay is 0 seconds). (Later on, some non-zero delay values are specified to schedule a new search based on the query generation frequency chosen by the user, using the TMN control panel, and some random offset value).

After the delay timeout, a random query from the query list is selected to perform a search. With some probability, the query is modified to be only the longest word or a negated word is concatenated to the query, such as "word1 word2 - word2" or quotation marks are added. Sometimes, if "Burst Mode" is enabled, a sequence of related queries might be generated from the selected query by omitting some keywords at random. These Burst Mode queries are sent within short intervals of time, so as to form a chain of related searches.

TMN maintains a list of headers and URLs for each search engine, and an entry in these lists gets updated with new headers and URLs when the user performs a search on the corresponding search engines. The previously selected and modified query is added to the URL, which is then encoded and an XML-HttpRequest is generated for the encoded URL with updated header fields. TMN saves this last query fired and displays it on the Firefox status bar; it also stores this URL in search history for later reference. When there is a state change in the XMLHttpRequest sent, i.e., when a response is received from the server, an appropriate action is taken based on the HTTP status response. If an error occurs, it is logged. If the HTTP status response is *OK*, based on some probability, TMN tries to simulate the user click-throughs. To this end, TMN identifies the links on the HTML response sent by the search engine, processes these links and picks one of them at random. After some delay, another XMLHttpRequest is generated with the selected link, thereby simulating the user behavior of clicking a link. TMN does not process the returned html response for this click-through link. If Burst Mode is enabled, TMN schedules the next search with the following keyword in sequence. If it is not under Burst Mode, the HTML response is processed, and keywords from the textual content on the web page are identified and extracted. TMN then picks at random a new keyword from this extracted keyword list and adds it to the query list by replacing a query at a randomly picked index in the querylist. This new query list is saved and written to the TMN seed file. TMN again schedules new search at a timeout value with an offset and this procedure is repeated.

In this way, the TMN seed file gets updated with keywords extracted from the web results returned by the search engine, for the queries fired by the user. In the long run, TMN gets adapted to a query content the user is interested in and generates better queries making it (potentially) much harder for the search engine to differentiate the noisy queries from the original user queries. Because some form of randomization occurs at each and every step, it is impossible for two TMN instances to generate the same set of TMN queries.

3   Experimental Study of TMN: Preliminaries

Based on our discussion in previous section, we find that TMN has taken necessary measures to simulate user's search behavior and generate noisy queries as similar as possible to user's queries. TMN has also evolved considerably over time resulting in a potentially robust and popular query obfuscation tool. In this work, we set out to investigate whether it is still possible (and to what extent) for an adversarial search engine – equipped with users search histories – to filter out TMN queries using off-the-shelf machine learning classifiers and thus undermine the privacy guarantees provided by TMN. In our *adversarial model*, we assumed that the search engine is adversarial and its goal is to distinguish between TMN and user queries for profiling and aggregation purposes. We also assumed that the engine would have access to user's search histories for a certain duration until the point the user starts using the TMN software. We considered a passive adversarial search engine, the one who only works with and analyses the queries received from the users, and in particular, does not inject manipulated responses to the user in an attempt to distinguish between TMN and user queries.

In order to pursue our study, we should work with real user queries. To this end, one possibility was to seek users who may volunteer to use TMN and let us record all outgoing (user as well as TMN) search queries fired from their machines. However, due to the privacy concerns (which form the basis for our work), it was not feasible to recruit such volunteering users.

To address the above problem, we used a novel experimental methodology. We worked with the AOL search data [1] and modeled or simulated the existing user queries in a way they would have appeared to the search engine if the users were using TMN. The AOL search data was well suited for this purpose because it consists of a large number of real user queries (21 million), corresponding to a large user base (650,000) and spanning over a reasonably long period of time (3 months). Though the AOL logs correspond to a different time period (year 2006), it does not affect our experiment because we concentrate on the query content alone and do not consider the associated query timestamps, as we discuss later in the paper (see Section 4.3). Since most queries do not have temporal dependence, we proceed with the use of historical AOL search logs for our experiments.

We selected a few users from the AOL logs and simulated their behavior of issuing queries to the search engine while TMN is installed and running on their machines. TMN is a Mozilla extension and these extensions, installed on a Firefox browser, operate only on one user profile – the one on which it was installed. Hence, we can have multiple Firefox user profiles, each with its own independent TMN instance, simulating a different user.

Due to the resource limitations on a single machine, it was difficult to run many Firefox user profiles simultaneously. To remedy this, we used the PlanetLab [16] system, a global distributed research network used by researchers to develop network applications and run network simulations. PlanetLab resources are assigned to the users as a resource slice, and these slices are instantiated by assigning nodes to it. Each of these nodes need to be configured with the experimental environment, which in our case is a working Mozilla Firefox browser with the TMN plugin installed.

3.1   Categorizing AOL Data

As mentioned earlier, the AOL logs span across three months: March, April and May of 2006. We use the last month's data for simulating the user and reserve the data from the first two months as the user history which we assume is available to the search engine before the user started using TMN. The former will be used as a test set and the latter as a training set, in case of our supervised machine learning classifiers (see Section 4.3). We selected a set of 60 test users from the AOL logs. This selection is based on AOL users' behavior as observed across four different categories (discussed below) so that a wide variety of users are covered. These categories are directly or indirectly related to TMN's query generation process. For obtaining the statistics across each category, we considered all the 650,000 AOL users, and thus each user falls into one user group in each category. While choosing our 60 test users, we made sure that there exist as few user intersections as possible across different categories so as to report the results for 60 different users.

Number of Queries: Over a period of time, different users fire different number of queries. TMN's efficiency in masking real user queries depends on the number of searches performed by the user. More the number of queries sent by the user, better are the chances for TMN to adapt itself to the user search categories and the content the user is interested in. We calculated the total number of searches performed by each user and plotted the number of users across different query bands. From Figure 1 (a power law distribution), we can see that most users lie below the 500 query mark with the bulk of them performing less than 100 searches over a three month duration. The rest are spread across the graph in small numbers. The same characteristics are also seen in the graphs plotting the maximum number of queries fired in a day, a week and one month versus the number of users in each query band. We thus combined these four into the same category (i.e., number of queries over a 3 month period).

Average Query Frequency: Users have different querying rates, which may turn out to be an identifying feature for TMN. TMN provides an option to set the frequency at which (noisy) queries are sent to the search engine. If this frequency varies significantly from the actual user's timing pattern, then it becomes easy to filter out the TMN queries. Hence, we computed the average timing difference between successive queries for each user and plotted the number of users across different time bands, as shown in Figure 2.

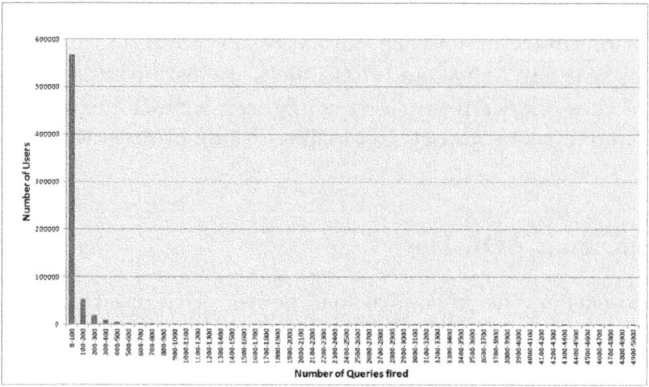

Fig. 1. Number of Queries

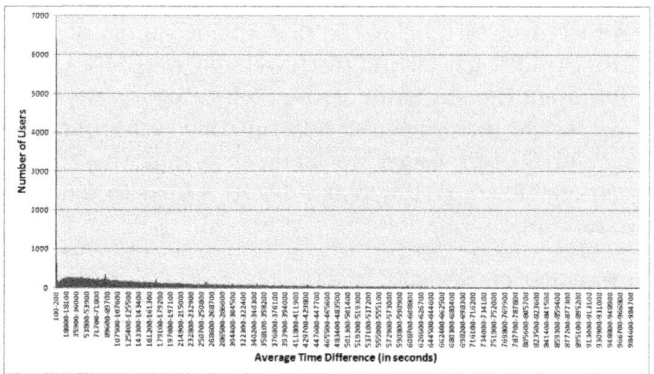

Fig. 2. Average Query Frequency

Sensitive Query Content: The contents of search queries obviously varies from user to user and TMN should be successful in masking these queries, especially those which are sensitive in nature. We considered two broad classes for the query content: sensitive and insensitive. Sensitive queries are those, which a user may not be willing to reveal to the outside world, such as his/her medical condition, interest in weaponry (considering the alarming increase in terrorism), those related to child abuse and pornography, and so on. On the other hand, a user may not mind the public taking notice of his/her insensitive queries, such as those related to movie interests, sports, and education.

Manually identifying the sensitive/insensitive query distribution for each user is very cumbersome. To remedy this, we resorted to machine learning techniques for classification of query content. We manually labeled a small subset of queries into sensitive and insensitive categories (we referred to various press articles discussing sensitive queries that appeared in the AOL logs [9,2]), and trained a Naive Bayes classifier with this data . This classifier was later used to classify the rest of the user queries. The cross-validation accuracy of this classifier on the manually labeled set was 68.0095%. Having identified each user's queries into the sensitive and insensitive categories, we plotted a graph indicating the number of users across different sensitive/insensitive percentages (see Figure 3). The graph is alarming and contrary to what one would normally expect. A large number of users were classified to be making sensitive queries. This anomaly could be because of the way we trained the classifier; while training, we labeled the complete query in the training set to be sensitive or insensitive instead of just selecting some relevant keywords, because we did not want the filtering mechanism to miss queries – such as "how to kill your wife" – which are not necessarily keyword sensitive.

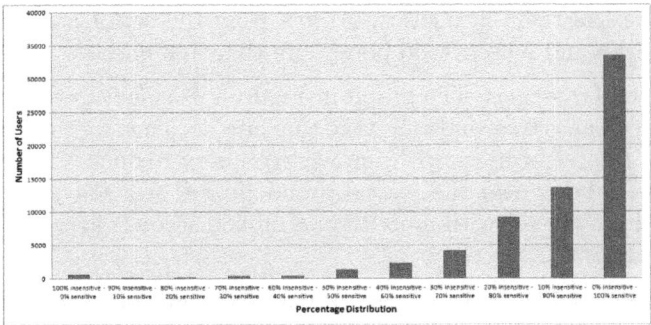

Fig. 3. Sensitive/Insensitive Distribution

Weekday/Weekend Distribution: Some users perform web search only during their office hours over the weekdays and some only over the weekends. If such users start using TMN on their desktop machines (neglecting laptops or notebooks, due to frequent periods of inactivity when these devices are put to sleep), it may be easier to separate out the TMN queries. Speculating this as an important issue, we calculated the number of queries fired by each user over weekdays and weekends. We categorized users into three groups – those who

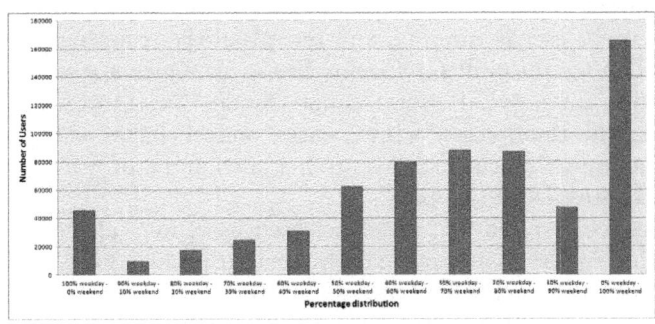

Fig. 4. Weekday/Weekend Distribution

search only over weekdays, those who search only over weekends and those who distribute their queries between weekdays and weekends. Figure 4 provides a graphical distribution of this data.

3.2   Selecting Users

Having observed different statistics, we next needed to select various users for our study. We decided to select 15 AOL users from each category discussed above, i.e., a total of 60 users.

Number of Queries: From Figure 1, we find that most users are below the 100 query mark, and of these, more than 70% perform less than 30 searches during the three month period. Thus, we selected 8 users at random from the set of users who fire less than 30 queries, 5 users from the set of users who fire less than 100 queries and 2 users who pose more than 100 queries.

Average Query Frequency: The graph in Figure 2 is smooth everywhere except for a sharp peak at 200 seconds. To take this into account, we randomly selected 5 users from the set of users with an average query frequency of less than 200 seconds, 5 users lying near the second rounded peak at 35000 seconds, and the remaining 5 from the set with more than a million seconds average gap between successive queries.

Sensitive Query Content: Since there are a large number of users in the 100% sensitive band (Figure 3), we randomly selected six users from this set. Five users are selected from the 30% insensitive - 70% sensitive band, two users from 10% sensitive - 90% insensitive band, and the remaining two from 100% insensitive query set.

Weekday/Weekend Distribution: Based on the distribution in Figure 4, we equally divided the choice of users among those who fire all their queries over weekdays, those who distribute 40% on weekday and 60% on weekend, and those who search only during weekends.

3.3   Experimental Set-Up and Implementation

After the user selection, the task ahead was to simulate the user logs while a TMN instance per user is running, and record all the resulting queries. We are using PlanetLab to run multiple Firefox instances. Once a resource "slice" has been assigned to a PlanetLab user account, "nodes" need to be allocated to the slice to utilize the resources. Each allocated node behaves as a separate Unix operating system, with basic utilities pre-installed and a provision to install any necessary softwares and updates.

Sixty nodes (corresponding to each selected user) were allocated to the slice, and each of these nodes maintains one Firefox user profile. Since Mozilla is a GUI application and X11 forwarding (necessary to run GUI applications over SSH connections) is not enabled on the PlanetLab machines due to security reasons, we had to install a VNC server on each of the nodes, which provides a GUI enabled remote access to these machines. Google was chosen as our (adversarial) search engine.

To simulate user's search behavior as per AOL log files, another Mozilla extension has been developed which reads the user logs and fires the queries at their respective timestamps listed in the logs. Similar to the TMN plugin, the new plugin also generates the user queries as XmlHttpRequests. The html response – from the server – to these queries is processed by TMN, since TMN does not find the corresponding request URL in its database (see Section 2). TMN treats the webpage to be a valid response to an actual user query and adapts itself to the new data – the exact behavior we need. Since the AOL user logs belong to a different time frame (year 2006), they were translated to the present time. The average query frequencies of TMN instances were chosen at random so as to keep them as close as possible to the real user behavior. We also ran 5 additional TMN instances with varying average TMN query frequency, for the same user, on our local machines in order to evaluate the effect of query frequency on the level of privacy provided by TMN. After configuring the necessary settings on PlanetLab machines, both the user log simulator and TMN were started. These experiments were conducted for a period of one month, and backup of the logs was taken at regular intervals.

4   Classification of User and TMN Queries

For our machine learning requirements, we used WEKA [23], an open source software which supports many machine learning algorithms and data preprocessing options. We used this off-the-shelf machine learning toolkit in order to estimate the accuracy with which we (adversarial search engine) can filter user queries, from the pool of user and TMN queries we obtained as described in previous section.

Two main categories of machine learning algorithms which can be used for our application are clustering and classification algorithms. Classification algorithms assign labels to quantities after being trained on a labeled training set. Clustering algorithms, without any prior knowledge of labeled data, try to group the data into groups (clusters), such that elements in a group share some common features. Classification is a supervised mechanism, where we need to train the classifier on some labeled training set, and determine its classification accuracy by labeling data in the test set. Clustering is the unsupervised version which gathers information about the data from an unlabeled training set and divides the test set into clusters [23].

4.1   Preparing the Data

The pool of simulated user and TMN query logs, collected over the one month period (as discussed in previous section), form our test data which needs to be clustered or classified. We labeled each query in the test data as a user or TMN query, since we want to test the accuracy of machine learning algorithms after categorizing the queries. The data includes the query, its label and the timestamp when the query was fired. For indicating the time, we used WEKA's DATE attribute in "yyyy-MM-dd HH:mm:ss" format. The queries are strings and WEKA can not directly handle string attributes. So we used a preprocessing filter, called *StringToWordVector*, which breaks down the words in the string and converts them into numeric attributes. Each string gets converted into a word vector of 1s and 0s in these attributes, where '1' indicates the presence and '0' indicates the absence of the word in the string.

4.2   Clustering Algorithms

We started with the unsupervised/clustering schemes since they are simple and potentially more powerful (as no labeled training is needed). We tested the performance of well known clustering algorithms, such as SimpleKMeans, Farthest First and EMClusterer [6] with *default parameters* using the *Classes-to-Clusters* evaluation mode. In this testing mode, the pre-assigned labels are masked and the data gets processed using the other attributes. Once the clusters are formed, the labels are unmasked and the majority class in each cluster is determined to find the accuracy of the algorithm as per these labels. However, the clustering algorithms with default parameters could not distinguish user queries from those of TMN and placed both types of queries into the same (TMN) cluster, for all of our test users. We note that it is possible to achieve better user query identification results by fine tuning the parameters of the clustering algorithms or applying other procedures, such as n-grams. However, since our goal is to identify the efficiencies using simple off-the-shelf machine learning tools with no parameter optimization, we defer this task to future work, and rather concentrate on classification algorithms.

4.3   Classification Algorithms

Since clustering with default parameters performed poorly, we decided to work with supervised/classification algorithms which are trained on prior labeled data. While training the classifiers, we need to have sample data corresponding to both the user and TMN classes (labels). If only one of user or TMN training data is used, all the queries would get classified into the same class since there are no identifying features available about the other class. The training set for the user queries was obtained from AOL two month user history, as discussed in Section 3.1. To obtain the TMN training set, we used the logs from a TMN instance which was run independently of all our simulations on a desktop machine for a period of one week.

With the training and test sets at our disposal, we next needed to choose the classifiers for our study. Out of several classifiers applicable to our scenario, based on their performance in few preliminary tests, we selected five algorithms: Logistic (Regression), Alternating Decision Trees (ADTree), Random Forest, Random Tree and ZeroR. For the sake of completeness, a brief description of each of these classifiers is provided below:

- *Logistic (Regression):* Regression classifier models are used to predict the probability of occurrence of an event by trying to fit the data to a logisitic curve. Logistic regression is mainly used when there are two classes of data, but multinomial versions also exist [5].
- *Alternating Decision Trees:* It is a decision tree algorithm containing decision and prediction nodes. These decision nodes specify a condition while the prediction nodes contain a number. In traditional decision trees, we travel along one path from the root, but here we simultaneously travel along many paths upto the leaf prediction nodes and the end result is determined by considering all the prediction node values covered [22].
- *RandomForest:* It is a collection of classification trees, in which the input is made to travel across all the trees and the final decision is made based on voting [13].
- *RandomTree:* It considers K randomly chosen attributes at each node in the tree and provides an estimation of class probabilities [8].
- *ZeroR:* This algorithm identifies the majority class label and classifies every element with the majority label, thereby providing the threshold accuracy that should be provided by other classifiers [7].

Query and Date Attributes: To check for the influence of each of the attributes (query and date) on the classification, we tested the performance of the above four classifiers (except ZeroR as its user accuracy is 0% due to a large TMN query set) across the following three settings for a couple of test users. Our goal was to determine to what extent these attributes might be useful for classification.

1. Considering only date and label value attributes
2. Considering only query and label value attributes
3. Considering both query and date along with label value attributes.

The results obtained are indicated in Table 1. (The percentages indicate the fractions of user queries correctly identified by the classifiers; the TMN query misclassification rates were close to 0% in most cases and are not listed). We can clearly see that out of the three settings, considering only query attribute along with label values provides the maximum accuracy. Including the date attribute reduces the accuracy and considering only the date attribute yields the worst accuracy. Therefore, for the analysis of rest of the experimental data, we neglect the date attribute and consider only query and label values as the data to be classified. Since Naive Bayes is a standard classifier which can be used when date attribute is not considered, we replaced ADTree with Naive Bayes classifier for the rest of our analysis.

TMN Average Query Frequency: To test for the effect of TMN's average query frequency in protecting users' privacy, we ran another 5 simulations apart from the 60 simulations considered before. Each of these 5 simulations, simulated the same user but with different TMN query frequencies – 10 per minute, 5 per minute, 1 per minute, 30 per hour and 1 per hour. After one month, these TMN logs were analyzed using the shortlisted classifiers. The results obtained

Table 1. % of user queries correctly classified with different attributes

| | | Classifier Accuracies | | | |
		Logistic	ADTree	Random Forest	Random Tree
User1	**Only Query**	92.59%	82.22%	92.59%	89.63%
	Only Date	14.44%	13.7%	13.7%	13.7%
	Both Query and Date	92.59%	13.7%	89.63%	46.30%
User2	**Only Query**	85.19%	85.71%	86.77%	86.24%
	Only Date	3.17%	0.53%	0.53%	0.53%
	Both Query and Date	10.58%	0.53%	68.25%	0.53%

for Naive Bayes and Logistic (Regression), which yielded the best accuracies, are depicted in Table 2. Though the performance of Naive Bayes was varying a little, the Logistic regression classifier was found to have a constant accuracy. This suggests that using different query frequencies would more or less provide the same level of accuracy. In other words, higher TMN frequency may not help in hiding user's query, contrary to one's intuition.

Table 2. % of user queries correctly classified for different TMN query frequencies

TMN Query Frequency	User Query Accuracies		TMN Query Misclassifications	
	Naive Bayes	Logistic (Regression)	Naive Bayes	Logistic (Regression)
10 per Minute	6.25%	56.25%	0%	0.06%
5 per Minute	0%	56.25%	0%	0.02%
1 per Minute	56.25%	56.25%	0%	0.12%
30 per Hour	56.25%	56.25%	0%	0%
10 per hour	56.25%	56.25%	0%	0%

Independent User History: Since using an independent TMN log for training the classifier turned out to be helpful in identifying the user queries with good accuracies, we performed a test to validate whether any user log data other than the actual user history would also give similar results (if this were the case, the search engine would not need access to every user's history of searches). To this end, we considered four users, $user_1$, $user_2$, $user_3$ and $user_4$, from the AOL log data. Now, instead of using a user's history to train the classifier for that user, we used the history of $user_4$ as the training data and tried to classify $user_1$, $user_2$ and $user_3$ simulated queries from their respective TMN query pools using Logistic, RandomForest, RandomTree and Naive Bayes (substituted with ADTree, as described before) classifiers. In all the cases, none of the user queries were identified correctly, however. That is, the accuracy turned out to be 0%.

Our analysis above shows that an independent user log is not helpful in distinguishing between user and TMN queries, but an independent TMN log is. One reason for this could be that the independent TMN log was functional around the same time frame as other TMN instances (i.e., it was run along with other TMN instances). Note that an adversarial search engine can also produce such updated TMN log from time to time for training the classifiers.

We note that many users are not likely to pay attention to the RSS feeds chosen for query generation and may use the default ones. Thus, in our experiments, we used the default RSS feeds thereby generating the same initial seed list of queries. We have not closed the browsers while conducting our experiments because of the common practice among users to put their computers to sleep and re-invoke them instead of switching them off and rebooting the machines each time, and also due to their tendency to continue using the browser without restarting unless it crashes. We acknowledge that not closing the browsers might affect the efficiency of TMN, because TMN updates the query list with new keywords from RSS feeds every time the browser restarts.

4.4 Classification Results

After collecting the query and label data from the 60 user simulations, we were ready to execute the selected classifiers. We built the training set with user history log and an independent TMN log as discussed previously. The results of classifiers over the test data are depicted in Table 3. For simplicity, we have not listed the results for all the classifiers; rather we only report the performance of the standard Naive Bayes classifier and the maximum accuracy achieved by the other three classifiers (Random Forest, Random Tree and Logistic). Also, the accuracies shown are the *mean accuracies* of the users belonging to different AOL

Table 3. Mean accuracies of user queries and mean misclassifications of TMN queries for each category of users

No. of Queries	Users	User Accuracy (%) Naive Bayes	Max.	TMN Misclassif. (%) Naive Bayes	Max.	Average Query Freq. (sec)	Users	User Accuracy (%) Naive Bayes	Max.	TMN Misclassif. (%) Naive Bayes	Max.
0-10	8	6.15	11.52	0	0.07	0-100	5	28.16	40.41	0.03	0.01
11-100	5	7.08	33.14	0	0.25	35000	5	30.83	71.86	0.01	0.01
100+	2	18.71	33.86	0.06	0.29	$> 10^6$	5	9.23	36.28	0	0

Senst. Query Content	Users	User Accuracy (%) Naive Bayes	Max.	TMN Misclassif. (%) Naive Bayes	Max.	Weekday/ Weekend Dist.	Users	User Accuracy (%) Naive Bayes	Max.	TMN Misclassif. (%) Naive Bayes	Max.
0%	2	60	60	0	0	Only weekdays	5	12.28	12.28	0	0
10%	2	61.46	64.79	0	0	Only weekends	5	23.2	99.99	57.26	0.08
70%	5	45.53	63.96	0.02	0.14	Distributed	5	1.22	99.92	86.94	0.08
100%	6	23.97	39.02	0	0.16						

categories (as defined in Section 3.2). We find that for all users, the classifiers did a very good job of correctly identifying almost all TMN queries; average TMN query misclassification rate was close to 0.02%. In other words, there were only a very few TMN queries which were wrongly classified.

The accuracies for identifying the user queries were not very high in general; average accuracy over all users was 48.88%. In most cases, the classifier was able to identify a reasonable fraction of user queries correctly. However, there were indeed some cases (e.g., the one for Sensitive Query Content and one for Average Query Frequency categories) where 100% accuracy was achieved in identifying the user queries. There were 4 other user instances for which more than 80% accuracies were achieved.

5   Discussion of Results

In this section, we discuss and attempt to interpret the results obtained in Section 4. The first key insight from our results is that the classifiers were very accurate in identifying the TMN queries (mean misclassification rate over all users was only 0.02%). In other words, very few TMN queries were wrongly identified as user queries. This is perhaps because the TMN query log – using which the classifiers were trained – consisted of a reasonably large number (42334) of TMN queries (although only corresponding to a week's period) which was likely sufficient to extract features for identifying TMN queries. Recall that this log was generated around the same time frame as our test user instances, which might have been helpful in correct classification of TMN queries. Note that an adversarial search engine can also produce such updated TMN log from time to time for training the classifiers. A very low rate of misclassification of TMN queries implies that any query classified as a user query is indeed a user query with a significantly high probability.

The classification accuracies for user queries, on the other hand, were not as good as they were for TMN queries (we obtained a mean user query identification accuracy of 48.88% over all users). One possible reason for relatively low accuracy in this case is that we were only able to leverage users' two-month history for training purposes. Since a large number of users only fired less than 100 queries (as seen from Figure 1) over 3 months, the classifiers did not have a large number of user queries to work with. Due to this reason, perhaps it was not possible to derive identifying characteristics for user queries in a number of cases. We believe that, in practice, the search engines can utilize long-term search histories available to them prior to a user starts using the TMN software, resulting in much better accuracies. Even with our current average identification rates of about 50%, the search engine can identify 50% of user queries (since almost no TMN queries were incorrectly classified, as discussed above) and still use them for profiling and aggregation purposes. Note also that our accuracies were found to vary significantly across different users. We observed that queries corresponding to some of the users could be identified with 100% and greater than 80% accuracies, whereas for others, the identification rate was less than

10%. Based on our current experiments, we can conclude that most users are susceptible to privacy violations even while using TMN, and some of these users are significantly more vulnerable than others (as we discuss below).

Looking at Table 3, we can make inferences regarding which users are possibly more vulnerable based on our different categories: number of queries, average query frequency, sensitive query content and weekday/weekend distributions. User query identification accuracies seem to be slightly improving with the number of queries posed by the users. Although the misclassification rates are increasing very slightly, we can ignore them considering a good improvement in user query classification rate. These results are justifiable because more the number of queries sent by a user, more are the chances to identify user query patterns and hence better are the accuracies. Users with very fast (less than 100 sec) and very slow (more than 1 million seconds) average querying frequencies seem significantly less vulnerable compared to those with mediocre (35,000 seconds) frequencies. The very fast and very slow category users are those who send very few queries in immediate succession or spread their queries across 3 months duration. Since the queries available for analysis are few, the accuracies are bound to be less for these users compared to the ones belonging to the mediocre category.

We do not notice any significant effect of the sensitivity of query content on classification accuracies. However, for users who did not pose any insensitive queries (based on our categorization in Section 3.1), accuracies were found to be relatively lower. Therefore, based on our sensitive query classification, the users who fire a larger fraction of sensitive queries were better camouflaged by TMN than those who fire a larger fraction of insensitive queries. This might be because of the presence of many sensitive queries in the initial query set generated from the default RSS feeds.

Users who engage in web search only during weekdays turned out to be much better protected compared to those who pose queries only over weekends (queries of such users can be identified with almost 100% success). This is because if users send queries only during weekends, then whatever queries are seen during weekday must be generated by TMN, allowing for easy identification. Finally, from Table 2, we also observed that using different TMN average query frequencies would more or less provide the same level of accuracy. In other words, higher TMN frequency may not help in hiding user's query, contrary to one's intuition.

In summary, our results indicate that TMN is very susceptible to machine learning attacks. In fact, TMN could be weaker than what our attacks imply. This is because we only used some simple off-the-shelf classifiers with default parameters and this itself resulted in considerable accuracies. Use of better and stronger machine learning algorithms, with optimized parameters, is very likely to further increase the accuracies.

6   Conclusions and Future Work

In this paper, we focused on TrackMeNot (TMN), a real-world search privacy tool based on query obfuscation. We demonstrated that a search engine, equipped with only a short-term history of user's search queries, can break the privacy guarantees of TMN by only utilizing off-the-shelf machine learning classifiers. More specifically, by treating a selected set of 60 users – from the publicly-available AOL search logs – as users of the TMN software, we showed that user queries can be identified with an average accuracy of 48.88%, while the average TMN query misclassification rate was only 0.02%.

In the future, we are interested in exploring designs of novel classifiers which can take into account other attributes (such as query timestamps) and possibly improve identification of users' queries. Classifier and clustering accuracies can be improved by selecting better classifiers and fine tuning their parameters. We defer this task of improving the efficiency by optimized parameter selection to future work.

Acknowledgments. We are grateful to our shepherd Rachel Greenstadt and PETS'10 anonymous reviewers for their insightful feedback. We also thank Lisa Hellerstein for discussion on machine learning classifiers and her helpful comments on our work, and the developers of TMN – Helen Nissenbaum and Vincent Toubiana – for their useful suggestions on a previous draft of the paper.

References

1. AOL Search Log Mirrors, http://www.gregsadetsky.com/aol-data/
2. Barbaro, M., Zeller, T.J.: A Face Is Exposed for AOL Searcher No. 4417749. The New York Times (August 9, 2006)
3. Schneier, B.: Schneier on Security: TrackMeNot. (2006), http://www.schneier.com/blog/archives/2006/08/trackmenot_1.html
4. Chow, R., Golle, P.: Faking contextual data for fun, profit, and privacy. In: ACM workshop on Privacy in the electronic society, WPES (2009)
5. DTREG - Software For Predictive Modeling and Forecasting. Logistic regression (Feburary 2010), http://www.dtreg.com/logistic.htm
6. Evans, R.: Clustering for Clasification. Master's thesis, Computer Science, University of Waikato (2007), http://adt.waikato.ac.nz/uploads/approved/adt-uow20070730.091151/public/02whole.pdf
7. Frank, E.: ZeroR (Feburary 2010), http://weka.sourceforge.net/doc/weka/classifiers/rules/ZeroR.html
8. Frank, E., Kirkby, R.: Random tree (Feburary 2010), http://weka.sourceforge.net/doc/weka/classifiers/trees/RandomTree.html
9. Hansell, S.: Marketers Trace Paths Users Leave on Internet. The New York Times (September 15, 2006)
10. Howe, D., Nissenbaum, H.: TrackMeNot: Resisting Surveillance in Web Search. In: Kerr, I., Lucock, C., Steeves, V. (eds.) On the Identity Trail: Privacy, Anonymity and Identity in a Networked Society (2008)
11. Jones, R., Kumar, R., Pang, B., Tomkins, A.: i know what you did last summer: query logs and user privacy. In: Conference on information and knowledge management, CIKM (2007)
12. Jones, R., Kumar, R., Pang, B., Tomkins, A.: Vanity fair: privacy in querylog bundles. In: Conference on Information and knowledge management, CIKM (2008)
13. Kirkby, R.: Random forest (Feburary 2010), http://weka.sourceforge.net/doc/weka/classifiers/trees/RandomForest.html

14. Kushilevitz, E., Ostrovsky, R.: Replication is not needed: single database, computationally-private information retrieval. In: Symposium on Foundations of Computer Science, FOCS (1997)
15. NYTimes: Google Resists U.S. Subpoena of Search Data, http://www.nytimes.com/2006/01/20/technology/20google.html?_r=1
16. PlanetLab: An open platform for developing, deploying, and accessing planetary-scale services, http://www.planet-lab.org/
17. Saint-Jean, F., Johnson, A., Boneh, D., Feigenbaum, J.: Private web search. In: ACM workshop on Privacy in Electronic Society (WPES) (2007)
18. Scroogle.org, http://scroogle.org/
19. Tor Anonymizing Network, http://www.torproject.org/
20. TrackMeNot: Browser Plugin, http://www.mrl.nyu.edu/~dhowe/trackmenot/
21. Trancer, B.: Click: What millions of people are doing online and why it matters. Hyperion (2008)
22. Wikipedia. Alternating decision tree (Feburary 2010), http://en.wikipedia.org/wiki/Alternating_decision_tree
23. Witten, I., Frank, E.: Data Mining–Practical Machine Learning Tools and Techniques, 2nd edn. Elsevier, Amsterdam (2005)
24. Ye, S., Wu, S.F., Pandey, R., Chen, H.: Noise injection for search privacy protection. In: Conference on Computational Science and Engineering, CSE (2009)

Private Information Disclosure from Web Searches

Claude Castelluccia[1], Emiliano De Cristofaro[2], and Daniele Perito[1]

[1] INRIA Rhone-Alpes, Montbonnot, France
[2] University of California, Irvine

Abstract. As the amount of personal information stored at remote service providers increases, so does the danger of data theft. When connections to remote services are made in the clear and authenticated sessions are kept using HTTP cookies, intercepting private traffic becomes easy to achieve. In this paper, we focus on the world largest service provider – Google. First, with the exception of a few services only accessible over HTTPS (e.g., Gmail), we find that many Google services are vulnerable to simple session hijacking attacks. Next, we present the Historiographer, a novel attack that reconstructs the web search history of Google users – Google's Web History – even though this service is supposedly protected from session hijacking by a stricter access control policy. The Historiographer uses a reconstruction technique inferring search history from the personalized suggestions fed by the Google search engine. We validate our technique through experiments conducted over real network traffic and discuss possible counter-measures. Our attacks are general and not only specific to Google, and highlight privacy concerns of mixed architectures mixing secure and insecure connections.

1 Introduction

With the emergence of cloud-based computing, users store an increasing amount of information at remote service providers. Cloud-based services often come at no cost for the users, while service providers leverage considerable amounts of user profiling information to deliver targeted advertisement. However, storing large amounts of personal information to external providers raises privacy concerns. Privacy advocates have highlighted the conceptual and practical dangers of personal data exposure over the Internet [12,14,15,16].

In this paper, we analyze private information potentially leaked from web searches to third parties, rather than focusing on data disclosed to service providers.

Being the world's largest service provider, we focus on the case of Google. In particular, we analyze one Google service: Web History: It provides users with personalized search results based on the history of their searches and navigation. The history is accessible at `http://google.com/history`.

Web searches have been shown to be often sensitive [16]. Any information leaked from search histories could endanger user privacy. For example, it is likely that search histories contain personal health-related information: a recent research has, in fact, successfully correlated the spread of influenza and the number of related search queries divided by region [18]. Similarly, searches may be related to political or religious views, sexual orientation, etc. Also, AOL's release in 2006 of 20 million nominally anonymized searches underlined that search queries contain private information [10].

M.J. Atallah and N. Hopper (Eds.): PETS 2010, LNCS 6205, pp. 38–55, 2010.

The privacy of personal data stored by service providers has been long threatened by the well-known attacks consisting of hijacking user's HTTP cookies.[1] These attacks have been addressed by Google in several ways. For instance, "sensitive" services such as Gmail now enforce secure HTTPS communication by default and transmit authentication cookies only over encrypted connections. Regarding Google Web History, the login page states: "To help protect your privacy, we'll sometimes ask you to verify your password even though you're already signed in. This may happen more frequently for services like Web History which involves your personal information". Frequently requesting users to re-enter their credentials can thwart the session hijacking attack. However, as illustrated in this paper, such an attack can still be effective if a user has just signed in. Moreover, we show that search histories can still be reconstructed even though the Web History page is inaccessible by hijacking cookies.

The Historiographer. To this end, we successfully design the Historiographer, an attack that reconstructs the history of web searches conducted by users on Google. The Historiographer uses the fact that users signed in any Google service receive suggestions for their search queries based on previously-searched keywords. Since Google Web Search transmits authentication cookies in the clear, the Historiographer—monitoring the network—can capture this cookie and use the search suggestions to reconstruct a user's search history. We refer to Section 3 for more details on the reconstruction technique.

Contributions. This paper makes the following contributions:

1. We show that the Google infrastructure is vulnerable to the Historiographer, a new attack that reconstructs part of the search history of users.
2. We show that the well known session hijacking attack is still applicable to many Google services. More specifically, we evaluate the security of several Google services, including Web History, against this simple attack and report the number of services vulnerable along with the amount and type of information potentially disclosed by each service.
3. We conduct an experimental analysis over network traces from a research institution, a Tor [1] exit node, and the 20 million anonymized searches released by AOL in 2006, in order to assess the number of potential victims and the accuracy of our attack. Results show that almost one third of monitored users were signed in their Google accounts and, among them, a half had Web History enabled, thus being vulnerable to our attack. Finally, we show that data from several other Google services can be collected with a simple session hijacking attack.

Paper Organization. The rest of the paper is organized as follows. Section 2 presents the necessary technical background. Section 3 details the new Historiographer attack. Section 4 describes our experimental evaluations on real network traffic, and estimates the number of potential victims and the accuracy of the Historiographer. Independently of Historiographer, this section also evaluates the additional information leaked from Google's services through simple session hijacking. Section 5 discusses possible countermeasures to thwart the Historiographer attack, while Section 6 overviews related

---

[1] In a session hijacking attack, an attacker monitoring the network captures an authentication cookie and impersonates a user. In Section 6, we will discuss several related vulnerabilities.

work. Section 7 concludes the exposition. Finally, in Section 8, we discuss the actions taken by Google in response to our findings.

2 Background

In the following, we present background information on several aspects discussed throughout the rest of the paper: the HTTP cookies, and the Google architecture.

2.1 HTTP Cookies

The need of maintaining sessions in HTTP emerged with the creation of the first web applications (e.g., e-commerce websites), as HTTP is a stateless protocol. RFC2109 [22] and RFC2965 [23] specified a standard way to create stateful sessions with HTTP requests and responses. They describe two new headers, Cookie and Set-Cookie, which carry state information between participating origin servers and user agents. A Cookie, which contains a unique identifier, is typically used to store user preferences or to store an authentication token. Cookies are set by the server as follows. After an incoming HTTP request, a server sends back a HTTP response containing an HTTP header, referred to as Set-Cookie, requesting the browser to store one or several cookies. Such a header is in the form of *name=value*, the so-called "cookie crumb". As a result, provided that the user agent enables cookies, every subsequent HTTP request to a server on the same domain will include the cookie in the Cookie HTTP header. A cookie may also include an expiration date[2], or a flag to mark it *secure*. In the latter case, the browser will send the secure cookie only over encrypted channels, such as SSL. A set-cookie header may optionally contain a *domain* attribute, which specifies the domain validity of the cookie. If this attribute is set, the cookie is referred to as domain cookie, as opposed to host cookie which is not specific to any particular sub-domain. For example, as we will present in Table 1, a user accessing Google's Calendar receives a domain cookie for `calendar.google.com` as an authentication token. Such a cookie is then to be included in every subsequent HTTP requests to the domain. In contrast, other Google's applications (such as the Search, History or Maps) only set host cookies, which are used across different services and domains. Finally, a set-cookie header may specify a path attribute to identify the subset of URLs for the cookie's validity. For example, as we will present in Table 2a, a user that signs in Google receives three cookies, namely `SID`, `SSID`, and `LSID`. While the latter only applies to the path "*/account*", the other two are can be used for different paths.

2.2 Google Architecture

As we mention in Section 1, we focus on the case of the world's largest service provider, i.e., Google. This section describes the Google architecture[3].

---

[2] If an expiration date is provided, cookies survive across browser sessions, and are then called "persistent". Otherwise, the cookie is deleted when closing the browser.

[3] Since not all the components of the Google architecture are public, some of the details presented in this section might not be completely accurate.

Google Web Products. Google offers more than 40 free Web services, including several search engines (e.g. Google Web Search), maps (Google Maps), as well as personalized subscription-based services like email (Gmail), documents (Google Docs), photos (Picasa), videos (Youtube), Web history. Even though some services can be used without registration (e.g., search), other are user-specific (e.g. Gmail) and require user authentication. Most of the services can be used by means of a single Google account, a combination of username and password. However, services that do not mandate registration provide extra features if users are signed in. For instance, an authenticated user can obtain personalized, potentially more accurate, search results on Google Maps based on her default location.

Google Web History. This *opt-out* service – previously known as Google Search History and Personalized Search – is implemented by Google to provide signed-in users with personalized search results based on the history of their searches and navigation. Furthermore, users typing search queries in the Web interface are prompted with *suggestions* resulting from their history. To this end, Google tracks all Web searches performed by a signed-in user (with Web History service enabled), as well as the target web pages clicked from the search result page. This service may be further enhanced by installing the Google Toolbar, allowing Google to also track *all* visited web sites, independently from the use of the search engine. Google Web History also provides a Web interface at google.com/history, allowing users to view and delete their history. Users are given the choice to *pause* Web History by accessing their account. Nevertheless, Google customizes searches and provides suggestions based on data recorded before pause. Note that Google is offering Personalized Search not only to signed-in but also to signed-out users. In fact, for these users Google performs the customization using the information linked to the user's browser with the help of an "anonymous" cookie. Specifically, Google stores up to 180 days of activity linked to such cookie. Again, users can explicitly disable this feature [3].

Google Authentication. Google services are accessible with a single set of credentials, composed by a pair username/password. Different services are usually hosted as subdomains of google.com (or other Top-Level Domains for different countries) and offer seamless integration between each other to minimize the need for users to re-enter their credentials. Integration is achieved through the Accounts service. In practice, requests to authenticate to a Google service are redirected to the Accounts page where the user is asked to enter her username and password. If authentication succeeds, a browser cookie is set (or refreshed) to track the session and the user is redirected back to the page that was originally requested. An illustration of this mechanism is provided in Fig. 1.

Access to Google Accounts is always secured using HTTPS. However, subsequent connections might revert back to simple HTTP depending on the requested service. For example connection to Maps Search are established with HTTP whereas HTTPS access to Gmail is enforced.

Table 1 compares several Google Services. It may be the case that services considered more sensitive are protected by HTTPS, whereas those judged less sensitive are left unencrypted. In particular, we noticed that the use of HTTPS is mandatory for some services (e.g., Gmail), while impossible for others (e.g., Search). Additionally, there are

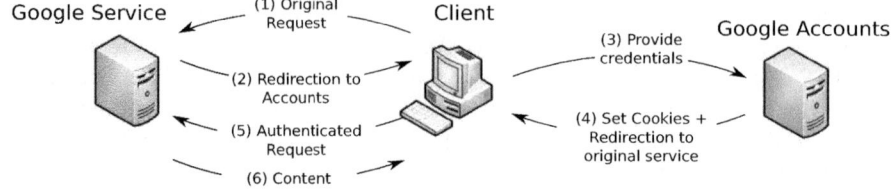

Fig. 1. The Google Accounts authentication management for Google services

Table 1. Some of Google's services

Service Name	Default Connect.	HTTPS Support	Domain specific cookie	Purpose
Search	HTTP	no	no	Web search
Maps	HTTP	no	no	Maps search
Reader	HTTP	yes	no	RSS/Atom feed reader
Contacts	HTTP	yes	no	Address book manager
History	HTTP	yes	no	Search history manager
Gmail	HTTPS	mand.	no	Web mail application
Accounts	HTTPS	mand.	no	Google account manager
News	HTTP	no	no	News aggregator
Bookmarks	HTTP	yes	no	Bookmark manager
Docs	HTTP	yes	yes	Office application
Calendar	HTTP	yes	yes	Calendar application
Groups	HTTP	yes	yes	Discussion groups application
Books	HTTP	no	no	Personalized digital library

services accessed on HTTP by default, but users may force a secure connection specifying `https://` in the URL.

Google cookies. Authenticated sessions are kept by means of cookies that are set by Accounts upon successful authentication. Two cookies, called `SID` and `SSID`, are used as authentication tokens across most services[4] for unencrypted and encrypted connections, respectively. We believe their names might stand for *Session ID* and *Secure Session ID*[5].

A description of several Google cookies is reflected in Tables 2a and 2b. Note that: (1) `SID` and `SSID` are valid for all Google sub-domains and are used to authenticate users to several services, (2) `SID` is not a secure cookie, i.e., it is sent on every connection to Google, while `SSID` is only sent over encrypted connections, and (3) `NID` represents the "anonymous" cookie used to track unlogged users. There are also a number of cookies not reported, which are used for miscellaneous purposes, e.g., to store language or search interface preferences.

In our study, we will focus on the `SID` cookie, providing authenticated access to most unencrypted services. In particular the `SID` cookie is sent in all web searches. It is

---

[4] All services that do not use domain cookies, such as Maps, History, Search, Reader, Books and Contacts – see Table 1.

[5] An additional list of domain-specific cookies, such as those for `docs.google.com` or `calendar.google.com`, are sent in the clear text but are *set* only over a secure connection upon user access.

Table 2. Description of the type and purposes of some cookies used in the Google platform

(a) Google's cookies for signed in users

Cookie-Name	Secure	Domain	Path	Purpose
SID	no	google.com	/	authentication token
SSID	yes	google.com	/	secure authentication token
LSID	yes	google.com	/accounts	secure authentication token

(b) Google's cookies for not signed in users

Cookie-Name	Secure	Domain	Path	Purpose
NID	no	google.com	/	track unlogged users
PREF	no	google.com	/	store search settings (e.g., language)

used by Google to identify the requesting account, populate the account's Web History and provide personalized web results and suggestions.

3   Historiographer: Reconstructing Search History

3.1   Attack Overview

In the following, we present the Historiographer, an attack aiming to reconstruct users' search histories stored by Google. The attack consists of two steps.

First, it hijacks a session stealing the victim's SID cookie. This can be done, for example, by eavesdropping on her traffic, and in particular on any request to a Google service, such as Google search. Eavesdropping can be performed by listening on a local wired network, an open wireless network, such as a campus network, or by deploying a Tor exit node (as detailed in Section 4). This does not necessary involve compromising nodes, and therefore does not require special skills.

Second, it reconstructs the Web History using a *partial precise* inference attack [17]. We recall that an inference attack is a technique used to disclose sensitive and protected information from presumably non-sensitive data. In this setting, we reconstruct part of the potentially privacy-sensitive Web History from web searches. The technique is *partial*, because, as shown in Section 3.2, it does not always reconstruct the whole history. Finally, it is *precise* since it infers accurate items from the Web History without introducing errors, as opposed to imprecise inference techniques that do it with a certain probability.

Note that any user, in particular if equipped with a mobile device, is likely to access the Internet via an unencrypted wireless channel at some point of time. As soon as she signs in Google when connected to such unprotected networks, she becomes vulnerable to our attack. Furthermore, the attack is effective even if the user is careful and never inputs sensitive information during "insecure" browsing sessions over unencrypted wireless channels.

Fig. 2. An example of Google Search Suggestions

3.2   Reconstructing the Web History through Inference

Web history access control. Authenticated users can consult, modify, pause or delete their complete history by accessing the Web History service. The history can be consulted as an HTML page or an RSS feed. However, as mentioned above, Google access control policy for Web History differs from the one implemented in other services. In fact, users are frequently asked to re-enter their credentials even though they are already authenticated. Preliminary tests showed that this mechanism is used quite frequently, and in such a case a session hijacker would be prevented from downloading the history.

Exploiting the search suggestion feature. However, a feature provided by Google, namely the *search suggestions*, helped us circumvent the access control enforced for Web History. As mentioned in Section 2, Google search engine offers contextual information in the search interface that can be derived from the user's search history. Specifically, whenever a prefix is typed in the search box, an Ajax [21] request is sent to a Google server, which replies with a list of associated keywords. Fig. 2 presents an example of a user typing the prefix "privac" in the search box. The user is then prompted with a list of related keywords to auto-complete the search, i.e., *search suggestions*. These keywords can either be based: (1) on Google's ranking of similarity (we call them *generic* search suggestions), or (2) on user's search history (we call them *history* search suggestions). Note that history search suggestions are only sent to the user if the typed prefix corresponds to search queries that are in the Web History and were followed by a "click" on one of the results. We call these queries: "clicked" queries. History search suggestions are visually distinguishable from the generic ones, since they include a link to remove them. This is reflected in the Javascript code, as history search suggestions have a flag set to differentiate them. The access to the web server that implements suggestions is carried out using Ajax and every request is authenticated sending an SID cookie, which can be easily eavesdropped and hijacked. Therefore, once an SID cookie has been captured, the user's Web History can be reconstructed using the suggestion service: Historiographer steals a user authentication cookie and then sequentially requests possible prefixes to the suggestion server to recover keywords coming from the history.

Reconstruction algorithms. In order to reconstruct a search history, the Historiographer needs to ask for suggestions for different prefixes. Hence, we need to carefully select the list of possible prefixes to use, since the keywords in the history are unknown. We encounter the following obstacles: (1) the number of requests for suggestions should be kept to a minimum, in order to be as stealthy as possible; (2) at most three replies come from the suggestion history upon each suggestion request, limiting the amount of information discovered with each request; and (3) suggestions are only returned for two-letter (or longer) prefixes, preventing from simply looking for all letters in the given alphabet. A naïve (*brute-force*) approach would involve requesting all the possible two- or three-letter prefixes to harvest the replies coming from the history. However, this would already require $26^2 = 676$ requests for two-letter and $26^3 = 17,576$ for three-letter combinations in the English alphabet, hence relatively high numbers that might lead to detection. Instead, the Historiographer employs a more sophisticated technique: it requests only prefixes that are common in a given language. For instance, if one considers English, there are only 7 words starting with the two-letter prefix oo, while no word starts with the prefix qr. Whereas, the most used prefix results to be co, used in 3223 words. It is then reasonable to expect that in the search history there are more entries starting with the letters co than with qr. As a result, we proceed as follows: We extract all two-letter prefixes from a reference corpus, order them by frequency, and we select only the prefixes in the $90th$ percentile. We used two different reference corpora in our experiments: the English dictionary and the AOL dataset of 20 million anonymized searches that was released in 2006 [10]. However, they both achieved very similar performance. For the English dictionary, this yields a total of 121 two-letter combinations and reduces the number of requests and the fingerprint of the attack[6]. Further, we notice that at most 3 search suggestions can come from the history for each requested prefix. Thus, if we get exactly 3 suggestions from the history, there are either 3 or more search queries starting with the corresponding prefix. This is a potential indication that this prefix is particularly frequent in the history, and it is worth being further explored. Hence, whenever we encounter a two-letter prefix producing 3 suggestions, we add another letter to the prefix and we repeat the request. Note that the resulting three-letter prefix is again generated by extracting the most common three-letter prefixes from the dictionary and not by simply adding every possible letter in the alphabet. Fig. 3 visually depicts this procedure: The prefix co produces 3 results and is further explored, contrary to de and ya who produce only 2 (resp., 1) results. A description of the achieved accuracy and the related overhead in terms of requests is provided in Section 4.2.

Implementation. We implemented the Historiographer as a Perl application. It is part of a more complete tool that: (i) captures traffic from a network interface, (ii) recognizes cookies sent to and from Google servers, and (iii) then uses them to hijack sessions and

---

[6] Different languages can be supported by simply changing the alphabet and the reference corpus.

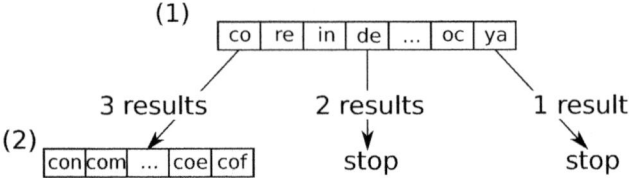

Fig. 3. Smart tree approach. To reconstruct large portions of the search history, we start with the most common two-letter prefixes (1). If a prefix produces 3 suggestions, then we descend in the tree (2).

retrieve personal information. Web History is only one of the services the software collects data from.

3.3   Beyond the Historiographer: Exploiting Personalized Results

The Historiographer attack uses Personalized Search to leak information from a user's Web History. However, one could also use the so-called Personalized Results, i.e., the fact that search queries on Google often produce different results based on the user's search history. We present an example of this in Fig. 4. If the results contain at least one linked page previously accessed by the user, the "View customizations" link appears at the top right corner of the result page. One can easily identify the visited linked pages (e.g., http://petsymposium.org/2010/ in Fig. 4) since they are marked with a tag reporting the number of visits (e.g., 8), and the date of the last visit (e.g., March 1st). Therefore, an adversary can verify that specific keywords belonging to a user's search history using the Personalized Results. We call such an attack a *targeted check*. Note that the adversary does not have to test the exact matching keyword searched by the user. It is enough to make a related search that includes the visited linked page in the results. For instance, assuming that a user has searched for *PETS 2010* and *Oakland 2010*, and has then clicked on the related links http://petsymposium.org/2010/ and http://oakland09.cs.virginia.edu/. A subsequent search for the keyword *Privacy* would produce a result page with the "View customizations" link. Looking at the result page produced by only one request, an adversary can find out that the above pages were visited and conclude that the user is interested in *privacy*, in *PETS 2010* and *IEEE Security and Privacy*. The adversary could then try other keywords and broaden the information leakage or profile user's interests. Note that this attack can be amplified with the exploitation of the new Google's **Star** service that allows users to mark their favorite web sites. With **stars**, a user can mark his favorite sites by simply clicking the star marker on any search result or map. As a result of this action, these sites will appear in a special list next time the identical or a related search is performed. This feature gives even more power to the adversary. Note that this attack only applies to signed-in Google users with Web History enabled (a significant proportion of Google users as showed in Sec. 4). However, as discussed in Sec. 2, Google provides customized searches to signed-out users too, using an "anonymous" cookie. Therefore,

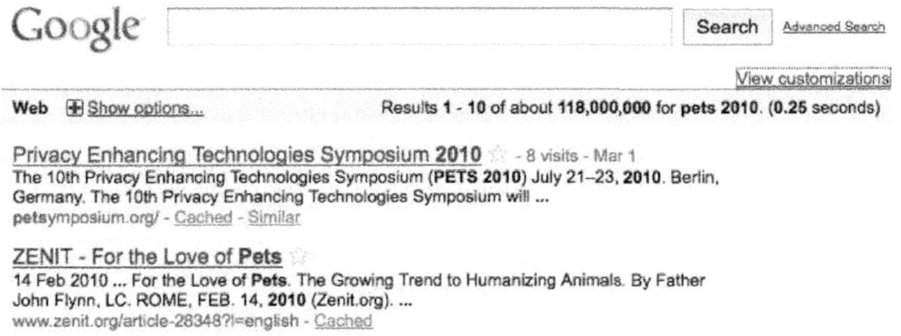

Fig. 4. An example of Google Personalized Results

we believe that a similar attack can be designed for signed-out users as well, although the history would be limited to the life of this cookie.

4 Measurements and Analysis

Given the private nature of the information gathered and the difficulty of having users willing to disclose them, we conducted four different experiments. These experiments were aimed at collecting data to estimate: (1) the number of potential victims that access Google services while being signed-in and, among them, how many have Web History enabled; (2) the accuracy and the cost of the Historiographer; (3) the amount of private data that can be retrieved from other services with the simple session hijacking attack; (4) the applicabity of the Historiographer on smart phones.

4.1 Estimating the Number of Potential Victims

In order to estimate the number of potential victims of our attack, we conducted an experimental analysis on the network traces collected from a research center with about 500-600 daily users and a Tor exit node. We collected one week of network traffic during February 2010. The goal was to measure the percentage of users using Google while signed-in, and that having the Web History service enabled. Note that only aggregate data was stored. The data collected from the research center was analyzed passively, i.e., no session was actually hijacked.

In order to count the number of users from a network trace, one needs reliable identifiers to filter out duplicate queries or changes of network identifiers, e.g. IP churn. Luckily we could use cookies gathered from the network captures to identify single users. As explained above, Google issues persistent cookies both to signed-in and not signed-in users. Among them we chose to use SID cookies to identify signed-in users and NID cookies to identify not signed-in ones. Furthermore, in order to count the number of users with history enabled, our application looked for a particular link to the History service that is included in each search result page. The results of test are presented in Table 3a. Around one third of the users resulted to be signed-in while using Google services, including web searches. Furthermore, about half of the users with

Table 3. Results from the three experiments

(a) Measurements on network traces

Experiment	Number of Google users	Number of users signed-in	Number of signed-in users with History enabled
Research center	1502	543 (36.1%)	223 (14.8%)
Tor Exit Node	1893	872 (46.1%)	441 (23.29%)

(b) Results from volunteers

User ID	n_h	n_c	n_s	Recall	$n_{requests}$	History Activation date
1	751	442	308	0.69	680	Aug 08, 2009
2	318	142	99	0.69	368	Mar 10, 2008
3	621	321	176	0.54	483	May 16, 2009
4	520	248	169	0.68	400	May 22, 2007
5	657	309	231	0.75	601	Feb 06, 2009
6	389	202	130	0.64	365	Fen 12, 2009
7	690	337	201	0.60	560	Jul 18, 2008
8	416	219	143	0.65	399	Aug 09, 2006
9	228	127	69	0.54	211	Aug 20, 2008
10	306	164	118	0.72	334	Sep 27, 2009
11	1567	930	506	0.54	740	Oct 26, 2009
12	1163	680	533	0.78	823	Dec 4, 2009

(c) Aggregate Information analyzed from 872 Tor users

Type of information leaked	Corresponding service	Number of Accounts accessible	Mean number of entries collected
Complete (unrestricted) Search History	History	45(5%)	123
Blogs followed on Reader	Reader	139(15%)	14
Address book	Contacts	766(87%)	189
Maps search history	Maps	696(79%)	22
Default address on Maps	Maps	52(5%)	1
Financial portfolio	Portfolio	11(1%)	8
First/Last name	Maps profile	661(75%)	1
Bookmarks	Bookmarks	236(27%)	79

an account have history enabled. The limited size and the lack of randomness in the choice of our sample, does not allow us to draw conclusions about the entire population of users. However, if we combine our results with the above mentioned popularity of Google services, it would appear that a significant portion of web users are at risk.

4.2   Estimating Historiographer's Accuracy

Volunteers. In order to evaluate the extent of potential leakage of private information from Google web searches, we turned to volunteers. It would have been otherwise impossible to conduct our study on uninformed users without incurring legal and ethical issues. We aimed at evaluating the accuracy of the Historiographer at reconstructing web histories. To this end, we "attacked" the accounts of 10 volunteers using our software and measured its accuracy. The performance of the Historiographer at reconstructing search histories can be measured in terms of *recall*. For every user u, we call H the set of entries in u's history, H_c the subset of searches whose results were clicked by u, and S the set of entries reconstructed from suggestions. We denote $n_h = |H|$, $n_c = |H_c|$

and $n_s = |S|$. Since suggestions are only given for "clicked" queries, the recall R of our reconstruction algorithm can be measured as the ratio $R = \frac{n_s}{n_c}$. Results are reflected in Table 3b. The Historiographer reconstructs a significant portion of a user's history, with a mean recall of 0.65. The mean number of requests per user to reconstruct the history was 440. Since users are kept signed-in for two weeks, these requests can be made at a low pace to increase stealthiness. For instance, an attacker could issue a request every hour and still expect to retrieve 65% of the "clicked" queries. Also, the recall can arbitrarily be increased by increasing the number of requests. On average, with about 2000 requests, we can obtain a mean recall of 0.81. The mean recall lowers to 0.34 when considering the ratio of reconstructed entries over the complete set H. Recall that the Historiographer can only recover "clicked" queries, although a complete history typically contains more information and additionally stores the time and the frequency of searches. We argue that only recovering "clicked" queries is not a tremendous limitation. When inspecting volunteers' history, we noticed that "clicked" queries are often corrections of generic or misspelled queries. A more accurate analysis of this phenomenon is left for future work. Note also that the Google's algorithm producing keyword suggestions is based on several parameters, such as dates and frequencies of searches and visited web sites. Therefore, we believe that the accuracy and the amount of information that can be retrieved by the Historiographer could be further improved with a deeper understanding of the underlying algorithm. On the other hand, it appears that the likelihood that an entry in the history is returned as a suggestion decreases over time, which could negatively affect the recall for older entries.

AOL Dataset. Next, we tested our attack on a wider sample. We used the anonymized query dataset released by AOL in 2006, containing 20 million searched made by 650,000 users. From the dataset, we constructed the search history of each user. Then, simulating the search suggestions fed by Google drawing from the histories, we estimated the recall of our reconstruction technique. The mean recall was 0.64, an accuracy similar to that obtained for the volunteers.

4.3 Additional Information Leakage via Session Hijacking

As mentioned above, in addition to the Historiographer, an attacker can hijack a user's session to access several Google services. This section evaluates the extent of the information leaked. We ran our software for a week on a Tor exit node, and we analyzed 872 Google accounts. We stress that our software only generated aggregate data automatically and discarded the information immediately. Note that we used Tor only as a way to collect anonymized network traces. This cannot, by any means, be considered as an attack against Tor. In fact, even considering a malicious Tor exit node, the attacks can be prevented by using the appropriate tool configuration to block cookies transmitted over HTTP. (For more information, we refer to [4,5]). However, we point out that a significant number of users are not aware of the dangers. In fact, they authenticate to Google while connected in Tor and do not block HTTP cookies, thus endangering their anonymity and privacy to potential malicious Tor exit nodes. In fact, a malicious entity could set up a Tor exit node to hijack cookies and reconstruct search histories. The security design underlying the Tor network guarantees that the malicious Tor exit node, although potentially able to access unencrypted traffic, is not able to learn the origin of such traffic. However, it may take the malicious node just one Google SID cookie to reconstruct a user's search history, the searched locations, the default location, etc., thus significantly increasing the probability of identifying a user. Additional example applications include RIAA tracking users that ever searched—although connected into Tor—for torrent files related to unlicensed material.

Session Hijacking Attack. By means of session hijacking, we tried to access the following information: locations searched on Maps (along with the "default location", when available); blogs followed on Reader; full Web History (when accessible without re-entering credentials); finance portfolio; bookmarks. For each of them, we counted the number of entries retrieved and reported the mean over the 872 accounts. Table 3c summarizes the obtained results. We point out that for 5% of the accounts, we accessed the Web History page without being asked to re-enter credentials (simply replaying the SID cookie). We stress that the session hijack had a significant success rate for many popular services. For instance, we retrieved 79% of the searched locations on Maps and the 87% of address books (Contacts). Also, we were able to retrieve the first and last name associated to the account in 75% of cases. Unfortunately, *these numbers translate into a significant amount of personal (and identifying) information leaked through session hijacking.* Notably, the information collected from the Maps service was composed of maps queries coming from the histories of the users. Similarly to history suggestions, users that access Maps are presented with entries that come from the locations they previously searched for. Differently from search suggestions, Maps suggestions are not the result of an prefix based Ajax query to a remote Google server. Instead, for signed-in users, the page at maps.google.com includes a Javascript array that includes *all* previous searches. Accessing this information only requires retrieving the web page once and does not require the use of the Historiographer. The provided information is very detailed and includes: the exact location searched (address:), the time, in seconds since the Epoch, it was searched (created:) and the number of times the location was searched (count:). The information collected this way is of the same kind of the one collected by the Historiographer but referred to maps searches instead of generic web searches. However, the specifics of the design of Maps suggestions make the attack on this service much easier. We can only speculate on the reasons behind such a design. One could be that, since Maps history is relatively small in mean size 3c, it is more efficient to send all the information at once, rather than relying on multiple Ajax requests and replies. Whatever the reasons, this design makes location information stored on Google more vulnerable to session hijacking than search history.

4.4   Web History and Smart Phones

With the increasing number of smart phones users, search history is likely to be strongly correlated with users' location of the users. We noticed that Google maintains a separated Web History when the search page is accessed from an iPhone. Such a history has a less strict access control policy. Similarly to Google Maps, the whole search history is sent as a Javascript list embedded in the page. Supposedly, this information is presented only when using the iPhone. However, one just needs to set the appropriate user agent string when accessing Google (for example through the User Agent Switcher Firefox extension [7]. Then, replaying the SID cookie, the whole Web History becomes accessible, with a single page access. We tested this strategy on the set of volunteers. We were able to retrieve their iPhone search history from a regular PC by switching the PC's browser user agent to an iPhone user agent, and hijacking the victims' SID cookies.

5 Possible Countermeasures

The vulnerability targeted by the Historiographer is difficult to address because of the complexity and scale of the Google architecture, as well as the performance and usability requirements. However, we discuss some possible countermeasures. For instance, users could take the following precautions, simultaneously: (i) always log out from any Google service when performing a search, (ii) disable the Web History service, and (iii) disable personalization from anonymous cookies or always delete Google cookies, similarly to what is suggested by the Electronic Frontier Foundation On the other hand, Google could either: (i) discontinue the Personalized Search service, or (ii) let the users choose to enforce HTTPS for web searches (for instance, by clicking on a special link when surfing from *insecure* networks) and trade off speed with privacy. However, one can argue that solutions preventing personalized searches may degrade the service, whereas the use of HTTPS on Web Search[7] may be too expensive to put in place. Evidence of this is given by the impossibility of accessing Google search page via HTTPS and by the concerns already expressed by Google regarding the performance of using HTTPS for Gmail [9].

Compartmentalized Searches. We propose an additional mitigation technique that would allow to keep the Personalized Search service. Specifically, we propose that Google could keep separate histories based on the networks from which user's searches originate. Then, it can provide different search suggestions (and personalized results) based on different locations. We imagine an extension to the google.com/history web page to allow a user to configure such locations and the privacy settings related to them. Although this would not solve all possible information leakage, it would compartmentalize user's private information: Consider for instance an employee reluctant to reveal personal information to her employer (e.g., that she is looking for another job). Fearing that her navigation within the company network is monitored, she might avoid accessing potentially "compromising" information. If she signs in Google from the company network, however, her search history —containing for instance "compromising" searches made from home—(and more) can be leaked.

Binding authentication cookies to IP addresses. Several web sites, e.g., LiveJournal [2], allow user agents to bind the authentication cookies to the current IP address. In other words, the server does not accept an authentication cookie that originates from a different IP address. However, this technique is not always enforced due to drawbacks on the usability of the service. For example, "mobile" users, whose IP address often changes, would be forced to frequently re-enter their credentials. However, depending on the network configuration, binding cookies to IP addresses could not be enough to

---

[7] Note that adopting HTTPS only for the Web History web page would not prevent the Historiographer, but only the access to the page.

prevent session hijack. For instance, an attacker operating on a local network could succeed by poisoning the ARP table on the local Ethernet switch. Note also that at the moment Google allows a single account to be signed-in from multiple locations and with multiple IP addresses (although some services such as Gmail display the number of simultaneous connections at the bottom of the page).

6   Related Work

To the best of our knowledge, this work is the first to focus on the private information leaked from web searches to third parties. In the following, we present the most relevant work to several concepts and tools that we use.

Session hijacking. Since their early appearances, the use of cookies to maintain authenticated sessions has lead the way to *session hijacking* attacks (see for instance [19]). These attacks are quite simple: an attacker monitoring network traffic may sniff an authentication cookie and replay it to impersonate another user. For this reason, sensitive web applications should always employ secure cookies, i.e., authentication cookies that are only transmitted over encrypted channels. However, this simple countermeasure is not always effective. For instance, in 2008 the Cookiemonster attack [24] highlighted vulnerabilities derived from an improper mixed support of secure and insecure connections. In response to this work, Google sett HTTPS in Gmail by default [26]. Although this attack—as well as simple session hijacking—could not be be used to hijack the Web History, it is an interesting example of vulnerabilities in web applications that do not *properly* provide mixed HTTP/HTTPS support.

Privacy Threats. Recent work has discussed potential privacy threats related to cloud service providers. For instance, [14] discussed potential threats and countermeasures associated with many forms of web activity—focusing on Google—related to the information collected by service providers. However, as opposed to our work, this paper focuses on the privacy threats against the service provider. Another direction was taken in [16,15] to assess user perception on alleged privacy threats by interviewing users. Among the other interesting results, it has been shown that more than 80% of users admitted to having conducted searches for information they would not want disclosed to their current or future employer. Finally, independently of our work, it was recently shown that popular online applications may leak private data to a network eavesdropper even over encrypted web connections [13]. In particular, an adversary could exploit the autocompletion mechanism of popular search engines to infer the victim's search queries. When a user types the first letter in a search query, the search engine sends that character to the server, and the server replies with a list of suggested completions. As the size of that list depends on the character typed, an attacker can deduce which letter was typed. When the second letter is entered, another request is sent to the server, and another encrypted response sent back to the client, which allows the attacker to infer the second character; and so on. As a result, the attacker guesses the search query, despite the communication is encrypted. This result is complementary to our work: It allows recovering search requests over encrypted channels. However, the attack does not work if the victim is logged-in and the suggestions received are personalized. In contrast, our attack retrieves parts of the victim's search history using these personalized suggestions, although our attack does not work over encrypted links.

Limiting personal information disclosure. Several techniques have been proposed to avoid user profiling and reduce the amount of information potentially leaked. For instance, the Firefox extension Trackemenot [20] periodically issues randomized search-queries to search engines to populate a user's search history with (non-clicked) queries and hide real queries. However, this would not prevent the Historiographer from retrieving "clicked" queries from the history and retrieve sensitive information.

7   Discussion

This paper has presented a study of the private information disclosed to third parties from web searches. We showed that the well known session hijacking attack is still applicable to many Google services, and we presented the Historiographer, an attack that reconstructs Google's search histories from simple web searches. We have validated our technique through a large-scale experimental analysis.

We argue that solutions should be quickly deployed to protect users against these two types of attacks. The session hijacking attack is harmful not only because it allows an attacker to collect a lot of private information, including sometimes the search history, but also because it can be exploited to add potentially *compromising* entries [25]. It can also be used to modify the search results displayed to the victim. In fact, Google allows to delete or promote—i.e., show as first—results using a button associated to them. An adversary hijacking a session cookie can perform searches on the victim's behalf and influence the results corresponding to these searches as she wishes. For instance, this attack can be a powerful tool for censorship, as it can be used to remove or promote some pages displayed after a Google search.

The Historiographer can be used to reconstruct part of the Web History, when, for example, the simple session hijacking attack is not applicable. In addition, it can be used as an oracle to perform *targeted checks*, e.g., to verify the existence in the search history of specific keywords. The Historiographer is an *amplification* attack, and therefore is much more powerful than a simple eavesdropping attack: It not only allows an attacker to eavesdrop on the victim's search requests, but also allows him to retrieve the victim's *previous* search requests, *possibly performed from different networks and even different computers*. Also, the Historiographer is *non-destructive*, i.e., it does not affect user data. The number of potential victims is very high, since any signed-in user is at risk as soon as she issues a single Google search request from an unencrypted network, such as an open wireless network at an airport or a cafe.

These attacks deserve serious attention since Web Histories contain sensitive information. Any information leaked from Web search histories could endanger user privacy. Information retrieved from the search history could also be combined with other publicly available data, such as that published on social networks to accurately profile and/or identify target users. Furthermore, since the Historiographer also works for Google searches performed from mobile devices and such searches contain also localized results, one could use location-based services to also track users' movements and locations.

Although the Historiographer builds on features specific to the Google architecture, our goal is not to attack Google nor any particular service provider. Instead, we highlight the general problem of protecting the privacy of sensitive data when using a mixed architecture with both secure and insecure connections. As mentioned in [8], Google is not the only provider which leaves its customers vulnerable to data theft and account hijacking. As a matter of fact, the Bing search engine recently added a similar functionality to Personalized Suggestions. Users receive suggestions based on their previous searches and they can access the full search history [6]. Differently from Google, Bing only uses anonymous cookies for this purpose and stores the search history only up to 29 days. However, in Bing the full history is accessible via a simple session hijacking. We defer to future work a complete analysis of Bing and other search engines.

8   Afterword

While this paper was under submission (March 2010) we disclosed it to Google to allow them to react to it. Google has been very responsive to our research and has taken some actions to fix some of the highlighted issues. After receiving a preliminary report, Google temporarily disabled the personalized suggestions (note, however, that they were never disabled on smart phones), and switched the Web History and Bookmark services to HTTPS (thus, preventing session hijacking on these services)[8]. Later on, Google countered the Historiographer attack by encrypting back-end server requests associated with the personalized Maps and Search suggestion services. We provide a detailed description and discussion on the possible shortcomings of this solution in [11]. We also detail a possible way the Historiographer could work against Google's solution, albeit with a different and slightly more powerful attacker. It is also noteworthy that the proposed solutions do not prevent potential leakage resulting from personalized results (see Section 4.3). Furthermore, as of today (beginning of May), searches conducted from smart phones are still vulnerable (see Section 4.4) and session hijacking is still effective on the following services: Reader, Contacts and Portfolio.

References

1. Tor: anonymity online, http://www.torproject.org/
2. LiveJournal,
   http://www.livejournal.com/support/faqbrowse.bml?faqid=135 (Retrieved February 2010)
3. Personalized search for everyone, http://googleblog.blogspot.com/2009/12/personalized-search-for-everyone.html (Retrieved February 2010)
4. Privoxy, http://www.privoxy.org/ (Retrieved February 2010)
5. Torbutton, http://www.torproject.org/torbutton/ (Retrieved February 2010)
6. Bing Autosuggest, http://bit.ly/bxPk9g (Retrieved March 2010)

---

[8] For more details on the ongoing development of this project, refer to
http://planete.inrialpes.fr/projects/
private-information-disclosure-from-web-searches

7. User Agent Switcher firefox plugin, `https://addons.mozilla.org/en-US/firefox/addon/59` (Retrieved March 2010)
8. Acquisti, A., et al.: Ensuring adequate security in Google's cloud based services (2009), `http://www.wired.com/images_blogs/threatlevel/2009/06/google-letter-final2.pdf`
9. Whitten, A. (Google): HTTPS security for web application (2009), `http://googleonlinesecurity.blogspot.com/2009/06/https-security-for-web-applications.html`
10. Barbaro, M., Zeller, T.: A face is exposed for AOL searcher no. 4417749. New York Times 9, 2008 (2006)
11. Castelluccia, C., De, E.D., Perito, D.: The historiographer reloaded. Technical report, INRIA (May 2010)
12. Cellan-Jones, R.: Web creator rejects net tracking (2008), `http://news.bbc.co.uk/2/hi/7299875.stm`
13. Chen, S., Wang, R., Wang, X., Zhang, K.: Side-Channel Leaks in Web Applications: a Reality Today, a Challenge Tomorrow. In: IEEE Security and Privacy Symposium 2010 (2010)
14. Conti, G.: Googling considered harmful. In: Workshop on New Security Paradigms, pp. 76–85 (2006)
15. Conti, G.: Googling Security: How Much Does Google Know About You? Addison-Wesley, Reading (2009)
16. Conti, G., Sobiesk, E.: An honest man has nothing to fear: user perceptions on web-based information disclosure. In: SOUPS 2007, pp. 112–121 (2007)
17. Farkas, C., Jajodia, S.: The inference problem: a survey. ACM SIGKDD Explorations Newsletter 4(2), 6–11 (2002)
18. Ginsberg, J., Mohebbi, M., Patel, R., Brammer, L., Smolinski, M., Brilliant, L.: Detecting influenza epidemics using search engine query data. Nature 457(7232), 1012–1014 (2008)
19. Graham, R.: SideJacking with Hamster (2007), `http://erratasec.blogspot.com/2007/08/sidejacking-with-hamster_05.html`
20. Howe, D., Nissenbaum, H.: TrackMeNot (2008), `http://mrl.nyu.edu/~dhowe/trackmenot/`
21. Garrett, J.J.: Ajax: A New Approach to Web Applications (2005), `http://www.adaptivepath.com/ideas/essays/archives/000385.php`
22. Kristol, D., Montulli, L.: RFC2109: HTTP State Management Mechanism. IETF (1997)
23. Kristol, D., Montulli, L.: RFC2965: HTTP State Management Mechanism. IETF (2000)
24. Perry, M.: CookieMonster: Cookie Hijacking (2008), `http://fscked.org/projects/cookiemonster`
25. Robertson, J.: Internet Virus Frames Users For Child Porn (2009), `http://www.huffingtonpost.com/2009/11/09/internet-virus-frames-use_n_350426.html`
26. Schillace, S.: Default https access for Gmail, `http://gmailblog.blogspot.com/2010/01/default-https-access-for-gmail.html` (Retrieved February 2010)

Collaborative, Privacy-Preserving Data Aggregation at Scale

Benny Applebaum[1,*], Haakon Ringberg[2], Michael J. Freedman[2], Matthew Caesar[3], and Jennifer Rexford[2]

[1] Weizmann Institute of Science
[2] Princeton University
[3] UIUC

Abstract. Combining and analyzing data collected at multiple administrative locations is critical for a wide variety of applications, such as detecting malicious attacks or computing an accurate estimate of the popularity of Web sites. However, legitimate concerns about privacy often inhibit participation in collaborative data aggregation. In this paper, we design, implement, and evaluate a practical solution for privacy-preserving data aggregation (PDA) among a large number of participants. Scalability and efficiency is achieved through a "semi-centralized" architecture that divides responsibility between a *proxy* that obliviously blinds the client inputs and a *database* that aggregates values by (blinded) keywords and identifies those keywords whose values satisfy some evaluation function. Our solution leverages a novel cryptographic protocol that provably protects the privacy of both the participants and the keywords, provided that proxy and database do not collude, even if both parties may be individually malicious. Our prototype implementation can handle over a million suspect IP addresses per hour when deployed across only two quad-core servers, and its throughput scales linearly with additional computational resources.

1 Introduction

Many important data-analysis applications must aggregate data collected by multiple participants. ISPs and enterprise networks may seek to share traffic mix information to more accurately detect and localize anomalies. Similarly, collaboration can help identify popular Web content by having Web users—or proxies monitoring traffic for an entire organization—combine their access logs to determine the most frequently accessed URLs [1]. Such distributed data analysis is similarly important in the context of security. For example, victims of denial-of-service (DoS) attacks know they have been attacked but cannot easily distinguish the malicious source IP addresses from the good users who happened to send legitimate requests at the same time. Since compromised hosts in a botnet often participate in multiple such attacks, victims could potentially identify the bad IP addresses if they combined their measurement data [39]. Cooperation is also useful for Web clients to recognize they have received a bogus DNS response

* Work done in part while visiting Princeton University. Supported by Koshland Fellowship, and NSF grants CNS-0627526, CNS-0831653, CCF-0426582 and CCF-0832797.

M.J. Atallah and N. Hopper (Eds.): PETS 2010, LNCS 6205, pp. 56–74, 2010.

or a forged self-signed certificate, by checking that the information they received agrees with that seen by other clients accessing the same Web site [34,41]. In this paper, we present the design, implementation, and evaluation of an efficient, privacy-preserving system that supports these kinds of data analysis.

Today, these kinds of distributed data aggregation and analysis lack privacy protections. Existing solutions often rely on a trusted (typically centralized) aggregation node that collects and analyzes the raw data, thereby learning both the identity and inputs of participants. There is good reason to believe this inhibits participation. ISPs and Web sites are notoriously unwilling to share operational data with one another, because they are business competitors and are concerned about compromising the privacy of their customers. Many users are unwilling to install software from Web analytics services such as Alexa [1], as such software would track and report every Web site they visit. Unfortunately, even good intentions may not translate to good privacy protections, demonstrated all too well by the fact that large-scale data breaches have become commonplace [35]. There certainly are non-Internet applications as well. Patients could benefit from the aggregated analysis of medical data, but significant privacy concerns— and regulation in the form of HIPAA and laws—understandably limit deployment in practice. As such, we believe that many useful distributed data-analysis applications will not gain serious traction unless privacy can be ensured.

Fortunately, many of these collaborative applications have a common pattern: aggregating participants' inputs on common input keys and potentially analyzing the resulting intersection. When designed with privacy in mind, we refer to this problem as *privacy-preserving data aggregation* (PDA). Namely, each participant p_j (or *client*) autonomously makes observations about *values* associated with *keys*, *i.e.*, input key-value tuples $\langle k_i, v_i \rangle$. The system jointly computes a two-column input table T. The first column of T is a set comprised of all unique keys belonging to all participants (the *key column*). The second, *value column* is comprised of values $T[k_i]$ that are the sum or union of all participant's values for k_i. This is akin to a database join on matching keys across each participant's input (multi)set.

We consider two different forms of this functionality: (1) *aggregation-only (PDA)*, where the output is just the value column, and (2) *conditional-release (CR-PDA)*, where the protocol also outputs a key k_i if and only if some evaluation function $f(\forall j | v_{i,j})$ is satisfied. For example, our botnet anomaly detection is an instance of over-threshold set intersection—also known as the heavy-hitter or iceberg detection problem—where the goal is to detect keys that occur more than some threshold number of times across all participants. Here, the keys k_i refer to IP addresses, each value $v_{i,j}$ is 1, and f is true iff its cardinality exceeds some threshold τ (*i.e.*, if values are aggregated as $T[k_i] \leftarrow T[k_i] + 1$, is $T[k_i] \geq \tau$?)[1]

---

[1] In fact, since CR-PDA also releases the value column of all keys, one can choose the function f based on the value table itself. (For example, in the case of anomaly detection the dataset may naturally expose a clear gap between frequency counts of normal and anomalous behavior, and so it makes sense to set the frequency threshold τ correspondingly.) This increases the utility of the system by letting the data operators "play" with raw data (without seeing the keys). However, one should note that in some scenarios this additional information may be seen as a privacy violation.

Table 1. Comparison of proposed schemes for privacy-preserving data aggregation

Approach	Keyword Privacy	Participant Privacy	Efficiency	Flexibility	Lack of Coordination
Garbled-Circuit Evaluation [42,3]	**Yes**	**Yes**	Very Poor	**Yes**	No
Multiparty Set Intersection [16,26]	**Yes**	**Yes**	Poor	No	No
Hashing Inputs [17,2]	No	No	**Very Good**	**Yes**	**Yes**
Network Anonymization [11]	No	**Yes**	**Very Good**	**Yes**	**Yes**
This paper	**Yes**	**Yes**	**Good**	**Yes**	**Yes**

A practical PDA system should provide the following:

- **Keyword privacy:** No party should learn anything about inputted keys. That is, given the above aggregated table T, each party should only learn the value column $T[k_i]$ at the conclusion of the protocol. In the case of CR-PDA, parties should only learn the keys k_i whose corresponding value $T[k_i]$ satisfies f.
- **Participant privacy:** No party should learn which key inputs belongs to which participant (except for information which is trivially deduced from the output of the function). This is formally captured by showing that the protocol leaks no more information than an ideal implementation that uses a trusted third party, a convention standard in secure multi-party computation [19].
- **Efficiency:** The system should scale to large numbers of participants, each generating and inputting large numbers of observations (key-value tuples). The system should be scalable both in terms of the bandwidth consumed (communication complexity) and the computational complexity of executing the PDA.
- **Flexibility:** There are a variety of computations one might wish to perform over each key's values $T[k_i]$, other than the sum-over-threshold test. These may include finding the maximum value for a given key, or checking if the median of a row exceeds a threshold. A single protocol should work for a wide range of functions.
- **Lack of coordination:** Finally, the system should operate without requiring that all participants coordinate their efforts to jointly execute some protocol at the same time, or even all be online around the same time. Furthermore, no set of participants should be able to prevent others from executing the protocol.

Classes of solutions. In this work, we consider privacy-preserving data aggregation as a form of the general *secure multiparty computation* problem, where multiple participants wish to jointly compute some value based on individually-held secret bits of information without revealing their secrets to one another. The theoretical cryptographic literature provides generic solutions for this problem which also satisfy very strong notions of security [42,20,4,7]. In general, however, these tools are not efficient enough to be used in practice. Few have ever been implemented ([28,18,3]), let alone operated in the real world [5]. Moreover, they do not scale well either to large data sets or to a large number of participants. More efficient solutions exist for special cases of the PDA problem, such as secure set intersection [13,30,27,16,26,15,23,10]. However, while some of these solutions are quite efficient when the number of participants is small (e.g., 2), none of them achieve practical efficiency in our setting where there are hundreds or thousands of participants each generating thousands of inputs.[2]

On the other extreme, ad-hoc solutions for PDA can be highly efficient. Rather than building fully decentralized protocols, we could aggregate data and compute results using a centralized server. One approach is to simply have clients first hash their keys before submitting them to the server (*e.g.*, using SHA-256), so that a server only sees $H(k_i)$ [2]. While it may be difficult to find the hash function's pre-image, brute-force attacks may be possible. In our intrusion detection application, for instance, a server can easily compute the hash values of all four billion IP addresses and build a simple lookup table. Thus, while efficient, this approach fails to achieve either keyword or participant privacy, with the latter not achieved because a client submits its inputs directly to the server. That said, one possible approach for participant privacy would be to proxy a client's request through one or more intermediate proxies that hide the client's identity (*e.g.*, its IP address), as done in network anonymity systems such as Tor [11].

Table 1 summarizes these design points. An important goal of this work is to provide a solution between these two extremes, *i.e.*, a protocol that is efficient enough to be used in practice and at large scale, yet also provide a meaningful level of security that is formally provable. There are various ways one could imagine weakening the strongest notions of secure multi-party computation, which provide privacy guarantees against *any* malicious participant. A standard relaxation would be to only guarantee privacy against *honest-but-curious* parties, in which participants learn no information provided that they faithfully execute the correct protocol. Another approach would be to provide privacy against all small coalitions of malicious parties. But in the large settings we consider, it may be easy for a single party to forge multiple identities and thus circumvent such protections, the so-called Sybil attack [12].

Instead, we focus on providing security against any malicious participant, provided that there exists a small set of well-known parties that do not collude. This is a natural model that already appears in real-world scenarios, such as Democrats and Republicans jointly comprising election boards in the U.S. political system. For our specific examples, business competitor ISPs like AT&T and Sprint could jointly provide a service like cooperative DoS detection. Or, it could be offered by third-party entities who have no incentive to collude. Such non-collusion assumptions already appear in several cryptographic protocols [8,14]. It should be emphasized that these well-known parties should not be treated as trusted: we only assume that they will not collude. Indeed, jumping ahead, our protocols do not reveal sensitive information to either party.

Contributions. In this paper, we *design, implement, and evaluate* privacy-preserving data aggregation—through logical centralization over a small number of non-colluding parties—that provably offers privacy-preserving data aggregation without sacrificing efficiency. Rather than full decentralization (as in secure multi-party computation) or full centralization (as typical in trusted-party solutions), our PDA architecture is split between well-known entities playing two different roles: a *proxy* and a *database* (DB). The proxy plays the role of obliviously blinding client inputs, as well as transmitting blinded inputs to the DB. The DB, on the other hand, builds a table that is indexed by

---

[2] For example, a careful protocol implementation of [16] found two sets of 100 items each took 213 seconds to execute [18].

the blinded key and aggregates each row's values (either incrementally or after some time). While most of the paper will focus on the case of only two entities—one proxy and one DB—we also show how to extend the protocol to larger numbers of parties.

The resulting system provides strong keyword and participant privacy guarantees, provided that the well-known entities—which operate the proxy and the database—do not collude. Specifically, we describe two variants of the protocol which provides the following notions of security (see Appendix A for more details):

- *Privacy of PDA against malicious entities and malicious participants*: Even an arbitrary coalition of malicious participants, together with either a malicious proxy or DB, learn nothing about other participants' inputs (except that implied by the protocols' output). Such a coalition may violate correctness in almost arbitrary ways, however. Similar notions of security have appeared before [32,15,23].
- *Privacy of CR-PDA against honest-but-curious entities and malicious participants*: Our CR-PDA protocol achieves full security in the "ideal-real" framework. This holds with respect to malicious coalitions of participants, as well as honest-but-curious coalitions between participants and the DB or proxy.

Using a semi-centralized architecture greatly reduces operational complexity and simplifies the liveness assumptions of the system. Clients can asynchronously provide inputs without our system requiring any complex scheduling. Despite these simplifications, the cryptographic protocols necessary to provide strong privacy guarantees are still non-trivial. Specifically, our solution makes use of oblivious pseudorandom functions [33,15,23], amortized oblivious transfer [31,24], and homomorphic encryption with re-randomization. In summary, the contributions of this paper include:

- We demonstrate a tradeoff between efficiency and security in multi-party computation. Our protocols achieve a relatively strong notion of provable security, while remaining practical for large numbers of participants with large input sets.
- At an abstract level, we introduce and implement a new cryptographic primitive that extends the notion of oblivious pseudorandom function (OPRF) as follows: A sender with input k communicates with a receiver *via* a mediator who holds a PRF key s. At the end of the protocol, the receiver learns $F_s(k)$, and the sender and mediator learn nothing. We believe that this notion, as well as our specific implementation, are of independent cryptographic interest and may be useful elsewhere.
- There are very few implementations of secure multi-party computation ([28,3,5]), and our system is one of the first to demonstrate practical efficiency. To our knowledge, it also includes the first implementation of some cryptographic machinery we use as sub-protocols (*e.g.*, amortized oblivious transfer [24]); our evaluation show that they realize significant benefits in practice.
- Finally, we illustrate that our system provides a level of performance that is sufficient for several applications of interest, including anomaly detection, certificate cross-checking, and distributed ranking.

The remainder of this paper is organized as follows. Section §2 describes our PDA protocols and sketches proofs of their privacy. We describe our system architecture and implementation in §3, evaluate its performance in §4, and conclude in §5. The appendix details some security definitions, protocol extensions, and proofs.

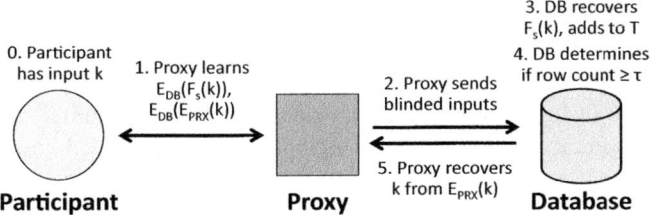

Fig. 1. High-level system architecture and protocol. Conditional release extensions to PDA are steps 4 and 5, as well as additional input in step 2 (all shown in blue). F_s is a keyed hash function whose secret s is known only to the proxy.

2 Our Protocols

In this section, we describe our protocols and analyze their security. We first describe a simplified version of the CR-PDA protocol that achieves somewhat weaker security properties, and we then extend this protocol to support a stronger notion of security. We conclude by explaining how to adopt the CR-PDA protocol to support the (simpler) case of the PDA functionality and sketch an extension to the case of $t > 2$ mutually-distrustful parties. Formal security proofs are deferred to the full version of this paper.

2.1 The Basic CR-PDA Protocol

Our protocol consists of five basic steps (see Figure 1). In the first two steps, the proxy interacts with the participants to collect the blinded keys together with their associated values encrypted under the DB's public key, and then passes these encrypted values on to the DB. Then, in the next two steps, the DB aggregates the blinded keys with the associated values in a table, and it decides which rows should be revealed according to a predefined function f. Finally, the DB asks the proxy to unblind the corresponding keys. Since the blinding scheme F_s is not necessarily invertible, the revealing mechanism uses additional information sent during the first phase. The specific steps are as follows.

- **Parties:** Participants, Proxy, Database.
- **Cryptographic Primitives:** A pseudorandom function F, where $F_s(k_i)$ denotes the value of the function on input k_i with a key s. A public-key encryption E, where $E_K(x)$ denotes an encryption of x under the public key K.
- **Public Inputs:** The proxy's public key PRX, the database's public key DB.
- **Private Inputs.** *Participant:* A list of key-value pairs $\langle k_i, v_i \rangle$. *Proxy:* key s of PRF F and secret key for PRX; *Database:* secret key for DB.

1. Each participant interacts with the proxy as follows. For each entry $\langle k_i, v_i \rangle$ in its list, the participant and the proxy run a sub-protocol for oblivious evaluation of the PRF (OPRF). At the end of this sub-protocol, the proxy learns nothing and the participant learns only the value $F_s(k_i)$ (and nothing else, not even s). The participant computes $E_{DB}(F_s(k_i))$, $E_{DB}(v_i)$, and $E_{DB}(E_{PRX}(k_i))$, and it sends them to the proxy. (The last entry will be used during the revealing phase.) The proxy adds this triple to a list and waits until most/all participants send their inputs.

2. The proxy randomly permutes the list of triples and sends the result to the DB.
3. The DB decrypts all the entries of each triple. Now, it holds a list of triples of the form $\left\langle F_s(k_i), v_i, E_{\text{PRX}}(k_i) \right\rangle$. If a value v_i is not valid (*i.e.*, $v_i \notin \mathcal{D}$, where $\mathcal{D}$ is the domain of legal values), the corresponding triple is omitted. The DB inserts the valid values into a table which is indexed by the blinded key $F_s(k_i)$. At the end, the DB has a table of entries of the form $\left\langle F_s(k_i), \mathsf{T}[k_i], \mathsf{E}[k_i] \right\rangle$. $\mathsf{T}[k_i]$ is some aggregation of all v_i's that appeared with k_i (*e.g.*, the actual values or, for threshold set intersection, simply the number of times that k_i was inputted). $\mathsf{E}[k_i]$ is a list of values of the form $E_{\text{PRX}}(k)$.
4. The DB uses some predefined function f to partition the table into two parts: R, which consists of the rows whose keys should be revealed, and H, which consists of the rows whose keys should remain hidden. It publishes the value column of the table H (without the blinded-keys) and sends R to the proxy.
5. The proxy goes over the received table R and replaces all the encrypted $E_{\text{PRX}}(k_i)$ entries with their decrypted key k_i. It then publishes the updated table.

Security Guarantees. This protocol guarantees privacy against the following:

Coalition of honest-but-curious (HBC) participants. Consider the view of an HBC participant during the protocol. Due to the security of the OPRF, a single participant sees only a list of pseudorandom values $F_s(k_i)$, and therefore this view can be easily simulated by using truly random values. The same holds for any coalition of participants. In fact, this protocol achieves reasonable security against malicious participants as well. The interaction of the proxy with a participant is completely *independent* of the inputs of other participants. Hence, even if participants are malicious, they still learn nothing about other participants' inputs. Furthermore, even malicious participants will be forced to choose their inputs *independently* of other honest participants. (See [31,23] for similar security definitions.) However, malicious participants can still violate the *correctness* of the above protocol. We fix this issue in the extended protocol.

HBC coalition of proxy and participants. The proxy's view consists of three parts: (1) the view during the execution of the OPRF protocol—this gives no information due to the security of the OPRF; (2) the tuples that the participants send—these values are encrypted under the DB's key and therefore reveal no information to the proxy; and (3) the value column of the table H and the key-value pairs that the DB sends during the last stage of the protocol (encrypted under the proxy's key)—this information should be revealed anyway as part of the the actual output of the protocol.

This argument generalizes to the case where the proxy colludes with HBC participants: their joint view reveals nothing about the inputs of the honest participants.

HBC database. The DB sees a blinded list of keys encrypted under his public key DB, without being able to relate blinded entries to their owners. For each blinded key $F_s(k_i)$, the DB sees the list of its associated values $\mathsf{T}[k_i]$ and encryptions of the keys under the proxy's key PRX. Finally, the DB also sees the key-values pairs that were released by the proxy (*i.e.*, , the table R which is chosen by f). The values $F_s(k_i)$ and $E_{\text{PRX}}(k)$ bear no information due to the security of the PRF and the encryption scheme. Hence, the DB learns nothing but the table R and the value column of H, as it should.

2.2   A More Robust Protocol

We now describe how to immunize the basic protocol against stronger attacks.

HBC coalition of participants and DB. The previous protocol is vulnerable against such coalitions for two main reasons.

First, a participant knows the blinded version $F_s(k_i)$ of its own keys k_i, and, in addition, the DB can associate all the values $\mathsf{T}[k_i]$ to their blinded keys $F_s(k_i)$. Hence, a coalition of a participant and a DB can retrieve all the values $\mathsf{T}[k_i]$ that are associated with a key k_i that the participant holds, even if this key *should not be revealed* according to f. To fix this problem, we modify the first step of the protocol. Instead of using an OPRF protocol, we will use a different sub-protocol in which the participant learns nothing and the proxy learns the value $E_{\mathrm{DB}}(F_s(k_i))$ for each k_i. This solves the problem as now that participant himself does not know the blinded version of his own keys. To the best of our knowledge, this version of an *encrypted-OPRF protocol* (abbreviated EOPRF and detailed in §2.3) has not previously appeared in the literature.

Second, we should eliminate subliminal channels, as these can be used by participants and the DB to match the keys of a participant to their blinded versions. To solve this problem, we use an encryption scheme that supports re-randomization of ciphertexts; that is, given an encryption of x with randomness b, it should be possible to recompute an encryption of x under fresh randomness b' (without knowing the private key). Now we eliminate the subliminal channel by asking the proxy to re-randomize the ciphertexts—$E_{\mathrm{DB}}(F_s(k_i))$, $E_{\mathrm{DB}}(v_i)$, and $E_{\mathrm{DB}}(E_{\mathrm{PRX}}(k_i))$—which are encrypted under the DB's public key (at Step 1). We should also be able to re-randomize the *internal* ciphertext $E_{\mathrm{PRX}}(k_i)$ of the last entry as well.

Coalition of malicious participants. As we observed, malicious participants can violate the correctness of our protocol, *e.g.*, by trying to submit ill-formed inputs. Recall that the participants are supposed to send to the proxy triples $\langle a, b, c \rangle$, of the form $a = E_{\mathrm{DB}}(F_s(k_i)), b = E_{\mathrm{DB}}(v_i)$ and $c = E_{\mathrm{DB}}(E_{\mathrm{PRX}}(k_i))$ for some k_i and v_i. However, a cheating participant might provide an inconsistent tuple, in which $a = E_{\mathrm{DB}}(F_s(k_i))$ while $c = E_{\mathrm{DB}}(E_{\mathrm{PRX}}(k_i'))$ for some $k_i' \neq k_i$. To prevent this attack, we let the proxy apply a consistency check to R in the last step of the protocol. The proxy makes sure that $E_{\mathrm{PRX}}(k_i')$ and $F_s(k_i)$ match, and otherwise omits the inconsistent values. Then the DB checks again if the corresponding row should still be revealed.

A cheating participant might also try to replace b with some "garbage" value $b' = E_{\mathrm{DB}}(v')$ which is not part of the legal domain $\mathcal{D}$ or for which he does not know the plaintext v'. (While this might not seem beneficial in practice, we must prevent such an attack to meet strong definitions of security.) To prevent such attacks, we use an encryption scheme which supports only messages taken from the domain $\mathcal{D}$, and ask the participant to provide a zero-knowledge proof of knowledge (ZK-POK) that he knows the plaintext v to which b decrypts. As seen later, this does not add too much overhead.

2.3   Concrete Instantiation of the Cryptographic Primitives

In the following section, we assume that the input keys are represented by m-bit strings. We assume that m is not very large (*e.g.*, less than 192–256); otherwise, one can hash the input keys and apply the protocol to resulting hashed values.

Public Parameters. We mostly employ Discrete-Log-based schemes. In the following, g is a generator of a multiplicative group $\mathbb{G}$ of prime order p for which the decisional Diffie-Hellman assumption holds. We publish (g, p) during initialization and assume that algorithms for multiplication (and thus for exponentiation) in $\mathbb{G}$ exist.

El-Gamal Encryption. We will use El-Gamal encryption over the group $\mathbb{G}$. The private key is a random element a from $\mathbb{Z}_p^*$, and the public key is the pair $(g, h = g^a)$. In case we wish to "double-encrypt" a message $x \in \mathbb{G}$ under two different public keys (g, h_1) and (g, h_2), we will choose a random b from $\mathbb{Z}_p^*$ and compute $(g^b, x \cdot h^b)$ where $h = (h_1 \cdot h_2)$. This ciphertext as well as standard ciphertexts can be re-randomized by multiplying the first entry (resp. second entry) by $g^{b'}$ (resp. $h^{b'}$), where b' is chosen randomly from $\mathbb{Z}_p^*$.

Goldwasser-Micali Encryption. The values v_i which are taken from the domain $\mathcal{D}$ will be encrypted under the Goldwasser-Micali (GM) Encryption scheme [21]. Specifically, if the domain size is 2^ℓ, we represent the values of $\mathcal{D}$ by all possible ℓ-bit strings, and encrypt such strings under GM in a bit-by-bit manner. The GM scheme provides ciphertext re-randomization, and it allows the party who generates a ciphertext c to prove in zero-knowledge that he knows the decryption of c and that c is valid (*i.e.*, decrypts to an ℓ bit string) [22]. Furthermore, both these operations and encryption cost only ℓ modular multiplications.[3] Decryption costs 2ℓ modular exponentiations, but ℓ is typically bounded by a very small integer in our protocols. Finally, the ZK proof consists of 3 moves and can run in parallel with the EOPRF.

Naor-Reingold PRF [33]. The key s of the function $F_s : \{0, 1\}^m \rightarrow \mathbb{G}$ contains m values $(s_1, \ldots, s_m)$ chosen randomly from $\mathbb{Z}_p^*$. Given m-bit string $k = x_1 \ldots x_m$, the value of $F_s(k)$ is $g^{\prod_{x_i=1} s_i}$, where the exponentiation is computed in the group $\mathbb{G}$.

Oblivious-Transfer [36,31] and Batched Oblivious Transfer [24]. To implement the sub protocol of Step 1, we need an additional cryptographic tool called Oblivious Transfer (OT). In an OT protocol a sender holds two strings (α, β), and a receiver has a selection bit c. At the end of the protocol, the receiver learns a *single* string: α if $c = 0$, and β if $c = 1$. The sender learns nothing (in particular, it does not learn c). In general, OT is an expensive public-key operation (*e.g.*, it may take two exponentiations per invocation and, in the above protocol, we would execute OT for each *bit* of the participant's input k_i). However, Ishai *et al.* [24] show how to reduce the amortized cost of OT to be as fast as matrix multiplication. This "batch OT" protocol uses a standard OT protocol as a building block; we implemented our batch OT on top of [31].

---

[3] For the case of zero-knowledge, the protocol of [22] provides only weak soundness at the cost of ℓ multiplications. However, [9] provides strong soundness guarantees with amortized cost of ℓ modular multiplications. Our setting naturally allows such an amortization.

2.4   The Encrypted-OPRF Protocol

Our construction is inspired by a protocol for oblivious evaluation of the PRF
F [15,30,31]. We believe that this construction might have further applications.

- **Parties:** Participant, Proxy.
- **Inputs.** *Participant:* m-bit string $k = (x_1 \ldots x_m)$; *Proxy:* secret key $s = (s_1, \ldots, s_m)$ of a Naor-Reingold PRF F.

1. Proxy chooses m random values $u_1, \ldots, u_m$ from $\mathbb{Z}_p^*$ and an additional random
   $r \in \mathbb{Z}_p^*$. In parallel, for each $1 \leq i \leq m$: the proxy and the participant invoke the
   OT protocol where proxy is the sender with inputs $(u_i, s_i \cdot u_i)$ and receiver uses x_i
   as his selector bit. (*i.e.*, the participant learns u_i if $x_i = 0$, and $s_i \cdot u_i$ otherwise.)
   The proxy also sends the value $\hat{g} = g^{r/\Pi u_i}$.
2. The participant computes the product M the values received in the OT stage. Then
   it computes $\hat{g}^M = (g^{\Pi_{x_i=1} s_i})^r = F_s(k)^r$, encrypts $F_s(k)^r$ under the DB's public
   key DB $= (g, h)$, and sends the result $(g^a, F_s(k)^r \cdot h^a)$ to the proxy.
3. The proxy raises the received pair to the power of r', where r' is the multiplicative
   inverse of r modulo p. It also re-randomizes the resulting ciphertext.

Correctness. Since $\mathbb{G}$ has a prime order p, the pair $(g^a, F_s(x)^r \cdot h^a)$ raised to the power
of $r' = r^{-1}$, results in $(g^{ar'}, F_s(k) \cdot h^{ar'})$, which is exactly $E_{DB}(F_s(k))$.

Privacy. All the proxy sees is the random tuple $(u_1, \ldots, u_m, r)$ and $E_{DB}(F_s(k)^r)$. This
view gives no additional information except of $E_{DB}(F_s(k))$. The participant, on the
other hand, sees the vector $(s_1^{x_1} \cdot u_1, \ldots, s_m^{x_m} \cdot u_m)$, whose entries are randomly
distributed over $\mathbb{G}$, as well as the value $\hat{g} = (g^{1/\Pi u_i})^r$. Since r is randomly and independently chosen from $\mathbb{Z}_p^*$, and since $\mathbb{G}$ has a prime order p, the element $\hat{g}$ is also
uniformly and independently distributed over $\mathbb{G}$. Hence, the participant learns nothing
but a sequence of random values. The protocol supports security against malicious participants (in the sense that was described earlier) and malicious proxy as long as the
underlying OT is secure in the malicious setting.

2.5   Efficiency of Our Protocol

In both the basic and extended protocol, the round complexity is constant, and the communication complexity is linear in the number of items. The protocol's computational
complexity is dominated by cryptographic operations. For each m-bit input key, we
have the following amortized complexity: The participant (who holds the input key),
proxy and DB compute a small constant number of exponentiations and perform $O(m)$
modular multiplication / symmetric-key operations. In the extended protocol, the DB
computes another $2 \lg |\mathcal{D}|$ exponentiations where $\mathcal{D}$ is the domain of legal values. (One
can optimize the exact number of exponentiations in the basic protocol by employing
RSA instead of El-Gamal.)

2.6   Extensions and Variations

PDA Protocol. Our PDA protocol is based on the CR-PDA protocol. The proxy and
participant first use an EOPRF to send the proxy a list of pairs $E_{DB}(F_s(k_i))$ and

$E_{\mathrm{DB}}(v_i)$. (The value $E_{\mathrm{DB}}(E_{\mathrm{PRX}}(k_i))$ is not needed in this case.) Then, the proxy passes the (randomly shuffled) list to the DB, which aggregates the tuples according to the blinded keys in the table $\left\langle F_s(k_i), \mathsf{T}[k_i] \right\rangle$ and outputs the tuples $\mathsf{T}[k_i]$ in a random order. Security analysis (details omitted) is similar to the previous: malicious behavior of either proxy or DB does not affect its own view or that of a colluding participant.

Using many mutually-distrustful servers. One might want a generalized protocol with $t > 2$ proxies/DBs (hereafter referred to as servers), in which privacy holds as long as *not all* of the servers collude. We now sketch one such simple extension of our PDA protocol which works for HBC servers. This change increases the complexity by a multiplicative factor of t, and so we get a smooth tradeoff between security and efficiency.

The basic idea is to make sure that both the key of the PRF (s) and the public key of the database (DB) remain hidden from any coalition of $t - 1$ servers. Specifically, each server holds a random share of an El-Gamal private key for DB (*i.e.*, the sum of the shares equals to the private key), and a key s_i for the Naor-Reingold PRF. We define a PRF $F_s(x)$ to be the product of $F_{s_1}(x), \ldots, F_{s_t}(x)$. The protocol proceeds as follows: (1) For each input $\langle k, v \rangle$, each participant performs the first EOPRF step of the previous PDA protocol with all the servers, and broadcasts the value $E_{\mathrm{DB}}(v)$. Thus, the i-th server learns the ciphertexts $\langle E_{\mathrm{DB}}(F_{s_i}(k)), E_{\mathrm{DB}}(v) \rangle$. In addition, the participant supplies to each server a POK for knowing a corresponding legal value v. (Some overhead can be saved here by using a *single* invocation of non-interactive ZK-POK.) (2) Now, the servers use the homomorphism properties of El-Gamal to compute $E_{\mathrm{DB}}(F_s(k))$; they can pass the $E_{\mathrm{DB}}(F_{s_i}(k))$'s to each other in a chain-like order or via a broadcast. (3) Then, the servers emulate the second step of the previous protocol to get a randomly-ordered list of decrypted pairs $\langle F_s(k), v \rangle$. This is done in t rounds: At the i-th round, the i-th server decrypts each pair under his share of the private key (removes the i-th "layer" of encryption), rerandomizes the encryption, shuffles the list in a random order, and passes the result to the next server. The final server aggregates the values according to the blinded keys and broadcasts the result.

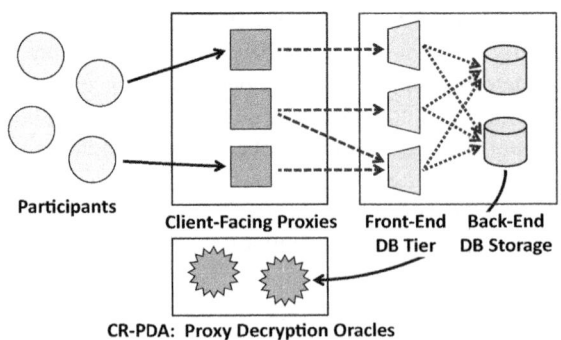

Fig. 2. Distributed proxy and database architecture

3 Distributed Implementation

This section describes our design and implementation of a scalable PDA architecture. For simplicity, we present the case of two administrative entities, one running a single logical proxy and the other a database. Both of these proxy and database logical components can be physically replicated in a relatively straightforward manner, however. In particular, our design can scale out horizontally to handle higher loads, by increasing the number of proxy and/or database replicas, and then distributing requests across these replicas. (Note that this replication strategy differs from the extension for $t > 2$ administrative entities, per Section 2.6.) Our distributed architecture is shown in Figure 2. Our current implementation covers all details described in the basic protocol, as well as some security improvements of the extended version (*e.g.*, including the EOPRF, but not ciphertext re-randomization, proofs of knowledge, or the final consistency check).

3.1 Proxy: Client-Facing Proxies and Decryption Oracles

One administrative domain can operate any number of proxies. Each proxy's functionality may be logically divided into two components: handling client requests and, in the case of CR-PDA, serving as decryption oracles for the DB when a particular key should be revealed. None of these proxies need to interact, other than having all client-facing proxies use the same secret s to key the pseudorandom function F and all decryption-oracle proxies use the same public/private key PRX. In fact, these two proxies play different logical roles and could even be operated by two different administrative domains. Currently, all proxies register with a single group membership server, although a fault-tolerant, distributed membership service could be implemented [6].

To discover a client-facing proxy, a client contacts this group membership service, which returns a proxy IP address in round-robin order (this could be replaced by any technique for server selection, including DNS, HTTP redirection, or a local load balancer). To submit its inputs, a client connects with this proxy and then executes an amortized Oblivious Transfer (OT) protocol on its input batch. This results in the proxy learning $\left\langle E_{\mathrm{DB}}(F_s(k_i)), E_{\mathrm{DB}}(v_i), E_{\mathrm{DB}}(E_{\mathrm{PRX}}(k_i)) \right\rangle$ for each input tuple, with the final element only present for CR-PDA protocols. The proxy pushes this tuple onto an internal queue. (While Section 2.3 only described the use of ElGamal encryption, its special properties are only needed for $E_{\mathrm{DB}}(F_s(k_i))$; the other public-key operations can be RSA, which we use in our implementation.) When this queue reaches a certain length—10,000 in our implementation—the proxy randomly permutes the items in the queue, and sends them to a database server.

Conditional-release PDA protocols have one final step. The database, upon determining that a key k_i's value satisfies f, sends $E_{\mathrm{PRX}}(k_i)$ to a proxy-decryption oracle. The proxy-decryption oracle decrypts $E_{\mathrm{PRX}}(k_i)$ and returns k_i to the database for storage and potentially for subsequent release to other participants in the system.

3.2 Database: Front-end Decryption and Back-end Storage

The database component can also be replicated. Similar to the proxy, we separate database functionality into two parts: the *front-end* module that handles proxy submissions and decrypts inputs, and a *back-end* module that acts as a storage layer. Each logical module can be further replicated in a manner similar to the proxy.

The servers comprising the front-end DB tier do not need to interact, other than being configured with the same public/private keypair DB. Thus, any front-end DB can decrypt the $E_{DB}(F_s(k_i))$ input supplied by a proxy, and the proxies can load balance input batches across these servers.

The back-end DB storage, on the other hand, needs to be more tightly coordinated, as we ultimately need to aggregate all $F_s(k_i)$'s together, no matter which proxy or front-end DB processed them. Thus, the back-end storage tier partitions the keyspace of all 1024-bit strings over all storage nodes (using consistent hashing). All such front-end and back-end DB instances also register with a group membership server, which the front-end servers contact to determine the list of back-end storage nodes. Upon decrypting an input, the front-end node determines which back-end storage node is assigned the resulting key $F_s(k_i)$, and sends the tuple $\langle F_s(k_i), v_i, E_{PRX}(k_i) \rangle$ to this storage node (the final element again present only for CR-PDA protocols). As these storage nodes each accumulate a horizontal portion of the entire table T, they can aggregate the values of each table row accordingly. In the case of CR-PDA, they can test the value column for their local table to see if any keys satisfy f. For each such row, the storage node sends the tuple $\langle F_s(k_i), T[k_i], E_{PRX}(k_i) \rangle$ to a proxy-decryption oracle.

3.3 Prototype Implementation

Our design is implemented in roughly 5,000 lines of C++. All communication is performed over TCP using BSD sockets, and concurrency is achieved through Linux pthreads. We use the GnuPG library for large numbers (bignums) and cryptographic primitives (*e.g.*, RSA, ElGamal, and AES). The Oblivious Transfer protocol (and its amortized variant) were implemented from scratch, comprising 625 lines of code. All RSA encryption used a 1024-bit key, and ElGamal used a 1024-bit group size. AES-256 was used in the batch OT and its underlying OT primitive. The back-end DB currently stores table rows only in memory.

4   Performance Evaluation

In this section, we evaluate system *throughput* (number of updates/queries per second) as a function of the number of keys and system participants. We also investigate how throughput scales with greater resources. In each case, we are concerned with both how long it takes for clients to send key-value pairs to the proxy during the OT phase (*proxy throughput*), as well as how long it takes for the DB to decrypt and identify keys with values that satisfy the function f (*DB throughput*). Our experiments were run on multiple machines. The proxy and DB were run on quad-core Intel Xeon 2 GHz machines running CentOS Linux. These machines can perform a 1024-bit ElGamal encryption in 2.2 ms, ElGamal decryption in 2.5 ms, RSA encryption in 0.5 ms, and RSA decryption in 2.8 ms. Clients were run on separate local machines.

As discussed earlier, our system can be used in different contexts. One potential application of collaborative anomaly detection. As modern botnets can range up to roughly

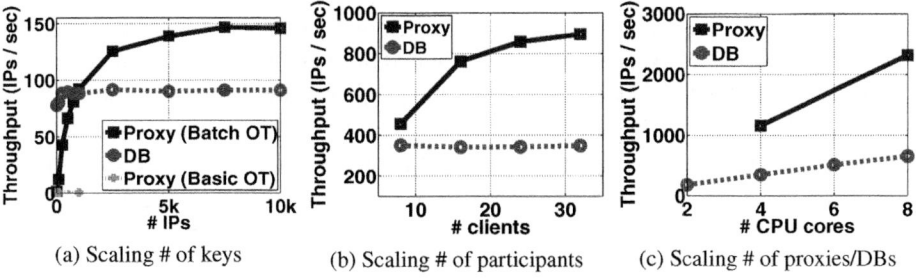

Fig. 3. Scaling effect of number of (a) keys, (b) participants, and (c) proxy/database replicas

100,000 unique hosts [37], we would like our system to be able to correlate suspicions of hundreds of participating networks within a few hours. Thus, our implementation should be able to process millions of keys in the span of hours, or hundreds of keys per second. We revisit the feasibility of supporting applications in Section 4.2.

4.1   Scaling and Bottleneck Analysis

Effect of number of keys (Figure 3a). Figure 3a measures throughput of a single proxy and DB (each running on a single core) as a function of the number of keys. The throughput of the OT primitive is exceedingly low—less than 1 key per second—and was thus not evaluated on the full range of input sizes. However, when using the amortized OT, proxy throughput significantly improves. Throughput increases with larger numbers of keys per batch, as the amortized OT calls the primitive OT a fixed number of times regardless of the number of input keys. DB throughput, on the other hand, does not increase with larger input batches. The DB must perform a fixed number of decryptions per input tuple—initiated when it receives a batch of encrypted inputs from the proxy—and thus its computational cost is relatively constant per input. Figure 3a shows our DB processes about 90 keys per second (and then becomes CPU limited).

The amortized OT protocol [24] introduces a trade-off between message overhead and memory consumption. The memory footprint of this protocol per client-proxy interaction for n keys is $n \times 32 \times 2 \times 1024/8 = 8196n$ bytes (*i.e.*, we assume 32 bits per key, the 2 values for the OT primitive, and 1024-bit encryption lengths). For $n = 10,000$ keys, for example, this requires 82 MB on both the proxy and the client. To reduce this memory footprint, a user of the protocol could choose to execute the amortized OT protocol in stages by sending k keys at a time.

Effect of number of participants (Figure 3b). We next evaluate the throughput of our system as a function of the number of clients submitting inputs. In this experiment, we limit the proxy and DB to one server machine each. Four client-facing proxy processes are launched on one machine and four front-end DB processes are launched on the other. Figure 3b shows that the proxy scales well with the number of clients, increasing by nearly a factor of two between 8 and 32 clients. When communicating with a single client, a proxy spends a substantial fraction of its time idling (largely while the client is performing its cryptographic operations). The four proxies in this experiment are not CPU limited until they handle 32 clients, at which time the throughput approaches 900 keys per second. The DB, however, is CPU-bound throughout these experiments. It has a throughput of about 350 keys per second, independent of the number of clients (a like amount of work per core as that seen in Figure 3a).

Effect of number of replicas (Figure 3c). Finally, we analyze how our distributed architecture scales with computing resources. Here, we provide up to 8 cores on 2 machines to each of the proxy and DB front-ends. While the proxy functionality alone is evaluated using 64 clients, computing resource constraints meant that the DB (which also required proxies to test) is evaluated using 32 clients. Performance of both the proxy and DB scale linearly with the number of CPU cores allocated to them, enabling a few servers to handle inputs on the order of a few million keys per hour.

Micro-benchmarks. To understand the factors limiting our design's performance, we instrumented the code to account for how CPU cycles are spent. While the DB is entirely CPU bound by the cost of decrypting inputs, the proxy and client engage in the oblivious transfer protocol whose bottlenecks are less clear. When communicating with a single client, we found that the client-facing proxy spends more than 60% of its time idling while waiting for the client (some of the OT time is also spent waiting on clients). The 60% idle time is primarily due to waiting for the client to encrypt k_i and $F_s(k_i)$. The single largest computational expense for the proxy is performing modular exponentiations at 16%; the remaining non-OT tasks add up to 15%. Given that concurrent clients will reduce the proxy's waiting state, achieving higher proxy throughput will require either more efficient cryptographic operations or faster bignum libraries.

We noted earlier that the GnuPG cryptographic library we used performed public-key operations in approximately 2.5–2.8 ms. On the same servers, we benchmarked the Crypto++ library to perform RSA decryption in only 1.2 ms, increasing speed by 130%. Crypto++ would also allow us to take advantage of elliptic curve cryptography, which would increase system throughput. In future work, we plan to modify our implementation to use this library.

4.2   Feasibility of Supporting Applications

Anomaly detection. Network operators commonly run systems to detect and localize anomalous behavior by dynamically tracking traffic characteristics. For example, Mao *et al.* [29] found that most DDoS attacks observed within a large ISP were sourced by fewer than 10,000 source IPs, and generated 31,612 alarms over a four-week period (0.8 events per hour). Ramachandran *et al.* [38] were able to localize 4,963 Bobax-infected host IPs sending spam from a single vantage point. We envision our system could be used to improve the accuracy of these techniques by correlating anomalies across ISP boundaries. This correlation may be done on the level of IP addresses (given DoS attackers typically do not spoof source IPs given ingress filtering [29] and for applications such as email spam that require bidirectional TCP connections), or on the level of subnets. Our system could handle 10,000 IP addresses as keys, with a request rate of several hundred keys per second, even with several hundred participants.

Cross-checking certificates. Multiple vantage points may be used to validate authenticity of information (such as a DNS reply or ssh certificate [34,41]) in the presence of "man-in-the-middle" attacks. Such environments demand privacy—DNS responses reveal domains that clients access, ssh keys reveal host connection patterns—as well as present scaling challenges due to the potentially large number of keys that could be inserted. Under typical workloads [25,40] (15 key updates per hour, with 30 keys per participating host), our system scales to support several hundred hosts with a single proxy. Extrapolating out to larger workloads, our system can handle tens of thousands of clients storing tens of thousands of keys with under fifty proxy/database pairs.

Distributed ranking. Search tools such as Alexa and Google Toolbar collect information about user behavior to refine search results returned to users. Users have incentive to install these tools, as they provide benefits (simplified searching and other features). However, they are sometimes labeled as *spyware* as they reveal information about the contents of queries performed by users. Our tool may be used to improve privacy of user submissions to these databases. Alexa Toolbar has an estimated 180,000 active users, and average web users browse 120 pages per day. Roughly extrapolating this data to our results and assuming that users batch their daily usage, our system could handle this daily workload with a single 4-core proxy and DB pair.

5   Conclusions

In this paper, we presented the design, implementation, and evaluation of a collaborative data-analysis system that is both scalable and privacy preserving. Since a fully-distributed solution would be complex and inefficient, our design divides responsibility between a small number of well-known, independent parties—most commonly, a proxy that obliviously blinds the client inputs and a database that aggregates the inputs based on the (blinded) keys. The functionality of both the proxy and the database can be easily distributed for greater scalability and reliability. Experiments with our prototype implementation show that our system performs well under increasing numbers of keys, participants, and proxy/database replicas. The performance is well within the requirements of our motivating applications for collaborative data analysis.

References

1. Alexa the Web Information Company (2010), http://www.alexa.com/
2. Allman, M., Blanton, E., Paxson, V., Shenker, S.: Fighting coordinated attackers with cross-organizational information sharing. In: HotNets (November 2006)
3. Ben-David, A., Nisan, N., Pinkas, B.: FairplayMP: A system for secure multi-party computation. In: CCS (October 2008)
4. Ben-Or, M., Goldwasser, S., Wigderson, A.: Completeness theorems for non-cryptographic fault-tolerant distributed computation. In: STOC (1988)
5. Bogetoft, P., Christensen, D.L., Damgard, I., Geisler, M., Jakobsen, T., Krøigaard, M., Nielsen, J.D., Nielsen, J.B., Nielsen, K., Pagter, J., Schwartzbach, M., Toft, T.: Secure multi-party computation goes live. In: Dingledine, R., Golle, P. (eds.) FC 2009. LNCS, vol. 5628, pp. 325–343. Springer, Heidelberg (2009)

6. Burrows, M.: The Chubby lock service for loosely-coupled distributed systems. In: OSDI (November 2006)
7. Chaum, D., Crépeau, C., Damgård, I.B.: Multiparty unconditionally secure protocols. In: Pomerance, C. (ed.) CRYPTO 1987. LNCS, vol. 293, pp. 462–462. Springer, Heidelberg (1988)
8. Chor, B., Goldreich, O., Kushilevitz, E., Sudan, M.: Private information retrieval. J. ACM 45(6) (November 1998)
9. Cramer, R., Damgård, I.: On the amortized complexity of zero-knowledge protocols. In: Halevi, S. (ed.) CRYPTO 2009. LNCS, vol. 5677, pp. 177–191. Springer, Heidelberg (2009)
10. Dachman-Soled, D., Malkin, T., Raykova, M., Yung, M.: Efficient robust private set intersection. In: Abdalla, M., Pointcheval, D., Fouque, P.-A., Vergnaud, D. (eds.) ACNS 2009. LNCS, vol. 5536, pp. 125–142. Springer, Heidelberg (2009)
11. Dingledine, R., Mathewson, N., Syverson, P.: Tor: The second-generation onion router. In: USENIX Technical (August 2004)
12. Douceur, J.R.: The Sybil attack. In: Druschel, P., Kaashoek, M.F., Rowstron, A. (eds.) IPTPS 2002. LNCS, vol. 2429, p. 251. Springer, Heidelberg (2002)
13. Fagin, R., Naor, M., Winkler, P.: Comparing information without leaking it. Comm. ACM 39(5) (1996)
14. Franklin, M.K., Reiter, M.K.: Fair exchange with a semi-trusted third party (extended abstract). In: CCS (April 1997)
15. Freedman, M.J., Ishai, Y., Pinkas, B., Reingold, O.: Keyword search and oblivious pseudorandom functions. In: Kilian, J. (ed.) TCC 2005. LNCS, vol. 3378, pp. 303–324. Springer, Heidelberg (2005)
16. Freedman, M.J., Nissim, K., Pinkas, B.: Efficient private matching and set intersection. In: Cachin, C., Camenisch, J.L. (eds.) EUROCRYPT 2004. LNCS, vol. 3027, pp. 1–19. Springer, Heidelberg (2004)
17. Friend-of-a-Friend Project (2009), http://www.foaf-project.org/
18. Garriss, S., Kaminsky, M., Freedman, M.J., Karp, B., Mazières, D., Yu, H.: RE: Reliable email. In: NSDI (May 2006)
19. Goldreich, O.: Foundations of Cryptography: Basic Applications. Cambridge University Press, Cambridge (2004)
20. Goldreich, O., Micali, S., Wigderson, A.: How to play any mental game (extended abstract). In: STOC (May 1987)
21. Goldwasser, S., Micali, S.: Probabilistic encryption. JCSS 28 (1984)
22. Goldwasser, S., Micali, S., Rackoff, C.: The knowledge complexity of interactive proof systems. SIAM J. Computing 18 (1989)
23. Hazay, C., Lindell, Y.: Efficient protocols for set intersection and pattern matching with security against malicious and covert adversaries. In: Canetti, R. (ed.) TCC 2008. LNCS, vol. 4948, pp. 155–175. Springer, Heidelberg (2008)
24. Ishai, Y., Kilian, J., Nissim, K., Petrank, E.: Extending oblivious transfers efficiently. In: Boneh, D. (ed.) CRYPTO 2003. LNCS, vol. 2729, pp. 145–161. Springer, Heidelberg (2003)
25. Jung, J., Sit, E., Balakrishnan, H., Morris, R.: DNS performance and the effectiveness of caching. IEEE/ACM Trans. Networking 10(5) (October 2002)
26. Kissner, L., Song, D.: Privacy preserving set operations. In: Shoup, V. (ed.) CRYPTO 2005. LNCS, vol. 3621, pp. 241–257. Springer, Heidelberg (2005)
27. Lindell, Y., Pinkas, B.: Privacy preserving data mining. In: Bellare, M. (ed.) CRYPTO 2000. LNCS, vol. 1880, p. 36. Springer, Heidelberg (2000)
28. Malkhi, D., Nisan, N., Pinkas, B., Sella, Y.: Fairplay: A secure two-party computation system. In: USENIX Security (August 2004)
29. Mao, Z., Sekar, V., Spatscheck, O., van der Merwe, J., Vasudevan, R.: Analyzing large DDoS attacks using multiple data sources. In: SIGCOMM LSAD (September 2006)

30. Naor, M., Pinkas, B.: Oblivious transfer and polynomial evaluation. In: STOC (May 1999)
31. Naor, M., Pinkas, B.: Oblivious transfer with adaptive queries. In: Wiener, M. (ed.) CRYPTO 1999. LNCS, vol. 1666, p. 573. Springer, Heidelberg (1999)
32. Naor, M., Pinkas, B.: Efficient oblivious transfer protocols. In: SODA (January 2001)
33. Naor, M., Reingold, O.: Number-theoretic constructions of efficient pseudorandom functions. In: FOCS (October 1997)
34. Poole, L., Pai, V.S.: ConfiDNS: Leveraging scale and history to improve DNS security. In: WORLDS (November 2006)
35. Privacy Rights Clearinghouse. A chronology of data breaches (January 2009), http://www.privacyrights.org/ar/ChronDataBreaches.htm
36. Rabin, M.: How to exchange secrets by oblivious transfer. Tech. Rep. TR-81, Harvard Aiken Computation Lab. (1981)
37. Rajab, M.A., Zarfoss, J., Monrose, F., Terzis, A.: My botnet is bigger than yours (maybe, better than yours): Why size estimates remain challenging. In: HotBots (April 2007)
38. Ramachandran, A., Feamster, N.: Understanding the network-level behavior of spammers. In: SIGCOMM (September 2006)
39. Ringberg, H., Soule, A., and Caesar, M. Evaluating the potential of collaborative anomaly detection (2008) (manuscript)
40. Schechter, S., Jung, J., Stockwell, W., McLain, C.: Inoculating SSH against address harvesting. In: NDSS (Feburary 2006)
41. Wendlandt, D., Andersen, D.G., Perrig, A.: Perspectives: Improving SSH-style host authentication with multi-path probing. In: USENIX Technical (June 2008)
42. Yao, A.C.: Protocols for secure computations. In: FOCS (November 1982)

A   Security Assumptions

We now motivate and clarify some security assumptions and privacy definitions.

Security against coalitions. We insist on providing security against any coalition of an arbitrary number of participants together with either the database or the proxy. This is essential as otherwise the DB (or proxy) can perform a Sybil attack [12], *i.e.*, create many dummy participants and use their views, together with his own view, to reveal sensitive information. On the other hand, in order to have an efficient and scalable system, we are willing to tolerate vulnerability against a coalition of the DB and the proxy, which could otherwise break participant and keyword privacy.

Power of the adversaries: honest-but-curious vs. malicious adversaries. In our CR-PDA protocol, both proxy and DB are expected to act as HBC. We believe this model is very appropriate for our semi-centralized system architecture. In many deployments, the DB and proxy may be well-known and trusted to act to the best of their abilities, as opposed to simply another participant amongst a set of mutually-distrusted parties. Of course, these trust assumptions do not extend to the potentially large number of participants, and therefore we require security against any coalition of *malicious participants* (who are allowed to deviate arbitrarily from the protocol). We mention that our PDA protocol provides security even when the DB or proxy are *malicious*. More generally, security holds against any arbitrary coalition of malicious participants that include either a malicious proxy or a malicious DB. Typically, security against fully malicious behavior comes at a great computational cost. We avoid this overhead by providing a weaker notion of security as discussed next.

Notions of security: ideal-real framework vs. input indistinguishability. In cryptography, the security of a protocol is usually defined via the ideal-real framework. Roughly speaking, the protocol should be as secure as an ideal-world implementation in which the players can employ a fully trusted party. This means that any attack that can be carried against the real protocol should be simulatable in the ideal world as well. This notion is very strong, as it shows that the protocol essentially achieves the highest possible level of security. Our CR-PDA protocol provides this notion of security.

A weaker notion (recently studied in [32,15,23]) tries to deal separately with privacy and correctness in order to improve efficiency. In particular, malicious parties are allowed to arbitrarily corrupt the correctness of the protocol as long as they do not learn anything about the inputs of honest players. (Formally, this is captured by an indistinguishability-based definition [23].) This is motivated by the fact that a malicious party can often violate semantic correctness in an ideal implementation, *e.g.*, by adding, changing, or omitting inputs to the function—by "lying," in more informal terms. Therefore, it may be reasonable to give up completely on correctness against malicious parties (proxies and DBs) and gain significant computational savings.[4]

---

[4] For technical reasons this relaxation makes sense mainly when the malicious parties do not get any output. Since in our PDA functionality only the DB gets an output, we may adopt this relaxed notion and provide *privacy* (at the form of input indistinguishability) against malicious participants and/or malicious proxy, and full *security* (at the form of the ideal-real framework) for coalitions that include a malicious DB.

Privacy-Preserving Queries over Relational Databases*

Femi Olumofin and Ian Goldberg

Cheriton School of Computer Science
University of Waterloo
Waterloo, ON, Canada N2L 3G1
{fgolumof,iang}@cs.uwaterloo.ca

Abstract. We explore how Private Information Retrieval (PIR) can help users keep their sensitive information from being leaked in an SQL query. We show how to retrieve data from a relational database with PIR by hiding sensitive constants contained in the predicates of a query. Experimental results and microbenchmarking tests show our approach incurs reasonable storage overhead for the added privacy benefit and performs between 7 and 480 times faster than previous work.

Keywords: Private information retrieval, relational databases, SQL.

1   Introduction

Most software systems request sensitive information from users to construct a query, but privacy concerns can make a user unwilling to provide such information. The problem addressed by private information retrieval (PIR) [3,9] is to provide such a user with the means to retrieve data from a database without the database (or the database administrator) learning any information about the particular item that was retrieved. Development of practical PIR schemes is crucial to maintaining user privacy in important application domains like patent databases, pharmaceutical databases, online censuses, real-time stock quotes, location-based services, and Internet domain registration. For instance, the current process for Internet domain name registration requires a user to first disclose the name for the new domain to an Internet domain registrar. Subsequently, the registrar could then use this inside information to preemptively register the new domain and thereby deprive the user of the registration privilege for that domain. This practice is known as *front running* [17]. Many users, therefore, find it unacceptable to disclose the sensitive information contained in their queries by the simple act of querying a server.

Users' concern for query privacy and our proposed approach to address it are by no means limited to domain names; they apply to publicly accessible databases in several application domains, as suggested by the examples above. Although ICANN claims the practice of domain front running has subsided [17],

---

* An extended version of this paper is available [22].

M.J. Atallah and N. Hopper (Eds.): PETS 2010, LNCS 6205, pp. 75–92, 2010.

we will, however, use the domain name example in this paper to enable head-to-head performance comparisons with a similar approach by Reardon et al. [23], which is based on this same example.

While today's most developed and deployed privacy techniques, such as onion routers and mix networks, offer anonymizing protection for users' identities, they cannot preserve the privacy of the users' queries. For the front running example, the user could tunnel the query through Tor [12] to preserve the privacy of his or her network address. Nevertheless, the server could still observe the user's desired domain name, and launch a successful front running attack.

The development of a practical PIR-based technique for protecting query privacy offers users and service providers an attractive value proposition. Users are increasingly aware of the problem of privacy and the need to maintain privacy in their online activities. The growing awareness is partly due to increased dependence on the Internet for performing daily activities — including online banking, Twittering, and social networking — and partly because of the rising trend of online privacy invasion. Privacy-conscious users will accept a service built on PIR for query privacy protection because no currently deployed security or privacy mechanism offers the needed protection; they will likely be willing to trade off query performance for query privacy and even pay to subscribe for such a service. Similarly, service providers may adopt such a system because of its potential for revenue generation through subscriptions and ad displays. As more Internet users value privacy, most online businesses would be motivated to embrace privacy-preserving technologies that can improve their competitiveness to win this growing user population. Since the protection of a user's identity is not a problem addressed by PIR, existing service models relying on service providers being able to identify a user for the purpose of targeted ads will not be disabled by this proposal. In other words, protection of query privacy will provide additional revenue generation opportunities for these service providers, while still allowing for the utilization of information collected through other means to send targeted ads to the users. Thus, users and service providers have plausible incentives to use a PIR-based solution for maintaining query privacy. In addition, the very existence of a practical privacy-preserving database query technique could be enough to persuade privacy legislators that it is reasonable to demand that certain sorts of databases enforce privacy policies, since it is possible to deploy these techniques without severely limiting the utility of such databases.

However, the rudimentary data access model of PIR is a limiting factor in deploying successful PIR-based systems. These models are limited to retrieving a single bit, a block of bits [3,9,18], or a textual keyword [8]. There is therefore a need for an extension to a more expressive data access model, and to a model that enables data retrieval from structured data sources, such as from a relational database. We address this need by integrating PIR with the widely deployed SQL.

Dynamic SQL is an incomplete SQL statement within a software system, meant to be fully constructed and executed at runtime [26]. It requires only a single compilation that *prepares* it for subsequent executions. It is therefore a flexible, efficient, and secure way of using SQL in software systems. We observe that the shape or textual content of an SQL query prepared within a system is not private, but the constants the user supplies at runtime are private, and must be protected. For domain name registration, the textual content of the query is exposed to the database, but only the textual keyword for the domain name is really private. For example, the *shape* of the dynamic query in Listing 1 is not private; the question mark ? is used as a placeholder for a private value to be provided before the query is executed at runtime.

Listing 1. Example Dynamic SQL query (database schema as in [22])

```
SELECT t1.domain, t1.expiry, t2.contact
FROM regdomains t1, registrar t2
WHERE (t1.reg_id = t2.reg_id) AND (t1.domain = ? )
```

Our approach to preserving query privacy over a relational database is based on hiding such private constants of a query. The client sends a *desensitized* version of the prepared SQL query appropriately modified to remove private information. The database executes this public SQL query, and generates appropriate cached indices to support further rounds of interaction with the client. The client subsequently performs a number of keyword-based PIR operations [8] using the value for the placeholders against the indices to obtain the result for the query.

None of the existing proposals related to enabling privacy-preserving queries and robust data access models for private information retrieval makes the noted observation about the privacy of constants within an otherwise-public query. These include techniques that eliminate database optimization by localizing query processing to the user's computer [23], problems on querying Database-as-a-Service [16,15], those that require an encrypted database before permitting private data access [25], and those restricted to simple keyword search on textual data sources [4]. This observation is crucial for preserving the expressiveness and benefits of SQL, and for keeping the interface between a database and existing software systems from changing while building in support for user query privacy. Our approach improves over previous work with additional database optimization opportunities and fewer PIR operations needed to retrieve data. To the best of our knowledge, we are the first to propose a practical technique that leverages PIR to preserve the privacy of sensitive information in an SQL query over existing commercial and open-source relational database systems.

Our contributions. We address the problem of preserving the privacy of sensitive information within an SQL query using PIR. In doing this, we address two obstacles to deploying successful PIR-based systems. First, we develop a generic data access model for private information retrieval from a relational database using SQL. We show how to hide sensitive data within a query and how to use

PIR to retrieve data from a relational database. Second, we develop an approach for embedding PIR schemes into the well-established context and organization of relational database systems. It has been argued that performing a trivial PIR operation, which involves having a database send its entire data to the user, and having the user select the item of interest, is more efficient than running a computational PIR scheme [1,27]; however, information-theoretic PIR schemes are much more efficient. We show how the latter PIR schemes can be applied in realistic scenarios, achieving both efficiency and query expressivity. Since relational databases and SQL are the most influential of all database models and query languages, we argue that many realistic systems needing query privacy protection will find our approach quite useful.

The rest of this paper is organized as follows: Section 2 provides background information on PIR and database indexing. Section 3 discusses related work, while Section 4 details the threat model, security, and assumptions for the paper. Section 5 provides a description of our approach. Section 6 gives an overview of the prototype implementation, results of microbenchmarking and the experiment used to evaluate this prototype in greater depth. Section 7 concludes the paper and suggests some future work.

2   Preliminaries

2.1   Private Information Retrieval (PIR)

PIR provides a means to retrieve data from a database without revealing any information about which item is retrieved. In its simplest form, the database stores an n-bit string X, organized as r data blocks, each of size b bits. The user's private input or query is an index $i \in \{1, ..., r\}$ representing the ith data block. A trivial solution for PIR is for the database to send all r blocks to the user and have the user select the block of interest at index i (i.e., X_i), but this carries a very poor communication complexity.

The three important requirements for any PIR scheme are correctness (returns the correct block X_i to the user), privacy (leaks no information to the database about i and X_i) and non-triviality (communication complexity is sublinear in n) [10]. An additional requirement, which is not often addressed in the published literature, is implementation (i.e., computational) efficiency [1,27]. While the performance of information-theoretic PIR schemes are generally better [14], this neglect of computational overhead has led to single-database PIR schemes that are slow for large databases [27]. On the other hand, multi-server information-theoretic PIR schemes are much more efficient than the trivial solution and their use is justified in situations where the user lacks the bandwidth and local storage for the trivial download of data. Recent attempts at building practical single-database PIR [31] using general-purpose secure coprocessors offers several orders of magnitude improvement in performance. Nevertheless, the potential application of PIR in several practical domains has been largely unrealized with no "fruitful" or "real world" practical application.

A related cryptographic construction to PIR is *oblivious transfer* (OT) [20,21]. In OT, a database (or sender) transmits some of its items to a user (or chooser), in a manner that preserves their mutual privacy. The database has assurance that the user does not learn any information beyond what he or she is entitled to, and the user has assurance that the database is unaware of which particular items it received. OT and the related *Symmetric* PIR (SPIR) [19] can thus be seen to be generalizations of PIR. Those protocols could easily be used in place of PIR in our work, with the concomitant extra computational cost.

2.2 Indexing

Data can be indexed by a key formed either from the values of one or more attributes or from hashes (generally not cryptographic hashes) of those values. Indices are typically organized into tree structures, such as B^+ trees where internal or non-leaf nodes do not contain data; they only maintain references to children or leaf nodes. Data are either stored in the leaf nodes, or the leaf nodes maintain references to the corresponding tuples (i.e., records) in the database. Furthermore, the leaf nodes of B^+ trees may be linked together to enable sequential data access during range queries over the index; *range queries* return all data with key values in a specified range.

Hashed indices are specifically useful for *point queries*, which return a single data item for a given key. For many situations where efficient retrieval over a set of unique keys is needed, hashed indices are preferred over B^+ tree indices. However, it is challenging to generate hash functions that will hash each key to a unique hash value. Many hashed indices used in commercial databases, for this reason, use data partitioning (bucketization) [16] techniques to hash a range of values to a single bucket, instead of to individual buckets. Recent advances [5,6] in *perfect hash functions (PHF)* have produced a family of hash functions that can efficiently map a large set of n key values (on the order of billions) to a set of m integers without collisions, where n is less than or equal to m.

3   Related Work

A common assumption for PIR schemes is that the user knows the index or address of the item to be retrieved. However, Chor et al. [8] proposed a way to access data with PIR using keyword searches over three data structures: binary search tree, trie and perfect hashing. Our work extends keyword-based PIR to B^+ trees and PHF. In addition, we provide an implemented system and combine the technique with the expressive SQL. The technique in [8] neither explores B^+ trees nor considers executing SQL queries using keyword-based PIR.

Reardon et al. [23] similarly explore using SQL for private information retrieval, and proposed the TransPIR prototype system. This work is the closest to our proposal and will be used as the basis for comparisons. TransPIR performs traditional database functions (such as parsing and optimization) locally on the client; it uses PIR for data block retrieval from the database server, whose function has been reduced to a block-serving PIR server. The benefit of TransPIR is that the database will not learn any information even about the textual content of the user's query. The drawbacks are poor query performance because the database is unable to perform any optimization, and the lack of interoperability with any existing relational database system.

An interesting attempt to build a practical pseudonymous message retrieval system using the technique of PIR is presented in [24]. The system, known as the Pynchon Gate, helps preserve the anonymity of users as they privately retrieve messages using pseudonyms from a centralized server. Unlike our use of PIR to preserve a user's query privacy, the goal of the Pynchon Gate is to maintain privacy for users' identities. It does this by ensuring the messages a user retrieves cannot be linked to his or her pseudonym. The construction resists traffic analysis, though users may need to perform some dummy PIR queries to prevent a passive observer from learning the number of messages she has received.

4   Threat Model, Security and Assumptions

4.1   Security and Adversary Capabilities

Our main assumption is that the shape of SQL queries submitted by the users is public or known to the database administrator. Applicable practical scenarios include design-time specification of dynamic SQL by programmers, who expect the users to supply sensitive constants at runtime. Moreover, the database schema and all dynamic SQL queries expected to be submitted to, for example, a patent database, are not really hidden from the patent database administrator. Simultaneous protection of both the shape and constants of a query are outside of the scope of this work, and would likely require treating the database management system as other than a black box.

The approach presented in this paper is sufficiently generic to allow an application to rely on any block-based PIR system, including single-server, multi-server, and coprocessor-assisted variants. We assume an adversary with the same capability as that assumed for the underlying PIR protocol. The two common adversary capabilities considered in theoretical private information retrieval schemes are the curious passive adversary and the byzantine adversary [3,9]. Either of these adversaries can be a database administrator or any other insider to a PIR server.

A curious passive adversary can observe PIR-encoded queries, but should be incapable of decoding the content. In addition, it should not be possible to differentiate between queries or identify the data that makes up the result of a query. In our context, the information this adversary can observe is the desensitized SQL query from the client and the PIR queries. The information obtained from the desensitized query does not compromise the privacy of the user's query, since it does not contain any private constants. Similarly, the adversary cannot obtain any information from the PIR queries because PIR protocols are designed to be resistant against an adversary of this capability.

A byzantine adversary with additional capabilities is assumed for some multi-server PIR protocols [3,14]. In this model, the data in some of the servers could be outdated, or some of the servers could be down, malfunctioning or malicious. Nevertheless, the client is still able to compute the correct result and determine which servers misbehaved, and the servers are still unable to learn the client's query. Again, in our specific context, the adversary may compromise some of the servers in a multi-server PIR scenario by generating and obtaining the result for a substitute fake query or executing the original query on these servers, but modifying some of the tuples in the results arbitrarily. The adversary may respond to a PIR request with a corrupted query result or even desist from acting on the request. Nevertheless, all of these active attack scenarios can be effectively mitigated with a byzantine-robust multi-server PIR scheme.

4.2   Data Size Assumptions

We service PIR requests using indexed data extracted from relational databases. The size of these data depends on the number of tuples resulting from the desensitized query. We note that even in the event that this *desensitized* query yields a small number of tuples (including just one), the privacy of the *sensitive part* of the SQL query *is not compromised*. The properties of PIR ensure that the adversary gains no information about the sensitive constants from observing the PIR protocol, over what he already knew by observing the desensitized query.

On the other hand, many database schemas are designed in a way that a number of relations will contain very few rows of data, all of which are meant to be retrieved and used by every user. Therefore, it is pointless to perform PIR operations on these items, since every user is expected to retrieve them all at some point. The adversary does not violate a user's query privacy by observing this public retrieval.

4.3   Avoiding Server Collusion

Information-theoretic PIR is generally more computationally efficient than computational PIR, but requires that the servers not collude if privacy is to be preserved; this is the same assumption commonly made in other privacy-preserving technologies, such as mix networks [7] and Tor [12]. We present scenarios in which collusion among servers is unlikely, yielding an opportunity to use the more efficient information-theoretic PIR.

The first scenario is when several independent service providers host a copy of the database. This applies to naturally distributed databases, such as Internet domain registries. In this particular instance, the problem of colluding servers is mitigated by practical business concerns. Realistically, the Internet domain database is maintained by different geographically dispersed organizations that are independent of the registrars that a user may query. However, different registrars would be responsible for the content's distribution to end users as well as integration of partners through banner ads and promotions. Since the registrars are operating in the same line of business where they compete to win users and deliver domain registry services, as well as having their own advertising models to reap economic benefits, there is no real incentive to collude in order to break the privacy of any user. In this model, it is feasible that a user would perform a domain name registration query on multiple registrars' servers concurrently. The user would then combine the results, without fear of the queries revealing its content. Additionally, individual service agreements can foreclose any chance of collusion with a third party on legal grounds. Users then enjoy greater confidence in using the service, and the registrars in turn can capitalize on revenue generation opportunities such as pay-per-use subscriptions and revenue-sharing ad opportunities.

The second scenario that offers less danger of collusion is when the query needs to be private only for a short time. In this case, the user may be comfortable with knowing that by the time the servers collude in order to learn her query, the query's privacy is no longer required.

Note that even in scenarios where collusion cannot be forestalled, our system can still use any computational PIR protocol; recent such protocols [1,31] offer considerable efficiency improvements over previous work in the area.

5   Hiding Sensitive Constants

5.1   Overview

Our approach is to preserve the privacy of sensitive data within the WHERE and HAVING predicates of an SQL query. For brevity, we will focus on the WHERE clause; a similar processing procedure applies to the HAVING clause. This may require the user (or application) to specify the constants that may be sensitive. For the example query in Listing 2, the domain name and the creation date may be sensitive.

Our approach splits the processing of SQL queries containing sensitive data into two stages. In the first stage, the client computes a public subquery, which is simply the original query that has been stripped of the predicate conditions containing sensitive data. The client sends this subquery to the server, and the server executes it to obtain a result for the subquery. The desired result for the original query is contained within the subquery result, but the database is not aware of the particular tuples that are of interest.

In the second stage, the client performs PIR operations to retrieve the tuples of interest from the subquery result. To enable this, the database creates a cached index on the subquery result and sends metadata for querying the index to the client. The client subsequently performs PIR retrievals on the index and finally combines the retrieved items to build the result for the original query.

Listing 2. Example query with a WHERE clause featuring sensitive constants

```
SELECT t1.contact, t1.email, t2.created, t2.expiry
FROM registrar t1, regdomains t2
WHERE (t1.reg_id = t2.reg_id) AND (t2.created > 20090101) AND
      (t2.domain = 'anydomain.com')
```

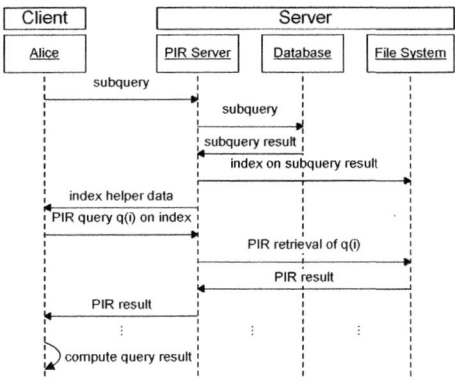

Fig. 1. A sequence diagram for evaluating Alice's private SQL query using PIR

The important benefits of this approach as compared with the previous approach [23] are the optimizations realizable from having the database execute the non-private subquery, and the fewer number of PIR operations required to retrieve the data of interest. In addition, the PIR operations are performed against a cached index which will usually be smaller than the complete database. This is particularly true if there are joins and non-private conditions in the WHERE clause that constrain the tuples in the query result. In particular, a single PIR query is needed for point queries on hash table indices, while range queries on B^+ tree indices are performed on fewer data blocks. Figure 1 illustrates the sequence of events during a query evaluation.

We note that often, the non-private subqueries will be common to many users, and the database does not need to execute them every time a user makes a request. Nevertheless, our algorithm details, presented next in Section 5.2, show the steps for processing a subquery and generating indices. Such details are useful in an *ad hoc* environment, where the shape of a query is unknown to the database *a priori*; each user writes his or her own query as needed. Our assumption is that revealing the shape of a query will not violate users' privacy (see Section 4).

5.2   Algorithm

We describe our algorithm with an example by assuming an information-theoretic PIR setup with two replicated servers. We focus on hiding sensitive constants in the predicates of the WHERE clause. The algorithm details for the SELECT query in Listing 2 follows. We assume the date 20090101 and the domain anydomain.com are private.

Step 1: The client builds an attribute list, a constraint list, and a desensitized SELECT query, using the attribute names and the WHERE conditions of the input query. We refer to the desensitized query as a *subquery*.

To begin, initialize the attribute list to the attribute names in the query's SE-LECT clause, the constraint list to be empty, and the subquery to the SELECT and FROM clauses of the original query.

- *Attribute list:* {`t1.contact, t1.email, t2.created, t2.expiry`}
- *Constraint list:* {}
- *Subquery:* `SELECT t1.contact, t1.email, t2.created, t2.expiry`
  `FROM registrar t1, regdomains t2`

Next, consider each WHERE condition in turn. If a condition features a private constant, then add the attribute name to the *attribute list* (if not already in the list), and add (attribute name, constant value, operator) to the *constraint list*. Otherwise, add the condition to the subquery.

On completing the above steps, the attribute list, constraint list, and subquery with reduced conditions for the input query become:

- *Att. list:* {`t1.contact, t1.email, t2.created, t2.expiry, t2.domain`}
- *Con. list:* {(`t2.created,20090101,>`),(`t2.domain,'anydomain.com',=`)}
- *Subquery:*
  `SELECT t1.contact,t1.email,t2.created,t2.expiry,t2.domain`
  `FROM registrar t1, regdomains t2 WHERE (t1.reg_id = t2.reg_id)`

Step 2: The client sends the subquery, a key attribute name, and an index file type to each server.

The key attribute name is selected from the attribute names in the constraint list — `t2.created, t2.domain` in our example. The choice may either be random, made by the application designer, or determined by a client optimizer component with some domain knowledge that could enable it to make an optimal choice. One way to make a good choice is to consider the *selectivity* — the ratio of the number of distinct values taken to the total number of tuples — expected for each constraint list attribute, and then choose the one that is most selective. This ensures the selection of attributes with unique key values before less selective attributes. For example, in a patent database, the patent number is a better choice for a key than the author's gender. A poor choice of key can lead to more rounds of PIR queries than necessary. Point queries on a unique key attribute can be completed with a single PIR query. Similarly, a good choice of key will reduce the number of PIR queries for range queries. For the example query, we choose `t2.domain` as the key attribute name.

For the index file type, either a PHF or a B^+ tree index type is specified. Other index structures may be possible, with additional investigation, but these are the ones we currently support. More details on the selection of index types is provided below.

Step 3: Each server: executes the subquery on its relational database, generates a cached index of the specified type on the subquery result, using the key attribute name, and returns metadata for searching the indices to the client.

The server computes the size of the subquery result. If it can send the entire result more cheaply than performing PIR operations on it, it does so. Otherwise, it proceeds with the index generation. For hash table indices, the server first computes the perfect hash functions for the key attribute values. Then it evaluates each key and inserts each tuple into a hash table. The metadata that is returned to the client for hash-based indices consists of the PHF parameters, the count of tuples in the hash table, and some PIR-specific initialization parameters.

For B^+ tree indices, the server bulk inserts the subquery result into a new B^+ tree index file. B^+ tree bulk insertion algorithms provide a high-speed technique for building a tree from existing data [2]. The server also returns metadata to the client, including the size of the tree and its first data block (the root). Generated indices are stored in a disk cache external to the database.

Step 4: The client receives the responses from the servers and verifies they are of the appropriate length. For a byzantine robust multi-server PIR, a client may choose to proceed in spite of errors resulting from non-responding servers or from responses that are of inconsistent length.

Next, the client performs one or more keyword-based PIR queries, using the value associated with the key attribute name from the constraint list, and builds the desired query result from the data retrieved with PIR.

The encoding of a private constant in a PIR query proceeds as follows. For PIR queries over a hash-based index, the client computes the hash for the private constant using the PHF functions derived from the metadata[1]. This hash is also the block number in the hash table index on the servers. This block number is input to the PIR scheme to compute the PIR query for each server. For a B^+ tree index, the user compares the private value for the key attribute with the values in the root of the tree. The root of the tree is extracted from the metadata it receives from the server. Each key value in this root maintains block numbers for the children blocks or nodes. The block number corresponding to the appropriate child node will be the input to the PIR scheme.

For hash-based indices, a single PIR query is sufficient to retrieve the block containing the data of interest from the hash table. For B^+ tree indices, however, the client uses PIR to traverse the tree. Each block can hold some number m of keys, and at a block level, the B^+ tree can be considered an m-ary tree. The client has already been sent the root block of the tree, which contains the top m keys. Using this information, the client can perform a single PIR block query to fetch one of the m blocks so referenced. It repeats this process until it reaches the leaves of the tree, at which point it fetches the required data with further PIR queries. The actual number of PIR queries depends on the height of the (balanced) tree, and the number of tuples in the result set. Traversals of B^+ tree indices with our approach are oblivious in that they leak no information about nodes' access pattern; we realize retrieval of a node's data as a PIR operation over the data set of all nodes in the tree. In other words, it does not matter which particular branch of a B^+ tree is the location for the next block to be retrieved. We do not restrict PIR operations to the subset of blocks in the subtree rooted

---

[1] Using the CMPH Library [5] for example, the client saves the PHF data from the metadata into a file. It reopens this file and uses it to compute a hash by following appropriate API call sequences.

at that branch. Instead, each PIR operation considers the set of blocks in the entire B^+ tree. Range queries that retrieve data from different subtrees leak no information about to which subtree a particular piece of data belongs. The only information the server learns is the number of blocks retrieved by such a query. Therefore, specific implementations may utilize dummy queries to prevent the server from leaning the amount of useful data retrieved by a query [24].

To compute the final query result, the client applies the other private conditions in the constraint list to the result obtained with PIR. For the example query, the client filters out all tuples with `t2.created` not greater than 20090101 from the tuple data returned with PIR. The remaining tuples give the final query result.

Capabilities for dealing with complex queries can be built into the client. For example, it may be more efficient to request a single index keyed on the concatenation of two attributes than separate indices. If the client requests separate indices, it will subsequently perform PIR queries on each of those indices, using the private value associated with each attribute from the constraint list. Finally, the client combines the partial results obtained from the queries with set operations (union, intersection), and performs local filtering on the combined result, using private constant values for any remaining conditions in the constraint list to compute the final query result. The client thus needs query-optimization capabilities in addition to the regular query optimization performed by the server.

6   Implementation and Microbenchmarks

6.1   Implementation

We developed a prototype implementation of our algorithm to hide the sensitive portions of SQL queries using generally available open source C++ libraries and databases. We developed a command-line tool to act as the client, and a server-side database adapter to provide the functions of a PIR server. For the PIR functions, we used the Percy++ PIR Library [13,14], which offers three varieties of privacy protection: computational, information theoretic and hybrid (a combination of both). We extended Percy++ to support keyword-based PIR. For generating hash table indices for point queries, we used the C Minimal Perfect Hash (CMPH) Library [5,6], version 0.9. We used the API for CMPH to generate minimum perfect hash functions for large data sets from query results; these perfect hash functions require small amounts of disk storage per key. For building B^+ tree indices for range queries on large data sets, we used the Transparent Parallel I/O Environment (TPIE) Library [11,30]. Finally, we base the implementation on the MySQL [28] relational database, version 5.1.37-1ubuntu5.1.

6.2   Experimental Setup

We began evaluating our prototype implementation using a set of six whois-style queries from Reardon et al. [23], which is the most appropriate existing microbenchmark for our approach. We explored tests using industry-standard database benchmarks, such as the Transaction Processing Performance Council (TPC) [29] benchmarks, and open-source benchmarking kits such as Open Source Development Labs Database Test Suite (OSDL DTS) [32], but none of the tests from these benchmarks is suitable for evaluating our prototype, as their test databases cannot be readily fitted into a scenario that would make applying PIR meaningful. For example, a database schema that is based on completing online orders will only serve very limited purpose to our goal of protecting the privacy of sensitive information within a query.

We ran the microbenchmark tests using two whois-style data sets, similar to those generated for the evaluation of TransPIR [23]. The smaller data set consists of 10^6 domain name registration tuples, and 0.75×10^6 registrar and registrant contact information tuples. The second data set similarly consists of 4×10^6 and 3×10^6 tuples respectively. We describe the two database relations and the evaluation queries, as well as the results for the smaller data set, in the extended version [22].

In addition to the microbenchmarks, we performed an experiment to evaluate the behaviour of our prototype on complex input queries, such as aggregate queries, BETWEEN and LIKE queries, and queries with multiple WHERE clause conditions and joins. Each of these complex queries has varying privacy requirements for its sensitive constants.

We ran the all experiments on a server with two quad-core 2.50 GHz Intel Xeon E5420 CPUs, 8 GB RAM, and running Ubuntu Linux 9.10. We used the information-theoretic PIR support of Percy++, with two database replicas. The server also runs a local installation of a MySQL database.

6.3   Result Overview

The results from our evaluation indicate that while our current prototype incurs some storage and computational costs over non-private queries, the costs seem entirely acceptable for the added privacy benefit (see Tables 1 and 2). In addition to being able to deal with complex queries and leverage database optimization opportunities, our prototype performs much better than the TransPIR prototype from Reardon et al. [23] — between 7 and 480 times faster for equivalent data sets. The most indicative factor of performance improvements with our prototype is the reduction in the number of PIR queries in most cases. Other factors that may affect the validity of the result, such as variations in implementation libraries, are assumed to have negligible impact on performance. Our work is based on the same PIR library as that of [23]. Our comparison is based on the measurements we took by compiling and running the code for TransPIR on the same experimental hardware platform as our prototype. We also used the same underlying PIR library as TransPIR.

6.4   Microbenchmark and Complex Query Experiments

For the benchmark tests, we obtained measurements for the time to execute the private query, the number of PIR queries performed, the number of tuples in the

Table 1. Experimental results for microbenchmark tests compared with those of Reardon et al. [23]. **BTREE** = timing for our B^+ tree prototype, **HASH** = timing for our hash table prototype, and **TransPIR** = timing from TransPIR [23]; **Time** = time to evaluate private query, **PIRs** = number of PIR operations performed, **Tuples** = count of rows in query result, **QI** = timing for subquery execution and index generation, **Xfer** = total data transfer between the client and the two PIR servers.

Query	Approach	Time (s)	PIRs	Tuples	QI (s)	Xfer (KB)
Q1	**HASH**	2	1	1	16	128
	BTREE	4	3	1	38	384
	TransPIR	25	2	1	1,017	256
Q2	**BTREE**	5	4	80	32	512
	TransPIR	999	83	80	1,017	10,624
Q3	**BTREE**	5	4	168	32	512
	TransPIR	2,055	171	168	1,017	21,888
Q4	**BTREE**	6	5	236	37	640
	TransPIR	2,885	240	236	1,017	30,720
Q5	**BTREE**	5	3	1	67	384
	TransPIR	37	3	1	1,017	384
Q6[†]	**BTREE**	5	4	168	66	512
	TransPIR	3,087	253	127	—[†]	32,384

query results, the time to execute the subquery and generate the cached index, and the total data transfer between the client and the two PIR servers.

Table 1 shows the results of the experiment. The cost of indexing (QI) can be amortized over multiple queries. The indexing measurements for BTREE (and HASH) consist of the time spent retrieving data from the database (subquery execution), writing the data (subquery result) to a file and building an index from this file. Since TransPIR is not integrated with any relational database, it does not incur the same database retrieval and file writing costs. However, TransPIR incurs a one-time preprocessing cost (QI) which prepares the database for subsequent query runs. Comparing this cost to its indexing counterpart with our BTREE and HASH prototypes shows that our methods are over an order of magnitude faster.

For the experiment on queries with complex conditions, we used a number of synthetic query scenarios having different requirements for privacy (see [22] for details). The measurements, as reported in Table 2, show execution duration for the original query without privacy provision over the MySQL database, and several other measurements taken from within our prototype using a B^+ tree index.

6.5   Discussion

The empirical results for the benchmark tests reflect the benefit of our approach. For all of the tests, we mostly base our comparison on the timings for query

---

† We reproduced TransPIR's measurements from [23] for query Q6 because we could not get TransPIR to run Q6 due to program errors. The '—' under QI indicates measurements missing from [23].

evaluation with PIR (Time), and sometimes on the index generation timings (QI). The time to transfer data between the client and the servers is directly proportional to the amount of data (Xfer), but we will not use it for comparison purposes because the test queries were not run over a network.

Our hash index (HASH) prototype performs the best for query Q1, followed by our B^+ tree (BTREE) prototype. The query of Q1 is a point query having a single condition on the domain name attribute.

Query Q2 is a point query on the expiry_date attribute, with the query result expected to have multiple tuples. The number of PIR queries required to evaluate Q2 with BTREE is 5% of the number required by TransPIR. A similar trend is repeated for Q3, Q4 and Q6. Note that the HASH prototype could not be used for Q2 because hash indices accept unique keys only; it can only return a single tuple in its query result.

Query Q3 is a range query on expiry_date. Our BTREE prototype was approximately 411 times faster than TransPIR. Of note is the large number of PIR queries that TransPIR needs to evaluate the query; our BTREE prototype requires only 2% of that number. We observed a similar trend for Q4, where BTREE was 480 times faster. This query features two conditions in the SQL WHERE clause. The combined measured time for BTREE — the time taken to both build an index to support the query and to run the query itself — is still 67 times faster than the time it takes TransPIR to execute the query alone.

Query Q5 is a point query with a single join. It took BTREE only about 14% of the time it took TransPIR. We observed the time our BTREE spent in executing the subquery to dominate; only a small fraction of the time is spent building the B^+ tree index.

Our BTREE prototype similarly performs faster for Q6, with an order of magnitude similar to Q2, Q3, and Q4.

In all of the benchmark queries, the proposed approach performs better than TransPIR because it leverages database optimization opportunities, such as for the processing of subqueries. In contrast, TransPIR assumes a type of block-serving database that cannot give any optimization opportunity. Therefore, in our system, the client is relieved from having to perform many traditional database functions, such as query processing, in addition to its regular PIR client functions.

Results for queries with complex conditions. We see from Table 2 that in most cases, the cost to evaluate the subquery and create the index dominates the total time to privately evaluate the query (BTREE), while the time to evaluate the query on the already-built index (Time) is minor. An exception is CQ2, which has a relatively small subquery result (rTuples), while having to do dozens of (consequently smaller) PIR operations to return thousands of results to the overall range query. Note that in all but CQ2, the time to privately evaluate the query on the already-built index is at most a few seconds longer than performing the query with no privacy at all; this underscores the advantage of using cached indices.

We note from our results that it is much more costly to have the client simply download the cached indices. We observe, for example, that it will take about 5

Table 2. Measurements taken from executing five complex SQL queries with varying requirements for privacy. **oQm** = timing for executing original query directly against the database, **BTREE** = overall timing for meeting privacy requirements with our B^+ tree prototype, **Time** = time to evaluate private query within BTREE, **PIRs** = number of PIR operations performed, **Tuples** = number of records in final query result, **rTuples** = number of indexed records in subquery result, **Xfer** = total data transfer between the client and the two PIR servers, **Size** = storage for index.

Query	oQm (s)	BTREE (s)	Time (s)	PIRs	Tuples	rTuples	Xfer (KB)	Size (MB)
CQ1	2	31	2	3	1	1,753,144	384	579.63
CQ2	1	15	13	41	3,716	72,568	5,248	25.13
CQ3	0	80	3	3	1	631,806	384	209.38
CQ4	2	25	5	3	1	1,050,300	384	348.63
CQ5	2	69	3	3	6	4,000,000	384	1,324.13

times as long, for a user with 10 Mbps download bandwidth, to download the index for CQ5. Moreover, this trivial download of data is impractical for devices with low bandwidth and storage (e.g., mobile devices).

One way to improve query performance is by revealing a prefix or suffix of the sensitive keyword in a query. Revealing a substring of a keyword helps to constrain the result set that will be indexed and retrieved with PIR. Making this trade-off decision in a privacy-friendly manner necessarily requires some knowledge of the data distribution in terms of the number of tuples there are for each value in the domain of values for a sensitive constant. These information can be included in the metadata a server sends to the client and the client can make this trade-off decision on behalf of the user based on the user's preset preferences. We are considering this extension as part of our future work.

6.6   Limitations

Our approach can preserve the privacy of sensitive data within the WHERE and HAVING clauses of an SQL query, with the exception of complex LIKE query expressions, negated conditions with sensitive constants, and SELECT nested queries within a WHERE clause. The complexity of complex search strings for LIKE queries, such as (LIKE 'do%abs%.c%m'), and negated WHERE clause conditions, such as (NOT registrant = 45444) are beyond the current capability of keyword-based PIR. Our solution to dealing with these conditions in a privacy-friendly manner is to compute them on the client, after the data for the computation has been retrieved with PIR; converting NOT = queries into their equivalent range queries is generally less efficient than our proposed client-based evaluation method. In addition, our prototype cannot process a nested query within a WHERE clause. We propose that the same processing described for a general SQL query be recursively applied for nested queries in the WHERE clause. The result obtained from a nested query will become an input to the client optimizer, for recursively computing the enclosing query for the next round.

There is need for further investigation of the approach for nested queries returning large result sets and for deeply nested queries.

7   Conclusion and Future Work

We have provided a privacy mechanism that leverages private information retrieval to preserve the privacy of sensitive constants in an SQL query. We described techniques to hide sensitive constants found in the WHERE clause of an SQL query, and to retrieve data from hash table and B^+ tree indices using a private information retrieval scheme. We developed a prototype privacy mechanism for our approach offering practical keyword-based PIR and enabled a practical transition from bit- and block-based PIR to SQL-enabled PIR. We evaluated the feasibility of our approach with experiments. The results of the experiments indicate our approach incurs reasonable performance and storage demands, considering the added advantage of being able to perform private SQL queries. We hope that our work will provide valuable insight on how to preserve the privacy of sensitive information for many existing and future database applications.

Future work can improve on some limitations of our prototype, such as the processing of nested queries and enhancing the client to use statistical information on the data distribution to enhance privacy. The same technique proposed in this paper can be extended to preserve the privacy of sensitive information for other query systems, such as URL query, XQuery, SPARQL and LINQ.

Acknowledgments

We would like to thank Urs Hengartner, Ryan Henry, Aniket Kate, Can Tang, Mashael AlSabah, John Akinyemi, Carol Fung, Meredith L. Patterson, and the anonymous reviewers for their helpful comments for improving this paper. We also gratefully acknowledge NSERC and MITACS for funding this research.

References

1. Aguilar-Melchor, C., Gaborit, P.: A Lattice-Based Computationally-Efficient Private Information Retrieval Protocol. Cryptol. ePrint Arch., Report 446 (2007)
2. Arge, L., Procopiuc, O., Vitter, J.S.: Implementing I/O-efficient Data Structures Using TPIE. In: Möhring, R.H., Raman, R. (eds.) ESA 2002. LNCS, vol. 2461, pp. 88–100. Springer, Heidelberg (2002)
3. Beimel, A., Stahl, Y.: Robust Information-Theoretic Private Information Retrieval. J. Cryptol. 20(3), 295–321 (2007)
4. Bethencourt, J., Song, D., Waters, B.: New Techniques for Private Stream Searching. ACM Trans. Inf. Syst. Secur. 12(3), 1–32 (2009)
5. Botelho, F.C., Reis, D., Ziviani, N.: CMPH: C minimal perfect hashing library on SourceForge, http://cmph.sourceforge.net/
6. Botelho, F.C., Ziviani, N.: External perfect hashing for very large key sets. In: ACM CIKM, pp. 653–662 (2007)

7. Chaum, D.L.: Untraceable electronic mail, return addresses, and digital pseudonyms. Commun. ACM 24(2), 84–90 (1981)
8. Chor, B., Gilboa, N., Naor, M.: Private information retrieval by keywords. Technical Report TR CS0917, Dept. of Computer Science, Technion, Israel (1997)
9. Chor, B., Goldreich, O., Kushilevitz, E., Sudan, M.: Private information retrieval. In: FOCS, October 1995, pp. 41–50 (1995)
10. Crescenzo, G.D.: Towards Practical Private Information Retrieval. In: Achieving Practical Private Information Retrieval (Panel @ Securecomm 2006) (August 2006)
11. Department of Computer Science at Duke University. The TPIE (Templated Portable I/O Environment), http://madalgo.au.dk/Trac-tpie/
12. Dingledine, R., Mathewson, N., Syverson, P.: Tor: the second-generation onion router. In: USENIX Security Symposium, p. 21 (2004)
13. Goldberg, I.: Percy++ project on SourceForge, http://percy.sourceforge.net/
14. Goldberg, I.: Improving the Robustness of Private Information Retrieval. In: IEEE Symposium on Security and Privacy, pp. 131–148 (2007)
15. Hacigümüş, H., Iyer, B., Li, C., Mehrotra, S.: Executing sql over encrypted data in the database-service-provider model. In: ACM SIGMOD, pp. 216–227 (2002)
16. Hore, B., Mehrotra, S., Tsudik, G.: A privacy-preserving index for range queries. In: VLDB, pp. 720–731 (2004)
17. ICANN Security and Stability Advisory Committee (SSAC). Report on Domain Name Front Running (February 2008)
18. Kushilevitz, E., Ostrovsky, R.: Replication is not needed: single database, computationally-private information retrieval. In: FOCS, p. 364 (1997)
19. Mishra, S.K., Sarkar, P.: Symmetrically Private Information Retrieval. In: Roy, B., Okamoto, E. (eds.) INDOCRYPT 2000. LNCS, vol. 1977, pp. 225–236. Springer, Heidelberg (2000)
20. Naor, M., Pinkas, B.: Oblivious transfer and polynomial evaluation. In: ACM Symposium on Theory of Computing, pp. 245–254 (1999)
21. Naor, M., Pinkas, B.: Efficient oblivious transfer protocols. In: ACM-SIAM SODA, pp. 448–457 (2001)
22. Olumofin, F., Goldberg, I.: Privacy-preserving Queries over Relational Databases. Technical report, CACR 2009-37, University of Waterloo (2009)
23. Reardon, J., Pound, J., Goldberg, I.: Relational-Complete Private Information Retrieval. Technical report, CACR 2007-34, University of Waterloo (2007)
24. Sassaman, L., Cohen, B., Mathewson, N.: The Pynchon Gate: a Secure Method of Pseudonymous Mail Retrieval. In: ACM WPES, pp. 1–9 (2005)
25. Shi, E., Bethencourt, J., Chan, T.-H.H., Song, D., Perrig, A.: Multi-Dimensional Range Query over Encrypted Data. In: IEEE SSP, pp. 350–364 (2007)
26. Silberschatz, A., Korth, H.F., Sudarshan, S.: Database System Concepts, 5th edn. McGraw-Hill, Inc., New York (2005)
27. Sion, R., Carbunar, B.: On the Computational Practicality of Private Information Retrieval. In: Network and Distributed Systems Security Symposium (2007)
28. Sun Microsystems. MySQL, http://www.mysql.com/
29. Transaction Processing Performance Council. Benchmark C, http://www.tpc.org/
30. Vengroff, D.E., Scott Vitter, J.: Supporting I/O-efficient scientific computation in TPIE. In: IEEE Symp. on Parallel and Distributed Processing, p. 74 (1995)
31. Williams, P., Sion, R.: Usable PIR. In: Network and Distributed System Security Symposium. The Internet Society (2008)
32. Wong, M., Thomas, C.: Database Test Suite project on SourceForge, http://osdldbt.sourceforge.net/

Achieving Efficient Query Privacy
for Location Based Services*

Femi Olumofin[1], Piotr K. Tysowski[2], Ian Goldberg[1], and Urs Hengartner[1]

[1] Cheriton School of Computer Science
University of Waterloo
Waterloo, Ontario, Canada N2L 3G1
{fgolumof,iang,uhengart}@cs.uwaterloo.ca
[2] Department of Electrical and Computer Engineering
University of Waterloo
Waterloo, Ontario, Canada N2L 3G1
pktysows@uwaterloo.ca

Abstract. Mobile smartphone users frequently need to search for nearby points of interest from a location based service, but in a way that preserves the privacy of the users' locations. We present a technique for private information retrieval that allows a user to retrieve information from a database server without revealing what is actually being retrieved from the server. We perform the retrieval operation in a computationally efficient manner to make it practical for resource-constrained hardware such as smartphones, which have limited processing power, memory, and wireless bandwidth. In particular, our algorithm makes use of a variable-sized cloaking region that increases the location privacy of the user at the cost of additional computation, but maintains the same traffic cost. Our proposal does not require the use of a trusted third-party component, and ensures that we find a good compromise between user privacy and computational efficiency. We evaluated our approach with a proof-of-concept implementation over a commercial-grade database of points of interest. We also measured the performance of our query technique on a smartphone and wireless network.

Keywords: Location based service, private information retrieval, various-size grid Hilbert curve.

1 Introduction

Users of mobile devices tend to frequently have a need to find Points Of Interest (POIs), such as restaurants, hotels, or gas stations, in close proximity to their current locations. Collections of these POIs are typically stored in databases administered by Location Based Service (LBS) providers such as Google, Yahoo!, and Microsoft, and are accessed by the company's own mobile client applications

---

* An extended version of this paper is available [27].

M.J. Atallah and N. Hopper (Eds.): PETS 2010, LNCS 6205, pp. 93–110, 2010.

or are licensed to third party independent software vendors. A user first establishes his or her current position on a smartphone such as a RIM BlackBerry, Apple iPhone, or Google Android device through a positioning technology such as GPS (Global Positioning System) or cell tower triangulation, and uses it as the origin for the search. The problem is that if the user's actual location is provided as the origin to the LBS, which performs the lookup of the POIs, then the LBS will learn that location. In addition, a history of locations visited may be recorded and could potentially be used to target the user with unexpected content such as local advertisements, or worse, used to track him or her. The user's identity may be divulged through the inclusion of the originating dynamic IP address, e-mail address, or phone number in requests to the LBS server so that the results of an LBS query can be routed back to the correct user via a TCP data connection, e-mail reply, or SMS reply, respectively. If a location can always be correlated to each request, then the user's current pattern of activity and even personal safety is being entrusted to a third party, potentially of unknown origin and intent. Although search engines routinely cache portions of previous queries in order to deliver more relevant results in the future, we are concerned when the user's exact location history is tracked, and not just the key words used in the search.

For many users, this constitutes an unacceptable violation of privacy, and efforts should be made to avoid it. As location technology becomes commonplace, users will become increasingly aware of and concerned about location privacy. Not only are privacy and personal safety important considerations, but recent advances in mobile advertising have even opened the possibility of location-based spam. In February 2010, the Energy and Commerce Joint Subcommittee of the U.S. House of Representatives held a joint hearing on the implications of location-based services on the privacy of consumers[1]. Our challenge has been to design a system whereby a user can retrieve useful POI information without having to disclose his or her exact location to a third party such as the LBS server. The user should also not have to reveal what particular POIs were searched for and found, as each POI record typically includes precise location coordinates. Thus, the server will be unable to infer the user's current location or likely destination, or accumulate a history of requests made for profiling purposes. Generally speaking, a user will typically be comfortable with a certain degree of privacy, meaning that the user could be expected to be anywhere within a certain geographic area, such as a city or neighbourhood without fear of discovery.

Today's smartphones have high-performing processors which are suitable for cryptographic operations that can enable location privacy. For instance, the Apple iPhone 3GS contains a Samsung ARM 833 MHz CPU, while the BlackBerry Storm 2 contains a Qualcomm 528 MHz CPU. However, these devices have limited memory and bandwidth. For instance, the iPhone and Storm are both limited to 256 MB of dynamic RAM, 32 GB of flash memory, and operate on 3G wireless networks no faster than the (theoretical) 7.2 Mbps HSDPA network. Consider these data limits with respect to a typical commercial POI database

---

for the U.S. and Canada, which can contain 6 to 12 million entries and require 1 to 2 GB or more of flash data storage. Requiring that the smartphone download the entire database for each request so as not to provide information about its current location is clearly not practical [31]; nor is requiring that it periodically download just the updated data to ensure accuracy of results, given the practical bandwidth limits, data usage limits, and associated overage charges (penalties for exceeding the limits) of smartphone data plans. Thus, it is desirable to provide a cryptographic way for a mobile user to request local information while preserving location privacy. Although extra server-side processing demands must be anticipated on a privacy-enhanced LBS server, it may easily be scaled to multiple computers in a distributed fashion, which is a reasonable tradeoff.

1.1 Requirements and Assumptions

Our basic scenario entails a mobile device user who operates a smartphone with location technology and wireless data transfer capability. The user searches for nearby POIs (i.e., nearest neighbour) by first constructing and sending a query to a known LBS server over the wireless network. The LBS server retrieves the query, performs a search of its POI database, and returns a set of results to the user containing all POIs found in the specified region. Our protocol must meet the following requirements:

- The LBS server must not learn the user's exact location. It may only identify a general region that is large enough, in terms of area and the number of POIs it contains, to confer a sufficient level of privacy to the user's satisfaction.
- There must be no third parties, trusted or otherwise, in the protocol between the user and the server.
- The implementation must be computationally efficient on hardware, such as smartphones, which are resource constrained. A user may be expected to tolerate a delay of no more than several seconds for any kind of query.
- The approach cannot rely on a secure processor that is not typically found on a commercial smartphone.

Clearly, these requirements present the need for a mechanism to directly retrieve information in a secure and private way without revealing the contents of the query results, and without the need for an intermediary between the user and the database server to provide some kind of a masking function. Fortunately, there is a branch of cryptography that is associated with retrieving information from a database without revealing which item is being retrieved; it is known as Private Information Retrieval (PIR) [7]. Our proposed solution is sufficiently generic to allow an application to rely on any PIR scheme. We make the same assumptions as that of the underlying PIR scheme, where retrieval is either by object index or keyword [6]. We describe a server that can find the relevant POI entries based on the user's location of interest included in the request; this is possible because the entries in the POI database are indexed by their location.

Although PIR satisfies our baseline privacy constraints, current implementations of it fail to satisfy our third condition, which is usable performance on modern smartphone hardware. Our challenge has been to complement PIR with a new algorithmic approach that effectively reduces the amount of computations without significantly sacrificing the user's location privacy.

Note that we make no effort to hide the user's identity from the location-based service. We assume that it is acceptable to reveal the user's identity for the purpose of routing the response to a location-based request, and for offering a customized LBS experience. A user that also wishes to hide his or her identity to some extent may wish to make use of an onion router, such as Tor [10]. However, we note that there are application domains where the protection of a user's location using our proposed technique is superior to anonymizing the user's identity. For example, it is easy to try to identify a user who made a query with a particular geographical coordinate, simply by looking up the user who lives at the corresponding residential address and assuming the request did not originate elsewhere. On the other hand, our proposed technique hides query contents from the LBS, and leaves no useful clues for determining the user's current location.

When a typical mobile phone accesses a third-party LBS provider through a wireless 3G data connection, we assume that it reveals only its identity and the query itself to the provider. Unavoidably, a mobile communications carrier is always aware of the user's location based on the cell towers in contact, and so it must not collude with the LBS provider. Our assumption relies on the LBS provider not being integrated into the carrier's infrastructure, such as a traffic reporting service using cell tower data that discovers a user's location passively. Our assumption is valid for the vast majority of LBS applications, which are unaffiliated with the carrier; these include search portals, social applications, travel guides, and many other types. When communicating with such an application, the mobile user's IP address is of no help in determining the user's physical location, as it is dynamically assigned independent of location. Only a central gateway that is administered by the telecommunications carrier will be identified. We assume that no other information will be gleaned by the LBS provider. In the case where a mobile user utilizes Wi-Fi instead, the user will be assigned an address that points to the nearby access point, however, and may need to employ other techniques, such as Tor, to mask the address.

1.2 Our Results

We propose a novel hybrid LBS technique that integrates location cloaking and private information retrieval. We have also implemented and evaluated our proposal to determine its practicality on resource-constrained hardware. The results show that users can achieve a good compromise between privacy and computational efficiency with our technique unlike all other existing LBS proposals.

2 Related Work

We provide a brief overview of cloaking- and PIR-based approaches for location privacy. A survey and classification of methods for location privacy in LBS can be found in [33]. Similarly, in a position paper in 2008 [11], Ghinita introduced a taxonomy for LBS privacy techniques.

2.1 Location Cloaking Techniques

Location cloaking in general seeks to prevent an attacker from being able to match queries to particular users and to thus compromise their privacy. The attacker may be in a position to observe traffic flowing through the network or even be situated at the LBS provider endpoint.

One popular cloaking technique is based on the principle of k-anonymity, where a user is hidden among k-1 other users. Queries from multiple users are typically aggregated at an anonymity server which forms an intermediary between the user and the LBS provider. This central anonymity server can provide spatial and temporal cloaking functions, so that an attacker will encounter difficulty matching multiple queries that are observed with users at particular locations and at particular points in time. Many cloaking solutions for location privacy suggest either a central anonymity server as described [18,34], or other means such as decentralized trusted peers [9] or distributed k-anonymity [35].

The chief problem is that the anonymity server must normally be part of the trusted computing environment and represents a single point of vulnerability. If it is successfully attacked, or collusion with the LBS server occurs, then the locations of all users may be divulged. It is also observed that although a cloaking technique by itself is advantageous in that it does not result in increased computational cost on the server, it can carry with it a high communication cost from the LBS provider to the client. This can mean a large and unacceptable penalty for mobile phone users. Finally, if a reduced sample population results from the number of active users in a particular geographic area, it may not suffice to satisfy the desired degree of anonymity. If the anonymity server delays execution of a request until the k-anonymity condition is satisfied, then this delay may prove to be unacceptable to the user from a feature interaction point of view.

2.2 PIR-Based Techniques

A PIR technique can be used to ensure that queries and their results are kept private. Specifically, PIR provides a user with a way to retrieve an *item* from a *database*, without the database (or the database administrator) learning any information about which particular item was retrieved. PIR satisfies our requirements for privacy and low communication cost. However, existing PIR techniques have drawbacks of high computational cost for applications that require low latency.

The PIR database is typically organized as an n-bit string, broken up into r blocks, each n/r bits long. The user's private input or query is typically an index $i \in \{1, ..., r\}$ representing the ith block of bits. A trivial solution for PIR is for the database to send all r blocks to the user and have the user select the desired block at index i, but this carries a maximum cost of communication and is unsuitable in a resource-constrained environment such as a wireless network.

When the PIR problem was first introduced in 1995 [7], it was proven that a single-database solution with information theoretic privacy and a sub-linear communication complexity (between the user and the database) is impossible to achieve. Information theoretic privacy assures user privacy even for an adversary with unlimited computational capability. Using at least two replicated databases, and some form of restrictions on how the databases can communicate, PIR schemes with information theoretic privacy are possible, and sometimes hold attractive properties like byzantine robustness [3,15]. The first single-database PIR proposal was in 1997 [5]; its PIR scheme only assures privacy against an adversary with limited computational capability (i.e., polynomially bounded attackers). The type of privacy protection known as computational privacy, where computational capability is expected to be limited, is a weaker notion of privacy compared to information theoretic privacy. Nonetheless, computational PIR (CPIR) [5,22] offers the benefit of fielding a single database. Basic PIR schemes place no restriction on information leaked about other items in the database that are not of interest to the user; however, an extension of PIR, known as *Symmetric* PIR (SPIR) [24], adds that restriction. The restriction is important in situations where the database privacy is equally of concern. The only work in an LBS context that attempts to address both user and database privacy is [12]. Although, not strictly an SPIR scheme, it adopts a cryptographic technique to determine if a location is enclosed inside a rectangular cloaking region. The goal of the paper was to reduce the amount of POIs returned to the user by a query. Unlike ours, the approach fails to guarantee a constant query result size which defeats correlation attacks, and it requires dynamic partitioning of the search space which may be computationally intensive. It also requires two queries to be executed, whereas a single query-response pair is sufficient in ours.

PIR has been applied to solving the problem of keeping a user's location private when retrieving location-based content from a PIR database. This content typically consists of points of interest (POI's), with each entry consisting of a description of a place of interest as well as its geographical location. The only work cited for PIR in the survey from [33] which does not utilize a third party is [13]. Our approach differs from the PIR approach in [13] in three important ways. First, the approach is specifically based on the 1997 computational PIR scheme by Kushilevitz et al. [22]. It would require considerable re-invention before it could be used with recent and more efficient PIR schemes. For instance, it re-organizes a POI database into a square matrix M despite the reduced communications costs attainable from using a rectangular matrix.

On the other hand, our approach is flexible and supports any block-based PIR schemes. Secondly, the costs of computation and communication with the approach are $O(n)$ and $O(\sqrt{n})$, respectively, where n is the number of items, or POIs, in the database. The user has no flexibility for dealing with this linear computational cost for large n and it reveals too many POIs to the user; it is too costly for low-bandwidth devices. Our hybrid technique departs from this one-size-fits-all approach and enables users to negotiate their desired level of privacy and efficiency with LBS providers. Thirdly, the scope of the approach did not consider a privacy-preserving partitioning approach for the data set. It considers partitioning with kd-tree and R-tree in the general sense, without specific privacy considerations (see Section 4.2 in [13]). On the other hand, we will show how to use a different method of partitioning of POI data that permits cloaking, and offers privacy protection when used in conjunction with PIR.

Most of the PIR-based approaches for location privacy rely on hardware-based techniques, which typically utilize a secure coprocessor (SC) at the LBS server host [1,19]. This hardware creates a computing space that is protected from the LBS, to realize query privacy. A major drawback of SC-based PIR is that it requires the acquisition of specialized tamperproof hardware and it usually requires periodic reshuffling of the POIs in the database, which is a computationally expensive operation [1,20].

2.3 Hybrid Techniques

Hybrid techniques [11] permit privacy-efficiency tradeoff decisions to be made by combining the benefits of cloaking- and PIR-based techniques. Chor et al. [8] conjectured a tradeoff between privacy and computational overhead as a means of reducing the high computational overhead for some application areas of PIR. Our work concretizes and validates their conjecture in the context of LBS, and also realizes the future work left open in [11], which is to further reduce the performance overhead of PIR techniques. The authors' own optimization of PIR in [13] (paper previously mentioned above) reuses partial computation results (i.e., multiplications of large numbers) and parallelizes the computations. This optimization reduces CPU cost by 40%, but the overall query response time is still impractical [23,29]. Ghinita [11] suggests improving the performance of PIR-based techniques for LBS privacy through a hybrid method that includes a PIR phase on a restricted subset of the data space. Our work answers the open question of how to reduce the processing cost of PIR, without requiring the LBS to have multiple CPUs to take advantage of parallelization. Parallel processors are not typically found on smartphones, either.

3 Our Tradeoff Solution

We have developed a hybrid solution that consists of PIR to achieve query privacy in the context of a location-based service, and a cloaking technique to reduce the computational cost of PIR to a feasible level. Our technique essentially describes how the user creates a cloaking region around his or her true location, and performs a PIR query on the contents of the cloaking region only. The benefits are numerous: the user's location is kept hidden from the server to an acceptable degree regardless of the number of other users in the area; there is no intermediary server that is responsible for cloaking and that would need to be trusted; and the computational cost of the cryptographic algorithms employed is still practical. We ensure that the user downloads only the POIs that are of interest to the smartphone, keeping wireless traffic to a minimum to reduce costs and conserve the battery. We describe our solution in this section.

The approach that we propose entails two phases. First, there is a pre-processing phase in which the system is set up for use. The pre-processing operation must be carried out whenever significant changes are made to the POI database on the server. In practice, it can occur every few months during a period of low usage on the server such as nighttime maintenance activities. Second, there is an execution phase, in which the LBS server responds to queries for POIs from users. At a high level, the pre-processing phase consists of the following steps:

1. A geographic region is projected onto a two-dimensional plane.
2. A suitable grid is formed on the plane.
3. A collection of POIs is saved in a database such that each row corresponds to one POI.
4. Each cell of the grid is mapped to a portion of the database, i.e., a particular set of database rows (each containing a POI).
5. The grid structure is transmitted and saved on the client device in a local mapping database so that it can be referenced in a subsequent query.

The execution phase, in which a query is made for a set of nearby POIs, consists of the following steps:

1. The user determines the area of interest, either based on the current physical position as determined through GPS, or some other arbitrary area that the user may be traveling to in the future.
2. The user chooses a desirable level of privacy.
3. The client creates a cloaking region corresponding to this level of privacy, which will enclose the area of interest.
4. The client sends the cloaking region to the server. Also, the client identifies which portion of the cloaking region contains the area of interest, in a way that is hidden from the server.
5. The server receives the request, and finds the database portion corresponding to the cloaking region. A block of rows is retrieved from this portion based on the user's specified location of interest. The POIs present in these rows are transmitted back to the client.
6. The client decodes the result, and automatically finds the nearest neighbour POI, or presents the full list of POIs returned to the user to choose amongst.

3.1   Level of Privacy for the PIR Query

To defeat a server's ability to narrow down the search space for the item of interest to the user, PIR protocols typically process every item, or POI, in the PIR database. This results in a computational complexity that is linear in n (where n is the number of items in the PIR database). This is the main hindrance to practical PIR deployment [31].

We propose a tradeoff, in the tradition of PIR development over the years, to make PIR-based solutions practical. For example, information theoretic privacy necessitates replacing a single database with at least two replicated databases; another option is to compromise information theoretic privacy for lower privacy (i.e., attain computational privacy). Our proposal is to offer users the choice of trading off privacy for better query performance, by specifying the levels of privacy that they want for their queries. A level of privacy for the query determines the number of items that the PIR server must process in order to provide a response. Setting levels of privacy is a common practice in several domains where privacy is important (e.g., web browsers). In the specific case of location privacy, we argue that resource-constrained device users are willing to trade off privacy to obtain reasonable performance. On the other hand, such users are equally willing to trade off some levels of performance to gain some levels of privacy support.

A user sets the desired privacy level by specifying the size of the cloaking region. The ratio of the number of POIs inside this region to the number of POIs in the entire POI database defines the level of privacy. The privacy level can be specified in terms of cities/towns (city level), states/provinces (provincial level), and so on, to enhance user-friendliness. Thus, a privacy level value of 1 indicates that the user desires query privacy at the same level as that offered by a typical PIR protocol. Similarly, if a user sets the query privacy level to 0.6, the PIR query will execute faster. Although the cost is still linear in the number of items in terms of computational complexity, the constant term is modified (i.e. in terms of Big-O notation), leading to significant performance gains. At the same time, it will be disclosed to the server that a particular amount of $0.4n$ items are not of interest to the user; this leakage of information does not necessarily constitute a significant breach of location privacy.

The cloaking region is thus identified as a subset of the entire world described by the database. If we imagine that the world is mapped as a grid of so-called geographic grid cells that are equally distributed, then one of these cells will be chosen to comprise the cloaking region. If a higher privacy level is desired, then the cloaking region may be expanded to include multiple geographic grid cells, and thus a larger portion of the database that describes the world. It is sufficient to identify each grid cell by its cell number if the mapping is static and published. The process of mapping the world to a geographic grid occurs during the pre-processing phase, described next.

3.2 Pre-processing and Location Cloaking

The first step in the pre-processing phase is to represent a geographic area such as the United States and Canada on a two-dimensional plane using a map projection method such as the commonly used Miller cylindrical projection [32]. Once that is done, the user's location of interest may be found on this plane. It is necessary to obscure the user's location by creating a cloaking area around the user's true position or area of interest. POIs will be found anywhere by the LBS server within this cloaking region. The region must be sufficiently large in order to achieve sufficient privacy for the user, but at the same time it must be sufficiently small to minimize the amount of computation required on the user's mobile device to process the query results, as well as to constrain the amount of wireless data traffic required to transport them.

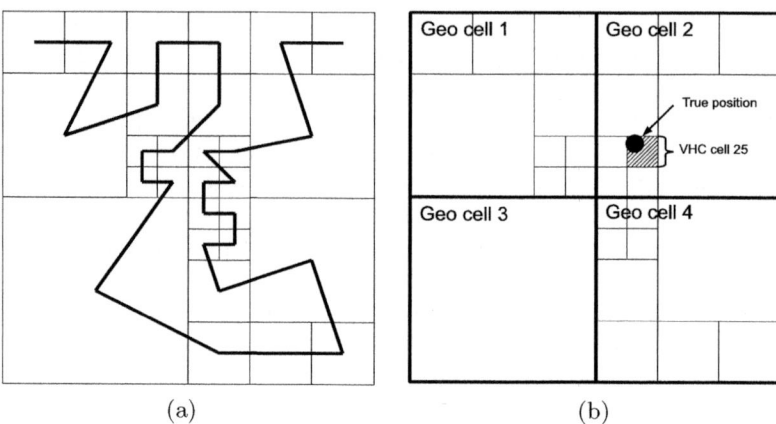

|(a)|(b)|

Fig. 1. (a) A Various-size-grid Hilbert Curve (VHC) mapping with uniform POI density. (b) A user's true position inside VHC cell 25 (shaded) and within a cloaking region bounded by the single geographical grid cell 2. The POI results for VHC cell 25 only will be returned in a query. If a larger cloaking region consisting of geographic grid cells 1 to 4 was specified (for privacy), the same POI results would still be returned.

Several techniques allow POIs to be mapped to a cloaking region. One technique is quad-tree mapping [18], but it has the disadvantage (from its use in Casper [25]) of forming an unnecessarily large cloaking region which can impair performance [2]. Another technique is called VHC (Various-size-grid Hilbert Curve) mapping [28], which suits our purpose. In particular, it solves the problem of the density of POIs varying by geographic area. If the density of POIs is significantly higher for a given region (such as a city), then a higher data traffic cost will result if the size of the cloaking region remains constant, and the query will be much slower. If on the other hand, the density becomes significantly lower (such as in a sparsely populated region like the countryside), then the result size may be so minimal that the server may guess the user's likely destination with a high degree of confidence, leading to loss of privacy. VHC solves this problem by creating variable-sized regions that can be used for cloaking, based on the density of the POIs in the geographic area.

Essentially, in VHC, the two-dimensional geographic grid is mapped to a one-dimensional space such that it has equal POI density everywhere (see Fig. 1a). Assume that a typical POI database that covers the regions of Canada and the U.S. will have 6 million POIs. If each VHC cell must contain the same number of POIs, such as 60, then there will be a total of 100,000 VHC cells that will cover this geographic region. Suppose that the lowest POI density found in the database is 60 POIs per 40,000 km^2. Thus, the maximum size of a VHC cell will be 40,000 km^2.

Now, we create a geographic grid overlaying the U.S. and Canada regions with fixed-size square cells that are 200 km in length (the area of each is 40,000 km^2).

This corresponds to the maximum size of a single VHC cell as described above. Each geographic grid cell, however, may contain any number of smaller-sized VHC cells if the POI density of the region is greater (see Fig. 1b).

Finally, the client determines a cloaking region based on a particular privacy level which will dictate the number of geographic grid cells to include inside the cloaking region. Suppose that the client chooses a privacy level such that the cloaking region consists of four geographic grid cells. The user's true location is in one of these grid cells. Inside of the geographic grid cell, there is a set of variable-sized VHC cells according to the distribution of the POIs in the geographic grid cell. The user's area of interest, in which POIs will be searched, will be the single current VHC cell found inside the geographic grid cell. The number of POIs per VHC cell is known, and in our case, it is 60. Thus, the user will initiate a request that will reference the cloaking region, as well as the specific VHC cell in which the user is located or interested in. The user will receive a set of 60 POIs that are found in his or her current VHC cell only. The server will only know that the location of interest is somewhere within the cloaking region defined by the geographic grid cells.

The geographic grid is useful in specifying the size of the cloaking region and for identifying which VHC cells will comprise the cloaking region. The level of privacy, defined from 0 to 1, establishes the size of the cloaking region. The client then sends this cloaking region to the server, by identifying the bounding coordinates (i.e., the longitude and latitude of the top-left and bottom-right corners). The server will then be able to identify which VHC cells belong to this cloaking region, and therefore which portion of the database must be read. The client must also encode the VHC cell containing the area of interest inside a PIR query. (Each VHC cell in the system is uniquely identified by a numeric value.) Fig. 2 further illustrates the relationships among a geographical grid, VHC cells and POIs.

Thus, our cloaking technique provides a way of reducing the search space of the POI database by employing multiple levels of database segmentation. The cloaking region itself is described as a single, or multiple, geographic grid cell or cells. Inside each geographic grid cell are found one or multiple VHC cells, the number depending on the POI density. The user's true location is inside one of these VHC cells, and the user retrieves POI's corresponding to that VHC cell only. As far as the LBS server is concerned, though, the user could be located anywhere within the larger geographic grid cell.

The geographic grid is fixed. The initial grid cell dimensions are configured based on the maximum size of each VHC cell, but once established, will not need to change. Both the client and server must have the same knowledge of the geographic grid. It can be distributed offline (along with the software for the user's smartphone). A simple approach to determining grid cell dimensions is to use a geographic coordinate system such as Degrees-Minutes-Seconds (DMS) [21]. For instance, each grid cell may be two latitude degrees in length, which roughly equates to 200 km at the 30 degree latitude. A population of tens of thousands to millions of users may typically inhabit and stay within the bounds of a grid cell that is 200 km^2 in size, leading to excellent privacy. Cells of larger size will afford province- and state-level privacy if desired.

VHC cell 1	POI 1	POI 2	...	POI 60
VHC cell 2	POI 61	POI 62	...	POI 120
VHC cell 3	POI 121	POI 122	...	POI 180
VHC cell 4	POI 181	POI 182	...	POI 240
VHC cell 5	POI 241	POI 242	...	POI 300
VHC cell 6	POI 301	POI 302	...	POI 360
VHC cell 7	POI 361	POI 362	...	POI 420
VHC cell 8	POI 421	POI 422	...	POI 480
⋮	⋮	⋮	⋮	⋮

Geo cell 1 { VHC cell 1–4

Geo cell 2 { VHC cell 5–8

Fig. 2. Illustration of the relationship between geographical grid cells, VHC cells, and POIs as stored in database rows

Both the client and server must agree on the same VHC mapping, and this mapping must be done off-line in advance. Because it is dependent on population density, it will remain relatively static over time even as the population grows, and can be dynamically updated on the client if necessary. In order to contain knowledge of the mapping to define the cloaking region, the user may make use of a pre-computed map file that is stored locally on the device. This mapping technique is a replacement for a cloaking region that is simply based on cells of constant size, and ensures that a constant and predictable number of results are returned for the user's grid cell.

The idea of using VHC to address the general problem of location privacy was proposed in [28], but in a way that is very different from ours. Specifically, VHC was used to map the user's current location to a 1-dimensional space. Random perturbation was then applied on the 1-dimensional value, which was then mapped back to 2-dimensional space according to the VHC mapping, to represent the user's true location. In essence, the random perturbation was applied to create confusion for an attacker about the user's true location. Our technique differs in that VHC is used for a different purpose; it defines the storage of POI entries of interest within a geographic cell, which comprises the cloaking region, in a way that allows proximate POIs to be stored as adjacent database entries. We then utilize this cloaking region within the context of a privacy-preserving PIR protocol. We do not perform perturbation of the location, which we argue would result in decreased privacy. Indeed, a non-stationary user whose true location is randomly perturbed is still subject to correlation attack. In our approach, we will demonstrate that the cost of computational and communication overhead through our use of PIR is acceptable, as we provide a method for retrieving only a subset of entries of the entire POI database for each query. Our technique is also impervious to correlation attacks.

The device must store a copy of the VHC map in local non-volatile memory, but the storage requirements are very reasonable. The current geographic grid cell encapsulating the user can be derived from the user's current latitude and longitude coordinate, if the mapping convention is known. A single coordinate for the intersection point of each VHC cell inside (i.e. one of its corners) can then be recorded. Hence, a single coordinate would suffice to store each VHC cell in device memory. For quick lookup and to minimize storage requirements, the coordinates of all VHC cells only in the current geographic cell could be stored. Assuming that the smallest VHC cell size is 1 km^2 in size, then the worst case is that 40,000 coordinates will need to be stored to account for all VHC's. Two bytes will be sufficient to store each VHC coordinate, because the origin of the geographic grid cell is known, so that the total cost will be approximately 80,000 bytes to store all VHC cells. This is the worst theoretical case; in practice, small VHC cells will only be encountered in very dense metropolitan areas, and they will not occupy an entire geographic cell.

3.3   Variable Level of Privacy

The size of the cloaking region and the performance of a query depend on the user's specified level of privacy. If the user wishes to obtain a higher level of privacy, then the size of the cloaking region can be defined to be larger, and to encompass a larger number of geographic grid cells (and thus VHC cells), but the amount of computation on the server will increase accordingly, delaying the response. Nevertheless, the chief benefit is that the processing time of the query on the server is predictable, because each VHC cell in each request contains the same number of POIs. The key fact is that the amount of data transmitted will be roughly proportional to the number of POIs in a single VHC cell (depending on the details of the PIR scheme being employed), but the server will only learn the client's location to the resolution of the cloaking region. The amount of variation allowed in the size of the cloaking region should be kept to a minimum, as this variable may be used to form part of a fingerprint of a target in a correlation attack. Allowing a one-cell or two-by-two-cell region only may be a good compromise. The latter could be employed by the user on a permanent basis to avoid the threat of inter-cell movement being discovered.

Our proposed algorithms for privacy-preserving queries, which allow the user to specify a level of privacy, are explained in detail in the extended version of this paper [27].

4   Experimental Evaluation

4.1   Implementations

We developed a C++ prototype and a Java prototype for our proposal using two available implementations of the PIR protocol. The evaluation of our approach in terms of feasibility and scalability is based on the C++ prototype. The point of the Java prototype is to demonstrate the successful porting of our implementation to a smartphone platform. We did not intend to compare these implementations or run them with the same set of parameters.

The C++ prototype is based on Percy++, an open source PIR protocol written in C++ [14,15]. The Percy implementation offers computational, information theoretic and hybrid (a mix of both) PIR. We modified Percy++ to support our proposal for allowing PIR queries to be based on a database portion defined by the cloaking region and added code for instrumentation. We measured the computational performance of the PIR algorithm when it does take into account the query level of privacy, and when it does not take it into account. We ran the PIR implementation against a database of 6 million synthetic POIs, the typical number of POIs in a commercial POI database for the U.S. and Canada [16,17]. We note that a similar experiment in [13] considers a much smaller database; only 10,000 and 100,000 POIs. A head-to-head comparison with [13] is infeasible because we used different PIR implementations and test data. Each POI consists of 256 bytes that we generated randomly. Again, this size is a conservative representation of practical POI sizes. In comparison, the POIs from [13] are only 64 bits in length. The (x, y) location coordinates are stored with each POI.

The Java prototype is based on a computational SPIR protocol implementation [30]. This SPIR protocol was derived from the oblivious transfer protocol by Naor and Pinkas [26] and is the only publicly available Java implementation to our knowledge. This second prototype development consists of both a server component and a client component that we deployed on a smartphone platform. Specifically, we ported the implementation from [30] to Google's Android smartphone platform, which supports the Java programming language. The only aspect of the implementation that could not be adapted without light modification was the RMI mechanism, which we replaced with HTTP socket communication between the Android client process and a server process running on a desktop computer.

4.2   Results and Discussion

We measured query roundtrip times for the C++ prototype on a machine with a 2.91 GHz dual-core AMD CPU, 3GB RAM, and running Ubuntu Linux. Since the Percy++ PIR uses replicated databases, we set the number of databases to 2 [15]. Fig. 3 shows query roundtrip times and levels of privacy for queries returning various numbers of POIs. The number of POIs returned for each query is equivalent to the number of POIs in a VHC cell. Similarly, the number of POIs returned by a query is equivalent of the number of blocks (in bytes), that a traditional PIR query returns. A block of 10 POIs is equivalent to 2560 bytes of data (each POI consists of 256 bytes).

The query roundtrip or response times for block sizes 5, 10, 25, 50, 100, 250, and 500, at query level of privacy 1, are between 25 and 70 seconds. This is because each PIR request runs against the entire database of 6 million synthetic POIs. However, the query roundtrip time improves with lower levels of privacy. For example, the query response times for the above block sizes at a privacy level of 0.17 are between 4 and 12 seconds. One must observe that setting the query level of privacy to 0.17 is equivalent to privately querying a block of POIs from a portion of the database consisting of 1.02 million POIs. If we assume there are equal number of POIs in all the provinces and states of Canada and US, a level of privacy set to 0.17 implies a cloaking region that covers approximately 10 provinces and/or states. Under a similar assumption, a user who intends to hide his or her query in a cloaking region consisting of one province or state will simply set his or her query level

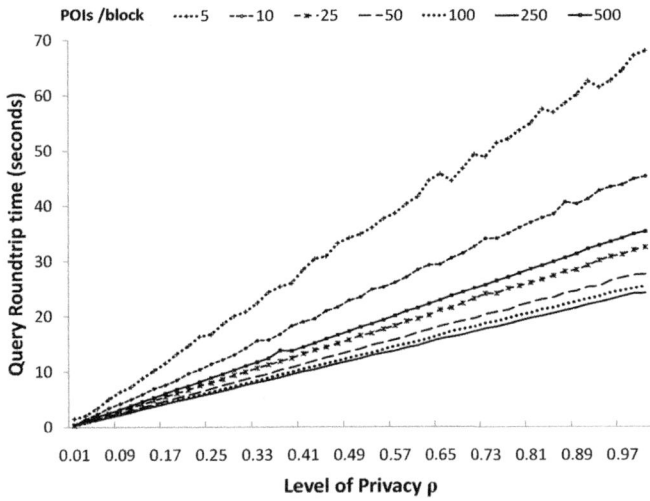

Fig. 3. Query roundtrip time and level of privacy for various numbers of POIs returned per query. A single measurement was taken per data point.

of privacy to a much lower value of 0.02. The query response time for this level of privacy is approximately 0.3 seconds for an optimal block size, which in our testing configuration consists of 256 POIs. It is easy to observe from the graph that the block that consists of 250 POIs gives the best performance. Furthermore, the worst performing block size is the one consisting of 5 POIs, the reason being that smaller block sizes require more rounds of computations to process the individual blocks, compared to larger block sizes. On the other hand, large block sizes, such as 500, carry performance penalties and overheads which depend on the characteristics of the underlying PIR scheme, and also on the resource constraints of the runtime hardware (e.g., RAM, disk and memory cache sizes, and network bandwidth). The network cost in the C++ implementation was negligible since the measurements were taken on a LAN.

We also installed the client for the Java prototype on a G1 Android smartphone from T-Mobile, which features a Qualcomm ARM processor running at 528 MHz, and includes 192 MB DDR SDRAM, and 256 MB flash memory. Although our locked smartphone was capable of running on T-Mobile's 3G network in the U.S., it did not support the 3G frequency bands in operation in Canada. We ran our tests using the Rogers EDGE network, which is slower by up to a factor of ten. We created an Android application with a user interface that allows the user to specify the server address and query parameters such as the size of the cloaking region and the size of the portion of the cloaking region to fetch. We observed that when the cloaking region was reduced to a quarter of its original size (i.e. a quarter of the POIs were returned), the query generation became 2.15 times slower, but the roundtrip time became 3.32 times quicker.

Overall, the implementation was usable even though it had not been originally designed and optimized for the Android platform, and we were restricted to a non-3G network. Further details of our implementation are available in [27].

4.3 Privacy and Size of the Cloaking Region

Our solution preserves the privacy of the user's location irrespective of the number of other users initiating queries for the same location. The server can infer only the user's location based on the cloaking region. The user may adjust the size of the cloaking region based on his or her personal preferences (i.e., the desired level of privacy, query performance, and cost), because a larger region will entail more computation.

The size of the cloaking region is based on a particular size of geographic area and does not need to be adjusted based on the known distribution of POIs within the region. The user only establishes a reasonable level of privacy based on the number of geographic grid cells that define a geographic area. The boundary of the cloaking region utilized in a request is established by the user and is based on the geographic cell map contained on the user's end and the level of privacy parameter. The size of the cloaking region and its boundaries are not controlled by the server.

5 Conclusions

In this paper, we have proposed an algorithm for private information retrieval that achieves a good compromise between user location privacy and computational efficiency. We have implemented and evaluated our algorithm and shown that it is practical on resource-constrained hardware. Our approach of using a variable-sized cloaking region divided into VHC cells results in greater location privacy than the traditional approach of a single cloaking region, while at the same time decreasing wireless data traffic usage from an amount proportional to the size of the cloaking region to an amount proportional to the size of a VHC cell. It also allows the user to dynamically choose various levels of privacy. Although increasing the size of the cloaking region does result in higher computation in processing the query, we believe that this tradeoff is very reasonable, given that the processing power of today's smartphones is still less of a concern than the speed and cost of wireless network connectivity.

Acknowledgments

We would like to thank the anonymous reviewers for their helpful comments for improving this paper. We also gratefully acknowledge NSERC and MITACS for funding this research.

References

1. Ali Khoshgozaran, H.S.-M., Shahabi, C.: SPIRAL, a scalable private information retrieval approach to location privacy. In: Proceedings of the 2nd International Workshop on Privacy-Aware Location-based Mobile Services, PALMS (2008)

2. Bamba, B., Liu, L., Pesti, P., Wang, T.: Supporting anonymous location queries in mobile environments with privacygrid. In: Proceeding of the 17th international conference on World Wide Web, New York, NY, USA, pp. 237–246 (2008)
3. Beimel, A., Stahl, Y.: Robust information-theoretic private information retrieval. J. Cryptol. 20(3), 295–321 (2007)
4. Bettini, C., Jajodia, S., Samarati, P., Wang, X.S. (eds.): Proceedings of the 1st International Workshop on Privacy in Location-Based Applications, Malaga, Spain, October 9. CEUR Workshop Proceedings, vol. 397 (2008)
5. Chor, B., Gilboa, N.: Computationally private information retrieval (extended abstract). In: STOC 1997: Proceedings of the twenty-ninth annual ACM symposium on Theory of computing, New York, NY, USA, pp. 304–313 (1997)
6. Chor, B., Gilboa, N., Naor, M.: Private information retrieval by keywords. Technical Report TR CS0917, Dept. of Computer Science, Technion, Israel (1997)
7. Chor, B., Goldreich, O., Kushilevitz, E., Sudan, M.: Private information retrieval. In: Proceedings of the 36th Annual Symposium on the Foundations of Computer Science, October 1995, pp. 41–50 (1995)
8. Chor, B., Kushilevitz, E., Goldreich, O., Sudan, M.: Private information retrieval. J. ACM 45(6), 965–981 (1998)
9. Chow, C., Mokbel, M.F., Liu, X.: A peer-to-peer spatial cloaking algorithm for anonymous location-based service. In: Proceedings of the 14th Annual ACM international Symposium on Advances in Geographic information Systems, New York, NY, USA, pp. 171–178 (2006)
10. Dingledine, R., Mathewson, N., Syverson, P.: Tor: the second-generation onion router. In: SSYM 2004: Proceedings of the 13th conference on USENIX Security Symposium, Berkeley, CA, USA, pp. 21–21 (2004)
11. Ghinita, G.: Understanding the privacy-efficiency trade-off in location based queries. In: SPRINGL 2008: Proceedings of the SIGSPATIAL ACM GIS 2008 International Workshop on Security and Privacy in GIS and LBS, New York, NY, USA, pp. 1–5 (2008)
12. Ghinita, G., Kalnis, P., Kantarcioglu, M., Bertino, E.: A hybrid technique for private location-based queries with database protection. In: Mamoulis, N., Seidl, T., Pedersen, T.B., Torp, K., Assent, I. (eds.) SSTD 2009. LNCS, vol. 5644, pp. 98–116. Springer, Heidelberg (2009)
13. Ghinita, G., Kalnis, P., Khoshgozaran, A., Shahabi, C., Tan, K.-L.: Private queries in location based services: anonymizers are not necessary. In: SIGMOD 2008: Proceedings of the 2008 ACM SIGMOD international conference on Management of data, New York, NY, USA, pp. 121–132 (2008)
14. Goldberg, I.: Percy++ project on SourceForge, http://percy.sourceforge.net/
15. Goldberg, I.: Improving the robustness of private information retrieval. In: SP 2007: Proceedings of the 2007 IEEE Symposium on Security and Privacy, Washington, DC, USA, pp. 131–148 (2007)
16. GPSmagazine. Garmin nuvi 780 GPS Review, http://gpsmagazine.com
17. GPSreview.net. POI– Points of Interest, http://www.gpsreview.net/pois/
18. Gruteser, M., Grunwald, D.: Anonymous usage of location-based services through spatial and temporal cloaking. In: MobiSys 2003: Proceedings of the 1st international conference on Mobile systems, applications and services, New York, NY, USA, pp. 31–42 (2003)
19. Hengartner, U.: Hiding location information from location-based services. In: 2007 International Conference on Mobile Data Management, May 2007, pp. 268–272 (2007)

20. Iliev, A., Smith, S.W.: Protecting Client Privacy with Trusted Computing at the Server. IEEE Security and Privacy 3(2), 20–28 (2005)
21. Kennedy, M., Kopp, S.: Understanding Map Projections. ESRI (Environmental Systems Research Institute) press (2000)
22. Kushilevitz, E., Ostrovsky, R.: Replication is not needed: single database, computationally-private information retrieval. In: FOCS 1997: Proceedings of the 38th Annual Symposium on Foundations of Computer Science, Washington, DC, USA, p. 364 (1997)
23. Lin, D., Bertino, E., Cheng, R., Prabhakar, S.: Position transformation: a location privacy protection method for moving objects. In: SPRINGL 2008: Proceedings of the SIGSPATIAL ACM GIS 2008 International Workshop on Security and Privacy in GIS and LBS, New York, NY, USA, pp. 62–71 (2008)
24. Mishra, S.K., Sarkar, P.: Symmetrically private information retrieval. In: Roy, B., Okamoto, E. (eds.) INDOCRYPT 2000. LNCS, vol. 1977, pp. 225–236. Springer, Heidelberg (2000)
25. Mokbel, M.F., Chow, C.-Y., Aref, W.G.: The new Casper: query processing for location services without compromising privacy. In: VLDB 2006: Proceedings of the 32nd international conference on Very large data bases, pp. 763–774 (2006)
26. Naor, M., Pinkas, B.: Oblivious transfer and polynomial evaluation. In: STOC 1999: Proceedings of the thirty-first annual ACM symposium on Theory of computing, New York, NY, USA, pp. 245–254 (1999)
27. Olumofin, F., Tysowski, P.K., Goldberg, I., Hengartner, U.: Achieving Efficient Query Privacy for Location Based Services. Technical report, CACR 2009-22, University of Waterloo (2009)
28. Pingley, A., Yu, W., Zhang, N., Fu, X., Zhao, W.: CAP: A Context-Aware Privacy Protection System For Location-Based Services. In: 29th IEEE International Conference on Distributed Computing Systems (June 2009)
29. Riboni, D., Pareschi, L., Bettini, C.: Privacy in georeferenced context-aware services: A survey. In: Bettini, et al. (eds.) [4]
30. Saint-Jean, F.: Java implementation of a single-database computationally symmetric private information retrieval (CSPIR) protocol. Technical Report YALEU/DCS/TR-1333A, Yale University, New Haven, CT, USA (2005)
31. Sion, R., Carbunar, B.: On the computational practicality of private information retrieval. In: Proceedings of the Network and Distributed Systems Security Symposium (2007)
32. Snyder, J.P.: Flattening the Earth, two thousand years of map projections. University of Chicago Press, Chicago (1993)
33. Solanas, A., Domingo-Ferrer, J., Martínez-Ballesté, A.: Location privacy in location-based services: Beyond TTP-based schemes. In: Bettini, et al. (eds.) [4]
34. Xu, T., Cai, Y.: Location anonymity in continuous location-based services. In: Proceedings of the 15th Annual ACM international Symposium on Advances in Geographic information Systems, New York, NY, USA, pp. 1–8 (2007)
35. Zhong, G., Hengartner, U.: A distributed k-anonymity protocol for location privacy. In: Proceedings of Seventh IEEE International Conference on Pervasive Computing and Communication (PerCom 2009), Galveston, TX, pp. 253–262 (2009)

Making a Nymbler Nymble Using VERBS⋆

Ryan Henry, Kevin Henry, and Ian Goldberg

Cheriton School of Computer Science
University of Waterloo
Waterloo, ON, Canada N2L 3G1
{rhenry,k2henry,iang}@cs.uwaterloo.ca

Abstract. We propose a new system modeled after Nymble. Like Nymble, our scheme provides a privacy-preserving analog of IP address blocking for anonymizing networks. However, unlike Nymble, the user in our scheme need not trust third parties to maintain their anonymity. We achieve this while avoiding the use of trusted hardware and without requiring an offline credential issuing authority to guarantee that users do not obtain multiple credentials.

We use zero-knowledge proofs to reduce the capabilities of colluding third parties, and introduce a new cryptographic technique that we call *verifier-efficient restricted blind signatures*, or VERBS, to maintain efficiency. Signature verification with our VERBS are 1–2 orders of magnitude faster than existing restricted blind signatures.

Keywords: Privacy, anonymity, authentication, anonymous blacklisting, revocation, anonymous credentials, zero-knowledge proofs.

1 Introduction

Anonymity networks provide users with a means to communicate privately over the Internet. The Tor network [13] is the largest deployed anonymity network; it aims to defend users against traffic analysis attacks by encrypting users' communications and routing them through a worldwide distributed network of volunteer-run relays [29].

The ability to communicate without fear of network surveillance makes it possible for many users to express ideas or share knowledge that they might otherwise not be willing to reveal for fear of persecution, punishment or simply embarrassment. On the other hand, some users use the veil of anonymity as a license to perform mischievous deeds such as trolling forums or cyber-vandalism. For this reason, some popular websites (for example, Wikipedia [33] and Slashdot [14]) proactively ban any user connecting from a known anonymous communications network from contributing content, thus limiting freedom of expression.[1]

⋆ An extended version of this paper is available [18].

[1] Some IRC networks also block access to anonymous users (for example, see
https://wiki.torproject.org/noreply/TheOnionRouter/BlockingIrc)

M.J. Atallah and N. Hopper (Eds.): PETS 2010, LNCS 6205, pp. 111–129, 2010.

Therefore, a real need exists for systems that allow anonymous users to contribute content online, while preserving the ability of service providers to selectively (and subjectively) ban individual users without compromising their anonymity. Not only would such a system benefit the estimated hundreds of thousands of existing Tor users, but it might also be a boon to wider acceptance of Tor. Indeed, the need for an anonymous blacklisting mechanism has been acknowledged by several key people involved with The Tor Project [11,12]. Thus, it is reasonable to expect that the operators of Tor might be willing to provide the infrastructure necessary to realize such a system, a situation that would greatly reduce the burden on service providers and lead to greater adoption.

Several schemes (e.g., [19,20,30,31,32]) have been proposed with the goal of allowing anonymous blacklisting of Tor users. The most well-known of these is Nymble [20,32], which is the system after which we model our own.

1.1   An Overview of Nymble

Suppose a user Alice wishes to connect anonymously to a *Service Provider* (SP), such as a website, while the SP will allow connections only if it can ban a misbehaving user by IP address. To facilitate this, the Nymble system introduces two TTPs, the *Pseudonym Manager* (PM) and the *Nymble Manager* (NM). Before connecting to the SP, Alice connects directly to the PM, thus proving she has control over the specified IP address. The PM then issues Alice a pseudonym called a *Nym*, which is deterministically generated from her IP in such a way that the NM is able to verify that the pseudonym was in fact issued to Alice by the PM, but learns no information about Alice's IP. Alice then connects to the NM over an anonymous channel and presents her Nym along with the name of the SP to which she wishes to connect. Using the pair (Nym, SP), the NM computes and issues to Alice a set of *nymbles* — one for each time period left in the current *linkability window*. Within a linkability window, each successive nymble is generated from the previous one using a one way function (a hash function) and two secrets; one secret is known only to the NM, while the other is shared by the NM and the SP. In order to connect to the SP, Alice presents the nymble which corresponds to the current time period. The shared secret allows the SP to verify the validity of Alice's nymble but not learn her IP address, nor compute or identify any of her other nymbles. Therefore, Alice's connections within a time period are linkable, while her accesses across different time periods are not. The SP records the nymble used during a session; if it is later found that Alice misbehaved, the SP can complain to the NM by presenting it with a copy of the recorded nymble. The NM then issues the SP a *linking token*, which is essentially a trapdoor that allows the SP to compute all of Alice's subsequent nymbles starting from the time period in which the complaint was made (up until the end of the linkability window). The one-way nature of hash functions guarantees that the trapdoor provides no way for the SP to compute *previous* nymbles; thus, backwards anonymity is preserved, while further connections from a misbehaving user can be detected and blocked.

1.2   The Not-So-Nymble Side of Nymble

Nymble provides an efficient framework for banning users of an anonymizing network; however, the simplicity and efficiency come at a cost. Recall that the PM knows the pair (IP, Nym) while the NM knows the pair (Nym, SP). Therefore, if the NM and PM collude, it is trivial for them to determine which SP the user associated with a given IP address is accessing. Further, because it is trivial for an NM to retroactively compute a user's nymbles, a colluding NM and SP can easily break backwards anonymity and link a user's connections. If all three parties collude (i.e., the PM, NM, and SP), they can trivially link all actions of a given user back to that user's IP, thus completely breaking anonymity.

1.3   Our Contributions

We present a new Nymble-like system, unimaginatively called *Nymbler*, that minimizes the capabilities of the PM, NM, and SP when colluding. This is accomplished through the use of anonymous credentials and a new *verifier-efficient* restricted blind signature scheme that we use to permit users to construct their own nymbles. Thus, our scheme eliminates the need to trust third parties with anonymity while maintaining the essential properties of Nymble.

Outline. The remainder of this paper is outlined as follows: Previous work related to restricted blind signature schemes and blacklisting anonymous users are presented in §2, followed by an overview of the approach taken in this work in §3. We describe in detail our approach to verifier-efficient restricted blind signatures in §4 while our Nymbler scheme and the protocols involved are described in §5. In §6 we suggest appropriate values for security parameters and analyze the performance of our system with these choices. We conclude in §7 and outline some potential areas for future work.

2   Related Work

2.1   Restricted Blind Signature Schemes

In his seminal work [9], Chaum introduced the notion of a blind signature scheme; the idea was later elaborated in [10], where the first construction (based on RSA signatures) was given. Chaum's scheme allows a user to obtain a cryptographic signature on a message without revealing *any* information about the message to the signer. Later, Brands [5] proposed *restricted blind signatures* in which a user obtains a blind signature on a message, while the signer gets to see certain parts of the structure of the message before signing. If this structure does not conform to certain rules, the signer can refuse to provide a signature; thus, the choice of message to be signed can be restricted by the signer. However, unlike Chaum's blind signature scheme, where verification costs just one modular exponentiation (where the exponent can be chosen to be as small as 3), verifying Brands' restricted blind signatures has a computational cost dominated by a multi-exponentiation where each exponent is essentially random (modulo a large prime) and depends on the message to be signed.

Camenisch and Lysyanskaya [7] presented a versatile signature scheme (CL-signatures) that allows a *re-randomizable* restricted blind signature to be issued. The well-known CL-credential [3,7] scheme is based on CL-signatures. In their scheme, the cost of verifying a signature is effectively one exponentiation and one multi-exponentiation, with each exponent approximately equal in size to the message to be signed.

Recently, Groth and Sahai [17] presented a zero-knowledge proof system based on bilinear pairings. Belenkiy et al. [2] proposed a restricted blind signature scheme called P-signatures and noninteractive anonymous credential system based on the Groth-Sahai framework. The cost of verification in their scheme is about one elliptic curve exponentiation and three pairing operations.

Our approach uses RSA-based signatures similar to Chaum's, combined with zero-knowledge proofs that allow the user to prove certain properties about the message before it is signed. The key advantage of our approach over other restricted blind signature schemes is its extremely low cost verification algorithm (i.e., almost as efficient as Chaum's *non-restricted* blind signatures with exponent 3). In particular, verifying a signature in our scheme costs just four modular multiplications, which is *1–2 orders of magnitude* faster than any previously proposed restricted blind signature scheme.[2]

2.2   Systems for Anonymous Blacklisting

Unlinkable Serial Transactions [28] was one of the first systems to allow anonymous blacklisting. The scheme prevents an SP from tracking the behaviour of its users, while protecting it from abuse due to simultaneous active sessions by a single user. Users are issued blind tokens from the SP and, in normal operation, these tokens are renewed at the end of a user's transaction. If a user is judged to have misbehaved, the SP can block future connections from that user by refusing to issue further tokens. However, the scheme provides no way for the SP to ban a user if misbehaviour is detected *after* the end of the session in which it occurred.

The Nym system [19] was a first attempt at solving the problem of allowing anonymous edits on Wikipedia; it represents one of the first attempts at bringing accountability to users of anonymity networks. Unlike later approaches, Nym only provides *pseudonymity*, and thus is not an ideal solution. Later schemes — most notably Nymble — improve upon Nym to provide full anonymity.

Blacklistable Anonymous Credentials (BLAC) [30], proposed by several of the authors of Nymble, provides an anonymous credential system that does not make use of any TTP who can revoke the anonymity of all users. Instead, the system allows an SP to add a credential to its blacklist if the owner of that

---

[2] In §6.2, we present experimental results indicating that the cost of verifying a signature in our scheme is almost forty times faster than computing a *single* modular exponentiation — an operation that is less expensive than the verification of any of the restricted blind signatures discussed above.

credential is judged to have misbehaved. However, BLAC suffers from two major drawbacks. The first of these is the loss of efficiency when compared to a system like Nymble; if the blacklist grows large, say one thousand users, then several hundred kilobytes of communication and several seconds of computation are required (per access) to prove that a user is not on the blacklist [32]. For large services with many users, such as Wikipedia, the performance of this approach is unacceptable. The second downside is that the credentials are not tied to an IP address. Instead, the system assumes that some offline credential issuing authority will ensure that no user obtains more than a single credential.

Privacy-Enhanced Revocation with Efficient Authentication (PEREA) [31] is another system proposed by the same authors as BLAC. It improves upon BLAC by providing similar functionality but utilizing a cryptographic accumulator to offer computational requirements at the SP that do not depend on the size of the blacklist. To make this possible the system makes use of an *authentication window*, which is similar in concept to that of a linkability window, except that it specifies the *maximum number of subsequent connections* a user may make before it becomes impossible to block them due to behaviour during a previous session, instead of *the maximum time duration* that can elapse. However, although the cost of verification at the SP is constant regardless of the size of the blacklist, it is still several orders of magnitude slower than Nymble, taking about 0.16 seconds per authentication when the authentication window is 30 [31]. Moreover, as with BLAC, the credentials used in PEREA are not tied to an IP address and are issued by an offline credential authority that ensures no user can obtain more than one credential. In the next section we touch on the technical reasons why BLAC and PEREA cannot be adapted to use IP addresses as a unique resource.

3   Our Approach

This section provides a high-level overview of our scheme. Further details about how this approach is realized are presented in §4 and §5.

As a first step, we replace the pseudonymous Nym with an anonymous credential; thus, the PM is replaced by a *Credential Manager* (CM). The CM learns Alice's IP address and issues a credential stating this fact, but the CM is unable to recognize this credential at a later time. This modification prevents the CM and NM from colluding to learn which SP a particular user is accessing.

We emphasize that our use of anonymous credentials — and the role of the CM in general — is fundamentally different from in BLAC and PEREA. For example, the CM is not required to keep track of the unique resources for which a credential has been issued; instead, the CM encodes each user's unique resource *directly in the credential* that it issues. This prevents the enrolment issues addressed in [30], wherein a user's credential is misplaced or compromised, from causing problems in our approach. In such a case, the CM simply issues the user with a new credential encoding the same unique resource, and all of their previous bans remain in effect. It is this property that allows us to continue to use IP addresses as the unique resource (as in Nymble). Note that in BLAC and PEREA this choice of unique resource is unrealistic, since in those schemes an SP would have no way to distinguish two credentials encoding the same IP address from ones encoding different IP addresses.

Using her credential, our scheme allows Alice to construct her own set of nymbles in such a way that the NM is convinced of their validity without ever actually seeing them. The NM then issues Alice with *verifier-efficient restricted blind signatures* (VERBS) on her nymbles so that the SP can also be convinced of their validity. Note that from a security point of view there is no reason why the NM, and not the SP, must be responsible for verifying the integrity of Alice's nymbles; indeed, the SP could verify Alice's proofs directly and thus eliminate the role of the NM at this stage. Our motivation for using the NM at this stage in the protocol is simply to offload work from the SP to the NM.

In the case that Alice misbehaves and the SP wishes to ban her, the SP can present a nymble to the NM, who then performs a non-trivial amount of computation — i.e., solving a discrete log — to recover sufficient information to calculate Alice's remaining nymbles. This is accomplished through the use of a trapdoor discrete log group, where parameters are selected so that performing discrete logs is possible using the NM's private key but even so is sufficiently expensive that wholesale deanonymization is impractical. We emphasize that although the NM can compute subsequent nymbles from a starting point, even with the ability to solve discrete logs the NM cannot go backwards. Thus, breaking backwards anonymity in our system is much more difficult than in Nymble.

4   Verifier-Efficient Restricted Blind Signatures

In this section we introduce *verifier-efficient restricted blind signatures* (VERBS), a restricted blind signature scheme with an efficient verification protocol. Our scheme makes use of *commitments*, which can be Feldman commitments [15] (the commitment to x is $\mathcal{CF}(x) = s^x$ for a known group element s) or Pedersen commitments [24] (the commitment to x is $\mathcal{CP}(x) = s^x r^\gamma$ for known group elements s, r where $\log_s r$ is unknown, and γ is random).

We use several standard zero-knowledge proofs from the literature; in particular, we use the standard proof of knowledge of a committed value (i.e., a discrete logarithm) [27], proof that a commitment opens to a product of committed values [8], and proof of knowledge of a committed value that lies in a particular range [4]. We note that no proof is necessary for addition or scalar multiplication of committed values, as those operations are easily accomplished by multiplication or exponentiation of the commitments, respectively.

We also utilize a proof of *nested commitments* (a "nest proof"); that is, given A, B, prove that you know x such that A is a commitment *to a commitment* to x and B is a commitment to the same x. That is (for simplicity, we only show the Feldman case; the Pedersen case is similar), that you know x and G such that $G = g^x$, $A = s^G$, and $B = t^x$. (All operations are in appropriate groups, and g, s, t are generators of those groups.)

This proof works the same way as the ordinary proof of equality of discrete logarithms: the prover chooses v and outputs g^v and t^v; the verifier (or a hash function if the Fiat-Shamir [16] method is used) chooses a challenge c; the prover outputs $r = v - cx$; the verifier accepts if $G^c g^r = g^v$ and $B^c t^r = t^v$. The twist in our scenario is that G is not available to the verifier; only its commitment $(A = s^G)$ is. We solve this problem by having the prover output s^{g^v} instead of g^v, and having the *prover* compute s^{G^c} (the commitment to G^c) and prove in zero-knowledge that it was done correctly (see below). Then the verifier checks that $(s^{G^c})^{g^r} = s^{g^v}$ (along with the unchanged $B^c t^r = t^v$). In the event that g and t have different orders (which will be true in general, and in our case), the above range proof is also utilized to show that $0 \le x < ord(t)$.

For the proof of an exponentiation of a committed value, we use a simplified version of the algorithm from [8]. In that paper, the *exponent* was also hidden from the verifier. In our situation, the exponent c is known, which makes matters considerably easier. The prover just performs any addition-and-multiplication-based exponentiation routine, and proves that each step was done correctly.

We next describe the four algorithms that make up VERBS. The full details are presented in [18]. We will state the algorithms in their noninteractive zero-knowledge form (such as by using Fiat-Shamir [16]); the adaptation of VERBS-Blind and VERBS-Sign to interactive zero-knowledge is straightforward. (The other two algorithms do not change.)

All computations are performed modulo an RSA number, ρ, whose factorization is known only to the signer. The **VERBS-Blind** algorithm is executed by the client. The algorithm takes as input a group element g, a commitment $\mathcal{C}(x)$ (either Feldman or Pedersen) to a secret value x, and x itself (plus γ in the case of a Pedersen commitment). The role of this algorithm, much like its Chaumian counterpart, is to produce the blinded message $S = f(\nu) \cdot \alpha^3 \bmod \rho$, where $\nu = g^x$ and the random blinding factor α are hidden from the signer, and $f(z) = z^2 + 1$ is a one-way function. (It is one-way since the factorization of the modulus ρ is unknown to the client.) It also produces Π, a zero-knowledge proof that the computation of S was performed correctly.

The **VERBS-Sign** protocol is run by the NM. It takes the tuple (S, p, q, ξ, Π) as input. $S \in \mathbb{Z}_\rho^*$ is a blinding of the message to be signed. p and q are the factors of ρ. $\xi \in \mathbb{Z}_\rho^*$ is a *context element* that encodes meta-information about the signature (see §5.1). Π is a zero-knowledge proof that S was correctly formed. It outputs the blinded signature $\sigma' = (\xi \cdot S)^{\frac{1}{3}} \bmod \rho$ if all proofs in Π are valid; otherwise, it outputs $\perp$. Note that σ' is essentially just a Chaum blind signature.

The **VERBS-Unblind** protocol is run by the client. The algorithm takes the tuple (σ', α) as input. σ' is a blind signature and α is the blinding factor used to blind the signature. It outputs $\sigma = \sigma' \cdot \alpha^{-1} \bmod \rho$, the unblinded signature.

The **VERBS-Verify** algorithm is run by the SP. It takes the tuple (ν, σ, ξ) as input; ν is the message that was signed, σ is the (unblinded) signature, and ξ is the context element. It outputs **true** iff $\sigma^3 \bmod \rho \stackrel{?}{=} \xi \cdot (\nu^2 + 1) \bmod \rho$. Note that the cost of VERBS-Verify is just four modular multiplications.

5   An Improved Nymble

We next present our new anonymous blacklisting scheme modeled after Nymble. Our scheme aims to meet the same goals as Nymble, while making deanonymization of a user infeasible, regardless of which subset of third parties might collude against her. Before describing the approach in any detail, we briefly describe the third parties involved and explain their roles. Note that the SP must trust third parties to properly carry out their respective responsibilities; however, unlike in the original Nymble, the user need not trust them not to collude in order for her anonymity to be maintained.

The third parties are called the *Credential Manager* (CM) and the *Nymble Manager* (NM). The CM is responsible for issuing an anonymous credential to the user which encodes two pieces of information: an obfuscated version of the user's IP address, and an expiration time. For added security, the CM may be distributed as outlined below. At any time before this expiration, the user can present her credential to the NM to receive a set of mutually unlinkable authentication tokens called *nymbles*, which can be used to anonymously access the services offered by a *Service Provider* (SP). The NM never sees the nymbles that it issues, but it does supply the user with a verifier-efficient restricted blind signature on each of them, which allows the user to efficiently convince the SP of their legitimacy. When the user connects to the SP over an anonymous channel she must present a valid nymble. The SP records the nymble that was used during each session. In the event of user misbehaviour, it presents a nymble to the NM, who then computes all subsequent nymbles for that user (and hence prevents her from connecting to the SP for the remainder of the *linkability window*).

5.1   System Parameters

In this subsection we introduce the system parameters used in our protocols. In §6.1 we discuss technical considerations in the selection of these parameters and suggest some reasonable values.

The system has a publicly known modulus n, where n is the product of two *unknown* (to anyone) large safe primes, and $N = 2n+1$ is prime. Such a modulus can be generated using a distributed protocol as described in [1], or with one-time trust in an entity which generates it, such as used in the erstwhile RSA Factoring Challenge [26]. Under the assumption that n is hard to factor, squaring modulo n is a *one-way function*. Thus, squaring modulo n is a one-way function that admits *efficient* zero-knowledge proofs of knowledge of preimages [8]. We fix $a, b \in QR_N$, the set of quadratic residues modulo N, so that $\log_a b \bmod N$ is unknown. Choosing $(a, b) = (4, 9)$ is fine.

Since IP addresses tend to change frequently, the system-wide parameter Δ_t specifies the maximum time period for which an issued credential is valid. That is, after a time period of Δ_t has elapsed, the user must reauthenticate with the CM to obtain a fresh credential encoding her current IP address, herein denoted IP.

As in the original Nymble, our scheme uses the concept of *linkability windows*. This prevents a malicious NM and SP from computing a trapdoor for a user that can be used to link that user's actions indefinitely. The duration W of each linkability window is a parameter that can vary from SP to SP based on their own policies; reasonable values for this parameter might be, for example, twenty-four hours or one week. Each linkability window is indexed by a value d, which is used in the computation of nymbles during that time period. For example, d might be equal to the current year concatenated with the current day of the year, or the current year concatenated with the current week of the year (if twenty-four hour or one-week linkability windows are used, respectively). The method used to determine d for a given date and time should be public and easily computable by any user. Each linkability window d is further subdivided into Γ uniform-sized *time periods*, denoted $\tau_{d,1}, \tau_{d,2}, \ldots, \tau_{d,\Gamma}$. A reasonable duration for these time periods might be fifteen minutes (in which case $W = \Gamma \cdot 15$ minutes). Their duration determines how often a user is able to unlinkably access the service, as exactly one unique and unlinkable nymble is issued per IP address per time period in each linkability window.

Each SP possesses a *linking list* $\mathcal{L}$ of the future nymbles associated with users who have misbehaved; these nymbles will not be accepted. The SP also possesses a *blacklist* $\mathcal{B}$, which contains one *canonical* nymble for each user in the linking list (i.e., that user's nymble for the last time period of the linkability window), and is signed by the NM and published by the SP. Before attempting to connect to the SP a user will download a copy of this blacklist and confirm that she is not presently banned. (This is important since otherwise, if a user does not realize she is presently on the blacklist, the SP could link the user's actions without her knowledge.) When receiving a request for a connection from a Nymble user, the SP consults the linking list to determine if the user is blacklisted. The techniques of [32] can be used to ensure that the user receives an up-to-date blacklist.

In our description of the protocols we assume that the credentials are Camenisch-Lysyanskaya (CL) credentials [3,7], although our approach could be easily adapted to other credential systems. The CM's public key is, therefore, the tuple (S, Z, R_1, R_2, m), where $m = m_p m_q$ is an ℓ_m-bit product of two large safe primes of equal size, $\langle S \rangle = QR_m$ (i.e., S is a randomly chosen generator of the group QR_m) and $Z, R_1, R_2 \in_R QR_m$ are randomly chosen quadratic residues modulo m. Here ℓ_m is a security parameter; in [3] the authors recommend $\ell_m = 2048$. The CM's private key is the tuple (m_p, m_q, sk), i.e., the factorization of m and a secret Message Authentication Code (**MAC**) key. For a distributed CM, each CM node would have an independent key pair.

The NM has public key $\rho = pq$, where ρ is an ℓ_ρ-bit product of ℓ_B-smooth primes p and q (that is, $p-1$ and $q-1$ are products of ℓ_B-bit primes), such that $R = 4\rho + 1$ is a prime.[3] It is required that $\rho > n$, but being just barely larger is sufficient. We note that a different ρ can be used in conjunction with each SP and linkability window, but for brevity, we will use a single ρ value in our

---

[3] We use $4\rho + 1$ because it is easy to see that p and q must be congruent to 2 mod 3, and so $2\rho + 1$ must be divisible by 3.

descriptions. Here ℓ_B is chosen so that computing discrete logarithms modulo ρ in subgroups of order $\approx 2^{\ell_B}$ is *costly but feasible*. In other words, given knowledge of the factorization of $p-1$ and $q-1$, computing discrete logs modulo p and q (and hence, modulo ρ) is feasible (but costly) using a technique like the parallel rho method of van Oorschot and Wiener [23]. g is a generator of QR_ρ, and r and s are generators of the order-ρ subgroup of $\mathbb{Z}_R^*$ such that $\log_r s$ is unknown. The NM's private key is then (p, q) and the factorization of $\phi(\rho)$ (into ℓ_B-bit primes), so $\mathbb{Z}_\rho^*$ is a trapdoor discrete logarithm group with the NM's private key as its trapdoor.

Each SP is tied to a value h, which changes once per linkability window. Here $h \in \mathbb{Z}_n^*$ and it is required that h has *large order* in $\mathbb{Z}_n^*$. More precisely, we require that $ord(h) \geq \frac{(p-1)(q-1)}{4}$. This requirement is guaranteed to hold if $\gcd(h, n) = \gcd(h^2 - 1, n) = 1$, which can easily be confirmed by any user. In practice, we also need to be sure that the relative discrete logarithm between the h values of different SPs, or the same SP at different linkability windows, is unknown. For this reason, we let h be the result of a strong cryptographic hash function applied to a concatenation of d and the SP's name (where d is the index of the linkability window for which nymbles derived from h will be valid). In the unlikely event that the result of the hash does not satisfy the order requirement, the hash is applied iteratively until an appropriate value for h is produced.

Every pair $(SP, \tau_{d,j})$ is associated with a *context element* denoted by $\xi_{d,j}^{SP} \in \mathbb{Z}_\rho^*$. As the notation suggests, this context element encodes the SP, linkability window, and time period for which a particular nymble is valid; without it, the SP has no way to distinguish, for example, nymbles issued for a time period that has already passed or those intended for a different SP altogether. The values for $\xi_{d,j}^{SP}$ can be precomputed and must be known by both the NM and the SP, as they are required in the VERBS-Sign and VERBS-Verify protocols. The client must also know $\xi_{d,j}^{SP}$ in order to verify its own nymbles. A reasonable value for $\xi_{d,j}^{SP}$ might be as simple as a hash of the SP's name, d, and j.[4]

5.2   Credential Issuing Protocol

When a user Alice wishes to gain anonymous access to an SP, she must first prove possession of IP to obtain a valid signed CL-credential from the CM. The following protocol describes this process.

1. Alice connects directly to the CM; this proves to the CM that Alice is in possession of IP.
2. The CM computes $x = \mathbf{MAC}_{sk}(\text{IP})$ and $t_{\exp} = t_{\text{cur}} + \Delta_t$, where $\mathbf{MAC}_{sk}(\cdot)$ denotes a Message Authentication Code keyed by the CM's private key sk[5],

---

[4] The security requirement is that the cube root modulo ρ of the ratio of any two of the ξ should be computable only with negligible probability if the factorization of ρ is unknown.

[5] A MAC of Alice's IP address is used instead of her plaintext IP address to frustrate brute-force attacks performed by a colluding NM and SP.

t_{cur} is the current time, and t_{exp} is the expiration time of the credential to be issued. The tuple (x, t_{exp}) is transmitted to Alice.

3. The CM then issues Alice a CL-credential $\mathbf{Cred}(x, t_{\text{exp}}) = (A, e, v)$ encoding x and t_{exp}, where $e \in_R [2^{\ell_e - 1}, 2^{\ell_e - 1} + 2^{\ell'_e - 1}]$ is a randomly chosen prime, $v \in_R \mathbb{Z}_{\phi(m)}$, and $A = \left(\dfrac{Z}{R_1{}^x \cdot R_2{}^{t_{\text{exp}}} \cdot S^v} \right)^{1/e} \bmod m$. Recall that R_1, R_2 and S and Z are part of the CM's public key. Here ℓ_e and ℓ'_e are security parameters; see §6.1 and [3] for more details.

5.3   Nymble Acquisition Protocol

Once a valid credential is obtained from the CM, the next step is for Alice to compute a set of nymbles and receive VERBS on each of them from the NM. These nymbles are computed using values associated with the SP to which she wishes to gain access, the time period and linkability window in which they will be valid, and Alice's IP address. Alice may choose to request any number of nymbles, provided that this number does not cause her nymble set to span multiple linkability windows and does not exceed a predefined limit K imposed by the particular SP. Let k be the number of nymbles which Alice requests, and let $j \geq 1$ be the index of the time period $\tau_{d,j}$ within the current linkability window (d), for which the first nymble will be valid.

1. Alice rerandomizes $\mathbf{Cred}(x, t_{\text{exp}})$ as follows [3]:
   (a) she chooses $v' \in_R \{0, 1\}^{\ell_m + \ell_\emptyset}$, where $\ell_\emptyset$ is a security parameter;
   (b) she computes $A' = A \cdot S^{v'} \bmod m$ and $v'' = v - ev'$ (in $\mathbb{Z}$).
   Her rerandomized credential is then $\mathbf{Cred}'(x, t_{\text{exp}}) = (A', e, v'')$.
2. Alice computes the public value h using the name of the SP and the index d of the linkability window during which she wishes to connect. That is, she computes $h = hash(d \| name)$, where $name$ is the canonical name associated with the SP. She also verifies that these values satisfy the order requirements from §5.1, and iteratively reapplies the hash function otherwise. She transmits $(h, name, k, j)$ to the NM.
3. The NM verifies that $k \leq K$ and $j + k \leq \Gamma$, and aborts otherwise.
4. Alice verifiably computes her unique *seed* value $h_j = h^{x2^j}$ as follows:
   (a) she picks a random $\gamma \in \mathbb{Z}_n$, computes the Pedersen commitment (to h_j)
   $$Y_j = a^{\left(h^{x2^j} \bmod n\right)} b^\gamma \bmod N,$$
   and transmits Y_j to the NM;
   (b) next she performs the statistical zero-knowledge proof of knowledge

$$PK \left\{ (e, v'', x, t_{\text{exp}}, \gamma) : \begin{array}{l} Z \equiv R_1{}^x \cdot R_2{}^{t_{\text{exp}}} \cdot S^{v''} \cdot (A')^e \bmod m \\ \wedge \; t_{\text{cur}} \leq t_{\text{exp}} \\ \wedge \; Y_j \equiv a^{\left(h^{x2^j} \bmod n\right)} b^\gamma \bmod N \\ \wedge \; x \in \pm\{0,1\}^{\ell_{\text{MAC}}} \\ \wedge \; t_{\text{exp}} \in \pm\{0,1\}^{\ell_t} \\ \wedge \; e - 2^{\ell_e - 1} \in \pm\{0,1\}^{\ell'_e + \ell_\emptyset + \ell_H + 2} \end{array} \right\}.$$

In the case of a distributed CM, this proof is repeated once for each CM node, except that the third statement is replaced by a single nest proof to the sum of the x values received from each CM. The first statement in this proof of knowledge convinces the NM that Alice does indeed possess a credential from the CM; the second statement asserts that this credential is not yet expired; the third statement (a nest proof) proves that Y_j does indeed encode the secret x from the credential and the first time period for which the credential should be valid; the remaining three statements are just length checks to show that the credential is validly formed. For full details on how this statistical zero-knowledge proof is performed we refer the reader to §4 and to [3].

If the proof succeeds, the NM is convinced that Y_j is a Pedersen commitment to $h_j = h^{x2^j} \bmod n$ and encodes the same secret x as Alice's credential; otherwise, the NM terminates. Note that the NM has learned no nontrivial information regarding the values of x and h_j.

5. Alice computes her sequence of nymbles using h_j as a seed value. This proceeds as follows:

   (a) Alice computes the sequence $(h_{j+i})_{i=1}^{k-1}$ where $h_{j+i} = \left(h_{j+(i-1)}\right)^2 \bmod n = h_j^{2^i} \bmod n$. Note that given any element of this sequence, it is easy to compute the next element, but being able to compute the previous element is equivalent to factoring n [22, Chap. 3]. She computes Pedersen commitments $Y_{j+i} = a^{h_{j+i}} b^{\gamma_{j+i}} \bmod N$ ($\gamma_{j+i} \in_R \mathbb{Z}_n$) to each h_{j+i} and transmits them, along with zero-knowledge proofs of multiplication to show that they were computed correctly, to the NM.

   (b) The NM verifies each of the proofs, and terminates if any proof fails.

6. Alice computes (but *does not send*) her nymbles $\nu_{j+i} = g^{h_{j+i}} \bmod \rho$, for $0 \le i < k$. (Here, the exponent is just taken as an integer in $[1, n)$.) She computes $(\alpha_{j+i}, S_{j+i}, \Pi_{j+i}) \leftarrow \mathsf{VERBS\text{-}Blind}(g, Y_{j+i}, \nu_{j+i}, \gamma_{j+i})$, and sends each blinded value S_{j+i} and proof Π_{j+i} to the NM.

7. For $0 \le i < k$, the NM computes (or looks up) its context element $\xi_{d,j+i}^{SP}$, and computes the blind signature $\sigma'_{j+i} = \mathsf{VERBS\text{-}Sign}(S_{j+i}, p, q, \xi_{d,j+i}^{SP}, \Pi_{j+i})$ (Recall that p, q is part of the NM's secret key, and $\rho = pq$.)

8. Alice unblinds the blind signatures σ'_{j+i} by computing
   $$\sigma_{j+i} = \mathsf{VERBS\text{-}Unblind}(\sigma'_{j+i}, \alpha_{j+i}) \text{ for } 0 \le i < k.$$

9. If all steps are completed successfully, the tuple $(\nu_{j+i}, \sigma_{j+i})$ is a valid nymble for time period $j+i$ for linkability window d and the given SP. Alice can verify the validity of the nymble by checking $\mathsf{VERBS\text{-}Verify}(\nu_{j+i}, \sigma_{j+i}, \xi_{d,j+i}^{SP})$.

10. If $j + k - 1 \ne \Gamma$ (i.e., $\tau_{d,j+k-1}$ is not the last time period in the current linkability window), then Alice also computes ν_Γ. This is the value that the NM will compute and place on the blacklist if Alice is, or becomes, banned from the SP. Note that the NM need not see or verify this value, nor provide a signature on it, since Alice will never be expected to present it to the SP.

5.4   Nymble Showing Protocol

The nymble showing protocol is extremely simple; Alice presents her nymble to the SP, the SP confirms that it is valid, that the associated context element $\xi_{d,i}^{SP}$ matches the current time period and linkability window, and that the nymble does not appear on the linking list. If each of these conditions is met, Alice is granted access.

1. Alice anonymously queries the NM for the current version number of the blacklist, and computes the current linkability window and time period $\tau_{d,i}$.
2. Alice then connects anonymously to the SP and requests a copy of the blacklist $\mathcal{B}$. She confirms its legitimacy and that it is up-to-date by verifying the version number and a signature from the NM encoded in the blacklist. Once convinced of the freshness of the blacklist, she verifies that she is not presently blacklisted. More specifically, she checks that $\nu_\Gamma \notin \mathcal{B}$. If she discovers that she *is* on the blacklist, she disconnects immediately. In this case, the SP learns only that "some blacklisted user" attempted to connect.
3. If she is not on the blacklist, Alice transmits the tuple (ν_i, σ_i) to the SP.
4. The SP consults the linking list $\mathcal{L}$ and confirms that Alice is not on the blacklist by checking that $\nu_i \notin \mathcal{L}$. If this check fails, the SP terminates and Alice is denied access.
5. The SP confirms that the given nymble is valid for the current time period i and linkability window d by confirming that $\mathsf{VERBS\text{-}Verify}(\nu_i, \sigma_i, \xi_{d,i}^{SP})$ is true. If so, Alice is granted access for the remainder of the time period; otherwise, Alice is denied access.
6. The SP adds the tuple (ν_i, σ_i, i) to a log file, so that if it determines at a later time (in the current linkability window) that Alice's behaviour in $\tau_{d,i}$ constitutes misbehaviour, it can present it to the NM to have Alice blacklisted.

5.5   Blacklisting Protocol

Suppose that Alice misbehaves in time period i^* and her misbehaviour is discovered in time period i' of the same linkability window. In this case, the SP initiates the following protocol with the NM to have Alice added to the blacklist.

1. The SP transmits the tuple $(SP, \nu_{i^*}, \sigma_{i^*}, i^*, h, \mathcal{B}, \mathcal{L})$ to the NM.
2. The NM verifies that h is valid for the SP and the current linkability window, that $\mathcal{B}$ and $\mathcal{L}$ are up-to-date, and that $\mathsf{VERBS\text{-}Verify}(\nu_{i^*}, \sigma_{i^*}, \xi_{d,i^*}^{SP})$ is true. If so, the NM uses its private knowledge (the factorization of $\rho = pq$ and the factorization of $\phi(\rho)$ into ℓ_B-bit primes) to solve the discrete logarithm of $\nu_{i^*} = g^{h_{i^*}} \bmod \rho$ with respect to g to recover the exponent h_{i^*}; otherwise, the NM terminates.
3. The NM then computes $h_{i^*+1}, \ldots, h_\Gamma$ using the recurrence equation $h_{i+1} = h_i^2 \bmod n$ and computes $\nu_{i'}, \ldots \nu_\Gamma$ as $\nu_i = g^{h_i} \bmod \rho$.
4. The NM computes the set $L = \{\nu_{i'}, \nu_{i'+1}, \ldots, \nu_\Gamma\}$ and then computes the new linking list $\mathcal{L}' = \mathcal{L} \cup L$ and the new blacklist $\mathcal{B}' = \mathcal{B} \cup \{\nu_\Gamma\}$.

5. The NM increments the version number and signs the new blacklist and then returns both the signed blacklist and the linking list to the SP.[6]

6   Implementation

We have implemented the key components of our system in order to measure its performance. In the next subsection we discuss reasonable choices for various system parameters, while in the following subsection we present performance benchmarks carried out using these values.

6.1   Parameter Choices

First let us examine the relevant computations in more detail. In order to place a user on the blacklist, the NM needs to compute a discrete log in a trapdoor group. We intentionally make this non-trivial in order to deter bulk deanonymization (in the sense that the users would become linkable, but not have their identities revealed); our target is about one minute of computation (wall-clock time) per discrete log computation. We also seek to ensure that, without the NM's private key, factoring and computing discrete logs mod ρ are infeasible; thus, we suggest setting $\ell_\rho = 1536$. The CM's public key n should be as large as possible, while ensuring that $n < \rho$, so we pick $\ell_n = 1534$.

The discrete log computation takes about $c \cdot \ell_\rho/\ell_B \cdot 2^{\ell_B/2}$ modular multiplications, which are almost completely parallelizable, for some constant of proportionality c. If the NM has a parallelism factor of P (i.e., P is the number of cores available to the NM), this will be about $\frac{\ell_\rho}{\ell_B} \cdot \frac{c \cdot 2^{\ell_B/2}}{P \cdot M}$ minutes to compute a discrete log, where M is the number of modular multiplications that can be computed by one core in one minute. So we want to choose ℓ_B such that

$$\frac{2^{\ell_B/2}}{\ell_B} \approx \frac{T \cdot M \cdot P}{\ell_\rho \cdot c}, \tag{1}$$

where T is the desired wall-clock time (in minutes) to solve a discrete log. (In §6.2, we measure $c \approx 0.57$ and M to be about 23.1 million for $\ell_\rho = 1536$.) Thus, for $T = 1$ and $P = 32$ we get $\ell_B \approx 50$; for $T = 1$ and $P = 64$ we get $\ell_B \approx 52$.

On the other hand, it takes at least about $\frac{3}{5} \cdot 2^{\ell_B}$ modular multiplications to factor ρ, taking advantage of its special form by using Pollard's $p - 1$ factoring algorithm [25]. However, this algorithm is inherently sequential [6]; only a small speedup can be obtained, even with a very large degree of parallelism.[7] This

---

[6] We adopt the same approach as the original Nymble system in order to ensure to the user that the blacklist they view is up-to-date, however, we omit many of the details here for brevity. In a later version of Nymble the authors propose the use of "daisies" to ensure blacklist freshness. This approach could easily be used in our scheme as well. The interested reader should consult [20,32] for these details.

[7] Of course, with *arbitrarily* large parallelism, other algorithms can factor ρ more quickly *without* taking advantage of the special form of ρ; massively parallel trial division is an extreme example.

means it will take about $\frac{3}{5} \cdot \frac{2^{\ell_B}}{M}$ minutes to factor ρ. Assuming $M = 23100000$, then $\ell_B = 50$ yields over 55 years to factor ρ, and $\ell_B = 52$ yields over 222 years to factor ρ. (Remember again that this is *wall-clock* time, not CPU time.) Note also that a different ρ can be used for each SP and for each linkability window, thus reducing the value of expending even that much effort.

The reason we seem to be making the unusual claim that 2^{50} security is sufficient is twofold: first, a minor point, these are counts of multiplications modulo an ℓ_ρ-bit modulus, each of which takes about $2^{12.8}$ cycles for our suggested $\ell_\rho = 1536$; thus, we are really proposing about 2^{62} security here. More importantly, these are counts of *sequential operations*. When one typically speaks of 2^{80} security (of a block cipher, for example), one assumes that the adversary can take advantage of large degrees of parallelism, which is not the case here.

Moreover, as noted in [21, §4], since the complexity of factoring increases with 2^{ℓ_B} while the complexity of computing discrete logs increases with $2^{\ell_B/2}$, as cores get faster (M increases) and more numerous (P increases), the time to factor ρ only goes *up* with respect to the time to compute discrete logs. In particular, if M can be increased by a factor of f, then this leads to a net security increase of a factor of f, whereas if P can be increased by a factor of g, this leads to a net security increase of a factor of g^2. These calculations suggest that the Nymbler construction will get *even more secure over time*.

Suggested values for parameters related to CL-credentials are taken directly from [3]. In particular, reasonable choices are $\ell_m = 2048$, $\ell_\emptyset = 80$, $\ell_e = 596$, $\ell'_e = 120$, and $\ell_H = 256$. We also suggest using $\ell_{\mathbf{MAC}} = 256$ and $\ell_t = 24$.

6.2 Performance Evaluation

In this subsection we present measurements obtained with our C++ implementation of the protocol. These include the average times taken to: 1) compute a nymble (and the associated proof of correct computation) at the client; 2) verify the client's proofs and issue a VERBS at the NM; 3) verify the signature on a nymble at the SP; and, 4) solve an instance of the discrete log problem at the NM. In order to compute M used in the previous subsection, and for comparison with other restricted blind signature schemes, we also show the time required to compute modular multiplications and exponentiations, respectively. Note that the bulk of the computation in our scheme is in the Nymble Acquisition Protocol — particularly in computing and verifying the zero-knowledge proofs.

We emphasize that our implementation is incomplete and unoptimized; it is used simply to demonstrate that both the time-sensitive and cost-intensive portions of our protocols can be carried out in an acceptable amount of time. In particular, there is still significant room for optimizations in our implementation of the VERBS-Blind algorithm and perhaps elsewhere in the protocols. For example, in order for the user to prove correct exponentiation of a committed value, our prototype implementation uses the naive "square-and-multiply" algorithm, but more efficient algorithms can be plugged in very simply. Moreover, all of our computations are single-threaded despite the highly parallelizable nature of the

Table 1. Timings for essential computations in Nymbler

Operation	Host	Mean Time	Trials	Reps/trial
Compute k nymbles	Client	360 ms + 397k ms ($R = .9974$)	10	1
Issue k blind signatures	NM	300 ms + 252k ms ($R = .9803$)	10	1
Verify signature	SP	11.2 μs $\pm$ 0.3 μs	10	100,000
Solve DL instance[a]	NM	25 m 38 s $\pm$ 2 m 16 s	10	1
Modular exponentiation[b]	—	403 μs $\pm$ 6 μs	10	100,000
Modular multiplication[c]	—	2.59 μs $\pm$ 0.02 μs	10	100,000

[a] This is the time to solve discrete logs with the parallel rho method on a single core and a 1536-bit 50-smooth modulus; using 32 cores should reduce this time to about 48 s $\pm$ 5 s. Solving for c in §6.1, Equation 1 with this value yields $c \approx 0.57$.

[b] Computed using a 1536-bit base, 160-bit exponent and 1536-bit modulus.

[c] Computed using random 1536-bit multiplicands and 1536-bit modulus; this yields $M \approx 23,100,000 \pm 100,000$ modular multiplications per minute.

protocols. Finally, we note that the as-of-yet unimplemented components of the system are not expected to significantly alter these measurements.

The performance benchmarks in Table 1 were obtained on a 2.83GHz Intel Core 2 Quad Q9550 running Ubuntu 9.10 64-bit.

These measurements compare favourably with BLAC and PEREA. In BLAC, the time required for a user to construct a proof that she is not banned, and for the SP to verify the proof, scales linearly with the size of the blacklist. In [30] the authors give measurements which indicate that the cost is about 1.8 ms and 1.6 ms *per entry on the blacklist*, at the user and SP, respectively. Thus, when the blacklist reaches a size of 385 entries[8], the cost per authentication in BLAC is roughly equal to the cost of obtaining a nymble in our scheme. (Half of the cost in our scheme is constant overhead which can be amortized over the cost of acquiring several nymbles.) We also note that, in this case, the cost at the SP is about 142 times higher in BLAC. In PEREA (with an authentication window of 30), [31] reports that an authentication takes about 160 ms at the SP (regardless of blacklist size) and up to 7 ms per entry on the blacklist for the user.

7 Conclusion and Future Work

We have presented a new system, inspired by Nymble, for providing an anonymous implementation of IP blocking over an anonymity network. Our approach is based on anonymous credentials, verifier-efficient restricted blind signatures, and a trapdoor discrete logarithm group. Compared to the original Nymble, our scheme severely limits the ability of malicious third parties to collude in order to break a user's anonymity. Although our system is not as efficient as the original

[8] An appendix in the extended version of this paper [18] gives recent usage and banning statistics from Wikipedia, which indicate that the average size of the blacklist is currently around 1200 entries — more than a factor of four larger than this figure.

Nymble, most of the added cost has been introduced in the Nymble Acquisition Protocol; verifying a nymble's authenticity at the SP is still very inexpensive.

One may pursue several directions to further improve our system.[9] For example, if the NM detects that a user has attempted to cheat in the Nymble Acquisition Protocol, we would like to be able to temporarily ban this user from any further use of Nymbler. One way that this could potentially be accomplished would be to use another Nymbler-like system (i.e., a *meta-Nymbler*) to allow blacklisting of Nymbler users from the system; however, this approach is actually overkill. Since this type of misbehaviour can always be detected *during* a session, a simpler technique, such as Unlinkable Serial Transactions [28], would be sufficient. We leave further investigation of this idea to future work.

Eventually, we envision that the CM services may be offered by the Tor directory servers, or the Tor entry nodes themselves, as they are already trusted with users' IP addresses. If we use P-signatures [2] instead of CL-signatures in the credentials obtained from the CM, each entry node can have its own public key, certified by the directory server, and the NM will not be able to tell which entry node certified the user's IP address. There are nontrivial issues with this simple proposal, however, and we leave addressing them to future work as well.

Acknowledgments. We would like to extend our thanks to Aniket P. Kate, Greg Zaverucha, Jalaj Upadhyay, Mark Giesbrecht, Femi Olumofin, Urs Hengartner, Greta Coger, and the PETS 2010 anonymous reviewers for their helpful suggestions which greatly improved this paper. This work is supported by NSERC, MITACS, and a David R. Cheriton Graduate Scholarship.

References

1. Algesheimer, J., Camenisch, J., Shoup, V.: Efficient computation modulo a shared secret with application to the generation of shared safe-prime products. In: Yung, M. (ed.) CRYPTO 2002. LNCS, vol. 2442, pp. 417–432. Springer, Heidelberg (2002)
2. Belenkiy, M., Chase, M., Kohlweiss, M., Lysyanskaya, A.: P-signatures and noninteractive anonymous credentials. In: Canetti, R. (ed.) TCC 2008. LNCS, vol. 4948, pp. 356–374. Springer, Heidelberg (2008)
3. Bichsel, P., Binding, C., Camenisch, J., Groß, T., Heydt-Benjamin, T., Sommer, D., Zaverucha, G.: Cryptographic protocols of the Identity Mixer Library, v. 1.0. Computer Science Research Report RZ3730, IBM Research GmbH, Zurich (2009)
4. Boudot, F.: Efficient proofs that a committed number lies in an interval. In: Preneel, B. (ed.) EUROCRYPT 2000. LNCS, vol. 1807, pp. 431–444. Springer, Heidelberg (2000)
5. Brands, S.A.: Untraceable off-line cash in wallets with observers. In: Stinson, D.R. (ed.) CRYPTO 1993. LNCS, vol. 773, pp. 302–318. Springer, Heidelberg (1994)
6. Brent, R.P.: Parallel Algorithms for Integer Factorisation. Number Theory and Cryptography, 26–37 (1990)

---

[9] The interested reader should consult the extended version of this paper [18] for a more comprehensive list of future research directions.

7. Camenisch, J., Lysyanskaya, A.: An efficient system for non-transferable anonymous credentials with optional anonymity revocation. In: Pfitzmann, B. (ed.) EUROCRYPT 2001. LNCS, vol. 2045, pp. 93–118. Springer, Heidelberg (2001)

8. Camenisch, J., Michels, M.: Proving in zero-knowledge that a number is the product of two safe primes (1998)

9. Chaum, D.: Blind signatures for untraceable payments. In: CRYPTO 1982, pp. 199–203 (1982)

10. Chaum, D.: Blind signature system. In: CRYPTO 1983, p. 153 (1983)

11. Dingledine, R.: Tor development roadmap, 2008–2011. Roadmap, The Tor Project (2008)

12. Dingledine, R., Mathewson, N., Syverson, P.: Deploying low-latency anonymity: Design challenges and social factors. IEEE Security and Privacy 5(5), 83–87 (2007)

13. Dingledine, R., Mathewson, N., Syverson, P.F.: Tor: The second-generation onion router. In: USENIX Security Symposium, pp. 303–320. USENIX (2004)

14. Dingledine, R.: Re: Banned from Slashdot, arma@freehaven.net, http://archives.seul.org/or/talk/Jun-2005/msg00002.html (Private e-mail message to Jamie McCarthy;June 1, 2005)

15. Feldman, P.: A practical scheme for non-interactive verifiable secret sharing. In: FOCS, pp. 427–437. IEEE, Los Alamitos (1987)

16. Fiat, A., Shamir, A.: How to prove yourself: Practical solutions to identification and signature problems. In: Odlyzko, A.M. (ed.) CRYPTO 1986. LNCS, vol. 263, pp. 186–194. Springer, Heidelberg (1987)

17. Groth, J., Sahai, A.: Efficient non-interactive proof systems for bilinear groups. In: Smart, N.P. (ed.) EUROCRYPT 2008. LNCS, vol. 4965, pp. 415–432. Springer, Heidelberg (2008)

18. Henry, R., Henry, K., Goldberg, I.: Making a Nymbler Nymble using VERBS. Tech. Rep. CACR 2010-05, Centre for Applied Cryptographic Research, Waterloo (2010), http://www.cacr.math.uwaterloo.ca/techreports/2010/cacr2010-05.pdf

19. Holt, J.E., Seamons, K.E.: Nym: Practical pseudonymity for anonymous networks. Internet Security Research Lab., Technical Report 2006-4, Brigham Young University, Provo, UT (2006)

20. Johnson, P.C., Kapadia, A., Tsang, P.P., Smith, S.W.: Nymble: Anonymous IP-address blocking. In: Borisov, N., Golle, P. (eds.) PET 2007. LNCS, vol. 4776, pp. 113–133. Springer, Heidelberg (2007)

21. Maurer, U.M., Yacobi, Y.: A non-interactive public-key distribution system. Designs, Codes and Cryptography 9(3), 305–316 (1996)

22. Menezes, A., van Oorschot, P.C., Vanstone, S.A.: Handbook of Applied Cryptography. CRC Press, Boca Raton (1996)

23. van Oorschot, P.C., Wiener, M.J.: Parallel collision search with application to hash functions and discrete logarithms. In: ACM CCS, pp. 210–218 (1994)

24. Pedersen, T.P.: Non-interactive and information-theoretic secure verifiable secret sharing. In: Feigenbaum, J. (ed.) CRYPTO 1991. LNCS, vol. 576, pp. 129–140. Springer, Heidelberg (1992)

25. Pollard, J.M.: Theorems on factorization and primality testing. Proceedings of the Cambridge Philosophical Society 76(03), 521 (1974)

26. RSA Laboratories: RSA Laboratories - the RSA factoring challenge FAQ, http://www.rsa.com/rsalabs/node.asp?id=2094(accessed 11-January-2010)

27. Schnorr, C.P.: Efficient identification and signatures for smart cards. In: Brassard, G. (ed.) CRYPTO 1989. LNCS, vol. 435, pp. 239–252. Springer, Heidelberg (1990)

28. Syverson, P.F., Stubblebine, S.G., Goldschlag, D.M.: Unlinkable serial transactions. In: Hirschfeld, R. (ed.) FC 1997. LNCS, vol. 1318, pp. 39–56. Springer, Heidelberg (1997)
29. The Tor Project, Inc.: Tor: Overview (accessed October 21, 2009), https://www.torproject.org/overview.html.en
30. Tsang, P.P., Au, M.H., Kapadia, A., Smith, S.W.: Blacklistable Anonymous Credentials: Blocking misbehaving users without TTPs. In: Ning, P., di Vimercati, S.D.C., Syverson, P.F. (eds.) ACM CCS, pp. 72–81. ACM, New York (2007)
31. Tsang, P.P., Au, M.H., Kapadia, A., Smith, S.W.: PEREA: Towards practical TTP-free revocation in anonymous authentication. In: Ning, P., Syverson, P.F., Jha, S. (eds.) ACM CCS, pp. 333–344. ACM, New York (2008)
32. Tsang, P.P., Kapadia, A., Cornelius, C., Smith, S.W.: Nymble: Blocking misbehaving users in anonymizing networks. In: IEEE TDSC (2009) (to appear)
33. Wikipedia: Wikipedia talk:blocking policy/tor nodes — Wikipedia, the free encyclopedia, http://en.wikipedia.org/wiki/Wikipedia_talk:Blocking_policy/Tor_nodes (accessed October 18, 2009)

Anonymous Webs of Trust

Michael Backes[1,2], Stefan Lorenz[1], Matteo Maffei[1], and Kim Pecina[1]

[1] Saarland University, Saarbrücken, Germany
[2] Max Planck Institute for Software Systems (MPI-SWS)

Abstract. Webs of trust constitute a decentralized infrastructure for establishing the authenticity of the binding between public keys and users and, more generally, trust relationships among users. This paper introduces the concept of anonymous webs of trust – an extension of webs of trust where users can authenticate messages and determine each other's trust level without compromising their anonymity. Our framework comprises a novel cryptographic protocol based on zero-knowledge proofs, a symbolic abstraction and formal verification of our protocol, and a prototypical implementation based on the OpenPGP standard. The framework is capable of dealing with various core and optional features of common webs of trust, such as key attributes, key expiration dates, existence of multiple certificate chains, and trust measures between different users.

1 Introduction

Over the last years, the Web has evolved into the premium forum for freely disseminating and collecting data, information, and opinions. Not all information providers, however, are willing to reveal their true identity: For instance, some may want to present their opinions anonymously to avoid associations with their race, ethnic background, or other sensitive characteristics. Furthermore, people seeking sensitive information may want to remain anonymous to avoid being stigmatized or other negative repercussions. The ability to anonymously exchange information, and hence the inability of users to identify the information providers and to determine their credibility, raises serious concerns about the reliability of exchanged information. Ideally, one would like to have a mechanism for assigning trust levels to users, allowing them to anonymously exchange data and, at the same time, certifying the trust level of the information provider.

Webs of trust. Webs of trust (WOT) constitute a well-established approach to bind public keys to their owners and, more generally, to establish trust relationships among users in a decentralized manner: Each participant decides which public keys are considered trustworthy. This trust is expressed by signing the trustworthy public keys along with a set of user and key attributes (e.g., user

M.J. Atallah and N. Hopper (Eds.): PETS 2010, LNCS 6205, pp. 130–148, 2010.

name and key expiration date). These certificates can be chained in order to express longer trust relationships:[1] For instance, the certificate chain

$$\mathsf{sig}((\mathsf{pk}_1, \mathcal{A}_1), \mathsf{sk}_2), \mathsf{sig}((\mathsf{pk}_2, \mathcal{A}_2), \mathsf{sk}_3)$$

says that the owner of pk_3 has certified the binding between the public key pk_2 and the set $\mathcal{A}_2$ of attributes, and the owner of pk_2 has certified the binding between pk_1 and $\mathcal{A}_1$. Such certificate chains are a salient technique for expressing transitive trust relationships, e.g., to use webs of trust to implement friendship relations in social networks such as Facebook, where transitive friendship relations are common; in this example, the owner of pk_1 would be a friend of a friend of the owner of pk_3.

After receiving a signature on message m that can be verified using pk_1, the owner of pk_3 knows that m comes from a user of trust level 2 bound to the attributes $\mathcal{A}_1$.[2] Hence for authenticating a message in the context of a WOT, the sender has to find a chain of certificates starting with a certificate released by the intended recipient and ending with a certificate for the sender's key.

Our contributions. In this work we introduce the concept of *anonymous webs of trust* – an extension of webs of trust that allows users to authenticate messages and determine each other's trust level without compromising their anonymity. Our framework comprises:

- a *cryptographic protocol* based on the Camenisch-Lysyanskaya signature scheme [14] and a novel zero-knowledge proof[3] that allows users to efficiently prove the existence of certificate chains without compromising user anonymity. For instance, given the certificate chain $\mathsf{sig}((\mathsf{pk}_1, \mathcal{A}_1), \mathsf{sk}_2), \mathsf{sig}((\mathsf{pk}_2, \mathcal{A}_2), \mathsf{sk}_3)$ and a message m that the owner of pk_1 wants to authenticate with the owner of pk_3, our protocol allows the owner of pk_1 to prove a statement of the form "there exist certificates C_1, C_2, a signature S, keys K_1, K_2, and attributes A_1, A_2 such that (*i*) C_1 is a certificate for (K_1, A_1) that can be verified with key K_2, (*ii*) C_2 is a certificate for (K_2, A_2) that can be verified with key pk_3, and (*iii*) S is a signature on m that can be verified with K_1". This statement reveals only the length of

---

[1] In the OpenPGP standard [13], trust relationships may be transitive and their validity is ruled by *trust signatures*, which we describe in Appendix A. In our setting, the trust relationship is more sophisticated and, in fact, it is parametrized by a number of factors including the length of the chain (i.e., the longer the chain, the smaller the conveyed trust). This allows us to accommodate fine-grained trust models, as discussed in Section 4.

[2] For the sake of simplicity, we identify the trust level of a certificate chain with its length here. In Section 4, we will consider the more sophisticated trust measure proposed in [18].

[3] A zero-knowledge proof combines two seemingly contradictory properties. First, it is a proof of a statement that cannot be forged, i.e., it is impossible, or at least computationally infeasible, to produce a zero-knowledge proof of a wrong statement. Second, a zero-knowledge proof does not reveal any information besides the bare fact that the statement is valid [29]. A non-interactive zero-knowledge proof is a zero-knowledge protocol consisting of one message sent by the prover to the verifier.

the chain, i.e., the trust level of the sender, the authenticated message m, and the public key pk_3 of the intended recipient. We provide a prototypical implementation of our protocol as an extension of the OpenPGP standard. The tool is freely available at [6].

- a number of *extensions* of our protocol to achieve fine-grained anonymity and trust properties. In some situations, a controlled release of additional information is desired or even required, e.g., proving that the keys involved in a chain have not expired. We propose variants of our zero-knowledge proof that allow for selectively revealing additional properties of the certificate chains, such as the validity of the keys with respect to their expiration date, the existence of multiple certificate chains, and the trust level that the certificate chains are assigned according to a realistic trust model. These extensions demonstrate the expressiveness and generality of our approach.

  The potential application scenarios of our protocol include distributed social networks, where people may want to share opinions or information in an anonymous fashion while being able to prove their trust relationships, applications for anonymous message exchange, and services for anonymous yet trustworthy reports or reviews.

- a *symbolic abstraction* and a *formal verification* of our protocol. We specify our protocol in the applied pi-calculus [3], and we formalize the trust property as an authorization policy and the anonymity property as an observational equivalence relation. We consider a strong adversarial setting where the attacker has the control over the topology of the web of trust, some of the protocol parties, and the certificate chains proven in zero-knowledge by honest parties. Security properties are verified using ProVerif [11], an automated theorem prover based on Horn clause resolution that provides security proofs for an unbounded number of protocol sessions and protocol parties.

Related work. Although the setting is different, our approach may at a first glance resemble the delegatable anonymous credential scheme [9]. This protocol relies on an *interactive* protocol between *each* pair of users along the certificate chain. In contrast, our protocol is fully non-interactive, and provers do not need any interactions with other principals except for the intended recipient. In addition, our approach allows the prover to selectively reveal partial information on attributes in the certificate chain, which is crucial to achieve anonymity in realistic trust models without compromising their expressiveness.

Group signature schemes [19,37,5,10] provide a method for allowing a member of a group to anonymously sign a message on behalf of the group. In contrast to our approach, these schemes require the presence of a group manager; moreover, two users in the same group are completely interchangeable. A similar argument holds for HIBE/HIBS schemes [27,12], where anonymity could be obtained by replacing user identifiers with generic anonymous attributes.

Ring signature schemes [34,31,32] are similar to group signatures but do not require a group manager. As for group signatures, two users in the same group are completely interchangeable. It would be interesting, nevertheless, to explore the usage of ring signature schemes to achieve k-anonymity in webs of trust.

Social networks constitute a particularly promising application scenario for our protocol; we thus briefly relate our approach to recent works on privacy and anonymity in social networks. The (somewhat) orthogonal problem of creating encrypted data that can be read by people who are n degrees away in a social network has been recently addressed [25]. Several techniques have been proposed to keep the social network graph private while enforcing access control policies based on trust degrees [22,21,41]. In contrast to our approach, the proposed protocols are interactive, similar to the delegatable anonymous credential scheme [9]. In other works, trust relationships are instead assumed to be public, e.g., [35,4,17]. Our approach does not put any constraints on the way certificates are distributed (for instance, they could be exchanged by private communication). We just assume that the prover can retrieve the certificates composing the chain proven in zero-knowledge. In the specific context of webs of trust such as GnuPG [38], public keys and attached certificates are uploaded on key servers and are thus publicly available. Finally, the recently proposed Lockr protocol [40] achieves access control and anonymity in social networks and file-sharing applications, such as Flickr and BitTorrent. Lockr provides weaker anonymity guarantees compared to our framework, since the prover has to reveal her identity to the verifier; moreover, Lockr does not support certificate chains but only direct trust relationships.

Outline of the paper. Section 2 introduces the notion of anonymous webs of trust and provides a high-level overview of our protocol. Section 3 describes the cryptographic setup and describes the implementation. Section 4 presents extensions of our protocol that accommodate some advanced properties of webs of trust. Section 5 proposes a symbolic abstraction of our protocol and conducts a formal security analysis. Section 6 concludes and gives directions of future research. The full-version of this paper is available at [6].

2   Anonymous Webs of Trust

In this section, we introduce the notion of anonymous webs of trust and we give an overview of our protocol.

A web of trust is a decentralized public-key infrastructure. Each user u holds a public key pk_u and a secret key sk_u. Trust is distributed via certificates. User u expresses her belief that a given public key pk_v actually belongs to user v by signing pk_v along with a set $\mathcal{A}_v$ of user and key attributes. Hence, certificates establish the relation between public keys and users and, depending on the applications, they can also be used to witness specific trust relationships between users. These certificates are attached to the signed public key and uploaded all together onto key servers. Every user having access to such a server can participate in the web of trust.

Trust into public keys not directly signed by a user is established using *certificate chains*. A certificate chain from A to B consists of all the certificates that link $(pk_A, \mathcal{A}_A)$ to $(pk_B, \mathcal{A}_B)$, thus establishing a trust relation between those keys.

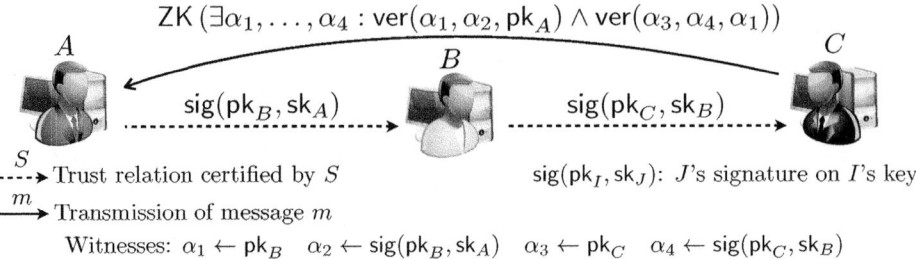

$$\mathsf{ZK}\left(\exists \alpha_1, \ldots, \alpha_4 : \mathsf{ver}(\alpha_1, \alpha_2, \mathsf{pk}_A) \wedge \mathsf{ver}(\alpha_3, \alpha_4, \alpha_1)\right)$$

S
$\cdots\!\!\rightarrow$ Trust relation certified by S $\mathsf{sig}(\mathsf{pk}_I, \mathsf{sk}_J)$: J's signature on I's key

m
$\longrightarrow$ Transmission of message m

Witnesses: $\alpha_1 \leftarrow \mathsf{pk}_B$ $\alpha_2 \leftarrow \mathsf{sig}(\mathsf{pk}_B, \mathsf{sk}_A)$ $\alpha_3 \leftarrow \mathsf{pk}_C$ $\alpha_4 \leftarrow \mathsf{sig}(\mathsf{pk}_C, \mathsf{sk}_B)$

Fig. 1. Protocol for anonymous proof of a certificate chain of length 2

Definition 1 (Certificate Chain). *A certificate chain or simply chain from* $(\mathsf{pk}_1, \mathcal{A}_1)$ *to* $(\mathsf{pk}_\ell, \mathcal{A}_\ell)$ *is a sequence of certificates* $\mathcal{C} = (C_1, ..., C_{\ell-1})$ *of length* $\ell - 1$, *where* $C_i = sig((\mathsf{pk}_{i+1}, \mathcal{A}_{i+1}), \mathsf{sk}_i)$ *and* $\ell \geq 2$. *We say that* $(\mathsf{pk}_\ell, \mathcal{A}_\ell)$ *has trust level* $\ell - 1$. *We assume to know the binding between* sk_1 *and* $(\mathsf{pk}_1, \mathcal{A}_1)$, *which can be captured by an additional self-generated certificate* $sig((\mathcal{A}_1, \mathsf{pk}_1), \mathsf{sk}_1)$.

The fundamental idea of our approach is to provide anonymity in webs of trust by deploying zero-knowledge proofs to demonstrate the existence of valid certificate chains without revealing any information that might compromise the anonymity of users. We consider a setting where users want to anonymously exchange messages, yet guaranteeing the receiver the trust level of the sender.

For the sake of simplicity, we initially focus on certificates on public keys without attributes. In Section 4, we will extend our zero-knowledge proof scheme to certificates binding a key to a set of attributes, and subsequently show how to selectively hide some of them while revealing the others.

In order to authenticate a message m with the owner of pk_1, the owner of pk_ℓ has to retrieve a certificate chain from pk_1 to pk_ℓ and to prove in zero-knowledge the existence of this chain as well as the knowledge of a signature on message m done with the signing key corresponding to pk_ℓ. Notice that the signature cannot be sent in plain, since this would compromise the anonymity of the sender. If we denote by $\mathsf{ver}(\mathsf{m}, C, \mathsf{pk})$ the successful verification of certificate C on message m with public key pk, the statement that the owner of pk_ℓ has to prove can be formalized by the following logical formula:

$$\mathsf{ver}(\mathsf{pk}_2, C_1, \mathsf{pk}_1) \wedge \left[\bigwedge_{i=2}^{\ell-1} \mathsf{ver}(\mathsf{pk}_{i+1}, C_i, \mathsf{pk}_i)\right] \wedge \mathsf{ver}(\mathsf{hash}(\mathsf{m}), \mathsf{sig}(\mathsf{hash}(\mathsf{m}), \mathsf{sk}_\ell), \mathsf{pk}_\ell) \quad (1)$$

which can be read as "the verification of signature C_1 on message pk_2 with verification key pk_1 succeeds and for all i from 2 to $\ell - 1$, the verifications of C_i on pk_{i+1} with pk_i succeed and the verification of the signature on the hash of m with pk_ℓ succeeds." For efficiency reasons, the sender signs the hash of the message she is willing to authenticate. Since the proof should not reveal the user identities, we weaken this statement by existentially quantifying over all secret witnesses:[4]

---

[4] Here and throughout the paper, we use the convention introduced in [16] that Greek letters denote those values that are kept secret by the proof.

$$\exists \; \alpha_1, ..., \alpha_{2\ell-1} :$$
$$\mathsf{ver}(\alpha_1, \alpha_2, \mathsf{pk}_1) \wedge \left[\bigwedge_{i=2}^{\ell-1} \mathsf{ver}(\alpha_{2i-1}, \alpha_{2i}, \alpha_{2i-3}) \right] \wedge \mathsf{ver}(\mathsf{hash}(\mathsf{m}), \alpha_{2\ell-1}, \alpha_{2\ell-3}) \qquad (2)$$

This statement only reveals the public key pk_1 of the intended recipient, the hash of the authenticated message m, and the length of the chain (i.e., the trust level of the sender). The zero-knowledge proof of this statement is sent to the verifier, who, after successful verification, will authenticate message m as coming from a principal of level $\ell - 1$. Figure 1 schematically shows our protocol for a certificate chain of length 2. To execute this algorithm, we solely assume that the prover can efficiently retrieve the certificates composing the chain. In an established web of trust, public keys and attached certificates are usually uploaded on key servers and are thus publicly available. Our approach, however, is general and does not put any constraints on the way certificates are distributed (for instance, they could be exchanged by private communication). We just require that the prover has access to the certificate chain linking her key to the verifier's one.

3   Cryptographic Protocol

For implementing the ideas described in the previous sections, we need (i) a digital signature scheme that allows for efficient zero-knowledge proofs and (ii) an expressive set of zero-knowledge proofs that can be combined together in conjunctive and disjunctive forms. For signing messages, we rely on the Camenisch-Lysyanskaya signature scheme [14] while, for proving statements about certificate chains, we propose a novel non-interactive zero-knowledge proof of knowledge based on Σ-protocols [30]. We first review the basic building blocks and subsequently describe the construction of our zero-knowledge proof scheme.

3.1   Camenisch-Lysyanskaya Signature

This signature scheme was introduced in [14] together with some zero-knowledge proofs. None of them, however, deals with situations in which every value involved in the verification (and, in particular, the verification key) must be kept secret, as required by the statements considered in this paper. This circumstance required us to develop a novel zero-knowledge proof.

We will now give a short overview of this signature scheme. A public key is a tuple $\mathsf{pk} = (a, b, c, n)$ where $n = p \cdot q$ is a special RSA modulus and a, b, c are random elements from a large subgroup of $\mathbb{Z}_n^*$. The corresponding secret key is $\mathsf{sk} = p$. Since factorizing n is assumed to be hard, the attacker cannot efficiently compute sk. To sign a given message $m \in [0, ..., 2^{\ell_m})$, one chooses a random prime e of length $\ell_e \geq \ell_m + 2$ and a random number $s \in [0, ..., 2^{\ell_m + \ell_n + \ell})$ where ℓ_n is the bit-length of n and ℓ is a security parameter. In practice, $\ell = 160$ is considered secure. Finally, one computes v such that:

$$v \equiv_n (a^m \cdot b^s \cdot c)^{1/e} \qquad (3)$$

Here and throughout this paper, we write $v \equiv_n u$ to say that u is equivalent to v modulo n. Notice that the factorization of n is used to efficiently compute $1/e$. The signature on message m is the tuple $\mathsf{sig}_m = (e, s, v)$. Given $\mathsf{pk} = (a, b, c, n)$, m, and $\mathsf{sig}_m = (e, s, v)$, the verification of the signature sig_m is performed by checking that $2^{\ell_e - 1} < e < 2^{\ell_e}$ along with the following equivalence:

$$v^e \equiv_n (a^m \cdot b^s \cdot c) \tag{4}$$

This equation constitutes the cryptographic instantiation of the symbolic predicate $\mathsf{ver}(m, \mathsf{sig}_m, \mathsf{pk})$ discussed in Section 2. Under the strong RSA assumption, the Camenisch-Lysyanskaya signature scheme is secure against existential forgery attacks. Security against existential forgery is the standard notion of security when dealing with signature schemes.

3.2   Zero-Knowledge Proofs and Σ-Protocols

Zero-knowledge proofs were first introduced in [30] and have since then become a key element of many cryptographic protocols. A zero-knowledge proof is an interactive proof system (P, V) between two parties: The prover P and the verifier V. Both parties obtain the statement to be proven as input, the prover additionally receives a witness to the given statement. Besides the usual completeness and soundness properties, the zero-knowledge property ensures that even a malicious verifier cannot learn any information on the prover's witness.[5] Our zero-knowledge scheme builds on a class of zero-knowledge protocols, called Σ-protocols [28,20], which allow one to prove certain properties of committed values without opening the commitments. We briefly review below the basic building blocks of our scheme.

Σ-protocols and their properties. The proofs outlined below belong to the class of Σ-protocols, i.e., protocols composed of three message exchanges: *commitment*, *challenge*, and *response*, sent by the prover, the verifier, and the prover respectively. These protocols enjoy the *special soundness* and the *special honest verifier statistical zero-knowledge (SHVSZK)* properties [28,20].

Special soundness is a strong form of *proof of knowledge* and guarantees that a prover is in possession of a witness. Honest verifier zero-knowledge is a variant of the zero-knowledge property where the verifier chooses the challenge uniformly at random from the according challenge space and, in particular, independently of the commitment sent by the prover.[6] We write $\{\mathsf{PK}(\widetilde{\alpha}) : S\}$ to denote a proof of knowledge of witnesses $\widetilde{\alpha}$ for statement S.

---

[5] The zero-knowledge property is formalized using a simulator that, without having access to the witness to a given statement, creates simulated proof transcripts that are indistinguishable from actual protocol transcripts. Intuitively, this guarantees that the proof cannot be used to gain any information on the witness.

[6] In general, zero-knowledge implies honest-verifier zero-knowledge but the converse does not necessarily hold. In our setting, however, focusing on honest verifiers does not restrict the power of the attacker since the proof will be eventually made non-interactive using the Fiat-Shamir heuristic [24], which lets the prover herself choose the challenge by using the random oracle, without interacting with the verifier.

As shown in [20], Σ-protocols can be combined together to prove logical conjunctions and disjunctions of their respective statements.

Lemma 1 (Logical Combination of Σ-protocols [20]). *Assume that (P_1, V_1) and (P_2, V_2) are SHVSZK and have special soundness and overwhelming completeness for relations R_1 and R_2 respectively. Assume that $M_1 \supseteq L_{R_1}$ and $M_2 \supseteq L_{R_2}$ where $L_R := \{(x, y) \mid xRy\}$. Assume that for both schemes, the verifier accepts the output of the simulator with overwhelming probability.*

Then there exist SHVSZK proof schemes for the relations $R_\wedge := R_1 \wedge_{M_1, M_2} R_2$ and $R_\vee := R_1 \vee_{M_1, M_2} R_2$.

Intuitively, the M_i represent well-formed inputs and are needed for completeness reasons.

Commitments. A commitment scheme consists of the commit phase and the open phase. Intuitively, it is not possible to look inside a commitment until it is opened (hiding property) and the committing principal cannot change the content while opening (binding property). We use the integer commitment scheme described in [33]. In the following, we let $[\![c]\!]$ denote the value committed to in c.

Range proofs. We use the range proofs proposed in [26]. A range proof guarantees that a certain committed value lies in the interval (A, B), where A and B are integers. This proof will be denoted by $\{\mathsf{PK}(\alpha) : [\![c]\!] = \alpha \wedge A < \alpha < B\}$ Notice that this proof does not reveal α, just the commitment c and the bounds A and B of the interval.

Proofs of arithmetic operations. Our protocol also uses some of the protocols presented in [15] for proving sums, multiplications, and exponentiations of committed values in zero-knowledge (i.e., without opening the commitments and revealing the witnesses). These proofs will be denoted by

$$\{\mathsf{PK}(\alpha, \beta, \delta, \nu) : [\![c_a]\!] = \alpha \wedge [\![c_b]\!] = \beta \wedge [\![c_d]\!] = \delta \wedge [\![c_n]\!] = \nu \wedge \alpha + \beta \equiv_\nu \delta\}$$
$$\{\mathsf{PK}(\alpha, \beta, \delta, \nu) : [\![c_a]\!] = \alpha \wedge [\![c_b]\!] = \beta \wedge [\![c_d]\!] = \delta \wedge [\![c_n]\!] = \nu \wedge \alpha \cdot \beta \equiv_\nu \delta\}$$
$$\{\mathsf{PK}(\alpha, \beta, \delta, \nu) : [\![c_a]\!] = \alpha \wedge [\![c_b]\!] = \beta \wedge [\![c_d]\!] = \delta \wedge [\![c_n]\!] = \nu \wedge \alpha^\beta \equiv_\nu \delta\}$$

3.3 Our Protocol

Our goal is to compute the verification equation (4) in zero-knowledge. This is achieved by the zero-knowledge protocol (5). We first recompute the exponentiations in the signature verification equation, i.e., $\tau_1 \triangleq a^m$, $\tau_2 \triangleq b^s$, $\tau_4 \triangleq a^m b^s$, and $\tau_3 \triangleq v^e$, and check if $v^e \equiv_n a^m b^s c$ (cf. line (a)). We then test whether the signed message and the verification prime number are in the appropriate ranges (cf. line (b)). This protocol constitutes the cryptographic instantiation of the symbolic proof for the statement $\exists\, \alpha_m, \alpha_{\mathsf{sig}}, \alpha_{\mathsf{pk}} : \mathsf{ver}(\alpha_m, \alpha_{\mathsf{sig}}, \alpha_{\mathsf{pk}})$ discussed in Section 2 with $\alpha_m = \mu$, $\alpha_{\mathsf{sig}} = (\nu, \sigma, \epsilon)$, and $\alpha_{\mathsf{pk}} = (\alpha, \beta, \gamma, \eta)$.

$$\left\{\begin{array}{l}
\mathsf{PK}(\alpha, \beta, \gamma, \epsilon, \eta, \mu, \nu, \sigma, \tau_1, \tau_2, \tau_3, \tau_4) : [\![c_a]\!] = \alpha \wedge [\![c_b]\!] = \beta \wedge \\
[\![c_c]\!] = \gamma \wedge [\![c_n]\!] = \eta \wedge [\![c_m]\!] = \mu \wedge [\![c_v]\!] = \nu \wedge [\![c_s]\!] = \sigma \wedge [\![c_e]\!] = \epsilon \\
\wedge [\![c_{(a^m)}]\!] = \tau_1 \wedge [\![c_{(b^s)}]\!] = \tau_2 \wedge [\![c_{(v^e)}]\!] = \tau_3 \wedge [\![c_{(a^m b^s)}]\!] = \tau_4 \\
\tau_1 \equiv_\eta \alpha^\mu \wedge \tau_2 \equiv_\eta \beta^\sigma \wedge \tau_3 \equiv_\eta \nu^\epsilon \wedge \tau_4 \equiv_\eta \tau_1 \cdot \tau_2 \wedge \tau_3 \equiv_\eta \tau_4 \cdot \gamma \qquad (a) \\
\wedge\ 0 \le \mu < 2^{\ell_m} \ \wedge\ 2^{\ell_m+1} < \epsilon < 2^{\ell_m+2} \qquad\qquad\qquad\qquad\quad (b)
\end{array}\right\} \quad (5)$$

Zero-knowledge proofs for single chain elements are combined together in conjunctive form to prove the existence of a valid certificate chain, as formalized in equation (2). In particular, every occurrence of value u is instantiated with the same commitment c_u. This ensures the equality of the values appearing in different chain element proofs. We reveal the public key of the verifier and the hash of the signed message by opening the corresponding commitments.

Theorem 1. *Let c_a, c_b, c_c, c_m, c_s, c_v, c_e, and c_n be integer commitments and let $c_{(a^m)}$, $c_{(b^s)}$, $c_{(v^e)}$, and $c_{(a^m b^s)}$ be auxiliary commitments. Then, the protocol from equation (5) is a special honest verifier statistical zero-knowledge proof with special soundness that the values committed to in c_a, c_b, c_c, c_m, c_s, c_v, c_e, and c_n fulfill the Camenisch-Lysyanskaya signature scheme verification equation.*

Proof. The completeness follows from inspection of the protocol and the verification equation of the signature scheme. Special soundness and SHVSZK follow from the special soundness and the SHVSZK property of the individual proofs by applying Lemma 1.

Finally, we apply the Fiat-Shamir heuristic [24] to make our protocol non-interactive.

3.4   Implementation

We implemented our protocol as an extension of the OpenPGP standard. Our system relies on key servers that provide standard OpenPGP functionality and additionally maintain the certificates from the anonymous web of trust. The authenticity of anonymous web of trust keys is established by OpenPGP certificates. Arithmetic operations are performed by using MIRACL [36]. The implementation is in Java and comprises roughly 6000 lines of code. A prototypical implementation is freely available at [6].

4   Partial Disclosure: Beyond the All-or-Nothing Barrier

The cryptographic protocol described so far allows the prover to show the existence of a certificate chain without revealing anything other than the length of the chain. In some situations, however, the length of the chain might reveal too much about the prover's identity while in some other scenarios, users might desire more precise trust measures, even at the price of sacrificing a little their anonymity. There is indeed an inherent trade-off between anonymity and trust. In this section we develop extensions of our protocol that allow users to fine-tune the degree of anonymity and trust.

Hiding the chain length. The length of the chain might actually reveal some information about the sender, depending on the topology of the web of trust. For instance, in the extreme scenario where the intended recipient has certified just one key and the length of the chain is 1, the intended recipient knows exactly the identity of the sender. In this case, the prover can arbitrarily increase the length of the chain proven in zero-knowledge by attaching self-generated certificates. Note that the keys used in these certificates need not be uploaded onto a server as the verifier does not need them to check the proof and, after the proof is generated, these keys can be discarded. Indeed, a proof for a certificate chain of length n does not guarantee that the prover is n hops away from the verifier, but that she is *at most* n hops away.

Partial release of secrets. To achieve fine-grained trust properties, we now consider certificate attributes, such as user name and key expiration date, and show how to reveal some of them while keeping the others secret. For instance, we might want to reveal the key expiration date while hiding confidential information such as the user name. We recall that participants in a web of trust place the signature on the concatenation of a public key and a set of attributes. Intuitively, instead of proving $\exists\ \alpha_m, \alpha_{sig}, \alpha_{pk} : \mathsf{ver}(\alpha_m, \alpha_{sig}, \alpha_{pk})$, we would like to prove a statement of the form $\exists\ \alpha_S, \alpha_{sig}, \alpha_{pk}, \alpha_K, \alpha_A.\mathsf{ver}(\alpha_S, \alpha_{sig}, \alpha_{pk}) \wedge \alpha_S = (\alpha_K, \alpha_A)$ and then reveal (part of) the attributes α_A. The concatenation of the public key and the attributes is implemented as $b = k \cdot 2^{\ell} + A$ where ℓ is an a priori fixed upper bound on the length of the attribute set. The idea is to split b in zero-knowledge and to reveal some of the components to the verifier. Given commitment c_{kA} on public key k and attributes A, commitment c_k on k, and commitment c_A on A, we execute the following zero-knowledge protocol:

$$\left\{\mathsf{PK}(\alpha, \kappa, \tau) : \ [\![c_k]\!] = \kappa \wedge [\![c_A]\!] = \alpha \wedge [\![c_{kA}]\!] = \tau \wedge \tau = \kappa \cdot 2^{\ell} + \alpha \wedge 0 \leq \alpha < 2^{\ell}\right\}$$

We can then open c_A and release all the attributes A to the verifier or apply the protocol again on c_A to select which attributes have to be revealed.

Dynamic trust relationships and key expiration. Since trust relationships may vary over time, it is important to provide users with the possibility to periodically update their certificates. Our system incorporates two distinct key expiration mechanisms.

The first mechanism is based on a global version number that is attached to all public keys as an attribute. Periodically after a fixed interval, all keys have to be generated from scratch, re-signed, and tagged with the updated version number. Proving a key valid translates into showing that it is tagged with the most recent version number. This version number is revealed using our partial secret release protocol. As the interval is globally fixed, revealing the version number does not leak any information about the key.

In order to provide the user with the possibility to independently decide the validity of each certificate, we also support a second mechanism based on a key expiration date. Users can use our partial secret release protocol to selectively reveal the expiration date of a key. Since the exact expiration date might uniquely identify the public key, one can also prove $\{\mathsf{PK}(\epsilon) : [\![c_e]\!] = \epsilon \wedge current\ date < \epsilon < ub\}$ given a commitment c_e on the expiration date attribute ϵ and a suitable upper bound ub for all possible key expiration dates.

Notice that the OpenPGP standard [13] incorporates a key revocation mechanism, which is implemented by a special signature (also called revocation

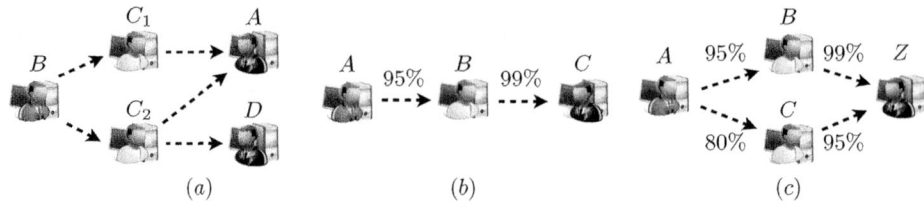

Fig. 2. Webs of trust

signature) that is attached to the revoked key by the revoking principal. Although conceptually appealing, such a revocation mechanism is not compatible
with our framework since there is no way to prove in zero-knowledge that a
certain key has not been revoked. In particular, even if revoked, the key and the
according certificates could still be used in our zero-knowledge proof.

Conjunctive and disjunctive statements over certificate chains. Σ-
protocols allow us to prove logical conjunction and disjunction of statements.
Proving a conjunctive statement over certificate chains strengthens trust at the
price of decreasing anonymity guarantees, whereas a disjunctive statement en-
hances the anonymity guarantees but diminishes trust.

In a way of example, consider Figure 2 (a) where A is trusted by both C_1 and
C_2, and D is only trusted by C_2. Assume A is interested in authenticating to a
party B trusting both C_1 and C_2 and suppose also that A does not know the
public key of B. If A proves that she is trusted by C_1 or C_2, a curious principal
will not be able to distinguish whether the message originated from D or A. The
trust guarantee provided by the proof, however, may be low if, for instance, the
link between C_2 and D is weak (cf. the following discussion on trust measures).

A proof that A is trusted by C_1 and C_2 strengthens the trust guarantee.
One can, however, compute the intersection of the principals trusted by C_1
and C_2, potentially reducing the anonymity guarantees. In this example, the
intersection uniquely identifies A as the prover. This example shows that there
is often an inherent trade-off between trust and anonymity. The expressiveness of
our zero-knowledge proof scheme is crucial to fine tune the security requirements
according to the application scenario.

Trust measures. In the following, we extend our approach to trust measures.
We will focus in particular on the trust model from [18]. The examples in this
section are intentionally borrowed from [18] in order to show the applicability of
our framework to existing trust models. Consider the web of trust in Figure 2 (b).
As shown by the weight of the two links, the trust of B in C is higher than the
trust of A in B. The trust measure proposed in [18] is based on the multiplication
of the trust values of the individual links. Therefore the trust degree provided
by the chain between A and C is $95\% \cdot 99\% = 94.05\%$.

We devise a proof that reveals the trust degree provided by a given chain,
without disclosing the weight of individual links, since this might compromise
the anonymity of participants. In case even the exact trust degree is considered

too informative on the identity of the parties involved in the chain, we can approximate this value using range proofs (cf. key expiration).

In addition to proving the validity of the certificate chain of Figure 2 (b), the prover executes the following protocol:

$$\{\mathsf{PK}(\alpha, \beta, \gamma) : \ [\![c_t]\!] = \alpha \wedge [\![c_{t_1}]\!] = \beta \wedge [\![c_{t_2}]\!] = \gamma \wedge \alpha \equiv_P \beta \cdot \gamma\}$$

where c_{t_1} and c_{t_2} are the commitments to the certificate attributes 95 and 99, P is a large publicly known prime, and c_t is a commitment to 9405, which is opened by the prover. Since we cannot reason on rational numbers and consequently on divisions,[7] the verifier has to perform the remaining computation on the value $[\![c_t]\!] = 9405$, namely, $1 - (1 - 9405/10000) = 94.05\%$.

We now show how our protocol can be extended to deal with even more complex scenarios. Consider the graph in Figure 2 (c): Z has to show that there exist two distinct paths from A to Z. The total trust degree is computed as $1 - (1 - 95\% \cdot 99\%) \cdot (1 - 80\% \cdot 95\%) \approx 98.6\%$.

The corresponding zero-knowledge proof is computed as follows. Given the commitments c_{s_1}, c_{s_2}, c_{s_3}, and c_{s_4} on the certificates $cert_{AB}$, $cert_{AC}$, $cert_{CZ}$, and $cert_{BZ}$, where $cert_{IJ}$ denotes the certificate issued by I on J's public key, and the commitments c_{t_1}, c_{t_2}, c_{t_3}, and c_{t_4} on the corresponding trust values, in addition to showing that both chains are valid we run the following protocol:

$$\left\{ \begin{array}{l} \mathsf{PK}(\alpha_1, \alpha_2, \alpha_3, \alpha_4, \beta_1, \beta_2) : \ [\![c_{t_1}]\!] = \alpha_1 \wedge [\![c_{t_2}]\!] = \alpha_2 \wedge [\![c_{t_3}]\!] = \alpha_3 \wedge [\![c_{t_4}]\!] = \alpha_4 \wedge \\ [\![c_{s_1}]\!] = \beta_1 \wedge [\![c_{s_2}]\!] = \beta_2 \wedge \beta_1 \neq \beta_2 \wedge [\![c_r]\!] \equiv_P ([\![c_{10000}]\!] - \alpha_1 \cdot \alpha_3) \cdot ([\![c_{10000}]\!] - \alpha_2 \cdot \alpha_4) \end{array} \right\}$$

Proving $[\![c_{s_1}]\!] \neq [\![c_{s_2}]\!]$ ensures that the first two signatures, and therefore the two chains, are different. The rest of the proof computes in zero-knowledge the total trust value as follows: $[\![c_r]\!] = (10000 - 95 \cdot 99) \cdot (10000 - 80 \cdot 95) = 1428000$ (c_{10000} is a commitment to 10000). The verifier then computes $(10^8 - [\![c_r]\!])/10^8 \approx 98.6\%$. Although the numbers grow quickly with the chain length and the number of parallel paths, $P \gg 10^{100}$ is large enough for any reasonably sized chain.

5   Formal Verification

The cryptographic proof from Section 3 ensures that our scheme enjoys the special soundness and honest verifier statistical zero-knowledge properties. It is important to verify, however, that the protocol as a whole guarantees the intended trust and anonymity properties. We conducted a formal security analysis by modeling our protocol in the applied pi-calculus [1], formalizing the trust property as an authorization policy and the anonymity property as an observational equivalence relation, and verifying our model with ProVerif [11,2], a state-of-the-art automated theorem prover that provides security proofs for an unbounded number of protocol sessions. We model zero-knowledge proofs following the approach proposed in [7], for which computational soundness results exist [8]. For

---

[7] Computing $1/m$ for a given m results in a number u such that $m \cdot u = 1 \mod q$, e.g., $1/4 = 5 \mod 19$.

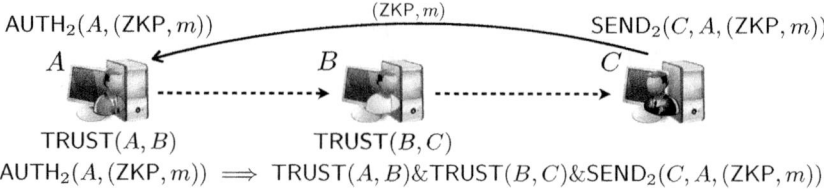

Fig. 3. Trust policy

easing the presentation, in this section we focus on certificate chains without attributes.

Attacker model. In our analysis, we consider a standard symbolic Dolev-Yao active attacker who dictates the certificates released by each party (i.e., the attacker controls the web of trust), the certificate chains proven in zero-knowledge, and the proofs received by each verifier.

Verification of trust. We partition the set of parties into honest and compromised. Honest parties generate a fresh key-pair, publish the public component, and engage in three distinct activities: Certificate generation, proof generation, and proof verification.

We decorate security-related protocol events with logical predicates, which constitute the building blocks of the authorization policy formalizing the trust property (cf. Figure 3). The event $\mathsf{TRUST}(x,y)$ describes the point in the protocol where the honest party associated with public key x releases a certificate for public key y. The event $\mathsf{COMPR}(x)$ tracks the compromise of the party associated with public key x (i.e., this party is under the control of the attacker, which also knows the corresponding private key). The event $\mathsf{SEND}_i(x,y,z)$ describes the point in the protocol where the party associated with public key x sends a zero-knowledge proof for a certificate chain of length i to the party associated with public key y to authenticate message z. Finally, the event $\mathsf{AUTH}_i(x,y)$ describes the point in the protocol where the party associated with public key x authenticates message y as coming from a party of trust level i. The trust property is formalized as the following authorization policy:

$$\mathsf{AUTH}_2(id2,x) \Rightarrow \mathsf{SEND}_2(id1,id2,x) \ \& \ \mathsf{TRUST}(id2,id3) \ \& \ \mathsf{TRUST}(id3,id1)) \quad (1)$$
$$| \ (\mathsf{TRUST}(id2,id3) \ \& \ \mathsf{TRUST}(id3,id1) \ \& \ \mathsf{COMPR}(id1)) \quad (2)$$
$$| \ (\mathsf{TRUST}(id2,id3) \ \& \ \mathsf{COMPR}(id3)). \quad (3)$$

For the sake of simplicity, we focus on certificate chains of length 2: The extension to arbitrary chain lengths is straightforward. This policy says that in all execution traces, the event $\mathsf{AUTH}_2(id2,x)$ has to be preceded by either (1) $\mathsf{SEND}_2(id1,id2,x)$ and $\mathsf{TRUST}(id2,id3)$ and $\mathsf{TRUST}(id3,id1)$ (i.e., all parties are honest), or (2) $\mathsf{TRUST}(id2,id3)$ and $\mathsf{TRUST}(id3,id1)$ and $\mathsf{COMPR}(id1)$ (i.e., all parties except for the prover are honest), or (3) $\mathsf{TRUST}(id2,id3)$ and $\mathsf{COMPR}(id3)$ (i.e., the party trusted by the verifier is compromised and the attacker has chosen to lengthen the certificate chain by an additional, possibly

Fig. 4. Anonymity game

fake, certificate). In other words, this policy says that whenever the verifier authenticates a message as coming from a party of trust level i, then indeed a party of trust level i or less has started a protocol session with the verifier to authenticate that message.

This authorization policy is successfully verified by ProVerif and the analysis terminates in 3 seconds. The formal analysis highlighted a couple of important requirements for the safety of our protocol. First, the verifier has to check that the authenticated message is not a public key,[8] otherwise the following attack would be possible: The attacker gathers a certificate chain of length $i + 1$ and builds a zero-knowledge proof for a certificate chain of length i, authenticating the public key signed in the $i + 1$-th certificate as coming from the party associated with the public key signed in the i-th certificate. For a similar reason, signatures on messages other than public keys cannot be sent in plain or must be tagged differently from the signatures proven in zero-knowledge.

Verification of anonymity. Intuitively, we formalize the anonymity property as a cryptographic game where two principals act in a web of trust set up by the attacker and one of them authenticates by proving in zero-knowledge a certificate chain chosen by the attacker. If the attacker cannot guess which of the two principals generated this zero-knowledge proof, then the protocol guarantees anonymity. Our model includes an arbitrary number of honest and compromised parties as well as the two (honest) principals engaging in the anonymity game.

The anonymity game is defined by two distinct processes that are replicated (i.e., spawned an unbounded number of times) and in parallel composition (i.e., concurrently executed). In the first process, each of the two principals releases certificates as dictated by the attacker. Since the attacker controls also the certificates released by the other parties in the system, both honest and compromised ones, the attacker controls the topology of the whole web of trust. In the second process, the two principals receive two (possibly different) certificate chains from the attacker. If both certificate chains are valid and of the same length, we non-deterministically choose one of the two principals and we let it output the corresponding zero-knowledge proof. The observational equivalence relation $\approx$ (cf. Figure 4) says that the attacker should not be able to determine which of the two principals output the zero-knowledge proof.

ProVerif successfully verifies this observational equivalence relation. This implies that our protocol guarantees the anonymity of users even against our strong adversarial model. Since processes are replicated and the two principals may

---

[8] We recall that parties sign the hash of messages and these are shorter than keys.

output an unbounded number of zero-knowledge proofs, our protocol additionally provides unlinkability, that is, the attacker is not able to tell if two zero-knowledge proofs come from the same principal or not.

6   Conclusion

We have proposed a cryptographic protocol for anonymous communication in webs of trust. We reconcile trust and anonymity, two seemingly conflicting requirements, using a novel zero-knowledge proof that allows the sender to prove the existence of a certificate chain without revealing her identity and the receiver to verify the trust level of the sender. The zero-knowledge proof scheme is general and accommodates different aspects of webs of trust, such as key expiration, trust measures, and existence of multiple certificate chains. We conducted a formal security analysis of our protocol, showing that trust and anonymity are guaranteed even in a strong adversarial setting.

Our approach inherently requires that the certificates comprising the certificate chain are accessible to the prover, since they have to be proven in zero-knowledge. While public relationships are not a problem in a company (e.g., boss, employee, trainee, etc.), there might be privacy issues in other settings, e.g., in the context of social networks where users may want to keep their social relationships secret. We stress that our approach does *not* require the whole relationship graph to be public; only the certificates used in the proof need to be accessible to the prover.

In a distributed social network, for instance, we envision the following *local* certificate distribution mechanism: A expresses her friendship with B by signing B's public key and sending the corresponding certificate C_{AB} to him. If A wants her profile to be available only to her friends (this corresponds to a "friends only" policy in Facebook [23]), then B is expected to keep C_{AB} to himself. Should A instead opt for a "friends of friends" policy (which is also available in Facebook [23]), then A authorizes B to release C_{AB} to his friends in order to let them anonymously authenticate with A (with a zero-knowledge proof of length 2). B's friends might express interest in authenticating with A, after looking at a preview of A's profile, which could be made available by B.

In general, there is an inherent trade-off between the privacy of the relationship graph and the anonymity guarantees of our scheme. On the one hand, if the relationship graph is fully private, then the prover does not know how many other principals have her own trust level. Hence, in the extreme scenario in which the verifier and all the principals in the chain have issued just one certificate, the prover is just anonymous in the set of principals occurring in the chain (due to the chain enlargement technique discussed in Section 4). On the other hand, if the relationship graph is public, as in GnuPG, the prover can be certain of her anonymity guarantees. As a future work, it would be interesting to investigate techniques to solve this tension, e.g., by selectively disclosing parts of the relationship graph in order to ensure meaningful anonymity properties.

Acknowledgments. This work was partially supported by the initiative for excellence and the Emmy Noether program of the German federal government and by Miur Project SOFT (*Security Oriented Formal Techniques*).

References

1. Abadi, M., Blanchet, B.: Secrecy types for asymmetric communication. In: Honsell, F., Miculan, M. (eds.) FOSSACS 2001. LNCS, vol. 2030, pp. 25–41. Springer, Heidelberg (2001)
2. Abadi, M., Blanchet, B., Fournet, C.: Automated verification of selected equivalences for security protocols. In: LICS 2005, pp. 331–340. IEEE, Los Alamitos (2005)
3. Abadi, M., Fournet, C.: Mobile values, new names, and secure communication. In: POPL 2001, pp. 104–115. ACM, New York (2001)
4. Ashri, R., Ramchurn, S.D., Sabater, J., Luck, M., Jennings, N.R.: Trust evaluation through relationship analysis. In: AAMAS 2005, pp. 1005–1011. ACM, New York (2005)
5. Ateniese, G., Camenisch, J., Joye, M., Tsudik, G.: A practical and provably secure coalition-resistant group signature scheme. In: Bellare, M. (ed.) CRYPTO 2000. LNCS, vol. 1880, pp. 255–270. Springer, Heidelberg (2000)
6. Backes, M., Lorenz, S., Maffei, M., Pecina, K.: Anonymous webs of trust (tool and long version) (2010), http://www.lbs.cs.uni-sb.de/awot/
7. Backes, M., Maffei, M., Unruh, D.: Zero-knowledge in the applied pi-calculus and automated verification of the direct anonymous attestation protocol. In: SSP 2008, pp. 202–215. IEEE, Los Alamitos (2008)
8. Backes, M., Unruh, D.: Computational soundness of symbolic zero-knowledge proofs against active attackers. In: CSF 2008, pp. 255–269. IEEE, Los Alamitos (2008)
9. Belenkiy, M., Camenisch, J., Chase, M., Kohlweiss, M., Lysyanskaya, A., Shacham, H.: Randomizable proofs and delegatable anonymous credentials. In: Halevi, S. (ed.) CRYPTO 2009. LNCS, vol. 5677, pp. 108–125. Springer, Heidelberg (2009)
10. Bellare, M., Shi, H., Zhang, C.: Foundations of group signatures: The case of dynamic groups. In: Menezes, A. (ed.) CT-RSA 2005. LNCS, vol. 3376, Springer, Heidelberg (2005)
11. Blanchet, B.: An efficient cryptographic protocol verifier based on Prolog rules. In: CSFW 2001, pp. 82–96. IEEE, Los Alamitos (2001)
12. Boneh, D., Boyen, X., Goh, E.-J.: Hierarchical identity based encryption with constant size ciphertext. In: Cramer, R. (ed.) EUROCRYPT 2005. LNCS, vol. 3494, pp. 440–456. Springer, Heidelberg (2005)
13. Callas, J., Donnerhacke, L., Finney, H., Shaw, D., Thayer, R.: OpenPGP message format. In: Request for Comments. IETF, vol. 4880 (2007)
14. Camenisch, J., Lysyanskaya, A.: A signature scheme with efficient protocols. In: Cimato, S., Galdi, C., Persiano, G. (eds.) SCN 2002. LNCS, vol. 2576, pp. 268–289. Springer, Heidelberg (2003)
15. Camenisch, J., Michels, M.: Proving in zero-knowledge that a number is the product of two safe primes. In: Stern, J. (ed.) EUROCRYPT 1999. LNCS, vol. 1592, pp. 107–122. Springer, Heidelberg (1999)
16. Camenisch, J., Stadler, M.: Efficient group signature schemes for large groups. In: Kaliski Jr., B.S. (ed.) CRYPTO 1997. LNCS, vol. 1294, pp. 410–424. Springer, Heidelberg (1997)

17. Carminati, B., Ferrari, E., Perego, A.: Rule-based access control for social networks. In: Meersman, R., Tari, Z., Herrero, P. (eds.) OTM 2006 Workshops. LNCS, vol. 4278, pp. 1734–1744. Springer, Heidelberg (2006)
18. Caronni, G.: Walking the web of trust. In: WETICE 2000, pp. 153–158. IEEE, Los Alamitos (2000)
19. Chaum, D., van Heyst, E.: Group signatures. In: Davies, D.W. (ed.) EUROCRYPT 1991. LNCS, vol. 547, pp. 257–265. Springer, Heidelberg (1991)
20. Cramer, R., Damgård, I., Schoenmakers, B.: Proofs of partial knowledge and simplified design of witness hiding protocols. In: Desmedt, Y.G. (ed.) CRYPTO 1994. LNCS, vol. 839, pp. 174–187. Springer, Heidelberg (1994)
21. Domingo-Ferrer, J., Viejo, A., Sebé, F., González-Nicolás, U.: Privacy homomorphisms for social networks with private relationships. Computer Networks 52(15), 3007–3016 (2008)
22. Domingo-Ferror, J.: A public-key protocol for social networks with private relationships. In: Torra, V., Narukawa, Y., Yoshida, Y. (eds.) MDAI 2007. LNCS (LNAI), vol. 4617, pp. 373–379. Springer, Heidelberg (2007)
23. facebook, http://www.facebook.com/
24. Fiat, A., Shamir, A.: How to prove yourself: Practical solutions to identification and signature problems. In: Odlyzko, A.M. (ed.) CRYPTO 1986. LNCS, vol. 263, pp. 186–194. Springer, Heidelberg (1987)
25. Frikken, K., Srinivas, P.: Key allocation schemes for private social networks. In: WPES 2009, pp. 11–20. ACM, New York (2009)
26. Fujisaki, E., Okamoto, T.: Statistical zero knowledge protocols to prove modular polynomial relations. In: Kaliski Jr., B.S. (ed.) CRYPTO 1997. LNCS, vol. 1294, pp. 16–30. Springer, Heidelberg (1997)
27. Gentry, C., Silverberg, A.: Hierarchical id-based cryptography. In: Zheng, Y. (ed.) ASIACRYPT 2002. LNCS, vol. 2501, pp. 548–566. Springer, Heidelberg (2002)
28. Goldreich, O.: Foundations of Cryptography: Basic Tools. Cambridge University Press, Cambridge (2001)
29. Goldreich, O., Micali, S., Wigderson, A.: Proofs that yield nothing but their validity or all languages in NP have zero-knowledge proof systems. Journal of the ACM 38(3), 690–728 (1991)
30. Goldwasser, S., Micali, S., Rackoff, C.: The knowledge complexity of interactive proof systems. SIAM Journal on Computing 18(1), 186–208 (1989)
31. Herranz, J.: Identity-based ring signatures from rsa. Theoretical Computer Science 389(1-2), 100–117 (2007)
32. Cottrell, L., Cypher, P., Finney, H., Goldberg, I., Laurie, B., Plumb, C., or Young, E.: Signing as one member of a set of keys, http://www.abditum.com/ringsig/
33. Pedersen, T.P.: Non-interactive and information-theoretic secure verifiable secret sharing. In: Feigenbaum, J. (ed.) CRYPTO 1991. LNCS, vol. 576, pp. 129–140. Springer, Heidelberg (1992)
34. Rivest, R.L., Shamir, A., Tauman, Y.: How to leak a secret. Communications of the ACM 22(22), 612–613 (2001)
35. Sabater-Mir, J.: Towards the next generation of computational trust and reputation models. In: Torra, V., Narukawa, Y., Valls, A., Domingo-Ferrer, J. (eds.) MDAI 2006. LNCS (LNAI), vol. 3885, pp. 19–21. Springer, Heidelberg (2006)
36. Scott, M.: Multiprecision Integer and Rational Arithmetic C/C++ Library, http://www.shamus.ie/
37. Song, D.X.: Practical forward secure group signature schemes. In: CCS 2001, pp. 225–234. ACM, New York (2001)

38. The GNU Privacy Guard Team. GnuPG, http://www.gnupg.org/
39. The GNU Privacy Guard Team. The GNU Privacy Handbook,
    http://www.gnupg.org/gph/en/manual.pdf
40. Tootoonchian, A., Saroiu, S., Ganjali, Y., Wolman, A.: Lockr: better privacy for
    social networks. In: CoNEXT 2009, pp. 169–180. ACM, New York (2009)
41. Wang, D.-W., Liau, C.-J., Hsu, T.-S.: Privacy protection in social network data
    disclosure based on granular computing. In: Fuzzy 2006, pp. 997–1003. IEEE, Los
    Alamitos (2006)

A   Trust Model

One of the core motivations behind webs of trust as public key infrastructures
is the fact that there is no central authority one has to trust. Every participant
bases trust decisions on her own policy.

However, this poses problems: Consider a simple web of trust where Alice
signed Bob's key and Bob signed Charlie's key. Alice trusts Bob only marginally,
i.e., she is not convinced that her signing policy is fully compatible with Bob's
policy. What does this say about Charlie's key? Probably Alice should not accept
it as a valid key if it is only signed by Bob. In the following, we use trust and
validity on the basis of the GnuPG Handbook [39]: *Trust* denotes the belief
that the owner of a key acts in accordance with our signing policy and *validity*
denotes our belief that a key actually belongs to the designated owner.

Our work is based on the OpenPGP standard [13], which stipulates a method
for conveying and expressing trust, namely, trust signatures. Such signatures
allow the signer to assert a *transitivity level* and a *trust level*. The former rules
the transitivity of trust relationships while the latter allows one to publicly
state the amount of trust set in the owner of a key. (Typical trust values are
unknown, no trust, marginal, and full.) For instance, a level one trust signature
on key k means that k can be used to sign another key k', which will inherit
the same trust level as k. Key k', however, is not trusted to sign further keys.
In general, a level n trust signature asserts that the owner of a key is trusted to
issue level $n-1$ trust signatures. Figure 5 depicts a trust signature chain with a
constant trust level. Note that the OpenPGP standard does not require the trust
level to remain constant throughout a chain. In practice, common transitivity
levels are 0 (direct friendship relation) and 1 (friend of a friend relation). A
level zero signature is equivalent to a standard signature in the web of trust.
Higher transitivity levels may be useful in certain applications where they have
a clear and meaningful interpretation (e.g., reflecting the hierarchical structure

$\mathcal{S}_{(i,j)}$: Trust signature with transitivity level i and trust level j

Fig. 5. Trust signature chain

of a company). PGP, since version 5, as well as GnuPG, depending on user preferences, use transitivity levels and trust levels to calculate the validity of keys. The specific details of these computations are implementation dependent.

Our approach is compatible with the trust signature mechanism and a variety of validity calculation algorithms. In fact, we can selectively reveal both transitivity levels and trust levels in our zero-knowledge proofs as well as compute in zero-knowledge the validity of keys as described in Section 4.

Taming Big Brother Ambitions: More Privacy for Secret Handshakes

Mark Manulis[1], Bertram Poettering[1], and Gene Tsudik[2]

[1] Cryptographic Protocols Group, TU Darmstadt & CASED, Germany
mark@manulis.eu, bertram.poettering@cased.de
[2] Computer Science Department, UC Irvine, USA
gts@ics.uci.edu

Abstract. In Secret Handshakes (SH) and Affiliation-Hiding Authenticated Key Exchange (AH-AKE) schemes, users become group members by registering with Group Authorities (GAs) and obtaining membership credentials. Group members then use their membership credentials to privately authenticate each other and communicate securely. The distinguishing privacy property of SH and AH-AKE is that parties learn each other's groups affiliations and compute common session keys only if their groups match. Current SH and AH-AKE schemes consider GAs to be fully trusted, especially, with regard to (i) security of the registration phase (no phantom members), (ii) secrecy of established session keys, and (iii) privacy. The impact of possible "big brother" ambitions of malicious GAs has not been investigated so far. In this paper, we discuss implications on group members' privacy and security of their communication in the presence of possible GA corruptions. We demonstrate problems arising from relaxed GA trust assumptions and propose an efficient — yet provably secure — AH-AKE protocol with enhanced privacy properties.

1 Introduction

Affiliation-Hiding Key Exchange. In the public-key setting, traditional Authenticated Key Exchange (AKE) protocols offer secure key establishment while usually revealing the identities and certificates of participants. Affiliation-Hiding AKE (AH-AKE) schemes [11,12] that combine Secret Handshakes (SH) [3,8,21,20,19,2,13,14] with secure key establishment offer stronger privacy guarantees. In both SH and AH-AKE, users are members of groups administrated by Group Authorities (GAs). Prior to participation, users register with the GA to obtain their membership credentials. The goal of SH and AH-AKE is to ensure private matching (e.g. exact, or dynamic matching [2]) between the affiliations (groups) of participants. Privacy stems from the requirement to hide these affiliations from outsiders or members of non-matching groups. AH-AKE protocols provide stronger privacy than Secret Handshakes, since they guarantee the affiliation-hiding property, even if established session keys are disclosed. Additionally, AH-AKE protocols provide traditional AKE-security goals [7] for the established keys. SH and AH-AKE schemes come in two flavors: linkable and

M.J. Atallah and N. Hopper (Eds.): PETS 2010, LNCS 6205, pp. 149–165, 2010.

unlinkable. Linkable protocols [3,8,11,12], which are useful if participants wish to be recognized across different sessions, employ re-usable pseudonyms that members obtain during the registration process with the GA. In contrast, unlinkable protocols [21,13,2,14] aim at preventing any correlation among multiple sessions of the same participant.

The GA Role. We assume that each GA manages one group. It is responsible for the registration of new members and for any subsequent membership revocation [3,8,21,12,14]. While in linkable AH-AKE members can be efficiently revoked by black-listing their pseudonyms on public revocation lists, unlinkable AH-AKE supports revocation either by restricting the number of unlinkable sessions of users, e.g. [21], or by regularly updating unrevoked membership credentials, e.g. [13].

Current protocols assume that GAs are fully trusted. This becomes clear by inspecting the underlying security models [13,12,14] where GA corruptions are not among the adversary's options. We first discuss what exactly the GA is trusted with, and whether this trust is justifiable and/or offers space for meaningful relaxations.

Security of Registration/Revocation. Among GA duties is the registration and revocation of group members. Clearly, if the GA misbehaves and introduces phantom members, then security of session keys computed by honest participants in sessions with phantom members can no longer represent a meaningful requirement. Therefore, GA must be trusted with regard to security of the registration (and revocation) in that it does not enroll phantom (or revoke honest) members. This is similar to the usual trust placed into the Certification Authority (CA) in public-key based AKE schemes.

However, we believe that possible GA misbehavior during registration of new (honest) members must be taken into account. Note that the registration process is the only step where GA interacts directly with users. Therefore, information obtained or issued by the GA during registration may be later misused to the detriment of members' privacy.

Security of Session Keys. An AH-AKE instance between two honest members should result in a secure session key. For obvious reasons, it is desirable for this key to be kept secret from the GA. This requirement subsumes forward secrecy of session keys with respect to any future GA corruptions. Although this issue has not been formally addressed so far, we note that some recent results [11,12] seem to satisfy this extended form of forward secrecy. Whereas, in many other protocols, e.g. [3,8,2], private secrets of the GA can be used to immediately recover session keys.

Privacy of Group Members. The central privacy requirement of AH-AKE protocols is to hide the group membership (affiliation) of participants from outsiders. However, it is also meaningful to extend this requirement towards the GA.

As long as GA is trusted with the security of the registration, it makes sense for transcripts of sessions among honest members not to reveal their affiliations to the GA. This requirement is of particular importance for linkable schemes where participants communicate via pseudonyms. Current linkable schemes, such as [3,8,20,12], do not provide this stronger privacy notion, since the GA learns (or even specifies) the pseudonyms of its members during the registration process.

Finally, there is an even more significant threat to privacy of group members, that stems from the fact that, during the registration process, GA learns users' real identities. In particular, we believe that handshake sessions involving honest members should not reveal any information about their real identities to the GA (even though the GA knows the real identities of all group members). In other words, users should remain *untraceable* throughout their communication sessions.

Untraceability is a new privacy requirement that does not appear in current AH-AKE security models; in fact, all current linkable protocols that we are aware of do not provide it. We observe that untraceability is an individual goal of members, while affiliation-hiding is a goal shared by all members of the same group. Therefore, untraceability is desirable even if the GA deliberately engages in sessions with genuine group members.

The above discussion shows that unconditional trust in GA by group members, as imposed by current AH-AKE security models, can be problematic and needs to be re-examined. In particular, mitigation of potential GA misbehavior (aimed to undermine privacy of group members and security of their communication) is an important goal which motivates our present work.

Contributions and Organization. Our work makes two contributions. First, in Section 2, we present three intuitive security goals for AH-AKE schemes (key secrecy, affiliation-hiding and user untraceability) that explicitly consider GA misbehavior. These goals can be viewed as strengthening those of the recent model of [12] where GA corruptions are not considered. We summarize two current protocols [12,8] and discuss why they are not strong enough to achieve these new goals. Based on this observation, as our second contribution, in Section 3 we propose a new AH-AKE scheme that operates in the Discrete Logarithm (DL) setting. Although some central design ideas are similar, the new protocol is fairly different from the one proposed by Castellucia, et al. [8]. In short, one novel factor is the decoupling of the registration phase, where pseudonyms are generated, from later protocol sessions by adopting blinding techniques for Schnorr signatures [18,17]. We show that an anonymized registration process is in fact necessary to preserve affiliation-hiding and untraceability against GAs. We also show that the latter can be achieved unconditionally. Efficiency and key security of our technique stem from a key establishment process where session keys are derived similarly to the Unified Model [4], thus achieving forward secrecy (not provided by [8]). Then, in Section 4, we prove security and privacy of our protocol in the random oracle model (ROM) using the computational variant of the Oracle Diffie-Hellman assumption from [1].

Related Work. Linkable Secret Handshake (LSH) schemes [3,8,20] provide group members with credentials composed of a pseudonym and additional secrets. These schemes have been designed with authentication in mind, and, although some of them offer session key establishment, no formal security treatment of the latter has been provided. Aforementioned schemes provide efficient revocation using certificate/pseudonym revocation lists. An extension of LSH to Linkable AH-AKE (LAH-AKE) schemes has been formally modeled and analyzed in [12]. The scheme in [12] works in the safe RSA setting and offers forward secrecy as well as revocation, under the trusted GA assumption.

In unlinkable Secret Handshakes [2,13,19,14] credentials are reused while still precluding the correlation of multiple sessions involving the same participant. The challenging part is the process of revocation of protocol participants, which is completely disregarded in [2], handled via synchronization of revocation epochs in [13], and addressed in [19] with group signatures and broadcast encryption. Jarecki and Liu [14] recently constructed a scheme that supports more efficient revocation and unlinkable reusable credentials using group signature-related techniques. We remark that unlinkability generally can be obtained from linkable protocols by using one-time pseudonyms; however, this is clearly impractical.

There are also a couple of Linkable Group Secret Handshake schemes [10,11] that extend the security model from two-party to multi-party authentication and key establishment scenarios. The approach in [10] uses credentials that employ Schnorr signatures issued by the GA (this is, in some sense, related to [8]), whereas, the scheme in [11] applies similar ideas to the RSA setting. Both approaches achieve session group key establishment based on a variant of the well-known Burmester-Desmedt [5] technique.

The first result on privacy protection against misbehaving GAs is due to Kawai, et al. [15]. It deviates from the traditional setting by splitting the GA role among the issue authority (responsible for registration and certificate issuance) and the tracing authority (responsible for tracing users based on their handshake transcripts). Since we treat the GA as a single instance, the setting of our work is more consistent with earlier results.

2   Malicious GAs: Impact and Challenges

After describing LAH-AKE syntax, we illustrate challenges stemming from malicious GAs using, as our running example, a concrete LAH-AKE scheme from [12]. We also highlight techniques necessary to protect against malicious GAs that are later used in our own construction.

2.1   SH and AH-AKE

The main syntactical difference between AH-AKE and SH schemes is the session key computation during protocol execution. Although many SH schemes provide participants with a session key, doing so is not mandatory for the purpose of pure authentication. An LAH-AKE scheme includes four components:

CreateGroup(1^κ) a probabilistic algorithm that sets up a new group G. It is executed by the corresponding GA. On input of the security parameter 1^κ, it generates a public/private group key-pair (G.pk, G.sk), initializes the group's pseudonym revocation list G.prl to $\emptyset$ and outputs public group parameters G.par $= (G$.pk, G.prl) along with the private key G.sk.

AddUser(U, G) a protocol executed between a prospective group member U and the GA of G. The algorithm on U's side is denoted AddUserU(U, G.par), and on GA's side by AddUserG(U, G.sk). Let π be a session of AddUserU or AddUserG. The *state* of π is represented with a variable π.state and can take running or accepted values. Initially π.state = running. Once AddUserU session π reaches π.state = accepted its variable π.result contains a pair (id, id.cred) where id is a *pseudonym* and id.cred is a *membership credential* enabling U to authenticate as id in group G in future Handshake sessions. A user can have several registered pseudonyms in the same group.

Handshake(params$_1$, params$_2$) a protocol (handshake) executed between two users, U_1 and U_2, on inputs params$_i = ((\text{id}_i, \text{id}_i.\text{cred}), G_i.\text{par}, r_i), i \in \{1, 2\}$, with G_i.par $= (G_i$.pk, G_i.prl), $r_1 = $ init and $r_2 = $ resp. Each U_i executes its own part Handshake'(param$_i$). Note that id$_i$ is the pseudonym previously registered to group G_i using the AddUser algorithm. The protocol verifies that both users are members of the same group (i.e. $G_1 = G_2$) and possess valid membership credentials. If so, the protocol accepts with an established shared session key. Otherwise, it rejects. Users keep track of the state of created Handshake protocols π through session variables that are initialized as follows: π.state $\leftarrow$ running, π.key $\leftarrow \perp$, π.id $\leftarrow$ id (where id is the own pseudonym) and π.partner $\leftarrow \perp$. At some point, the protocol completes and π.state is updated to either rejected or accepted. In the latter case, π.key is set to the established session key (of length κ) and the pseudonym of the handshake partner is assigned to π.partner. State accepted cannot be reached if the protocol partner is revoked (π.partner $\in G$.prl).

Revoke(G.sk, G.prl, id) a revocation algorithm executed by the GA of G. It outputs the updated pseudonym revocation list G.prl $\leftarrow G$.prl $\cup \{$id$\}$.

Definition 1 (Correctness). *Suppose that two users, U_1 and U_2, register as members of groups G_1 and G_2, and obtain their credentials (id$_1$, id$_1$.cred) and (id$_2$, id$_2$.cred), respectively, via corresponding AddUser executions. Further suppose that U_1 and U_2 participate in a Handshake protocol and let π_1 and π_2 denote their corresponding sessions. The LAH-AKE scheme is called correct if (a) π_1 and π_2 complete in the same state: accepted iff $G_1 = G_2$ and id$_1 \notin G_2$.prl and id$_2 \notin G_1$.prl and $r_1 \neq r_2$, and (b) if both sessions accept, then (π_1.key, π_1.partner, π_1.id) = (π_2.key, π_2.id, π_2.partner).*

2.2 Impact of GA Corruptions

LAH-AKE with Honest GAs. One state-of-the-art LAH-AKE scheme is due to Jarecki, et al. [12]. It is very efficient and offers a number of valuable security properties. In particular, it satisfies the following standard requirements, which we state here informally.

Authenticated Key Exchange (AKE) Security with Forward Secrecy. It should be infeasible for an active PPT adversary to distinguish the session key computed in some test session from a random key with a probability non-negligibly exceeding $\frac{1}{2}$. AKE-security has been modeled in [12] following the general approach for key exchange protocols (e.g. [7]) via an indistinguisha-bility game, that precludes all "trivial" attacks via which the adversary could obtain the key computed in the test session. The (sub)requirement of forward secrecy is typically modeled by allowing user corruptions, while preventing active participation of the adversary in the test session.

Linkable Affiliation-Hiding (LAH). It should be infeasible for an active PPT adversary to decide the group membership of an uncorrupted user from its handshake sessions or from knowledge of computed session keys. This requirement has been modeled in [12] via the simulation approach where the simulator executes handshake sessions without knowing the affiliation (and secret membership credentials) of participants.

We now briefly overview the LAH-AKE scheme from [12]. During setup, the GA creates public group parameters (n, g, e), where n is a safe RSA modulus of length $2\kappa''$, i.e., an RSA modulus $n = pq$ where p, q are safe κ'' bit primes, and $e \in \mathbb{Z}_{\varphi(n)}$ is an RSA exponent satisfying $\gcd(e, \varphi(n)) = 1$. Element $g \in \mathbb{Z}_n^*$ is chosen such that $\mathbb{Z}_n^* = \langle -1 \rangle \times \langle g \rangle$ (and hence $\mathrm{ord}(g) \approx n/2$). In addition, for each group, a specific hash function $H_n : \{0,1\}^* \to \mathbb{Z}_n^*$ is specified. When a user registers with the group, the pseudonym id it obtains is just a random string in $\{0,1\}^\kappa$. The corresponding credential id.cred $= \sigma_{\mathsf{id}}$ issued by the GA is the RSA signature on the full-domain hash of id: $\sigma_{\mathsf{id}} = H_n(\mathsf{id})^d \bmod n$ (where $d = e^{-1} \bmod \varphi(n)$). The handshake protocol is sketched in Figure 1. Note that H_1 is a hash function $\{0,1\}^* \to \{0,1\}^\kappa$, and pad is a probabilistic function that maps its first argument θ' to a random element θ within a certain interval such that $\theta \equiv \theta' \pmod{n}$. This padding function is necessary to hide the RSA modulus sent in protocol messages. Correctness follows from $r_A = g^{2ex_A x_B} = r_B$ which holds iff both participants employ valid credentials and consistent group parameters (n, g, e).

This protocol satisfies AKE- and LAH-security in the appropriate formal model, assuming random oracles and the hardness of the RSA problem with safe moduli. In our context, it is more important that the [12] model does not allow the adversary to corrupt relevant GAs. Our goal is to illustrate the impact of corrupted GAs on protocol sessions of honest users. We stress that our discussion does not mean that the original scheme is insecure. In our description, we distinguish between GAs malicious from the beginning (which is important if one considers that group parameters might be generated in some rogue way) and GAs that generate group parameters honestly but misbehave later.

Impact of GA corruptions on AKE-Security. Suppose that the GA is malicious during setup. In particular, it might choose RSA modulus n or generator g

User A	User B
Input: $(n_A, g_A, e_A), \mathrm{id}_A, \sigma_{\mathrm{id}_A}, \mathsf{init}$	**Input:** $(n_B, g_B, e_B), \mathrm{id}_B, \sigma_{\mathrm{id}_B}, \mathsf{resp}$
$(b_A, x_A) \xleftarrow{\$} \{0,1\} \times \mathbb{Z}_{n_A}$	$(b_B, x_B) \xleftarrow{\$} \{0,1\} \times \mathbb{Z}_{n_B}$
$\theta'_A \leftarrow (-1)^{b_A} (g_A)^{x_A} \sigma_{\mathrm{id}_A} \bmod n_A$	$\theta'_B \leftarrow (-1)^{b_B} (g_B)^{x_B} \sigma_{\mathrm{id}_B} \bmod n_B$
$\theta_A \leftarrow \mathsf{pad}(\theta'_A, n_A)$	$\theta_B \leftarrow \mathsf{pad}(\theta'_B, n_B)$

$$m_1 = (\theta_A, \mathrm{id}_A) \longrightarrow$$
$$\longleftarrow m_2 = (\theta_B, \mathrm{id}_B)$$

$\mathsf{sid}_A \leftarrow m_1 \,\|\, m_2$	$\mathsf{sid}_B \leftarrow m_1 \,\|\, m_2$
$r_A \leftarrow \left((\theta_B)^{e_A} H_{n_A}(\mathrm{id}_B)^{-1}\right)^{2x_A}$	$r_B \leftarrow \left((\theta_A)^{e_B} H_{n_B}(\mathrm{id}_A)^{-1}\right)^{2x_B}$
$v_A \leftarrow H_1(r_A \,\|\, \mathsf{sid}_A \,\|\, \mathsf{init})$	$v_B \leftarrow H_1(r_B \,\|\, \mathsf{sid}_B \,\|\, \mathsf{resp})$

$$v_A \longrightarrow$$
$$\longleftarrow v_B$$

accept with $K = H_1(r_A \,\|\, \mathsf{sid}_A)$ if	accept with $K = H_1(r_B \,\|\, \mathsf{sid}_B)$ if
$v_B = H_1(r_A \,\|\, \mathsf{sid}_A \,\|\, \mathsf{resp})$; else reject.	$v_A = H_1(r_B \,\|\, \mathsf{sid}_B \,\|\, \mathsf{init})$; else reject.

Fig. 1. RSA-based Handshake protocol from [12]

in a way that later facilitates computing session keys exchanged between honest members. For instance, if g is chosen to have small order (this is trivially feasible if n has more than two factors, or, if the factors are not safe primes), then the CDH-analog of computing r_A from θ'_A and θ'_B becomes tractable. Therefore, in general, public verifiability of group parameters is desirable for the registration of new members. In the RSA-based setting of [12], this is achievable using slight modifications of the zero-knowledge proofs from [6], as presented in [16]. However, this makes the registration process less efficient and, since our construction uses a DL-based setting, we refrain from investigating this idea further. As mentioned in Section 1, a malicious GA can always create phantom members and compute session keys exchanged between them and honest members. This is unavoidable since GA is typically trusted not to introduce new users to the system (similar to the CA in the classical PKI-setting). However, GA may be interested in learning the communication contents between two honest members and, in this sense, the protocol should ensure security of session keys in the presence of a passive GA that can corrupt group members. This requirement also implies forward secrecy with respect to GA corruptions. We observe that [12] provides this protection since the session key is derived from the ephemeral secret $g^{2e x_A x_B}$ (assuming that public group parameters have been generated correctly). Nevertheless, forward secrecy against GA corruptions is an important security goal and should be considered in the design of AH-AKE schemes. For example, the SH scheme of [8], which we modify to obtain our solution, is not forward secure if the GA is malicious.

Impact of GA Corruptions on LAH-Security. It seems impossible for affiliation of honest members to remain secret if these members are involved in handshake sessions with phantom members created by the malicious GA. In fact, this is similar to the case where the adversary corrupts a member and communicates with other users on behalf of that member. This case is typically excluded from the definition of LAH-security. On the other hand, it is still desirable for sessions between two honest users not to reveal their affiliations to the GA, i.e., no information about the affiliation of a handshake participant should be derivable from a session transcript. Considering the registration process in [12], we observe that, since the GA learns the pseudonym id of each new member U, it can always decide whether some honest handshake participant is a member of its group by simply observing the communication and the transmission of pseudonyms in the clear. A possible remedy is to prevent the GA from learning pseudonyms of group members upon their registration. This can be achieved by *blinding* the registration process. One natural approach (in the context of [12]) it to combine blind RSA signatures coupled with a full-domain hash [9,17]. However, the adversary could then register *any* pseudonym with any group. In particular, the adversary would be able to obtain membership credentials for some pseudonym id that is already in use by an honest group member, without explicitly corrupting any parties. This, in turn, would allow the adversary to mount (active) attacks on LAH-security and AKE-security of honest group members (since the adversary would be able to impersonate honest users without corrupting them or the GA). We stress that, in [12], this problem would arise not because of the blind registration process, but due to the specific construction of pseudonyms. In fact, our approach includes a blind registration process where no such problems occur, due to certain differences in pseudonym generation.

Impact of GA Corruptions on Traceability. As noted in Section 1, consideration of malicious GAs motivates a new privacy requirement — member untraceability, which we define informally as follows:

> *Member Untraceability:* It is infeasible for an active PPT adversary to learn the real identity U of an honest group member from handshake sessions involving that member. Note that untraceability is an individual privacy goal motivated by the fact that the GA learns members' real identities during their registration processes.

In [12], untraceability is not provided for the same reason that handshake transcripts reveal the participants' affiliation to the GA: the link between a member's real identity U and its pseudonym id is known by the GA from the registration process. We believe that this is avoidable by adopting a blinded registration process. However, it requires us to further examine group membership revocation. In LAH-AKE schemes, revocation is attained by adding members' pseudonyms to the revocation list maintained by the GA. In schemes like [12] where the GA knows the link between U and id anyway, there is no difference between revoking members and revoking their pseudonyms. The consequence of untraceability is that revoking a specific member U is no longer possible (since neither the GA nor a protocol participant can link U to id). However, it is still possible for the GA to revoke pseudonyms. Since members participate in handshakes using pseudonyms and revocation can be seen as a tool to prevent misbehavior of participants, it is still sufficient for the GA to revoke "misbehaving" pseudonyms, effectively preventing further participation of the member who "owns" them. This works only if the scheme ensures uniqueness of pseudonyms. However, if the scheme of [12] is amended with blind signatures in the registration process, uniqueness of pseudonyms can no longer be guaranteed. Although some workaround might be possible [16] (commensurate with lower efficiency), we do not investigate this direction, since our approach (which builds upon [8]) does not have such problems.

2.3   Challenges and Design Rationale

Based on our discussion above, we identify some issues and sketch potential solutions. The first issue is how to avoid possible attacks resulting from rogue generation of group parameters by the GA. Since, in the RSA setting (e.g., [12]), a suitable solution would have to involve inefficient zero-knowledge proofs, it seems that moving to the DL-based setting would be more advantageous. The second issue is how to blind the registration process, while ensuring uniqueness of pseudonyms. An intuitive solution based on blind signatures works only if the registration process prevents the prospective member from choosing its pseudonyms freely. For reasons alluded to above, the scheme in [12] does not yield a straightforward solution to these issues. On the other hand, we observe that the SH scheme in [8] is amenable to modifications that do not introduce significant overhead. Below, we briefly describe this scheme and the design rationale for our modifications, introduced in the subsequent section.

Let $\mathcal{G} = \langle g \rangle$ denote a cyclic group of prime order q. Let $H : \{0,1\}^* \to \mathbb{Z}_q$ and $H_1 : \{0,1\}^* \to \{0,1\}^\kappa$ denote hash functions. Upon group initialization, the GA picks a private key $x \in \mathbb{Z}_q \setminus \{0\}$ and publishes its public key $y_G = g^x$. To issue a credential for pseudonym id the GA computes a Schnorr signature (ω, t) on id, i.e. $(\omega, t) = (g^r, r + xH(\omega \| \mathrm{id}))$ for some $r \in_R \mathbb{Z}_q \setminus \{0\}$, and hands it out to the corresponding user. Note that $g^t = \omega(y_G)^{H(\omega\|\mathrm{id})}$. In [8], element ω is considered as a public value associated with id from which g^t can be computed as described above, while t acts as a trapdoor for this value and is only known to the owner of id. The handshake protocol shown in Figure 2 treats (g^t, t) as public/private key pair for ElGamal encryption. In essence, it is the protocol proposed in [8], expanded from a four-move to a six-move protocol, for the sake of better readability.

Since its goal is Secret Handshakes, this scheme has not been analyzed with regard to session key security. We note that this scheme does not provide forward secrecy, since the session key is derived from encrypted nonces, which can be decrypted later upon corruption of participants. Similar to [12], it does not provide affiliation-hiding and member untraceability in the face of GA corruptions.

Section 3 describes our LAH-AKE protocol which incorporates two important modifications to [8] that address aforementioned challenges stemming from GA corruptions. First, we introduce a blinded registration process using blind Schnorr signatures [18,17]. One nice property of blind Schnorr signatures is that both the signer and the verifier (i.e., the GA and the new member) contribute to the values (ω, t) of the resulting signature (see Figure 3). It follows that ω can serve as the unique identifier of a group member. Therefore, we consider as

$$
\begin{array}{c|c}
\textbf{User } A & \textbf{User } B \\
\textbf{Input: } (\mathsf{id}_A, \omega_A), t_A & \textbf{Input: } (\mathsf{id}_B, \omega_B), t_B \\
n_A \xleftarrow{\$} \{0,1\}^\kappa & n_B \xleftarrow{\$} \{0,1\}^\kappa \\[2mm]
\end{array}
$$

User A	User B
Input: $(\mathsf{id}_A, \omega_A), t_A$	**Input:** $(\mathsf{id}_B, \omega_B), t_B$
$n_A \xleftarrow{\$} \{0,1\}^\kappa$	$n_B \xleftarrow{\$} \{0,1\}^\kappa$

$$\xrightarrow{\quad \mathsf{id}_A, \omega_A, n_A \quad}$$
$$\xleftarrow{\quad \mathsf{id}_B, \omega_B, n_B \quad}$$

$y_B = \omega_B \, (y_{G_A})^{H(\omega_B \| \mathsf{id}_B)}$	$y_A = \omega_A \, (y_{G_B})^{H(\omega_A \| \mathsf{id}_A)}$
$r_A \xleftarrow{\$} G, x_A \xleftarrow{\$} \mathbb{Z}_q$	$r_B \xleftarrow{\$} G, x_B \xleftarrow{\$} \mathbb{Z}_q$
$(C_{A,1}, C_{A,2}) \leftarrow (g^{x_A}, r_A \, y_B^{x_A})$	$(C_{B,1}, C_{B,2}) \leftarrow (g^{x_B}, r_B \, y_A^{x_B})$

$$\xrightarrow{\quad (C_{A,1}, C_{A,2}) \quad}$$
$$\xleftarrow{\quad (C_{B,1}, C_{B,2}) \quad}$$

$r_B \leftarrow C_{B,2}/(C_{B,1})^{t_A}$	$r_A \leftarrow C_{A,2}/(C_{A,1})^{t_B}$
$v_A = H_1(r_A \| r_B \| n_B)$	$v_B = H_1(r_A \| r_B \| n_A)$

$$\xrightarrow{\quad v_A \quad}$$
$$\xleftarrow{\quad v_B \quad}$$

accept with $K = H_1(r_A \| r_B)$ if $v_B = H_1(r_A \| r_B \| n_A)$; else reject.	accept with $K = H_1(r_A \| r_B)$ if $v_A = H_1(r_A \| r_B \| n_B)$; else reject.

Fig. 2. DL-based Handshake protocol from [8]

user pseudonyms only the ω part of the signature, excluding all other identifiers. In other words: member pseudonyms together with secret user credentials form Schnorr signatures on the empty string. Our second tweak concerns the way session keys are computed. In our protocol they are derived from ephemeral Diffie-Hellman keys and only their authentication is performed using group credentials. The construction is similar to the Unified Model [4] and ensures forward secrecy with regard to later corruptions of both the GA and group members.

3 Untraceable LAH-AKE Protocol with Untrusted GAs

Our untraceable LAH-AKE scheme is inspired by the Secret Handshake protocol from [8] in which membership credentials are defined via Schnorr signatures. In order to meet stronger security and privacy requirements we make several substantial changes to the registration and key exchange procedures (for differences and design rationale see Section 2). We proceed with the description of algorithms and protocols.

Algorithm $\mathsf{Setup}(1^\kappa)$. This algorithm selects and publishes global parameters that are common to all users and group authorities. This is done by selecting security parameter κ' (polynomially dependent on κ), and by specifying a prime order cyclic group $(\mathcal{G}, g, q) \leftarrow \mathsf{GGen}(1^{\kappa'})$ and two hash functions $H^* : \{0,1\}^* \rightarrow \mathbb{Z}_q$ and $H : \{0,1\}^* \rightarrow \{0,1\}^{3\kappa}$.

Algorithm $\mathsf{CreateGroup}(\ )$. The group authority GA picks a random secret key $G.\mathsf{sk} \xleftarrow{\$} \mathbb{Z}_q \setminus \{0\}$ and calculates the public key as $G.\mathsf{pk} = g^{G.\mathsf{sk}}$. The algorithm initializes the group's revocation list $G.\mathsf{prl}$ to $\emptyset$ and outputs $G.\mathsf{par} = (G.\mathsf{pk}, G.\mathsf{prl})$ as public group parameters, and $G.\mathsf{sk}$ as private group key.

Protocol AddUser(U, G). This protocol admits an user U to group G. The protocol as specified in Figure 3 is basically the blind variant of the Schnorr signature scheme [18,17] where the empty message is signed by the group authority's secret key G.sk. The communication between U and G is assumed to be authentic. Due to the blinding factors α and β the resulting signature (r', s') remains unknown to both eavesdroppers and the group authority. The output of this algorithm is the pair $(\mathsf{id}, \mathsf{id.cred}) = (r', s') \in \mathcal{G} \times \mathbb{Z}_q$ where id will be used as U's pseudonym in group G and id.cred as his secret credential. Note from inspection of the protocol that from $r' = g^{k+\alpha+\beta G.\mathsf{sk}}$ and $s' = k + (H^*(r') + \beta)G.\mathsf{sk} + \alpha$ it follows that

$$\mathsf{id}(G.\mathsf{pk})^{H^*(\mathsf{id})} = r'(G.\mathsf{pk})^{H^*(r')} = g^{s'} = g^{\mathsf{id.cred}}.$$

Note that neither U nor GA have exclusive control over the resulting values for id and id.cred.

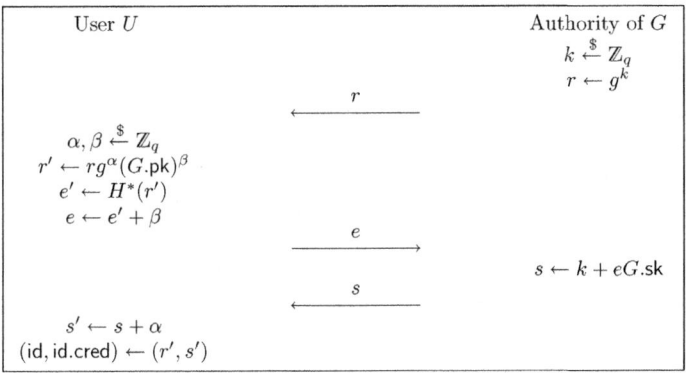

Fig. 3. Specification of our AddUser(U, G) protocol

Protocol Handshake($(\mathsf{id}_A, \mathsf{id}_A.\mathsf{cred}, G_A.\mathsf{par}, \mathsf{init}), (\mathsf{id}_B, \mathsf{id}_B.\mathsf{cred}, G_B.\mathsf{par}, \mathsf{resp})$).
The handshake protocol is executed between two users A and B, holding pseudonyms id_A and id_B, private credentials $\mathsf{id}_A.\mathsf{cred}$ and $\mathsf{id}_B.\mathsf{cred}$ and public group parameters $G_A.\mathsf{par} = (G_A.\mathsf{pk}, G_A.\mathsf{prl})$ and $G_B.\mathsf{par} = (G_B.\mathsf{pk}, G_B.\mathsf{prl})$, respectively. The protocol is specified in Figure 4. Observe that the equality $L_A = g^{\mathsf{id}_A.\mathsf{cred} \cdot \mathsf{id}_B.\mathsf{cred}} = L_B$ is implied by property $\mathsf{id}(G.\mathsf{pk})^{H^*(\mathsf{id})} = g^{\mathsf{id.cred}}$, which is inherent for the correctness of the protocol.

Algorithm Revoke($G.\mathsf{sk}, G.\mathsf{prl}, \mathsf{id}$). The revocation of a pseudonym id from the group is handled by the particular group authority by including id in the corresponding pseudonym revocation list $G.\mathsf{prl}$. It is assumed that this list is distributed authentically.

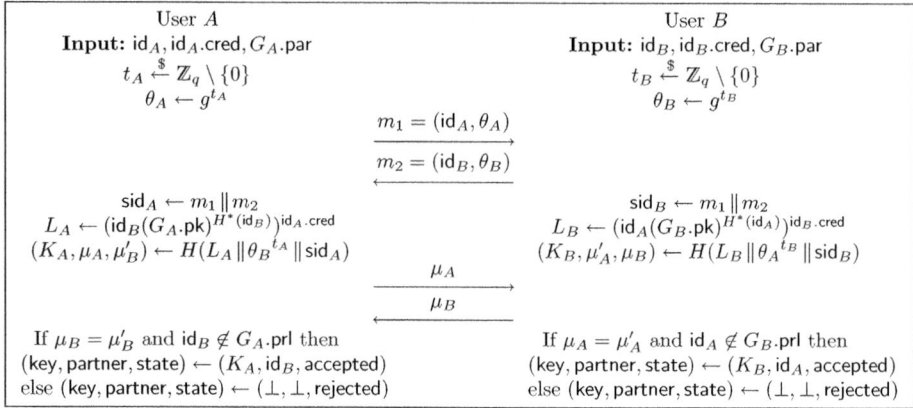

Fig. 4. Specification of our $\mathsf{Handshake}(U_A, U_B)$ protocol

4   Security Analysis and Performance Comparison

Security Analysis of our Protocol. In order to prove security of our protocol, we need an extension of the classical CDH assumption where we provide CDH-adversary $\mathcal{A}$ with two exponentiation oracles H'_a and H'_b (that will be realized with a hash function H' and modeled as random oracles). The stronger decisional version of this assumption was named Oracle Diffie-Hellman Assumption in [1], for which it has been shown that, in the random oracle model, such hash oracles do not provide additional advantage for distinguishing the challenge. Therefore, it seems reasonable to assume that these oracles are not helpful for breaking the CDH challenge either.

Definition 2 (Oracle CDH (OCDH) Assumption). *Let* $\mathsf{GGen}(1^{\kappa'})$ *denote an algorithm that outputs the specification of a group* $(\mathcal{G}, \cdot) = \langle g \rangle$ *of prime order* $q \geq 2^{\kappa'}$, *let* $H' : \mathcal{G} \to \{0,1\}^{\kappa}$ *denote a public hash function where* κ *is polynomial in* κ'. *We define* $\mathsf{Succ}^{\mathsf{ocdh}}_{\mathsf{GGen}, H'}(\kappa') =$

$$\max_{\mathcal{A}} \Pr\left[(\mathcal{G}, g, q) \leftarrow \mathsf{GGen}(1^{\kappa'}); \; a,b \xleftarrow{\$} \mathbb{Z}_q; \; h \leftarrow \mathcal{A}^{H'_a, H'_b}_{\mathcal{G}}(g^a, g^b) \text{ with } h = g^{ab} \right]$$

where $H'_a : x \mapsto H'(x^a)$ *and* $H'_b : x \mapsto H'(x^b)$ *are oracles available to* $\mathcal{A}$. *The OCDH assumption states that there exist* GGen *and* H' *such that* $\mathsf{Succ}^{\mathsf{ocdh}}_{\mathsf{GGen}, H'}(\kappa')$ *is negligible in* κ'.

Presuming the hardness of the OCDH problem, our construction presented in Section 3 satisfies the AKE-/LAH security and Untraceability goals introduced in Section 2 and formalized in the full version of this paper. The proof of Theorem 3 (with estimated attack probability) is given in Appendix A.3. For proofs of Theorems 1 and 2 we again refer to the full version.

Theorem 1 (AKE-Security). *Our LAH-AKE scheme is AKE-secure in the random oracle model under the OCDH assumption.*

Theorem 2 (LAH-Security). *Our LAH-AKE scheme is LAH-secure in the random oracle model under the OCDH assumption.*

Theorem 3 (Untraceability). *Our LAH-AKE scheme is unconditionally untraceable.*

Efficiency of our Protocol. Our protocol offers strong security and privacy for users and remains very efficient at the same time. Some computations can be even further optimized. The registration protocol is performed only once per user and takes three exponentiations in $\mathcal{G}$. The handshake protocol requires two exponentiations for the computation of the Diffie-Hellman value $g^{t_A t_B}$ plus two additional exponentiations for the computation of the shared long-term authentication key $L_A = g^{\mathrm{id}_A \cdot \mathrm{cred} \cdot \mathrm{id}_B \cdot \mathrm{cred}} = L_B$. The latter two exponentiations can be omitted in future sessions with the same partner by caching long-term keys. Furthermore, if user pseudonyms are publicly listed then long-term keys can be pre-computed.

Comparison with [8] and [12]. Table 1 compares security, privacy, and efficiency of the three protocols treated in this paper. We see that in respect to key security forward secrecy (FS) is provided only by [12] and our protocol, presuming honest behavior of the GA — denoted by hGA — for the former (otherwise, small group order attacks would be possible, see Section 2.2). In contrast, our protocol offers AKE security with forward secrecy even in the presence of corrupted GAs — denoted by cGA. As the user registration process in [8] and [12] is not blinded both protocols cannot provide LAH security if GAs are corrupted (as malicious GAs could record AddUser transcripts and later recognize affiliated pseudonyms). The same holds for user untraceability. The converse is correct for our protocol, which offers both properties even in the presence of corrupted GAs. As pointed out in Section 2.2, through the deployment of the blinding process revocation can be only performed based on pseudonyms.

The security advantage of our protocol is gained very efficiently: our protocol has best message and computational complexity (using optimal arrangement of messages and not counting cacheable computations). In practice security parameters $\kappa = 80$, $\kappa'' = 1024$ and $\kappa' = 1024$ (standard group setting) or $\kappa' = 2\kappa = 160$ (ECC group setting) would be chosen. In the latter case our protocol has the

Table 1. Security and Performance Comparison with [8] and [12]

Protocol	Security & Privacy				Revocation of	Complexity		
	AKE[1]	FS[2]	LAH[3]	UT[4]		Transf. bits[5]	# passes[6]	# exps[7]
CJT [8]	hGA	✗	hGA	✗	users,pseudonyms	$2(3\kappa' + 3\kappa)$	4	3 short
JKT [12]	hGA	✓	hGA	✗	users,pseudonyms	$2(\kappa'' + 3\kappa)$	3	2 long
Ours	cGA	✓	cGA	✓	pseudonyms	$2(2\kappa' + \kappa)$	3	2 short

[1]AKE-Security; [2]Forward Secrecy; [3]LAH-Security; [4]Untraceability; [5]Total number of transferred bits per handshake; [6]Number of message passes per protocol run; [7]Number of exponentiations (with short ($\approx 2\kappa$ bit) or long ($\approx \kappa''$ bit) exponents)

smallest bandwidth complexity of all named protocols (of about $10\kappa = 800$ bits per full handshake).

5   Conclusion

SH and AH-AKE schemes provide useful privacy-preserving authentication mechanisms coupled with the establishment of secure session keys. These schemes are becoming more important due to the increasing popularity of multi-user collaborative and group-based applications. Existing approaches and security models assume unconditional trust in Group Authorities. In this paper, we demonstrated that such trust assumptions might become problematic. We illustrated that these assumptions can be relaxed in a meaningful way resulting in more secure and private (yet efficient and practical) AH-AKE schemes. Our work opens a new research direction: Consideration of untrusted Group Authorities in unlinkable [2,13,14] and multi-party AH-AKE schemes [10,11].

References

1. Abdalla, M., Bellare, M., Rogaway, P.: The Oracle Diffie-Hellman Assumptions and an Analysis of DHIES. In: Naccache, D. (ed.) CT-RSA 2001. LNCS, vol. 2020, pp. 143–158. Springer, Heidelberg (2001)
2. Ateniese, G., Kirsch, J., Blanton, M.: Secret Handshakes with Dynamic and Fuzzy Matching. In: Network and Distributed System Security Symposium (NDSS 2007). The Internet Society (2007)
3. Balfanz, D., Durfee, G., Shankar, N., Smetters, D.K., Staddon, J., Wong, H.-C.: Secret Handshakes from Pairing-Based Key Agreements. In: IEEE Symposium on Security and Privacy 2003, pp. 180–196. IEEE CS, Los Alamitos (2003)
4. Blake-Wilson, S., Johnson, D., Menezes, A.: Key Agreement Protocols and their Security Analysis. In: Darnell, M.J. (ed.) Cryptography and Coding 1997. LNCS, vol. 1355, pp. 30–45. Springer, Heidelberg (1997)
5. Burmester, M., Desmedt, Y.: A Secure and Efficient Conference Key Distribution System. In: De Santis, A. (ed.) EUROCRYPT 1994. LNCS, vol. 950, pp. 275–286. Springer, Heidelberg (1995)
6. Camenisch, J., Michels, M.: Proving in Zero-Knowledge that a Number is the Product of Two Safe Primes. In: Stern, J. (ed.) EUROCRYPT 1999. LNCS, vol. 1592, pp. 107–122. Springer, Heidelberg (1999)
7. Canetti, R., Krawczyk, H.: Analysis of Key-Exchange Protocols and their Use for Building Secure Channels. In: Pfitzmann, B. (ed.) EUROCRYPT 2001. LNCS, vol. 2045, pp. 453–474. Springer, Heidelberg (2001)
8. Castelluccia, C., Jarecki, S., Tsudik, G.: Secret Handshakes from CA-Oblivious Encryption. In: Lee, P.J. (ed.) ASIACRYPT 2004. LNCS, vol. 3329, pp. 293–307. Springer, Heidelberg (2004)
9. Chaum, D.: Blind Signatures for Untraceable Payments. In: CRYPTO 1982, pp. 199–203. Plenum Press, New York (1983)
10. Jarecki, S., Kim, J., Tsudik, G.: Authentication for Paranoids: Multi-Party Secret Handshakes. In: Zhou, J., Yung, M., Bao, F. (eds.) ACNS 2006. LNCS, vol. 3989, pp. 325–339. Springer, Heidelberg (2006)

11. Jarecki, S., Kim, J., Tsudik, G.: Group Secret Handshakes or Affiliation-Hiding Authenticated Group Key Agreement. In: Abe, M. (ed.) CT-RSA 2007. LNCS, vol. 4377, pp. 287–308. Springer, Heidelberg (2006)
12. Jarecki, S., Kim, J., Tsudik, G.: Beyond Secret Handshakes: Affiliation-Hiding Authenticated Key Exchange. In: Malkin, T.G. (ed.) CT-RSA 2008. LNCS, vol. 4964, pp. 352–369. Springer, Heidelberg (2008)
13. Jarecki, S., Liu, X.: Unlinkable Secret Handshakes and Key-Private Group Key Management Schemes. In: Katz, J., Yung, M. (eds.) ACNS 2007. LNCS, vol. 4521, pp. 270–287. Springer, Heidelberg (2007)
14. Jarecki, S., Liu, X.: Private Mutual Authentication and Conditional Oblivious Transfer. In: Halevi, S. (ed.) CRYPTO 2009. LNCS, vol. 5677, pp. 90–107. Springer, Heidelberg (2009)
15. Kawai, Y., Yoneyama, K., Ohta, K.: Secret Handshake: Strong Anonymity Definition and Construction. In: Bao, F., Li, H., Wang, G. (eds.) ISPEC 2009. LNCS, vol. 5451, pp. 219–229. Springer, Heidelberg (2009)
16. Manulis, M., Poettering, B., Tsudik, G.: Affiliation-Hiding Key Exchange with Untrusted Group Authorities. In: Zhou, J. (ed.) ACNS 2010. LNCS, vol. 6123, pp. 402–419. Springer, Heidelberg (2010)
17. Pointcheval, D., Stern, J.: Security Arguments for Digital Signatures and Blind Signatures. Journal of Cryptology 13(3), 361–396 (2000)
18. Schnorr, C.P.: Efficient Identification and Signatures for Smart Cards. In: Brassard, G. (ed.) CRYPTO 1989. LNCS, vol. 435, pp. 239–252. Springer, Heidelberg (1989)
19. Tsudik, G., Xu, S.: A Flexible Framework for Secret Handshakes. In: Danezis, G., Golle, P. (eds.) PET 2006. LNCS, vol. 4258, pp. 295–315. Springer, Heidelberg (2006)
20. Vergnaud, D.: RSA-Based Secret Handshakes. In: Ytrehus, Ø. (ed.) WCC 2005. LNCS, vol. 3969, pp. 252–274. Springer, Heidelberg (2006)
21. Xu, S., Yung, M.: k-Anonymous Secret Handshakes with Reusable Credentials. In: 11th ACM Conference on Computer and Communications Security (CCS 2004), pp. 158–167. ACM, New York (2004)

A   Model and Proof for Untraceability

In the appendix of the full version of this paper formal security models and proofs for AKE-security, LAH-security and Untraceability are given. While, in respect to the two former models, we extend the work of [12], the property of untraceability is newly introduced here. Due to space limitations, in this version, we restrict the focus on model and proof of the latter.

A.1   Adversary Model

The adversary $\mathcal{A}$ is modeled as a PPT machine that interacts with parties via the set of the following basic queries. Unless explicitly noted, we assume that $\mathcal{A}$ always has access to up-to-date exhaustive (system-wide) lists of groups GLi and pseudonyms IDLi (these lists do not disclose the mapping between pseudonyms and groups).

CreateGroup() This query sets up a new group G and publishes its public parameters G.par. The group is added to GLi.

AddUserU(U, G.par) This query models the actions of U initiating the AddUser protocol with given target group G. A new protocol session π is started. Optionally, a first protocol message M is output. G is also added to GLi if it is a new group; this allows $\mathcal{A}$ to create its own groups with arbitrary (possibly malicious) public parameters.

AddUserG(G, U) This query differs from AddUserU in that it models GA's actions on the AddUser protocol. We require that G has been already established through the CreateGroup query.

Handshake(id, G.par, r) This query lets pseudonym id start a new session π of the Handshake protocol. It receives as input the public parameters of the group G wherein the handshake shall take place (given that id has credentials for that group) and a role identifier $r \in \{\text{init}, \text{resp}\}$ that determines whether the session will act as protocol initiator or responder. Optionally, this query returns a first protocol message M.

Send(π, M) Message M is delivered to session π. After processing M, the eventual output is given to $\mathcal{A}$. This query is ignored if π is not waiting for input. Note that π is either an AddUserU, an AddUserG or a Handshake protocol session. If π is an AddUserU session and accepts after processing M then id from π.result is added to IDLi.

Reveal(π) This query is defined only if π is a handshake session. Then, if π.state $\neq$ running it returns π.state and π.key; otherwise the query is ignored.

Corrupt($*$) The input is either a pseudonym id or a group identifier G:

Corrupt(id): If id $\in$ IDLi then, for any group G where id is registered, the corresponding credential id.cred is given to $\mathcal{A}$.

Corrupt(G): For a group G created by CreateGroup() this query hands G's long term secret G.sk and control over G's revocation list G.prl over to $\mathcal{A}$.

Revoke(G, id) This query lets the GA of G include id $\in$ IDLi in its pseudonym revocation list G.prl.

A.2   Definition of Untraceability

The idea behind untraceability is that, even in the presence of a malicious GA, any member remains untraceable throughout its AH-AKE sessions. As discussed in Section 1, this is a new (individual) privacy requirement, distinct from AKE- and LAH-security. We formalize it using the indistinguishability approach: we let $\mathcal{A}$ specify group parameters for a group G and pick two users U_0 and U_1 that are then enrolled into G by the challenger that obtains their respective pseudonyms id_0 and id_1. Untraceability means the inability of $\mathcal{A}$ to trace id_b where $b \in_R \{0, 1\}$.

Definition 3 (Untraceability).   *Let* LAH-AKE $= \{$CreateGroup, AddUser, Handshake, Revoke$\}$, *b a randomly chosen bit, and* $\mathcal{Q} = \{$CreateGroup, AddUserU, AddUserG, Handshake, Send, Reveal, Corrupt, Revoke$\}$ *the set of queries available* to $\mathcal{A}$. By $\mathsf{Game}^{\mathrm{trace},b}_{\mathcal{A},\mathsf{LAH\text{-}AKE}}(\kappa)$ we denote the following interaction of $\mathcal{A}$ with participants, where, for obvious reasons, we prevent $\mathcal{A}$ from accessing the up-to-date pseudonym list IDLi:

- $\mathcal{A}^{\mathcal{Q}}(1^{\kappa})$ interacts with all participants using the queries in $\mathcal{Q}$ and outputs a triple $(G.\mathsf{par}, U_0, U_1)$ where $G.\mathsf{par}$ are public parameters of a group G and U_0 and U_1 are two distinct users.
- U_0 and U_1 are admitted to G through the execution of $\mathsf{AddUser}(U_0, G)$ and $\mathsf{AddUser}(U_1, G)$ protocols in which the corresponding pseudonyms id_0 and id_1 are generated. Note that, during this process, protocol sessions on behalf of G can be executed by $\mathcal{A}$, however, the game does not proceed until the corresponding protocol sessions executed on behalf of U_0 and U_1 accept.
- $\mathcal{A}$ is given id_b and continues to interact with all participants via queries until it terminates and outputs bit b', which is also the output of the game.

We define: $\mathsf{Adv}^{\mathrm{trace}}_{\mathcal{A},\mathsf{LAH\text{-}AKE}}(\kappa) := \left| 2\Pr[\mathsf{Game}^{\mathrm{trace},b}_{\mathcal{A},\mathsf{LAH\text{-}AKE}}(\kappa) = b] - 1 \right|$

and denote by $\mathsf{Adv}^{\mathrm{trace}}_{\mathsf{LAH\text{-}AKE}}(\kappa)$ the maximum advantage over all PPT adversaries $\mathcal{A}$. We say that $\mathsf{LAH\text{-}AKE}$ is untraceable if this advantage is negligible (in κ).

A.3   Proof of Untraceability (Theorem 3)

It is well known that blind Schnorr signatures (see Figure 3) offer unconditional blinding [18,17]. In fact the two blinding values α and β as used in the AddUser protocol act as one-time-pad encryption in $\mathbb{Z}_q$ and therefore offer perfect secrecy. It follows directly that the group authority of G cannot learn any information about id or id.cred as established by an AddUser protocol session. Therefore, the probability that for a given pseudonym id_b in $\mathsf{Game}^{\mathrm{trace},b}_{\mathcal{A},\mathsf{LAH\text{-}AKE}}(\kappa)$ an Untraceability adversary $\mathcal{A}$ can output $b = b'$ is strictly the probability of a random guess, i.e. $1/2$. Hence our LAH-AKE protocol offers unconditional untraceability, i.e. we have

$$\mathsf{Adv}^{\mathrm{trace}}_{\mathcal{A},\mathsf{LAH\text{-}AKE}}(\kappa) = 0 \qquad \text{(for all } \kappa\text{)}$$

Observe that Handshake sessions are completely independent of the user running them and depend solely on the deployed pseudonym id and membership credential id.cred. Even a Corrupt(id) query does not reveal the owning user of the given id.

Preventing Active Timing Attacks in Low-Latency Anonymous Communication
(Extended Abstract)

Joan Feigenbaum[1,*], Aaron Johnson[2,**], and Paul Syverson[3,***]

[1] Yale University
Joan.Feigenbaum@yale.edu
[2] The University of Texas at Austin
ajohnson@cs.utexas.edu
[3] Naval Research Laboratory
syverson@itd.nrl.navy.mil

Abstract. Low-latency anonymous communication protocols in general, and the popular onion-routing protocol in particular, are broken against simple timing attacks. While there have been few proposed solutions to this problem when the adversary is active, several padding schemes have been proposed to defend against a passive adversary that just observes timing patterns. Unfortunately active adversaries can break padding schemes by inserting delays and dropping messages.

We present a protocol that provides anonymity against an active adversary by using a black-box padding scheme that is effective against a passive adversary. Our protocol reduces, in some sense, providing anonymous communication against active attacks to providing a padding scheme against passive attacks.

Our analytical results show that anonymity can be made arbitrarily good at the cost of some added latency and required bandwidth. We also perform measurements on the Tor network to estimate the real-world performance of our protocol, showing that the added delay is not excessive.

1 Introduction

Anonymous communication protocols are designed primarily to allow *users* to communicate with *destinations* anonymously. They face, however, the challenge of optimizing over several competing criteria: anonymity, latency, and bandwidth. High latency and limited bandwidth are unacceptable for many popular Internet applications, and onion routing [12], despite its vulnerability to correlation attacks, has become a successful protocol for anonymous communication on

---

* Supported in part by NSF grants 0331548 and 0716223 and IARPA grant FA8750-07-0031.
** Supported by NSF grant 0716223.
*** Supported by ONR.

M.J. Atallah and N. Hopper (Eds.): PETS 2010, LNCS 6205, pp. 166–183, 2010.

the Internet. To design a useful protocol, we focus on providing better anonymity than onion routing while maintaining acceptable latency and bandwidth.

Low-latency protocols in general have been vulnerable to several attacks based on the timing of events in the system. Typically, the user in these protocols chooses a set of *routers* to mediate between the user and the destination, forwarding data between the two and obscuring their relationship. The essential problem is that timing patterns in these data are conserved between the source and destination. Therefore an adversary only needs to observe the incoming *stream* of data (the consecutive messages exchanged during a communication session), from the user and the outgoing stream of data to the destination to use patterns to link the two. In a *passive* timing attack, an adversary relies on timing patterns that are generated by the user. Because the user creates these patterns, he can prevent this attack by adding dummy packets and delays into the stream to make his traffic look similar to the traffic of other users [27]. However, the adversary can defeat this by performing an *active* attack, in which he inserts timing patterns into the traffic as it passes through routers under his control.

As a result of this sort of active attack, existing low-latency anonymity protocols do not provide anonymity when the adversary controls the routers that the user communicates with directly and the routers that the destination communicates with directly. Suppose the adversary controls a fraction b of the network. In onion routing, users select routers uniformly at random, and the adversary compromises anonymity with probability b^2.

This probability is fixed and cannot be improved by trading off performance elsewhere, and it can be quite insufficient. Consider Tor [7], the popular implementation of onion-routing and the associated volunteer network. In Tor, a user sends a message over a sequence of routers he sets up in advance called a *circuit*. Suppose the adversary runs just two routers. If we take into account the way Tor chooses circuits, the size of the network [28], and the number of users observed on Tor in one day [17], we expect the adversary to compromise 15 users at least once in that day. If the adversary provides the top two routers by bandwidth, the expected number of compromised users increases to 9464.[1] Thus, the system

---

[1] Roughly, circuits are selected in Tor as follows: the first hop is chosen from a set of *guard* routers, the second hop is chosen from the entire network, and the third and final hop is chosen from a set of *exit* routers. As of April 2010, the Tor network consists of around 1500 routers, of which around 250 are guard routers and around 500 are exit routers. Suppose that the adversary runs one guard router and one exit router. McCoy et al. observed 7571 unique clients while running a guard router for one day. The expected number of these that would lose anonymity is $7571/500 = 15.142$. Moreover, Tor weights by bandwidth, and so suppose that the adversarial routers are the top two by bandwidth. McCoy et al. observed that the top 2% of routers transported about 50% of the traffic. Then, very roughly, the probability of choosing the adversary in a guard set would increase from $1/250$ to $.5/(250*.02)$, and so the expected number of users observed would be $25*7571=189275$. By similar rough approximation, for every circuit, the adversary's exit router would be selected with probability $.5/(500*.02)=.05$, and so the expected number of deanonymized users would be $189275*.05=9463.75$.

provides poor anonymity against a wide variety of realistic opponents, such as governments, ISPs, and criminals willing to purchase the use of botnets.

We consider the very weak anonymity provided by low-latency protocols against an active adversary to be a fundamental and critical challenge in anonymous communication. In this paper, we present a low-latency protocol that provides arbitrarily good anonymity against an adversary that can observe and create timing patterns. The protocol makes black-box use of a padding scheme to prevent passive timing attacks. Several padding schemes that defeat passive timing attacks have been proposed [27,25,30], and furthermore we believe that there is still potential for substantial improvement. The protocol provides two-way stream communication.

A two-way protocol requires different defenses, depending on the direction of communication, because of an asymmetry in the communication between the user and destination. The user can talk directly to many routers and will add padding correctly. We will require that the destination communicate with just one router, and that router can't be trusted to pad the stream correctly. As a result, our protocol uses a somewhat different scheme for traffic on the way *from* the user as on the way *to* the user. The essential features of our solution are

1. Packets have timestamps with their intended send time.
2. Packets from the user to the destination are sent in several copies over a *layered mesh* topology . This balances limiting view of the stream to a small number of routers while providing redundancy against malicious delays.
3. Packets from the destination to the user are sent over a path that performs in-stream padding.

For simplicity, we describe forming the layered mesh as a *cascade*: a fixed arrangement of routers that all users use to send data. The biggest drawback to using cascades is that the resource constraints of the cascade routers obviously limit the number of feasible users and therefore limit anonymity. Another drawback is that cascades make long-term intersection attacks easier because only two known endpoints need to be watched. Giving users freedom to choose the meshes, analogous to *free routes*, is an important future extension to our scheme.

We evaluate the anonymity provided by our protocol in a network model that incorporates timing and an active adversary. The theoretical results suggest that the approach has good asymptotic efficiency and that a promising next step is to optimize within the framework of the scheme we describe. Moreover, because we are concerned with eventual practicality, we do measure a component of the system over which we have no control and which could have made our protocol unusable, delay variations in the host network. Specifically, we measured the likely latency costs of running our protocol on the existing Tor [7] network. This provides a strenuous, real-world scenario to evaluate our protocol's performance.

Our results are therefore a mix of the theoretical and experimental:

1. We show that the user can be made anonymous with arbitrarily high probability as long as b is less than $1/2$. The user is anonymous within the set of users with identical traffic patterns as produced by the input padding scheme.

2. We prove that our mesh topology in the forward direction is optimal for anonymity in a limit sense.
3. The latency of our protocol is proportional to the length of the mesh and return path. We show that the probability of compromise decreases to zero polynomially in that length. This compares well with onion routing, which adds latency proportional to its path length.
4. The bandwidth used is $2w + (l-1)w^2 + 1$, where l is the mesh/path length, and $w = \Theta(\log l)$. This compares well asymptotically to the $l+2$ copies that are sent in an onion-routing path of the same total length.
5. For most of our measurements, we observe that added packet delay would need to be less than a factor of two to achieve satisfactory reliability.

The results suggest that our approach indeed has the potential to mitigate active timing attacks. Our results are presented here without proofs and detailed measurement procedures because of space limitations. Please see our Technical Report [9] for these details.

2   Related Work

Timing attacks are a major challenge in low-latency anonymous communication [16]. They have been observed in some of the earliest low-latency systems [1], including initial versions of onion routing [12]. These attacks are also closely related to traffic analysis in mix networks [24].

In a passive timing attack, the adversary observes timing patterns in a network flow, and then correlates them with patterns in other traffic that it observes. If the adversary is able to observe both the user and the destination, he can thereby link the two. The ability of the adversary to perform this correlation has been experimentally demonstrated several times [32,16,23,21,2].

A solution to passive timing attacks is to get rid of identifying patterns in the traffic by padding and delaying it. The drawbacks to such an approach are added latency and bandwidth overhead. Our protocol relies on the existence of some acceptable and effective padding scheme. Constant-rate padding, in which traffic is sent at a constant rate by filling in the gaps with dummy packets, is probably the most obvious such scheme. It has appeared multiple times in the literature [27,11,16]. Levine et al. [16] propose a "defensive dropping" mechanism which adds dummy packets at the start of the circuit and drops them at various routers before the end. This reduces the correlation between any patterns in the incoming streams and patterns in the outgoing streams. Shmatikov and Wang [25] propose a variable-rate padding scheme. In their scheme, packets from the user are forwarded with little delay, and dummy packets are added by the intermediate routers according to a probability distribution on the packet inter-arrival times. Wang et al. [30] describe a link-padding scheme for low-latency systems, but their system is designed for a situation in which the adversary is not active and the destination participates in the protocol. This situation does not reflect the kind of Internet communications that have proven useful and that we target.

All of these schemes are vulnerable to an adversary that actively delays packets from the user. Yu et al. [31] show that this can be done in a way that makes it difficult for the user or the system to detect that the attack is occurring. One approach to this problem is to change the timing patterns within the network by adding, dropping, or delaying packets ([25,16]). However, dropping or delaying packets can't hide very long delays without adding unacceptable latency or bandwidth overhead. Adding dummy packets can, in our case, be detected by the final router, and therefore do not help. A final router can detect them because, in our case, the destination does not participate in the protocol; there must be one last router in the system that provides the point of contact to the destination. Moreover, Wang et al. [29] experimentally show that many such schemes for internal traffic shaping are still vulnerable to an active timing attack.

Simply delaying packets that pass directly through adversarial routers isn't the only active timing attack that has been demonstrated. Murdoch and Danezis [20] show that in onion routing the adversary can actively add delay patterns to the data by sending bursts of traffic through a router. This can be used to determine the routers on a given circuit. Fu et al. [10] describe how the presence of a flow on a router can also be determined by ping times to the router. Borisov et al. [4] look at the case that the adversary doesn't just delay, but drops packets in a denial-of-service (DoS) attack aimed at forcing users to move to circuits that the adversary can deanonymize. Such an attack was also discussed by Dingledine et al. [8]. We do not address such attacks in this paper, and they are outside of our model.

A related timing attack by Hopper et al. [13] uses congestion to exploit different network latencies between hosts. They show that the latencies from multiple hosts to a user can be very identifying. The user in our protocol communicates with several routers as a first hop, and in light of this attack we took care not to allow the adversary to infer these latencies.

One key feature of our protocol is the use of a layered mesh to provide redundancy. The use of redundancy for several purposes has been also explored in previous protocols. Syverson [26] suggests using router "twins," pairs of routers that share the same key, to provide a backup in case a router fails. Two redundancy schemes to manage failures, K-Onion and Hydra-Onion, are proposed by Iwanik et al. [14]. Redundancy to support failure is not our goal, and such schemes are in some ways complementary to our own. However, the redundancy in our protocol does protect against honest node failures as well as malicious ones. Nambiar and Wright [22] use redundancy in the host lookup of Salsa to protect against route capture. Interestingly, an analysis by Mittal and Borisov [19] of this technique uncovers the tradeoff between preventing active and passive attacks that we face as well.

Another critical feature of our protocol is the use of explicit timing to coordinate the users and routers. This is similar to the timing instructions of Stop-and-Go mixes [15]. Such mixes are given a time window within which the packets must arrive, and they delay forwarding by an exponentially-distributed amount of time. Although the techniques are similar, this scheme is designed for mix networks and not stream communication, and this scheme does give the adversary some slack time within which a timing signature could possibly be placed. Moreover, the lack of any redundancy means that any slowdowns within the network, even of benign origin, can quite easily kill a connection.

The timing approach we take is also similar to the use of synchronicity in mix networks by Dingledine et al. [8]. They describe synchronous batching on free routes and show that it typically provides better anonymity than cascades. Our scheme can be viewed as low-latency synchronous batching.

3   Model

We will express and analyze our anonymity protocol in a model of network and adversary behavior. A particular advantage of this approach is the ability to make convincing guarantees of security when we cannot predict the tactics that an adversary will use.

3.1   Network

Let the network consist of a set of onion routers R, a user population U, and a set of destinations D. The network is completely connected, in that every host can send a message directly to every other host. Each event in the network occurs at some global time. We assume that each user and router has a local clock that accurately measures time, and that these clocks have run some sort of synchronization protocol [18]. Let δ_{sync} be the largest difference between two synchronized clocks in the network.

There is some probabilistic network delay $d_{net}(r, s)$ between every pair (r, s) of routers. This models the unpredictable delay between routers due to factors such as route congestion and route instability. There is also some probabilistic processing delay $d_{proc}(r)$ at every router r. This reflects changes in delay at a router due to local resource contention among anonymous messages and among multiple processes. The delay of a message is the sum of delays drawn independently from these two distributions. We also let the delay of one message be independent of the delays of the other messages. We assume the distributions of both sources of delay is known to the system. In practice, this may be achievable via network measurements.

We assume that all hosts (in particular, all destinations) respond to a simple connection protocol. One host h_1 begins the connection by sending to another host h_2 the pair $< n, M >$, where $n \in N^+$ is a number and M is a message. Any responses M' from h_2 are sent back as $< n, M' >$. Once established, connections in the anonymity protocol cannot be closed by anyone to prevent distinctions of one from another by open and close times. All connections thus stay open for a fixed amount of time and then close automatically. Application connections running over these can of course be closed by the ultimate source and destination; although this will not close the anonymity circuit, and padding messages will continue to be sent until connection timeout.

3.2   Users

User communication drives the operation of the anonymity network. We view the communication of a user as a sequence of connections. Each connection is to one destination, and it includes messages to and from the destination. 'User' refers to both human users and software running on their behalf.

3.3   Adversary

The adversary controls some subset $A \subseteq R$ of the routers, where $b = |A|/|R|$. It seems plausible that an adversary can run routers that are at least as fast as the other routers on the network, and that it may dedicate them to running the protocol. Therefore, in contrast to non-adversarial routers, we pessimistically assume that the adversary has complete control over the processing delay $d_{proc}(a)$ of routers $a \in A$. If needed, we reflect compromise of links between routers by the compromise of an adjacent router.

3.4   Padding Scheme

The padding scheme $\mathcal{P}$ is a black box that initially takes as input a connection start time and outputs the timing of the return traffic. Then every time step it takes the presence of data from the user and returns whether or not a packet should be sent. Note that this requires the scheme to determine in advance the length of the connection. Let S_u be the set of users that start connections at the same time as user u and have the same traffic pattern. Our proposed protocol relies on the effectiveness of the padding scheme. At best, it makes u indistinguishable within the set S_u supplied by $\mathcal{P}$.

Some of the padding schemes previously proposed in the literature can provide the black box $\mathcal{P}$. For example, to use basic constant-rate padding, in which packets get sent at constant rate in both directions, we simply need to choose a fixed length for the connection when it starts. This approach typically causes high added latency and/or message overhead, however. As another example, the padding scheme of Shmatikov and Wang [25] could be used by fixing the connection length and return scheme. In this padding scheme, inter-packet delays are sampled from a distribution, which is adjusted if a packet arrives early. Dummy packets are sent after the sampled delay, and real packets from the user are sent immediately. In the direction from the user, this scheme could be used directly. In the return direction, we could just skip shifting the distribution for early packets. Then we would send each return router the same sequence of random bits to use in sampling the distribution. Alternatively, we could relax our requirements for the return scheme and allow it to be updated periodically. The user could then use the forward mesh to update the distribution of packet arrival times.

It is not hard to conceive of novel padding schemes that might satisfy these requirements, although getting a good mix of anonymity and performance certainly does not seem easy.

4   Problem

The problem in this model is to design an anonymity protocol that supports the low-latency, two-way, stream communication that has made Tor [7] popular. In order to allow communication with hosts that are ignorant of the protocol, we require that only one host communicates with the final destination, and that the communication is only the original messages generated by the user. We evaluate our protocol by three criteria: anonymity, latency, and the amount of data transferred. We evaluate the anonymity in our protocol according to its *relationship anonymity*, that is, the extent to which it prevents an adversary from determining which user-destination pairs are communicating. For latency, we consider the amount of time it takes for a message to reach the destination from a user. For the amount of data transferred, we consider the total amount of data that to be transferred during a single user connection.

5   A Time-Stamping Solution

The padding scheme gives us sets of users that have traffic streams with identical timing patterns. However, the model we have described gives the adversary the ability to modify these patterns as the traffic travels through its routers towards the destination. To prevent this, we try to enforce the desired timing pattern on packets sent by including the times that the routers should forward them. Any honest node that receives the packet will obey the instructions, removing any delays inserted by the adversary. For traffic sent from the user to the destination we can trust the user to correctly encode the padding-scheme times. Traffic sent from the destination to the user must, by our requirements, pass initially through a single router. Because it may be compromised, we cannot trust it to use a proper padding scheme. However, this traffic is destined for an anonymity-protocol participant, the user; therefore, unlike traffic from the user, we can destroy inserted timing patterns by re-padding it all the way to the user. Observe that re-padding does not work for traffic from the user, because the final router sees which packets are real and which are padding.

5.1   From the User

First, consider what we could do if propagation and processing delays were deterministic. The user could send through a path in the network a layered data structure called an *onion* which, for each packet, includes in the ith layer the time that the onion should arrive at the ith router. Then each router on the path could unwrap the onion to make sure that the initial timing sequence was being preserved and, if so, forward the onion.

Unfortunately, in real networks, delays are somewhat unpredictable. For example, an onion might be delayed by congestion in the underlying network. However, if the distribution of delays is known, we know how long we need to wait at a router for onions to arrive with any fixed probability. We will set that probability to balance decreasing added latency with decreasing the chance of a successful timing attack. Then we add in this buffer time to the send time.

Another problem is that the adversary could drop onions entirely in a pattern the propagates down the path. Our approach to this problem is to send multiple copies of an onion down redundant, intersecting paths. A router on a path needs only one copy of the onion to arrive in time from any incoming path in order to forward it by its send time.

This approach has limits, because each redundant router adds another chance for the adversary to observe an entire path from source to destination. For example, suppose that we simply send onions over k paths of length l that intersect at a final router, where every router is chosen uniformly at random. Let b be the fraction of routers that are controlled by the adversary. The probability that at least one path is entirely composed of compromised routers is $b(1 - (1 - b^{l-1})^k)$. This quickly goes to b as k increases. We use a layered-mesh topology to balance the ability of the adversary to passively observe a path with his ability to actively perform a timing attack.

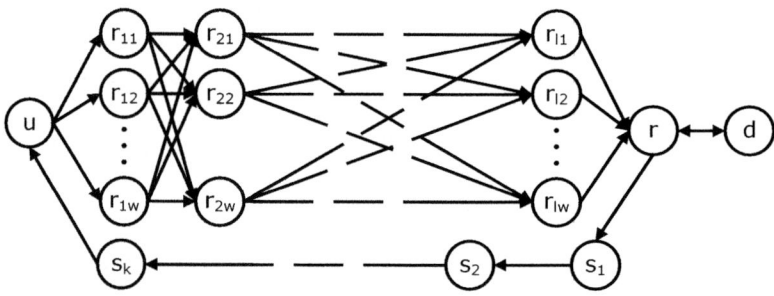

Fig. 1. Layered-mesh topology

Topology. The layered-mesh topology we propose is pictured in Figure 1. For some length l and width w, user u sends a copy of each onion to the w members r_{1j} of the first layer. Then, in layer i, each router r_{ij} sends one copy of every onion it receives to each router $r_{(i+1)k}$ of the next layer. Finally, the routers r_{lj} in the last layer send a copy of each onion received to a single router r, which finishes decrypting them and sends the data on to the destination d. We call this structure the *layered mesh*.

Timestamps. As described, the user sets timestamps to instruct routers to maintain a specific timing pattern. A user may have different latencies to the different routers in the first layer. If the time that one of these routers is instructed to forward the packet only depended on the network and processing delays of that router, the first-layer routers could send copies of the same packet at different times. This would provide information to the next layer about the identity of the user. Similarly, the adversary could use different times between layers to link other layers in the mesh. Therefore, we set the send time for each layer to be the send time of the previous layer plus the longest delay at our chosen reliability level p. We must also add some extra delay to allow for clock skews.

Let $d^*(r, s)$ be the amount of delay we need to ensure that a packet from r is processed at s with success probability p:

$$p = Pr[d_{net}(r, s) + d_{proc}(s) \leq d^*(r, s)].$$

At time t, let user u be instructed by $\mathcal{P}$ to send a message. The user chooses the same send time for all routers in the same layer. The send time for routers r_{1j} in the first layer is

$$t_1 = t + \max_j d^*(u, r_{1j}) + \delta_{sync}.$$

The send time for routers r_{ij} in the ith layer is

$$t_i = t_{i-1} + \max_{j,k} d^*(r_{(i-1)j}, r_{i,k}) + \delta_{sync}.$$

If a router receives its first copy of an onion after the send time has passed, it immediately forwards the onion to the routers in the next layer. At worst, the delay is the result of attempts by the adversary to delay certain packets. Sending the packet later or not at all in that case would only make it easier for the adversary to observe its lateness later in the mesh. Forwarding it immediately might even allow the onion to eventually get back on schedule. At best, the delay is just a result of network delays and forwarding has no effect on anonymity.

Onions. Let M be the message to be sent. We will encrypt the message with a public key shared by all members of a layer. Given that the layers are set up in advance and known to all, such a key can be generated by a trusted third party or by electing a leader to do it. Let $\{M\}_{r_i}$ denote the encryption of M with the public key of layer i. Let $n_{r_i}, n_{s_1} \in \mathbb{N}$ be random numbers and k_r be a private key. Then the onion that u sends to the routers in layer 1 is

$$\{n_{r_1}, t_1, \{n_{r_2}, t_2, \cdots \{n_r, d, n_{s_1}, k_r, M\}_r \cdots \}_{r_2}\}_{r_1}$$

For each layer i, a user generates the random number $n_{r_i} \in \mathbb{N}$ as an onion identifier. The routers keep track of the onion identifiers they have seen. When they receive an onion, they decrypt it and examine the identifier. Routers only forward an onion if its identifier n_i has not been seen before. n_{s_1} is the identifier that r should use with s_1 when sending back any reply, and k_r is a private key that will let r encrypt the return message for u.

The onion encoding and forwarding scheme should hide routing information, prevent forgery, prohibit replay attacks, and hide message content. For clarity of presentation, we have described a simple scheme that achieves this. We observe, however, that several improvements to the protocol could be made. For example, the protocol could do a more explicit stream open and close to reduce the lists of identifiers that routers have to maintain. Also, symmetric keys could be exchanged to speed up onion processing. Another improvement that we could incorporate is forward secrecy. Numerous cryptographic details must be carefully set out (*e.g.* as in [5]) for our protocol to have a cryptographically secure and efficient implementation. These are not the focus of this paper.

5.2   To the User

Traffic returning to the user from the destination must first pass through the one router that is selected to communicate directly with the destination. This router may be compromised, and it may try to insert timing patterns in the return traffic. We manage this by giving the intermediate routers the pattern of the return traffic. They enforce it by fitting the return onions into the pattern, adding dummy packets when necessary. We note again that this doesn't work for the traffic from the user because any added delays translate into delays in the underlying data, and this can be viewed by the final router. We choose a simple path of length k for the return traffic (Fig. 1), because there is no anonymity advantage to adding redundancy here. We call this structure the *return path*.

   To communicate the desired traffic pattern to the return path, we take advantage of the one-way communication protocol already developed. The user takes the return traffic pattern that is given by the padding scheme $\mathcal{P}$ and sends it via the layered mesh to every router in the return path. At the same time, the user generates the random numbers $n_{s_i} \in \mathbb{N}, 1 \leq i < k$, and sends two random numbers $n_{s_i}, n_{s_{i+1}}$ and a key k_{s_i} to each router s_i. The numbers will be the incoming and outgoing identifiers for the onion. The user also sends n_k and u to s_k. Let M be the message to be sent back from d to u. The return onion sent to s_i is

$$O_i = < n_{s_i}, \{ \cdots \{ \{ M \}_{k_r} \}_{k_{s_1}} \cdots \}_{k_{s_{i-1}}} > .$$

After r receives M from d, it will take n_{s_1} and k_r out of the inbound onion from the user and send O_1 to s_1. When s_i receives O_i it looks for a matching n_{s_i} in the pairs of number it has received and then forms O_{i+1} to send when the padding scheme instructs it to.

5.3   Choosing the Routes

A simple method to select the layered mesh and return path is for it to be chosen by the network and shared among all users. This is analogous to cascades in mix networks [3]. A disadvantage of cascades is that number of users that can be confused with one another, *i.e.*, the size of the anonymity set, is at most the number of users that can simultaneously be handled by a router [8]. Allowing users to choose the cascades with some freedom should allow anonymity sets to grow with the size of the network, similar to free routes in onion routing, but we leave this to future work.

6   Analysis

The purpose of our protocol is to provide better anonymity than onion routing at reasonable cost in latency and bandwidth. A major drawback to onion routing is that the probability of compromise is b^2 and cannot be improved, *e.g.* by choosing a longer path. We will show how in fact our scheme can provide arbitrarily good probability by increasing the length and width of the layered mesh.

First, the design of the protocol onions essentially limits the adversary to traffic analysis. For traffic from the user, the use of encryption and unique identifiers forces onions to be passed through the required layers and limits them to being forwarded by an honest router at most once. It also hides the source and destination from all but the first and last routers, and it makes messages leaving one layer unlinkable to messages leaving another layer. For traffic to the user, the source and destination are not included in the packets, and encryption prevents messages leaving one router from being linked with messages leaving another router.

For the adversary to break a user's anonymity, then, he will need to either observe traffic on an entire path between source to destination or link traffic at different steps on that path. The latter depends on his ability to introduce delays in the packet stream. To evaluate this possibility, we will make the simplifying assumption that the network and processing delay between two routers r, s never falls above the time allowed for it $d^*(r, s)$. In our model, such failures can happen with probability $1 - p$, where p can be set arbitrarily close to 1. Certainly, if the adversary can deanonymize a user even under this assumption, he can do so with possible link failures. When such failures do occur, they open up the chance for an adversary to successfully delay packets and insert a timing pattern. However, late packets are typically irrelevant because the same packet will have been forwarded by another router in the previous layer. Also, late packets that are the first of their type to arrive are immediately forwarded, thus benign delays are somewhat self-correcting, and we estimate that they do not open up a large opportunity for an active timing attack. However, if we wish to make a conservative estimation, we can expect that for any given packet a fraction $1 - p$ of the packet copies will fail to arrive in time. We can estimate the combined probability of malicious or benign delay or dropping of packets by $(1 - p) + b$.

Assuming no link failures, then, the anonymity of a user only depends on which routers the adversary controls. Because all users on the same cascade use the same routers, the adversary can either deanonymize all users in the anonymity set S_u, or he can not deanonymize any of them. Because the routers in the cascade are selected randomly, there is some probability that the adversary can deanonymize the users. Let $\mathcal{C}$ be the event that the adversary can compromise anonymity. We can quantify the probability of $\mathcal{C}$.

Theorem 1

$$Pr[\mathcal{C}] = b^{k+1} + b(1 - b^k)\left[b^w \frac{1 - (1 - (1 - b)^w - b^w)^l}{b^w + (1 - b)^w} + (1 - (1 - b)^w - b^w)^l\right]$$

Theorem 1 shows that, when less than half of the routers are compromised, we can make the probability that a user is anonymous arbitrarily high by setting w, l, and k large enough. (Recall that all proofs are in our technical report [9].)

Corollary 2

$$\lim_{w,l,k \to \infty} Pr[\mathcal{C}] = \begin{cases} 0 & b < 1/2 \\ 1/4 & b = 1/2 \\ b & b > 1/2 \end{cases}$$

Corollary 2 shows that anonymity can be made arbitrarily good when $b < 1/2$, but that it is worse than onion routing when $b \geq 1/2$. Therefore assume from now on that $b < 1/2$. We would like to determine how big the layered mesh and return path grow as we increase our desired level of anonymity. First, we will consider how wide the mesh must be for a given depth to achieve optimal anonymity. This affects the number of messages that need to be sent. Also, it will allow us to evaluate anonymity as a function of the lengths k and l, quantities which we would like to keep small to provide good latency. Luckily, it turns out that the optimal width w^* grows slowly as a function of l.

Theorem 3. $w^* = O(\log(l))$

Thm. 3 shows that the total number of messages sent for every message from the user is $O(2\log(l) + (l-1)\log(l)^2 + 1)$. This compares well asymptotically to the $l + 2$ copies that are sent in an onion-routing path of the same total length.

Network users are particularly sensitive to latency, and each additional step in the layered mesh and return path represents a potentially global hop on our network. To keep the lengths l and k of the mesh and return path small, then, we would like for $Pr[\mathcal{C}]$ to converge quickly to its limit. As suggested by Thm. 3, let $w = \log l$, and consider the convergence of $Pr[\mathcal{C}]$. It is clear that the first term shrinks exponentially with k. The convergence time of the second term is polynomial, although it does improve as b gets smaller.

Theorem 4. Let $c_1 = \log b$ and $c_2 = \log(1 - b)$. Then

$$Pr[\mathcal{C}] = \Theta(l^{c_1 - c_2}).$$

Table 1 compares the performance of our mesh topology to that of onion routing using some reasonable parameter values. In it, we let both the mesh length and the onion-routing-path length be l, we let the length of the return path from the mesh equal the mesh length (*i.e.* $k = l$), and the width w of the mesh is set to optimize

Table 1. Mesh routing vs. Onion routing

			Mesh		Onion Routing	
b	l	w	$Pr[\mathcal{C}]$	Msgs.	$Pr[\mathcal{C}]$	Msgs.
.05	3	3	.0002	29	.0025	8
.05	4	3	.00003	39	.0025	10
.1	4	3	.0007	39	.01	10
.25	4	2	.0303	22	.0625	10

anonymity. We use small values of l to make the number of hops close to the three hops that have proven to be usable in the current Tor system. The numbers show clear decreases in the probability of compromise when using the mesh, especially with larger values of l. We can see that larger compromised fractions b will require somewhat longer paths for significantly improved anonymity. The total number of messages sent in each scheme for every message-response pair between the user and destination is also given.

Our analysis shows how our scheme can provide arbitrarily good probability for $b < 1/2$. Is it possible to improve this to include values of b greater than $1/2$? First, we observe that some other plausible topologies do not perform as well. For example, suppose the user sends onions to k routers, each of which forwards it to the same next router, and then from then on there is a path to the destination. The probability that anonymity is compromised in this situation is $b^2(1 - (1 - b)^k + b^{k-1}(1 - b))$. As k grows, the anonymity goes to b^2, the probability that the second-layer router and final router are both compromised. As another example, consider using a binary tree, where the user sends to the leaves of the tree, and each node forwards to its parent at most one copy of the onions it receives. It can be shown that as the depth of the tree increases the probability that anonymity is compromised goes to zero when $b \leq 1/4$, $b(4b - 1)$ when $1/4 \leq b \leq 1/2$, and b when $b \geq 1/2$.

The following theorem shows that the layered mesh is optimal in the limit among all topologies.

Theorem 5. *Let $c(b)$ be the probability of anonymity compromise in some forwarding topology when the fraction of adversarial routers is b. Then, if $b < 1/2$, $c(b) < \epsilon$ implies that $c(1 - b) > 1 - b - \frac{1-b}{b}\epsilon$.*

Theorem 5 implies that if the probability of compromise for a topology goes to zero for $b \in [0, \beta]$, then it must go to b for $b \in [1 - \beta, 1]$. This is achieved by the layered-mesh topology for the largest range of b possible, $[0, 1/2)$.

7   Latency Measurements

Our protocol requires routers to hold messages until a specified send time. Latency between routers varies, and therefore this send time must be set high enough to guarantee that with sufficiently high probability that it occurs after the packet actually arrives. The amount of time that packets spend being delayed before the send time depends on the variability of latency. Because network performance is critical to realizing effective anonymous communication [6], we wish to evaluate the latency in our protocol.

In order to do so, we have measured latency in the Tor [7] network. Performance data in the Tor network gives us reasonable estimates for the performance of our protocol because the essential router operation in both protocols is decrypting and forwarding packets and the network is globally distributed and therefore includes a wide variety of network and host conditions.

7.1   Methodology

During each experiment, we made three measurements on all Tor routers from our test host. First, we measured *round-trip time* (*RTT*) by opening TCP connections to the hosts. Second, we measured the *connection delay*, that is, the time between sending the stream-open request to the router and receiving the

TCP connection from the router, by creating a circuit from our test host to the router and opening a TCP stream over that circuit from the router back to the test host. Third, we measured *packet delay* by sending five 400-byte segments of data up the established TCP stream.

We took measurements hourly in the Tor network from February 22, 2009, to March 21, 2009.

7.2   Results

Round-trip times for the experiments are shown in Figure 2(a), with the top 1% removed to show the rest in greater detail. The mean of these times is 161ms and the median is 110ms. We see a peak bin centered at 100ms. A histogram of all the connection delays measured is shown in Figure 2(b), with the top 5% of delays removed. It shows that nearly all delays are less than 1s. Also, we can see that the distribution is bimodal, with peaks at about 120ms and 860ms. The connection delays over time for a one such router - *b0b3r* (193.221.122.229) - is shown in Figure 2(c). The clear and uniform timing stratification suggests a cause other than varying Internet-route congestion or host-resource contention. We believe that this is due to read/write rate-limiting that Tor servers manage by periodically filling global token buckets. We can use the RTT and connection delay measurements, assuming they are independent, to estimate the distribution of host processing delays. Considering the distribution over all routers, there is almost a 40% probability of having a processing delay of nearly zero. Thus

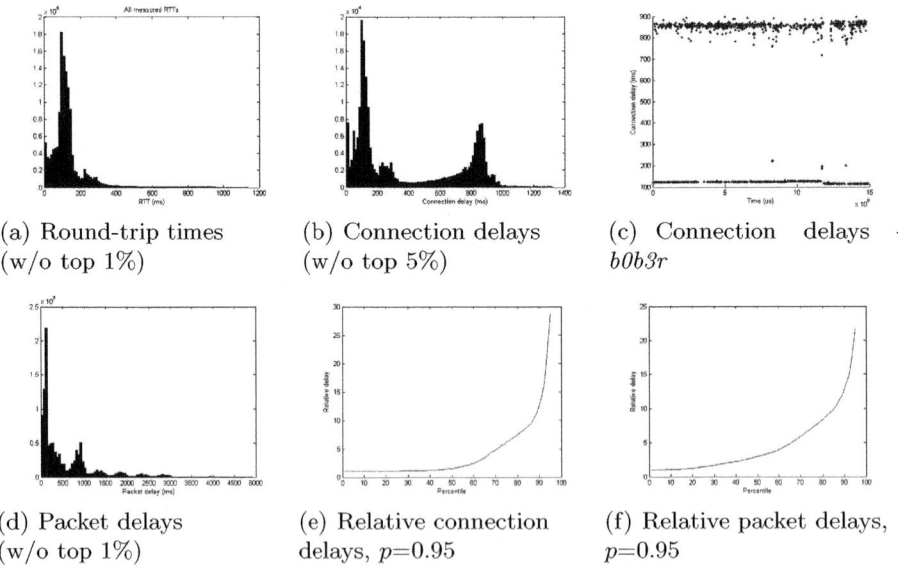

(a) Round-trip times (w/o top 1%)   (b) Connection delays (w/o top 5%)   (c) Connection delays - *b0b3r*

(d) Packet delays (w/o top 1%)   (e) Relative connection delays, $p=0.95$ (f) Relative packet delays, $p=0.95$

Fig. 2. Measurement results

processing delays are due to limited resources at the routers and not to inherent costs of the protocol.

The delays of the 400-byte packets that were successfully forwarded is shown in Figure 2(d). We again see times that cluster around certain levels. Here, there are six obvious levels. If we examine the delay time series of individual routers we see that again the different levels are interleaved. Thus, this phenomenon is probably due to the same mechanism underlying the similar pattern in connection delays.

From the delay measurements we can estimate the added delay that would have resulted from our protocol. The protocol chooses a time t that must elapse from the time the packet is originally sent before the packet is forwarded. It is set such that with some success probability p the packet arrives at the forwarding router in less than t time. In our data, we examine the tradeoff that varying t sets up between the fraction p of packets that arrive in time and the forwarding delay that gets added to them.

We divide the delay measurements by router and into 6 hour periods. Within each period, to achieve success probability p we set the send time t to be the smallest value that is larger than at least a fraction p of delays. We look at the relative increase in delay, *i.e.*, the total new delay divided by the original delay.

The distribution over all successfully-opened streams of relative connection delays to achieve a success probability of 0.95 is shown in Figure 2(e). At the 50th percentile, the relative connection delay is less than 1.48. Also, at the 50th percentile, we observe a failure rate of less than 0.005. The data for relative packet delays appears in Figure 2(f). At the 50th percentile, the relative packet delay is just over 2.95. The failure rate stays below 0.005 until the 99th percentile. The reason for this is that packet sends are not even attempted when the connection fails.

8   Future Work

There are several developments that fit within our approach and have to potential to make it truly useful and effective. Foremost among these is to design and evaluate a usable padding scheme, with large anonymity sets and low overhead. It should also allow a predetermined, or perhaps only periodically updated, return padding scheme. Also, we have avoided for now optimizing the efficiency of processing at the routers. Onion routing, in particular, has developed good techniques to make this aspect of the protocol fast. For example, we could use persistant circuits to speed up detecting duplicate packets, or we could switch to private keys. Our analysis could be improved in some areas as well. First, we could consider the positive effect of forwarding late packets immediately. Understanding this process better could improve the expected anonymity of the protocol. Also, Tor is not optimized for latency, and therefore understanding its resource congestion issues would help us better determine the added latencies of our protocol.

References

1. Back, A., Möller, U., Stiglic, A.: Traffic analysis attacks and trade-offs in anonymity providing systems. In: Moskowitz, I.S. (ed.) IH 2001. LNCS, vol. 2137, pp. 245–257. Springer, Heidelberg (2001)
2. Bauer, K., McCoy, D., Grunwald, D., Kohno, T., Sicker, D.: Low-resource routing attacks against Tor. In: Proceedings of the 2007 ACM Workshop on Privacy in Electronic Society (WPES 2007), pp. 11–20 (2007)
3. Berthold, O., Pfitzmann, A., Standtke, R.: The disadvantages of free MIX routes and how to overcome them. In: Designing Privacy Enhancing Technologies, International Workshop on Design Issues in Anonymity and Unobservability, pp. 30–45 (2000)
4. Borisov, N., Danezis, G., Mittal, P., Tabriz, P.: Denial of service or denial of security? In: Proceedings of the 14th ACM Conference on Computer and Communications Security (CCS 2007), pp. 92–102 (2007)
5. Camenisch, J., Lysyanskaya, A.: A formal treatment of onion routing. In: Shoup, V. (ed.) CRYPTO 2005. LNCS, vol. 3621, pp. 169–187. Springer, Heidelberg (2005)
6. Dingledine, R., Mathewson, N.: Anonymity loves company: Usability and the network effect. In: 5th Workshop on the Economics of Information Security, WEIS 2006 (2006)
7. Dingledine, R., Mathewson, N., Syverson, P.: Tor: The second-generation onion router. In: Proceedings of the 13th USENIX Security Symposium, pp. 303–320 (2004)
8. Dingledine, R., Shmatikov, V., Syverson, P.: Synchronous batching: From cascades to free routes. In: Martin, D., Serjantov, A. (eds.) PET 2004. LNCS, vol. 3424, pp. 186–206. Springer, Heidelberg (2005)
9. Feigenbaum, J., Johnson, A., Syverson, P.: Preventing active timing attacks in low-latency anonymous communication. Technical Report TR-10-15, The University of Texas at Austin (2010),
ftp://ftp.cs.utexas.edu/pub/techreports/TR-1965.pdf
10. Fu, X., Graham, B., Bettati, R., Zhao, W.: Active traffic analysis attacks and countermeasures. In: 2003 International Conference on Computer Networks and Mobile Computing (ICCNMC 2003), pp. 31–39 (2003)
11. Fu, X., Graham, B., Bettati, R., Zhao, W.: Analytical and empirical analysis of countermeasures to traffic analysis attacks. In: Proceedings of the 2003 International Conference on Parallel Processing, pp. 483–492 (2003)
12. Goldschlag, D.M., Reed, M.G., Syverson, P.F.: Hiding routing information. In: Anderson, R. (ed.) IH 1996. LNCS, vol. 1174, pp. 137–150. Springer, Heidelberg (1996)
13. Hopper, N., Vasserman, E.Y., Chan-TIN, E.: How much anonymity does network latency leak? ACM Transactions on Information and System Security 13(2), 1–28 (2010)
14. Iwanik, J., Klonowski, M., Kutylowski, M.: DUO–onions and hydra–onions – failure and adversary resistant onion protocols. In: Communications and Multimedia Security: 8th IFIP TC-6 TC-11 Conference on Communications and Multimedia Security, pp. 1–15 (2004)
15. Kesdogan, D., Egner, J., Büschkes, R.: Stop-and-go-MIXes providing probabilistic anonymity in an open system. In: Aucsmith, D. (ed.) IH 1998. LNCS, vol. 1525, pp. 83–98. Springer, Heidelberg (1998)

16. Levine, B.N., Reiter, M.K., Wang, C., Wright, M.K.: Timing attacks in low-latency mix-based systems (extended abstract). In: Juels, A. (ed.) FC 2004. LNCS, vol. 3110, pp. 251–265. Springer, Heidelberg (2004)
17. McCoy, D., Bauer, K., Grunwald, D., Kohno, T., Sicker, D.: Shining light in dark places: Understanding the Tor network. In: Borisov, N., Goldberg, I. (eds.) PETS 2008. LNCS, vol. 5134, pp. 63–76. Springer, Heidelberg (2008)
18. Mills, D.: Network time protocol (version 3) specification, implementation. RFC 1305, Internet Engineering Task Force (March 1992)
19. Mittal, P., Borisov, N.: Information leaks in structured peer-to-peer anonymous communication systems. In: Proceedings of the 15th ACM Conference on Computer and Communications Security (CCS 2008), pp. 267–278 (2008)
20. Murdoch, S.J., Danezis, G.: Low-cost traffic analysis of Tor. In: 2005 IEEE Symposium on Security and Privacy (SP 2005), pp. 183–195 (2005)
21. Murdoch, S.J., Zieliński, P.: Sampled traffic analysis by internet-exchange-level adversaries. In: Borisov, N., Golle, P. (eds.) PET 2007. LNCS, vol. 4776, pp. 167–183. Springer, Heidelberg (2007)
22. Nambiar, A., Wright, M.: Salsa: a structured approach to large-scale anonymity. In: Proceedings of the 13th ACM Conference on Computer and Communications Security (CCS 2006), pp. 17–26 (2006)
23. Øverlier, L., Syverson, P.: Locating hidden servers. In: 2006 IEEE Symposium on Security and Privacy (SP 2006), pp. 100–114 (2006)
24. Raymond, J.-F.: Traffic analysis: Protocols, attacks, design issues, and open problems. In: Federrath, H. (ed.) Designing Privacy Enhancing Technologies. LNCS, vol. 2009, pp. 10–29. Springer, Heidelberg (2001)
25. Shmatikov, V., Wang, M.-H.: Timing analysis in low-latency mix networks: Attacks and defenses. In: Gollmann, D., Meier, J., Sabelfeld, A. (eds.) ESORICS 2006. LNCS, vol. 4189, pp. 18–33. Springer, Heidelberg (2006)
26. Syverson, P.: Onion routing for resistance to traffic analysis. In: Proceedings of the 3rd DARPA Information Survivability Conference and Exposition (DISCEX-III), vol. 2, pp. 108–110 (2003)
27. Syverson, P., Tsudik, G., Reed, M., Landwehr, C.: Towards an analysis of onion routing security. In: Federrath, H. (ed.) Designing Privacy Enhancing Technologies. LNCS, vol. 2009, pp. 96–114. Springer, Heidelberg (2001)
28. TorStatus - Tor network status (April 2010), http://torstatus.kgprog.com/
29. Wang, X., Chen, S., Jajodia, S.: Network flow watermarking attack on low-latency anonymous communication systems. In: 2007 IEEE Symposium on Security and Privacy (SP 2007), pp. 116–130 (2007)
30. Wang, M.M.W., Srinivasan, V.: Dependent link padding algorithms for low latency anonymity systems. In: Proceedings of the 15th ACM Conference on Computer and Communications Security (CCS 2008), pp. 323–332 (2008)
31. Yu, W., Fu, X., Graham, S., Xuan, D., Zhao, W.: DSSS-based flow marking technique for invisible traceback. In: 2007 IEEE Symposium on Security and Privacy (SP 2007), Washington, DC, USA, pp. 18–32 (2007)
32. Zhu, Y., Fu, X., Graham, B., Bettati, R., Zhao, W.: On flow correlation attacks and countermeasures in mix networks. In: Martin, D., Serjantov, A. (eds.) PET 2004. LNCS, vol. 3424, pp. 207–225. Springer, Heidelberg (2005)

Impact of Network Topology on Anonymity and Overhead in Low-Latency Anonymity Networks

Claudia Diaz[1], Steven J. Murdoch[2], and Carmela Troncoso[1]

[1] K.U. Leuven/IBBT, ESAT/SCD-COSIC
firstname.lastname@esat.kuleuven.be
[2] Computer Laboratory, University of Cambridge, UK
Steven.Murdoch@cl.cam.ac.uk

Abstract. Low-latency anonymous communication networks require padding to resist timing analysis attacks, and dependent link padding has been proven to prevent these attacks with minimal overhead. In this paper we consider low-latency anonymity networks that implement dependent link padding, and examine various network topologies. We find that the choice of the topology has an important influence on the padding overhead and the level of anonymity provided, and that Stratified networks offer the best trade-off between them. We show that fully connected network topologies (Free Routes) are impractical when dependent link padding is used, as they suffer from feedback effects that induce disproportionate amounts of padding; and that Cascade topologies have the lowest padding overhead at the cost of poor scalability with respect to anonymity. Furthermore, we propose an variant of dependent link padding that considerably reduces the overhead at no loss in anonymity with respect to external adversaries. Finally, we discuss how Tor, a deployed large-scale anonymity network, would need to be adapted to support dependent link padding.

1 Introduction

Anonymous communication systems protect the privacy of their users by hiding who is communicating with whom. These systems support applications with strong privacy requirements such as e-voting protocols, intelligence gathering (e.g., law enforcement agents infiltrated in criminal organizations) or high security military communications. Additionally, anonymous communication systems help individuals in difficult situations (e.g., journalists who must protect their sources) and provide privacy for ordinary people seeking to protect themselves from unwanted eavesdropping. The importance of such systems is increasing, and the largest deployed anonymity network, Tor [6], has attracted an estimated 250 000 users.

Many network services, such as web-browsing or online chat, require low-latency communication to remain usable. Low-latency anonymous communication networks are vulnerable to timing analysis, which can be performed by a

M.J. Atallah and N. Hopper (Eds.): PETS 2010, LNCS 6205, pp. 184–201, 2010.

passive adversary to find correlations between streams and uncover communication partners [10,12]. Furthermore, an active adversary can trace communications by embedding a 'watermark' on the packet flow by delaying, dropping or adding packets to influence these timings [9,24].

A common solution to thwart timing analysis is the use of padding, i.e., dummy packets indistinguishable from (encrypted) real data. In this paper we consider Dependent Link Padding (DLP), a variant of padding in which the amount of dummy traffic generated at the output of a node depends on its input traffic.

We examine low-latency anonymous communication networks that implement DLP. We find that the topology of the network has a strong influence on both overhead and anonymity. Cascade networks introduce the lowest overhead, but at the cost of poor scalability in terms of anonymity. Fully connected networks (Free Routes) offer high anonymity, but suffer from feedback effects that cause huge overhead. Stratified networks are the best anonymity vs. overhead trade-off. Of all topologies, this provides the best level of anonymity, and its overhead is much lower than Free Routes. We introduce a restricted variant of the Stratified topology that further reduces the overhead at almost no cost in anonymity. Moreover, restricted topologies have better scalability.

In anonymity networks, connections between two routers are commonly encrypted and carry multiple data flows. We propose Reduced Overhead Dependent Link Padding (RO-DLP), a variant of dependent link padding that takes advantage of this property. RO-DLP provides the same level of protection as DLP towards external adversaries – who can observe communications but do not control any router – while substantially reducing the overhead. In the case of Stratified topologies the overhead factor is reduced from 27 using DLP to 8 using RO-DLP, and in its restricted version the reduction is from 23 to just 1.5.

Finally, we argue that, while the onion routing network protocol used by Tor supports padding, it is not compatible with DLP. We outline the modifications that are needed for supporting dependent link padding, and discuss their practical implications.

The remainder of the paper is organized as follows: we give an overview of anonymous communications, padding, and anonymity metrics in Section 2. Our system and adversary models are presented in Section 3. Section 4 introduces RO-DLP, our variant of dependent link padding. Section 5 describes our experimental setup, and we present the results in Section 6. We discuss the applicability of dependent link padding to Tor in Section 7. Finally, we conclude in Section 8.

2   Background and Related Work

Low-latency Anonymous Communications. Goldschlag, Reed, and Syverson introduced *onion routing* in 1996 [8], and a second generation protocol [6] has been implemented in the Tor network. Onion routing is designed to provide a bidirectional, low-latency anonymous communication channel that can be used for applications like web browsing. Onion routers perform cryptographic operations on the data they relay, so that the relationship between input and output data packets cannot be inferred from analyzing their content. The feasibility for delaying and reordering packets in onion routing is however limited by latency constraints, and therefore incoming and outgoing packets may be linked in these systems by means of timing analysis or end-to-end correlation attacks [10].

An important property of a multi-hop anonymity network is the *network topology*. One approach is Cascades, as adopted by AN.ON/JonDo [1], where clients select one out of several entry routers, but after that point the path through the remaining routers is fixed. An alternative is Free Routes, as adopted by Mixmaster [11], Mixminion [4], and Tor [6], where all routers in the network are connected to each other. Intermediate solutions have also been proposed, such as Restricted routing topologies based on expander graphs [3], or Stratified networks [7]. Dingledine *et al.* [7] showed that the topology of a high-latency anonymity network has a significant impact on traffic analysis resistance, reliability, scalability, and resistance to compromise. However, neither Cascades nor Free Routes have been shown to be conclusively superior, and the issue has long been a matter of debate [2].

Padding to Resist Timing Analysis. Let us consider a low-latency onion routing network that carries data flows of variable rate. To satisfy quality of service requirements, packets cannot be delayed too much, or dropped. Therefore, to conceal the relationship between incoming and outgoing flows, *dummy traffic* (padding) must be added to the data flows. Data packets leaving each node are augmented by *dummy packets* which the adversary cannot distinguish from (encrypted) real data packets. In addition, the start and end time of the flows must be obscured to prevent traffic analysis attacks based on correlating the timing of these events [12]. This can be achieved by synchronizing session start and end between all clients [13].

With respect to the rate of the padding, research in this field has centered on *Independent Link Padding* (ILP,) where all flows in the network are padded to a pre-arranged rate [13,19,21]. Because the timing and rate of packets in outgoing flows is not dependent on the timing and rate at the input, an adversary cannot correlate inputs and outputs. These padding strategies are however impractical if the traffic flows being routed by the network are bursty (e.g., web traffic), as any lulls would need to be filled with padding, at the same rate as the maximum throughput.

A more promising approach is *Dependent Link Padding* (DLP.) As with ILP, all traffic flows leaving a router are at the same rate, so as to provide timing analysis resistance. However, unlike ILP, this rate is different for each router, and it is a function of the traffic it is routing. This approach permits the amount of padding to be reduced, because when there is no input traffic, no output traffic needs to be generated. Similarly, bursts of traffic are permitted, and the burst is transmitted on all outputs.

An algorithm for performing DLP, whilst guaranteeing a maximum latency Δ at each node, and minimizing the amount of padding, was independently discovered by Venkitasubramaniam and Tong [22] and Wang *et al.* [23]. Their algorithm is to, when a packet is received at time t, check whether a padding packet has been scheduled to be transmitted on the corresponding outgoing link. If it is, the padding packet is replaced with the real packet. If not, the real packet is scheduled at time $t + \Delta$ and padding packets are scheduled at the same time on all other outgoing links. In this way, no packet will be delayed for more than Δ and the scheme is optimal (as proven in [23]) in that it achieves mixing with the minimal amount of padding.

Besides packet timing, it is also important to consider other properties of padding schemes, such as the source and destination of padding, and which entities can distinguish dummy packets from real ones. Several variants have been proposed in the literature to address different trust and adversary models. For example, ISDN Mixes [13] use dummy traffic only in the link between the initiator and the local exchange, which discards the dummy packets, and assumes that at least one router in the path is honest. Partial-route padding and defensive dropping [10,19] propose that dummy traffic be generated by the initiator and dropped by intermediate routers – and consider that some routers in the path may be malicious.

In both adaptive padding [18] and DLP schemes [22,23], dummy packets are generated by intermediate routers, instead of the initiator. Subsequent routers cannot distinguish these dummy packets from (encrypted) real packets, and thus they are routed all the way to the end recipient, who discards them. The padding schemes in [18,22,23] consider trusted recipients and resist adversaries who compromise a subset of the routers.

Anonymity Metrics. By observing – or actively attacking – an anonymous communication system, the adversary typically obtains a probability distribution linking the initiator of a communication to all possible recipients, and vice versa. Then, one can use *Shannon entropy* [17] (or simply "entropy") as a measure of the adversary's uncertainty on who is the initiator (or recipient) of a communication [5,16].

The analysis presented by Wang *et al.* [23] studied a single-node network, which offers high anonymity but no resistance to router compromise, low resilience to failures, and poor scalability. The anonymity provided by a single node is straightforward to compute with the metrics in [5,16]: in a single-hop network routing C circuits, the probability of an initiator corresponding with each recipient is uniformly distributed, and anonymity is maximum (the entropy of the distribution is $\log_2(C)$.) Venkitasubramaniam and Tong [22] did examine multi-hop networks, but considered only the "information leaked by the timing of packets within a flow." "Anonymity" as defined in [22] is assumed to be maximum when the timing of packets does not leak any information – as is the case when dependent link padding is implemented.

Computing the anonymity of communications in complex networks while taking into account all information available to the adversary is infeasible to do analytically [15], as it requires enumerating all possible combinations of internal states in the routers, as well as initiator-recipient relationships. Previous comparisons of network topologies [7] avoided this problem by simplifying the analyzed scenario – e.g., assuming that the load on each internal link within the network is exactly equal to the statistically expected load given a particular network topology. The Markov Chain Monte Carlo methodology recently proposed in [20] is based on sampling possible internal states and initiator-recipient correspondences that satisfy all constraints. This allows the efficient estimation (for a given confidence interval) of the adversary's probability distribution, taking into account all the available information. The model in [20] considers high-latency threshold mix networks. We note that the adversary's observation of a low-latency anonymity network that implements DLP, and has synchronous starts and ends of connections, is equivalent to that of a high-latency network made of threshold mixes. Therefore, the methodology can be used without major modifications to extend the analysis in [22] to consider routing constraints.

3   Model

System Model. We consider an anonymity system based on onion routing that implements dependent link padding and has synchronous starts and ends of connections. For simplicity, we assume that the path length of circuits is always three and require that all three routers in the path are distinct, but we note that our analysis is generalizable to other routing constraints [20].

When a client wishes to make a request, the system works as follows. First, it constructs a route selecting three routers (*nodes*) from the list of all available nodes, subject to topology constraints. It then connects to the first node (*entry,*) and exchanges keys to form an encrypted tunnel. Over this encrypted tunnel, the client connects to the second node (*middle,*) and then the third node (*exit,*) exchanging keys at each point such that each node knows the previous and next hops, but no more.

The connection through the three nodes, along with the corresponding keys, is known as a *circuit.* Once the circuit is established, the client requests that the last node creates a *stream* to carry the application data. Data is packaged into fixed length *cells* which are subsequently encrypted under the keys shared with the recipient, exit, middle, and entry nodes, and sent to the entry node. At each hop, one layer is removed until the recipient finally decrypts the payload. Note that DLP requires that the recipient be able to decrypt data cells, and to discard the dummy cells that have been added to the stream.

Multiple circuits may be carried on the *link* between any given pair of nodes. In addition to the circuit-level cryptography, which is end-to-end, there is also hop-by-hop link-level cryptography protecting the traffic between nodes. An external adversary will therefore not be able to tell, based on content, whether two cells correspond to the same circuit or to different ones.

Attacker Model. We assume that the adversary is *global*: it observes traffic on all communication links and knows the number of circuits routed over each of them. Furthermore, the adversary is *active*, and may introduce, delay, or drop cells. We note that DLP [22,23] protects against active attacks, as all streams coming out of a node are identical – e.g., if the adversary deploys traffic watermarking attacks [9,24], then all outgoing streams will carry the watermark.

Throughout the analysis, we also assume that all nodes are trustworthy, and thus the adversary is *external* and has no knowledge of node keys or other internal state information.

Note that denial of service attacks, long-term disclosure attacks, attacks involving corrupted nodes, and attacks on other protocol layers (e.g., dropping cells to force end-to-end retransmissions,) are not considered in this paper and left as a subject of future work.

4   RO-DLP: Reducing Padding Overhead in DLP

In the original DLP proposals [22,23], nodes pad every outgoing circuit in the same way, independently of whether or not some circuits are being multiplexed over the same link. In anonymity networks however, nodes typically use link encryption, which hides the correspondence of cells to circuits within a link. In this section we present the *Reduced Overhead Dependent Link Padding* (RO-DLP) algorithm.[1] Compared to simple DLP, RO-DLP reduces the amount of dummy traffic sent over links that multiplex several circuits, while achieving the same level of security against global external adversaries that do not control nodes.

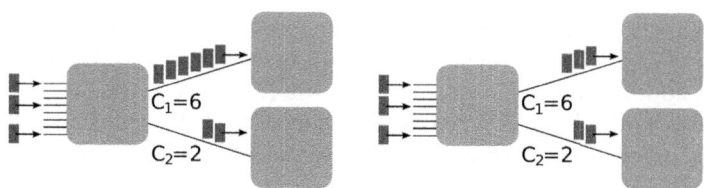

Fig. 1. Original DLP (left) and RO-DLP (right)

The goal of link padding is to prevent the adversary from learning the correspondence between incoming and outgoing circuits. Given that at time t the node forwards R_t cells, we show that it is enough to send R_t cells over links that contain a number c_i of circuits that is larger than R_t.

Let us consider a node n that routes C circuits over L links (note that $L \leq C$,) and let c_i denote the number of circuits multiplexed over the same link l_i ($1 \leq i \leq L$, and $\sum_{i=1}^{L} c_i = C$.) Initially, RO-DLP schedules a cell for each of the C outgoing circuits, as in DLP. Thus, at time t a set of C cells are scheduled, of which R_t correspond to cells that are being forwarded, and $C - R_t$ are dummy cells generated by node n. RO-DLP removes r_i dummy cells from link l_i as follows:

---

[1] We note that the term "Link Padding" has been used in the past [6] to mean padding that exists only on a single link and is not relayed to other nodes. In this paper, we use the terminology introduced by Wang et al. [23] where Dependent Link Padding refers to padding that, once generated, travels along the path until the end destination.

$$r_i = \begin{cases} 0 & \text{if} \quad c_i \leq R_t \\ c_i - R_t & \text{if} \quad c_i > R_t \end{cases}$$

The intuition behind this algorithm is the following. The adversary monitors the number of cells arriving at node n and can predict the number R_t of cells that will be forwarded at time t. When $c_i > R_t$ cells are sent over link l_i, the adversary knows that (at least) $c_i - R_t$ of these are dummy cells generated by n, and thus these do not provide any additional protection.

Consider a node that routes eight circuits over two outgoing links, such that $c_1 = 6$ and $c_2 = 2$, as shown in Figure 1. If only one cell is to be forwarded at time t (i.e., $R_t = 1$,) it is enough to send one cell on each of the outgoing links for the adversary to gain no information on the destination of the forwarded cell. One of the two cells sent will be the real cell, and the other will be a dummy cell going on one of the circuits of the other link. If, as in the example shown in the figure, three real cells are to be sent (i.e., $R_t = 3$,) then no padding can be removed from l_2, but we can still save three dummy cells in link l_1. From the perspective of the adversary, no additional information is leaked on the destination of the forwarded cells, compared to the case in which six cells are sent over l_1: in both cases, it could be that the three circuits for which there is a cell are routed over l_1, that one is routed over l_1 and two over l_2, or that two are routed over l_1 and one over l_2.

Note that if each link contains only one circuit, then no dummies can be removed and RO-DLP's overhead is the same as DLP's [22,23]. If all circuits going through a node are routed over one single link (e.g., in a Cascade topology,) then no dummies would be sent by that node and RO-DLP would not generate any overhead. In Section 6.3 we present an evaluation of the reduction in overhead when RO-DLP is used with real traffic streams.

5   Experimental Setup

We have implemented a simulator to evaluate the anonymity and dummy traffic overhead in anonymity networks that implement dependent link padding. Our simulator generates networks of N nodes, where N is an input parameter. Users create circuits that traverse three nodes before reaching their destination. We call *entry node* the first node in the circuit path, *middle node* the second, and *exit node* the third and last node. We consider four possible topologies, shown in Figure 2:

– **Free Routes (FR):** Any combination of three distinct nodes is a valid circuit path. Given an entry node, we choose, uniformly at random, a middle node from the remaining $N-1$ nodes, and an exit node from the remaining $N-2$ nodes.
– **Stratified (S):** Nodes are divided into entries, middle nodes, and exits ($N/3$ nodes in each category,) such that any entry connects to any middle, and any middle to any exit. Given an entry node, we choose uniformly at random one of the $N/3$ middle nodes, and one of the $N/3$ exits.

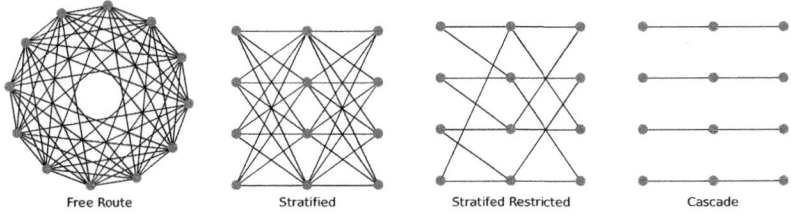

Fig. 2. Network topologies for $N = 12$

- **Stratified Restricted (SR):** As in the previous case, nodes are divided
  into entry, middle and exit nodes. We have chosen values of N of the form
  $N = 3K^2$, where K is an integer. Each entry node is connected to $K =
  \sqrt{N/3}$ middle nodes, and each middle node to K exits. An entry node i
  $(0 \leq i \leq N/3 - 1)$ is connected to middle nodes $N/3 + [(i + j) \mod N/3]$,
  with $j = 0 \ldots K - 1$; and a middle node i $(N/3 \leq i \leq 2N/3 - 1)$ is connected
  to exit nodes $2N/3 + [(i + j \cdot K) \mod N/3]$, with $j = 0 \ldots K - 1$. Given an
  entry node we construct the circuit paths choosing uniformly at random one
  of the $N/3$ exits, and then finding the middle node that connects the entry
  to the exit (in this topology each entry is connected to each exit by exactly
  one middle node.) The intuition behind this topology is to allow every entry
  node to connect to any exit node, while minimizing the number of links.
- **Cascades (C):** We consider $N/3$ parallel cascades of three nodes each.
  Given an entry node, the middle and exit nodes are fixed by the topology.

To make our evaluation as realistic as possible, we use as input real traffic data
logged by a deployed Tor [6] node for a period of 24 hours. In particular, we have
logged a timestamp and a circuit identifier[2] for each cell routed by the node. We
consider *sessions* of 60 seconds – i.e., we divide the input into slices of 60-seconds
duration, and assume that the traffic of sessions sufficiently separated in time is
independent. We take into account both the forward and the backward traffic
(i.e., requests and responses) in the bi-directional circuits that appear in that
session.

We consider that the comparison of network topologies is fair when both individual nodes, as well as the network as a whole, carry the same amount of traffic,
and we design our experiments in such a way that this condition is fulfilled. In
the Stratified and Cascade topologies, we feed each of the $\frac{N}{3}$ entry nodes with
the traffic of a session, with that node as first in the path, and the remainder of
the path selected according to the network topology constraints. In Free Routes
we follow a slightly different approach in order to keep the comparison fair: we
distribute the circuits of a session among three entries. In this way, both individual nodes and the overall network route the same amount of real traffic as in the

---

[2] To anonymize the logs, the circuit ID and peer IP address were encrypted on collection, under a key which was discarded after logging was completed. This dataset
will be made available by the authors upon request.

other topologies. In Stratified and Cascade networks, nodes route (on average) C circuits either as entry, middle or exit node, and the total number of circuits in the network is $C_T = C \cdot \frac{N}{3}$ ($\frac{N}{3}$ is the number of entry nodes.) In Free Routes, each node routes (on average) $\frac{C}{3}$ circuits as entry (plus $\frac{C}{3}$ as middle and $\frac{C}{3}$ as exit,) and the total number of circuits is $C_T = \frac{C}{3} \cdot N$ (all N nodes are entry nodes.)

The nodes in our simulator implement the DLP and RO-DLP algorithms. We record the amount of traffic routed by the network per second, distinguishing between real and dummy traffic; and between intra-network traffic (sent between nodes) and traffic at the edge of the network (between nodes and end destinations.)

6   Results

We examine networks in terms of *anonymity loss* and dummy traffic (padding) *overhead factor*. The anonymity loss is the difference between the maximum achievable anonymity given the total number of circuits routed by the network and the actual anonymity that the network provides to its circuits. We note that when DLP is deployed, the timing of packets does not leak any information, and the anonymity provided by the system depends only on the routing constraints. Given a circuit c_x, we compute its anonymity loss as $H_{\mathrm{loss}} = H_{\mathrm{max}} - H(c_x)$. The maximum achievable anonymity is given by $H_{\mathrm{max}} = \log_2(C_T)$, where C_T is the total number of circuits routed by the network [5,16]. For Stratified and Free Route networks, $H(c_x)$ is estimated by the method presented in [20], using the obtained lower bound as our estimation. In Cascades, we compute the anonymity $H(c_x)$ of a circuit c_x routed by $\mathrm{cascade}_i$ as $H(c_x) = \log_2(C_i)$, where C_i is the number of circuits routed by $\mathrm{cascade}_i$ (note that $\sum_i C_i = C_T$.)

To present the results for the dummy traffic (padding) overhead, we use the *overhead factor*, which is computed as $\frac{Dum}{Real}$, where Dum is the number of dummy cells sent in the network every second, and $Real$ is the number of real data cells sent over the same time period. Thus, the overhead factor indicates the number of padding cells sent for each real data cell.

6.1   Feedback Effects in Free Route Networks

If dependent link padding is implemented in a Free Route network, feedback effects are likely to happen. The feedback effect occurs both with DLP and RO-DLP, and it provokes dummy traffic to be generated even in the absence of real traffic (this case leads to infinite padding overhead.) To illustrate this effect, consider two nodes routing two circuits in opposite directions, as shown in Figure 3. One real cell ■ is sent into node A, on circuit Y. This cell is relayed ⊢→ to node B. Node B will, after a delay of Δ, relay this cell onto the next hop of circuit Y, but also generate a padding cell ☐ on circuit X. When node A receives this cell, it cannot tell that the cell is padding. Thus, A sends it onto the next hop of circuit X, and also generates a new dummy cell that is sent back to B, repeating the cycle. Note that feedback loops may form not only between pairs of nodes, but also in more complex structures involving several nodes.

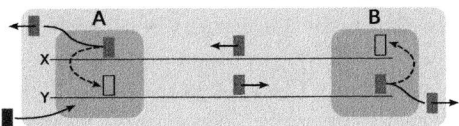

Fig. 3. Feedback loop with two nodes

Figure 4(a) compares the total traffic (number of cells per second) in a Stratified and a Free Route network that route the same input traffic (the networks have $N = 12$ nodes, route a total of $C_T = 12$ circuits, and there are 10 cells per circuit within the first 3 seconds.) Although there is no more input traffic after $t = 4$, we can see that the Free Route network continues to generate dummy traffic that quickly becomes stationary. In the Stratified network, traffic stops once the last real cell has left the network (this happens at most $3 \cdot \Delta$ seconds after it has entered, and in our case Δ is 1 second and thus the last cell leaves before $t = 7$.)

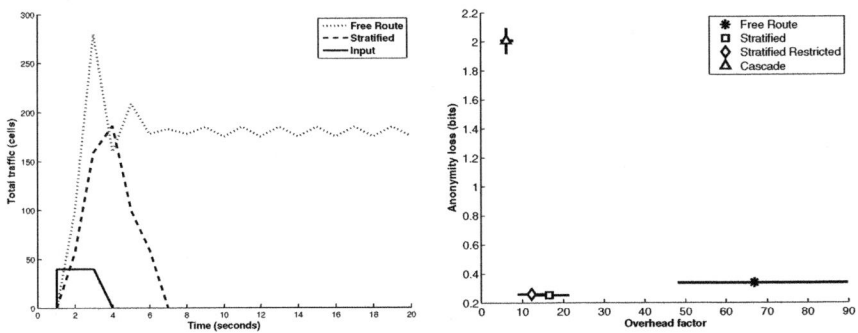

Fig. 4. Traffic in a Free Route and a Stratified network with the same input traffic (left.) Anonymity / Overhead tradeoffs for different topologies (right)

6.2   Comparison of Network Topologies

It is common for anonymity systems to offer a clear tradeoff between the level of anonymity and cost (with cost being in terms of delay and/or dummy traffic overhead,) such that more anonymity comes at a higher cost. In the scenarios considered in our analysis, the delay costs are fixed and identical for all the network topologies, and thus we focus on the tradeoff between anonymity and dummy traffic overhead.

Figure 4(b) shows the tradeoff offered by the four considered topologies in a network with 12 nodes that implement RO-DLP. The x axis shows the overhead factor (i.e., number of padding cells sent in the network for each real cell, taking into account both the traffic between nodes and the traffic in the edges of the network.) The y axis shows the anonymity loss with respect to the maximum achievable level in each of the experiments (note that the maximum depends on the total number of circuits C_T routed by the network in each experiment.) Therefore, lower values in the y axis correspond to networks that come closer to providing maximum anonymity to the circuits they are routing. The symbol at the center of the plot for each topology represents the median values for anonymity and overhead, the lines indicate the first and third quartiles. Although it is not shown in the figure, the overhead of Free Routes tends to infinity when the real traffic is very low.

As we can see in the figure, the overhead is lowest in Cascades, and it increases as more routes are possible in the network (i.e., the next best is Stratified Restricted, then Stratified, and worst is Free Route.) This is rather intuitive, as restricting the routing implies that more circuits are routed (multiplexed) over fewer links, and thus less overhead is generated by the RO-DLP algorithm. The fact that Free Routes has a much higher overhead than the other topologies is due to the feedback effects explained in the previous section.

A more interesting effect appears when we look at anonymity. *A priori*, one could expect topologies with more overhead to provide better anonymity. However, this is not the case: the best anonymity is provided by Stratified topologies (closely followed by its Restricted variant,) instead of Free Routes. In Stratified networks, circuit routes going through the same node are always mixed, because the node is in the same path hop for both routes. In Free Routes however, circuits may pass by the same node and not be mixed if the node is at a different hop in the circuit paths. Consider for example a node n that is the entry node for circuit c_a and exit node for circuit c_b. Given that routes always have three hops, the adversary knows that the circuit c_a entering the network at n cannot go out of the network immediately, and thus the outgoing c_b cannot possibly be the exit of c_a – i.e., c_a and c_b are not mixed in n.

We note that all topologies except Cascades consistently provide very high anonymity levels: the anonymity loss is less than 0.4 bits, and its variance is very small. For Cascades, the median loss is 2 bits, which corresponds to partitioning the anonymity set in four. Indeed, a network consisting of four parallel cascades partitions the total anonymity set of circuits in four subsets, with each subset being routed by a separate cascade.

Overall, Stratified topologies provide the best anonymity / overhead tradeoffs, with restrictions in the routing reducing the overhead at the cost of slightly worse anonymity. Cascades are better than Stratified topologies in terms of overhead, but this comes at a high cost in anonymity (a problem that becomes worse as the network grows, as shown in Section 6.4.) Free Routes are worse than Stratified topologies *both* in terms of anonymity as well as overhead.

6.3   Dummy Traffic Overhead with DLP and RO-DLP

In Section 4 we proposed a RO-DLP algorithm to reduce the overhead when several circuits are multiplexed over the same link. We note that multiplexing only happens in the links between network nodes, which typically carry many circuits. In our experiments, we assume that the links on the edges of the network – i.e., between nodes and external entities (initiators and responders) – carry only one circuit. Therefore, no multiplexing happens on the network edges and RO-DLP produces a similar overhead to DLP.

The boxplots[3] of Figure 5(a) show the intra-network overhead (i.e., only considering links between nodes) of RO-DLP compared to DLP. The results were obtained performing several dozens of simulation experiments on networks of 12 nodes, using real traffic as input, and having each node route the same amount of traffic as the Tor router from which the data was collected.

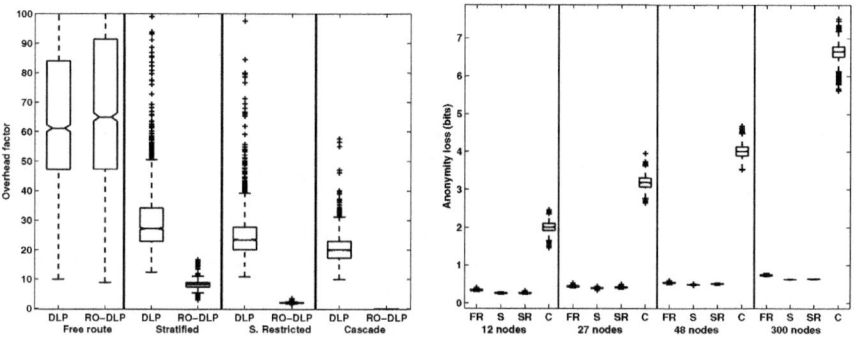

Fig. 5. Overhead (traffic on intra-network links only) of DLP and RO-DLP (left.) Network scalability vs. anonymity (right.)

In Cascades, all circuits going through a node are multiplexed over one link leading to the next node, which explains why RO-DLP reduces the intra-network overhead factor from 20 to zero (note that RO-DLP still generates padding cells on the edges, which is not shown, and thus the overall overhead is greater than zero.)

The overhead reduction of RO-DLP over DLP is rather significant in Stratified networks too. In Stratified Restricted topologies, the median overhead factor is reduced from 23 to 1.5 (i.e., from sending 23 padding cells for each real cell, to just sending 1.5 padding cells per real cell;) and in Stratified from 27 to 8. As we can see, there is a very direct relationship between the number of possible routes (i.e., amount of circuit multiplexing) and the reduction in overhead: the fewer the possible routes, the lower the overhead.

---

[3] The line in the middle of the box represents the median of the distribution of values over many experiments. The lower and upper limits of the box correspond, respectively, to the first and third quartiles of the distribution.

RO-DLP does not have a beneficial effect in Free Route topologies though. This is due to two effects. First, because Free Routes allow many more possible circuit paths, circuits are more spread over links and thus links multiplex fewer circuits. This mitigates to a large extent the benefits of RO-DLP. Furthermore, RO-DLP fails to counter the feedback effects explained in Section 6.1, because it only affects the removal of padding cells at the node where they are generated. Once these cells have been sent to other nodes, they are treated as real traffic and bounced back and forth in the network (just as in simple DLP.)

6.4 Network Scalability: Anonymity and Overhead

We have performed most of our experiments on networks of only 12 nodes, given that the simulation time of experiments on bigger networks increases rapidly with the network size. In this section we show results on how anonymity and overhead varies with the size of the network that implements RO-DLP.

Figure 5(b) shows the anonymity loss for the four topologies and network sizes of 12, 27, 48 and 300 nodes. The y axis represents the anonymity loss in these networks with respect to the maximum achievable $H_{max} = \log_2(C_T)$, where C_T is the total number of circuits routed by the network. Note that larger networks route more circuits and thus have a bigger H_{max}. We can see in Figure 5(b) that Stratified, Stratified Restricted, and Free Route topologies scale very well in terms of anonymity – their anonymity remains very close to the maximum when the network size grows. In networks of 300 nodes, the anonymity loss for any of those topologies is less than one bit.[4]

Cascade topologies however, have poor scalability in terms of anonymity. In this topology a larger network implies more parallel cascades. Given that cascades are independent of each other, they provide a constant level of anonymity, and thus a bigger anonymity loss as H_{max} increases. Consider a network consisting of N nodes and $\frac{N}{3}$ cascades, and assume for simplicity that all cascades route the same number C of circuits; i.e., the total number of circuits routed by the network is $C_T = \frac{N}{3}C$. The anonymity provided by the cascades is $H_{cascade} = \log_2(C)$, and the maximum achievable anonymity is $H_{max} = \log_2(C_T) = H_{cascade} + \log_2(\frac{N}{3})$. The anonymity loss is thus $\log_2(\frac{N}{3})$ on average; i.e., $\log_2(4) = 2$ bits for $N = 12$ nodes, $\log_2(9) = 3.17$ bits for $N = 27$ nodes, etc.

We show in Figure 6(a) and Figure 6(b) the overhead in intra-network links (that multiplex several circuits,) and at the edge of networks of 12, 27 and 48 nodes. As expected, overhead is unaffected by the growth of the network in Cascade topologies. The overhead factor remains at zero in the links between cascade nodes, as all circuits are multiplexed over a single link; and it remains constant at the network edges, as circuits routed by parallel cascades do not mix with each other: bursts in the traffic of one circuit only produce padding in the circuits going through the same cascade.

---

[4] An anonymity loss of one bit is equivalent to the adversary partitioning the anonymity set of C_T circuits in two subsets.

In the other three topologies, we can observe that network size has a negative impact on the overhead factor of the network. This is because a traffic burst in a single circuit produces a burst of dummy traffic in all other circuits, and as more circuits are routed by the network, bursts occur at a higher frequency. The overhead factor is particularly large for the traffic on the edges of the network (Figure 6(a)) because links to clients and destinations contain a single circuit, and thus do not benefit from the optimization based on circuit multiplexing. In the case of intra-network traffic (Figure 6(b),) we can see that Stratified restricted topologies manage to keep the overhead factor just over 8 when the network grows to 48 nodes – while overhead reaches 30 in Stratified networks, and over 80 in Free Routes.

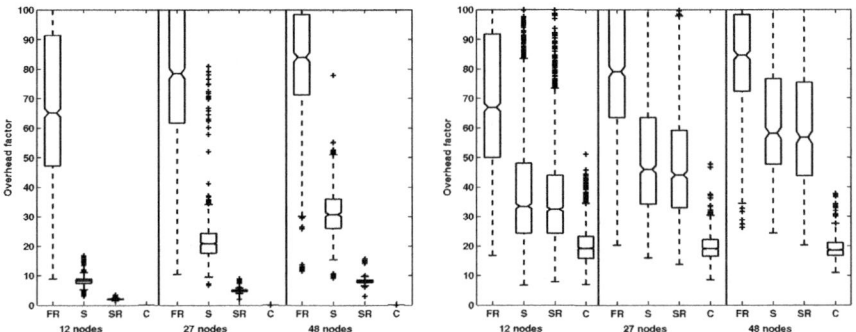

Fig. 6. Network scalability: overhead in intra-network links (left.) Overhead at the network edge right.)

7   Applying DLP to Tor

Although Tor is the most widely deployed anonymity network, it offers fairly weak protection against a global adversary, because traffic is not mixed. Tor aims to minimize latency and network load, so nodes neither add padding nor delay cells, hence it is trivial to perform timing analysis, either on an end-to-end or hop-by-hop basis. The Tor designers made these choices because latency would make interactive use intolerable, and existing ILP schemes had unacceptable overhead. However DLP, with the optimizations we have proposed in this paper, is a more promising approach.

In DLP, edge nodes need not generate padding, but they do need to consume it. Moreover, an adversary should not be able to distinguish padding from normal traffic. If we consider only internal circuits – where both the initiator and destination run the Tor software, though they do not necessarily need to route anyone else's traffic – DLP is straightforward to implement. Tor already uses internal circuits for connecting to hidden services (where the destination server wishes to hide its identity), and when the destination server is known to be running a Tor node.

It may also be possible to implement DLP without the destination being aware of Tor, provided there is end-to-end encryption and the exit node can inject padding which will be ignored by the destination. This option is more complex, because it requires that the exit node be aware of the encryption protocol. In particular, if the end-to-end encryption scheme implemented at the destination silently drops malformed packets, then it can consume padding without any changes being necessary.

Network Topology. The original Tor design was a free-route network, however for efficiency reasons it has now moved to a more complex topology. Currently only a subset of nodes can act as the entry (because they must be fast and be highly reliable), and only a subset can act as the exit (because nodes must opt in to allowing exit traffic). To balance load over the network, nodes which can neither be entry nor exit are preferentially selected as middle nodes. Strictly speaking, entry and exit nodes can be selected for the middle position, provided that there is sufficient entry and exit bandwidth, respectively. However, most of the time this is not the case and in practice Tor has a network topology very close to Stratified. For this reason, it would not be a significant change to move to a fully Stratified topology.

Implementation of Padding Modes in Tor. In order to implement DLP, it is necessary that connections between nodes are encrypted, so that an external adversary cannot tell whether two cells belong to the same circuit or different ones. Tor uses TLS for protecting both confidentiality and integrity on links, so complies with this requirement.

With respect to the creation of padding, the Tor protocol does permit dummy cells to be inserted, although the current implementation does not generate padding nor are there any plans to do so. Two types of padding cells are offered: link padding and circuit padding. However neither meet our requirements; the former is detected as padding by nodes and dropped, and the latter can only be injected by the initiator. There is no way for a node to inject a padding cell such that subsequent nodes on the path cannot distinguish it from data cells sent by the initiator.

The fundamental problem for implementing DLP in Tor is that the variant of onion routing adopted uses a stream cipher. Each Tor relayed cell contains a circuit ID that identifies which circuit the message pertains to, and an encrypted payload. On receiving such a cell, the Tor node checks if a key has been negotiated for the given circuit ID. If so, the node uses AES CTR mode to decrypt the cell with the counter being the number of ciphertext blocks seen in that circuit. Then, the node verifies whether a 32 bit digest in the cell matches the SHA-1 hash of all valid cells in the circuit.

Therefore, if a cell is injected by an intermediate node, the counter will be desynchronized, the data corrupted, and the digest check will fail. To resolve this problem, a simple addition to the Tor protocol would be another type of link padding cell which triggers a new padding cell to be emitted for the same circuit on the output link. In this way, each hop could add their own padding, which would be maintained all the way to the last hop. As links are protected using TLS, an adversary cannot distinguish padding cells from real cells, and so the goal of the padding would be maintained. In the implementation, care would need to be taken that the processing time for a padding cell would be identical to that for a real cell, to resist side-channel attacks leaking information on cell type.

This approach would resist the external adversary considered in the anonymity analysis of RO-DLP. However, in a more realistic scenario the adversary may control some routers, and any corrupt node on the path would be able to trivially tell which cells are padding. Circuit padding cannot be used to resolve this weakness because intermediate nodes cannot inject new cells. However, if instead of CTR mode, a per-cell IV was used, this problem would not exist – i.e., padding would not affect the decryption of other cells. Intermediate nodes do not know the key shared by the sender and other nodes in the path, hence the padding will fail the integrity check at the final hop and be discarded. A node would therefore be able to add padding cells with a random IV, and intermediate nodes will be unable to distinguish them from real data cells. A downside of this approach is that there is the overhead of a IV per-cell. Nevertheless, it has the advantage that there is no longer any need for a reliable transport protocol between nodes, provided there is an end-to-end error recovery mechanism. Moving from TCP to UDP for node-to-node communication has been shown to offer significant performance benefits, especially under congestion [14].

8   Conclusions and Future Work

Dependent link padding prevents timing analysis in low-latency anonymity networks while minimizing the overhead. However, the impact of complex topologies [2,7] on the performance of this technique had not yet been assessed. In this work we have analyzed anonymity / overhead trade-offs in low-latency anonymity systems that implement dependent link padding, and compared three topologies: Cascades, Free Routes and Stratified networks.

We have found that feedback effects appear in Free Route networks, leading to disproportionate padding overhead – a phenomenon not previously discussed in the literature. In contrast, Stratified networks and Cascades do not suffer from this problem, making them substantially more efficient. However, the level of anonymity provided by Cascades decreases severely when the network grows – while the other topologies maintain high anonymity, with Stratified networks being the best. We conclude that Stratified topologies offer the best trade-off between anonymity and overhead.

We have introduced a Restricted topology based on Stratified networks, which further reduces the overhead with almost no loss of anonymity. In addition, we have proposed RO-DLP, which takes advantage of circuit multiplexing in anonymity networks to reduce the amount of padding. Our experiments show that in Stratified Restricted topologies, RO-DLP reduces the overhead factor from 23 to just 1.5.

While dependent link padding is ideal for onion routing, as it offers good security without causing high latency, we have argued that the current Tor protocol cannot accommodate it. We have outlined modifications to the Tor protocol, such as moving from a per-stream IV to a per-cell IV, and discussed other applicability issues.

In this work we have assumed that all the nodes in the network are trustworthy. This is essential for RO-DLP to achieve the same level of protection against an external adversary, when compared to previous dependent link padding proposals. If the adversary has control over some of the nodes in the network [7], she would see partially padded circuits, and potentially correlate traffic based on timing analysis. Strategies for assigning padding to circuits in ways that minimize the effectiveness of this attack are left for future work.

Acknowledgements. The authors would like to thank George Danezis for early valuable discussions. C. Diaz and C. Troncoso are funded by the Fund for Scientific Research in Flanders (FWO). S. Murdoch is funded by The Tor Project. This work was supported in part by the IAP Programme P6/26 BCRYPT of the Belgian State.

References

1. Berthold, O., Federrath, H., Köpsell, S.: Web MIXes: A system for anonymous and unobservable Internet access. In: Federrath, H. (ed.) PET 2000. LNCS, vol. 2009, pp. 115–129. Springer, Heidelberg (2001)
2. Bohme, R., Danezis, G., Diaz, C., Kopsell, S., Pfitzmann, A.: Mix cascades vs. peer-to-peer: Is one concept superior? In: Martin, D., Serjantov, A. (eds.) PET 2004. LNCS, vol. 3424, pp. 243–255. Springer, Heidelberg (2005)
3. Danezis, G.: Mix-networks with restricted routes. In: Dingledine, R. (ed.) PET 2003. LNCS, vol. 2760, pp. 1–17. Springer, Heidelberg (2003)
4. Danezis, G., Dingledine, R., Mathewson, N.: Mixminion: Design of a Type III Anonymous Remailer Protocol. In: Proceedings of the IEEE Symposium on Security and Privacy, pp. 2–15. IEEE Computer Society, Los Alamitos (2003)
5. Diaz, C., Seys, S., Claessens, J., Preneel, B.: Towards measuring anonymity. In: Dingledine, R., Syverson, P.F. (eds.) PET 2002. LNCS, vol. 2482, pp. 54–68. Springer, Heidelberg (2003)
6. Dingledine, R., Mathewson, N., Syverson, P.: Tor: The second-generation onion router. In: Proceedings of the USENIX Security Symposium, pp. 303–320 (2004)
7. Dingledine, R., Shmatikov, V., Syverson, P.: Synchronous batching: From cascades to free routes. In: Martin, D., Serjantov, A. (eds.) PET 2004. LNCS, vol. 3424, pp. 186–206. Springer, Heidelberg (2005)
8. Goldschlag, D., Reed, M., Syverson, P.: Hiding routing information. In: Anderson, R. (ed.) IH 1996. LNCS, vol. 1174, pp. 137–150. Springer, Heidelberg (1996)
9. Houmansadr, A., Kiyavash, N., Borisov, N.: RAINBOW: A robust and invisible non-blind watermark for network flows. In: Proceedings of the Network and Distributed System Security Symposium (NDSS 2009). The Internet Society (2009)
10. Levine, B.N., Reiter, M., Wang, C., Wright, M.: Timing attacks in low-latency mix systems. In: Juels, A. (ed.) FC 2004. LNCS, vol. 3110, pp. 251–265. Springer, Heidelberg (2004)

11. Möller, U., Cottrell, L., Palfrader, P., Sassaman, L.: Mixmaster Protocol – Version 2. In: IETF Internet Draft (2003)
12. Murdoch, S.J., Zieliński, P.: Sampled traffic analysis by Internet-exchange-level adversaries. In: Borisov, N., Golle, P. (eds.) PETS 2007. LNCS, vol. 4776, pp. 167–183. Springer, Heidelberg (2007)
13. Pfitzmann, A., Pfitzmann, B., Waidner, M.: ISDN-MIXes: Untraceable communication with small bandwidth overhead. In: Kommunikation in Verteilten Systemen, Grundlagen, Anwendungen, Betrieb, GI/ITG-Fachtagung, pp. 451–463. Springer, Heidelberg (1991)
14. Reardon, J.: Improving Tor using a TCP-over-DTLS tunnel. Master's thesis, University of Waterloo (2008)
15. Serjantov, A.: On the Anonymity of Anonymity Systems. PhD thesis, University of Cambridge (2004)
16. Serjantov, A., Danezis, G.: Towards an information theoretic metric for anonymity. In: Dingledine, R., Syverson, P.F. (eds.) PET 2002. LNCS, vol. 2482, pp. 41–53. Springer, Heidelberg (2003)
17. Shannon, C.: A mathematical theory of communication. The Bell System Technical Journal 27, 379–423 (1948)
18. Shmatikov, V., Wang, M.-H.: Timing analysis in low-latency mix networks: Attacks and defenses. In: Gollmann, D., Meier, J., Sabelfeld, A. (eds.) ESORICS 2006. LNCS, vol. 4189, pp. 18–33. Springer, Heidelberg (2006)
19. Syverson, P.F., Tsudik, G., Reed, M., Landwehr, C.: Towards an analysis of onion routing security. In: Federrath, H. (ed.) PET 2000. LNCS, vol. 2009, pp. 96–114. Springer, Heidelberg (2001)
20. Troncoso, C., Danezis, G.: The Bayesian analysis of mix networks. In: Proceedings of the ACM Conference on Computer and Communications Security (CCS 2009), p. 11. ACM, New York (2009)
21. Venkitasubramaniam, P., He, T., Tong, L.: Relay secrecy in wireless networks with eavesdroppers. In: Proceedings of the Allerton Conference on Communication, Control and Computing (2006)
22. Venkitasubramaniam, P., Tong, L.: Anonymous networking with minimum latency in multihop networks. In: Proceedings of the IEEE Symposium on Security and Privacy, pp. 18–32. IEEE Computer Society, Los Alamitos (2008)
23. Wang, W., Motani, M., Srinivasan, V.: Dependent link padding algorithms for low latency anonymity systems. In: Proceedings of the ACM Computer and Communications Security Conference (CCS 2008), pp. 323–332. ACM, New York (2008)
24. Wang, X., Chen, S., Jajodia, S.: Network flow watermarking attack on low-latency anonymous communication systems. In: Proceedings of the IEEE Symposium on Security and Privacy, pp. 116–130. IEEE Computer Society, Los Alamitos (2007)

Drac: An Architecture for Anonymous Low-Volume Communications

George Danezis[1], Claudia Diaz[2], Carmela Troncoso[2], and Ben Laurie[3]

[1] Microsoft Research Cambridge
gdane@microsoft.com
[2] K.U. Leuven/IBBT, ESAT/SCD-COSIC
firstname.lastname@esat.kuleuven.be
[3] Google, Inc.
ben@links.org

Abstract. We present Drac, a system designed to provide anonymity and unobservability for real-time instant messaging and voice-over-IP communications against a global passive adversary. The system uses a relay based anonymization mechanism where circuits are routed over a social network in a peer-to-peer fashion, using full padding strategies and separate epochs to hide connection and disconnection events. Unlike established systems, Drac gives away the identity of a user's friends to guarantee the unobservability of actual calls, while still providing anonymity when talking to untrusted third parties. We present the core design and components of Drac, we discuss the key ways in which it challenges our current concepts of anonymity and provide an initial simulation-based security analysis.

1 Introduction

Anonymous communications are important since the addressing, timing and volume of traffic can in some cases leak as much information as its content [37]. This is particularly true for real-time communications, as instant messages or phone calls can be indicative of imminent intentions or plans, e.g. in military command and control systems, or sensitive personal information, like medical status or family life, in civilian settings. Despite this, few systems have been proposed to provide strong anonymity against global passive adversaries for private communications.

Drac aims to provide strong anonymity and traffic analysis guarantees for real-time communications. This is achieved though a peer-to-peer relay based architecture. We assume that the traffic relayed is regular or low volume such as voice-over-IP (VoIP) or instant messaging (IM) respectively. This allows us to use a traffic padding regime and destroy any information leaking from patterns of traffic. Communication sessions are started and ended synchronously to further limit the information leakage.

We also design the trust model of Drac around a friend-of-a-friend architecture: communications between friends are unobservable, and communications

M.J. Atallah and N. Hopper (Eds.): PETS 2010, LNCS 6205, pp. 202–219, 2010.

with further contacts in the network are anonymous. Despite the anonymity sets being smaller, they are harder than random anonymity sets, in that they are correlated between sessions and an adversary has to infiltrate the social circle of a user to perform insider attacks. Finally, we assume that both parties to a conversation use Drac for their communications and have incentives to stay on-line and relay third party traffic even when they are not communicating: this provides unobservability [27] and is a natural architecture to support incoming voice calls or instant messages.

The aim of this work is to introduce the Drac design and provide a preliminary analysis of anonymity and unobservability. Unobservability is an unusual property, and even defining it or measuring it in a system represents novel challenges. Three aspects of the system are studied though simulations: the anonymity provided against the presence system, and the anonymity and unobservability of communications towards a global passive adversary.

The paper is organised as follows: Sect. 2 presents previous work and building blocks used in Drac; Sect. 3 presents a high level model of Drac and its components; Sect. 4 shows the preliminary evaluation results; finally we discuss some further aspects of Drac in Sect. 5 and offer our conclusions in Sect. 6.

2 Drac and Related Work

High-latency anonymous communications were introduced by David Chaum [6], and have been implemented in deployed systems such as mixmaster [22] and later mixminion [8]. Those systems are economical in that they do not require cover traffic. On the downside, they delay communications significantly, making it difficult to have a real-time conversation as is required for IM or VoIP.

Onion Routing systems, including Tor [13], provide low latency communications for web-browsing cheaply, by sacrificing security against a global passive adversary. Yet such adversaries are realistic and can be implemented through sampling [24], indirect network measurements [23], or eavesdropping on key Autonomous Systems (AS) [15]. Web browsing loads are bursty and high-bandwidth such that any traffic padding regime would be uneconomical. IM and VoIP loads on the other hand are more regular, or simply low-bandwidth, allowing link and end-to-end padding strategies to be affordable if high security is required.

The ISDN-mix system [26] was specifically designed to provide real-time anonymous communications. As ISDN-mixes, Drac creates connections synchronously in epochs to maintain connection anonymity, but does not implement cascades and does not use the custom ISDN infrastructure to support its operation – instead we assume that the communications are taking place over IP, using off-the-shelf routers.

In this work we are not overly concerned with the cryptographic details of Drac. There exist well established, provably secure, cryptographic constructions to support relaying anonymized messages [9] and extending anonymous connections [16,18]. Similarly we assume that a padding regime is established that makes the output channels traffic statistically independent of the input channels [31,34,36]. This can be done simply by sampling a traffic schedule for the output channel independently and before even seeing the input channels, and sticking to it by adding cover traffic if there is not enough, or dropping messages if the queues become too long.

The trust model Drac uses is a version of restricted routes [7], where paths are created over friendship links. The impact of social networks on anonymity has been studied before [12], and recent work [17] has looked at modifying the global trust assumption common in contemporary anonymous channels. Yet we are the first to propose boldly making use of a social network as the backbone of anonymous paths.

Finally, the analysis we provide follows the information theoretic metrics proposed in [30,11]. The probabilistic analysis we perform is very much a first analysis of the system, as it is heuristic, and does not take into account all constraints known to the adversary. A full Bayesian analysis [32] would be required to do this, and is the subject of future work. A full analysis of the impact of long term disclosure attacks [19] is also necessary: Drac is designed to provide smaller, but harder anonymity sets, than other systems. The fact that anonymity sets of different epochs are highly correlated (as routing is embedded over a social graph) invalidates previous results and performance bounds of these attacks [25]. These models have so far assumed anonymity sets contain random users, whereas in Drac these are highly correlated and composed of the social surroundings of users.

3   The Drac System

At the core of Drac we have a social network formed by N *users* (or *nodes.*) Each user u_i in this social network is connected to a set of *friends* $\mathcal{F}_i$. We assume that friends have a strong trust relation, and that they use each other to relay communications. For this purpose, friends share cryptographic keys (or at least a weak secret to bootstrap a cryptographic key) that they can use to establish secure communication *links*. Besides communicating with her friends, a user u_i also interacts with a set of *contacts* $\mathcal{C}_i$ to whom she is not connected in the social network. Contacts are people that a user may wish to talk to, but does not necessarily trust for relaying her connections (e.g., a relationship between a patient and her doctor.) We consider that contacts exchange their pseudonyms and establish a long term symmetric key offline (e.g., the patient meets the doctor at the clinic.) Finally, we assume that relationships with friends are public, thus known to the adversary (e.g., extracted from a social network web site [3],) but that relationships with contacts are secret and must be concealed by Drac.

3.1   Establishing Communications with Drac

Upon connection to the network, a user establishes low bandwidth bi-directional *heartbeat connections* with each of her friends in order to make her availability known to them. These connection are padded at a very low rate, and are used for signaling purposes (creating and extending connections, starting communications, etc,) as well as for establishing connections with the private presence server (as explained in Sect. 3.2.) In Drac we strictly separate the control plane from the data plane: signalling and presence packets are embedded and routed in the heartbeat traffic such that an external observer cannot differentiate between dummy heartbeat packets and actual messages. Figure 1(left) shows the heartbeat connections between six users $\{u_A, \ldots, u_F\}$ in which $\mathcal{F}_A = \{u_C, u_F\}$, $\mathcal{F}_B = \{u_C, u_E\}$, $\mathcal{F}_C = \{u_A, u_B, u_D\}$, and so forth. By observing heartbeat connections, an adversary does not gain extra knowledge about users, as the friendships are considered public, and the timing and volume of heartbeat traffic does not leak any further information.

Users wish to communicate with contacts, but they are not connected to them in the network. For this purpose each u_i has an *entry point* E_i that she uses to indirectly establish communications. In each epoch users build a *circuit* of depth D to their entry points (using their heartbeat channels.) We describe the circuit creation process using the example network shown in Fig. 1:

1. User u_A selects at random one of her friends to be the first hop of the circuit. Say she chooses u_C from $\mathcal{F}_A = \{u_C, u_F\}$. They establish a secure *link* using their long-term key K_{AC}, and generate a session key k_{AC}.
2. u_A requests u_C to choose a friend at random and extend the circuit to her.
3. User u_C selects a friend at random, say u_D, and creates a new secure link using K_{CD}. Through the extended circuit, u_A and u_D establish a session key k_{AD}. As u_C chooses one of her friends at random to route u_A's traffic, it may be the case that u_A is chosen to participate in her own circuit.
4. Steps 2 and 3 are iterated D times using friends of friends as next hops in the path. The last user in the circuit is the entry point E_A of u_A. In the example above, if $D = 2$, we say that u_D is u_A's entry point E_A. As members of the circuit are chosen at random, u_A may end up being her own entry point.

We note that u_A needs to know her entry point to establish communications with contacts, and thus E_A needs to provide its identity to u_A at the end of the circuit creation process.

The circuit depth D is a security parameter of the system. Longer circuits increase the anonymity provided by Drac as they make tracing communications to their originator more difficult, while shorter circuits result in smaller anonymity sets, as shown in Sect. 4. We consider that the adversary can observe all links, and knows how many circuits are routed through each of them, but does not know the correspondences between inputs and outputs at each node.

Friends communicate with each other through direct links. To ensure that the communication is fully unobservable, both users still establish circuits of depth D in the network, but at least one of them has to choose the other as first hop. When a user u_i with entry point E_i, wants to communicate with one of her contacts u_j with entry point E_j, she requests E_i to extend the circuit to E_j. We call the connection between two entry points *bridge*, and denote it as B_{ij}. We note that bridges between users that are not friends are visible, as they stand out with respect to the edges in the underlying social network, and the heartbeat channels that the adversary observes. If the entry points of u_i and u_j are friends, an adversary can still observe that there is an extra circuit in the

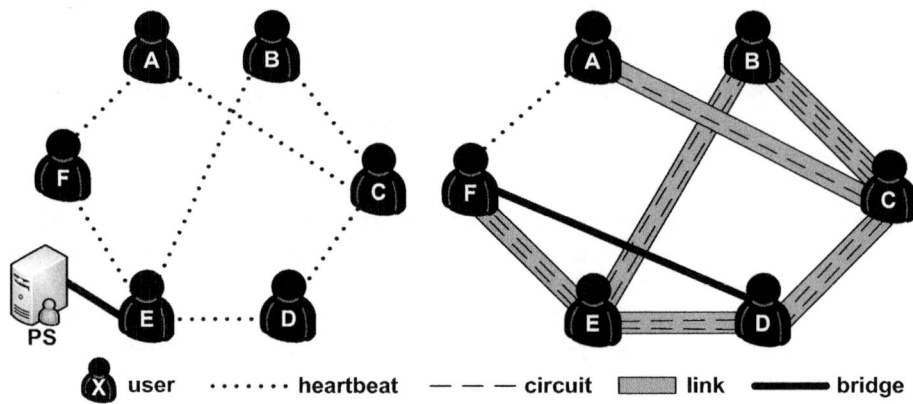

Fig. 1. Underlying social network and connection to the presence server (left.) Adversary's observation of an epoch (right.)

system. However, she cannot distinguish this bridge from other links that are part of a connection between a user and her entry point. Further, when E_i is the same as E_j, no bridge is created and an adversary cannot detect that there is a communication.

To ensure confidentiality of communications, u_i and u_j encrypt messages using the keys that they share with each other, and with the nodes that they use for transit. We denote by $\mathrm{E}_k(M)$ the encryption of message M under key k. Upon receiving a message, an intermediate node processes it using the session key shared with the originator of the message. After processing, the node checks whether the message is addressed to itself. If the result is still a ciphertext the message is relayed to the next node in the circuit, or dismissed at the last node.

Example. Let us consider that u_X talks to u_W through two of her friends u_Y and u_Z (which whom she shares session keys k_{XY} and k_{XZ} respectively,) and two of u_W's friends u_U and u_V (with whom u_W shares k_{WU} and k_{WV}.) u_X and u_W share a session key k_{XW} that they create as explained in Sect. 3.2. The route can be depicted as:

$$u_X \to u_Y \to u_Z \Rightarrow u_U \to u_V \to u_W$$

where a bridge B_{XW} has been created between u_Z and u_U.

If u_X wishes to package a message M for u_W she encrypts it under k_{XW}, k_{XZ}, and k_{XY}, and sends:

$$u_X \to u_Y : \mathrm{E}_{k_{XY}}(\mathrm{E}_{k_{XZ}}(\mathrm{E}_{k_{XW}}(M)))$$

The message gets relayed and decrypted by u_Y and u_Z. User u_Z sends to u_U $E_{k_{XW}}(M)$ through the bridge B_{XW}. Then, the message is encrypted under the keys of u_U and u_V. The following message arrives to u_W:

$$u_V \to u_W : \mathrm{E}_{k_{WV}}(\mathrm{E}_{k_{WU}}(\mathrm{E}_{k_{XW}}(M)))$$

3.2 Private Presence Server

Users can establish communications with their friends or contacts, and thus need to be reachable by them. To communicate with friends, users can use their direct heartbeat channels. For initiating communications with a contact, we require a private presence server that allows u_i to be reachable by her contact u_j. The presence server is assumed to be cooperative (i.e., follows the protocols) but untrustworthy (i.e., it could be colluding with the adversary in order to deanonymize its users.) In our scheme, we draw some ideas from the Apres [20] system, but we introduce several modifications in order to adapt it to the context of Drac. For simplicity, we only consider one presence server in this work, but we note that Drac could be trivially extended to support several servers.

Each user u_i has a long term identifier ID_i that is known by all her contacts, but not by the presence server. We note that a user u_i may have several IDs, each corresponding to a circle of contacts, so that contacts belonging to different "circles" cannot find out that they know the same user. In order to have unlinkability between time periods and avoid long-term pseudonymous profiling by the presence server, the identifier IDJ_i of u_i in a given time period T is computed as $IDJ_i = H(T, ID_i)$, where $H(x, y)$ is an HMAC of x with key y. As T is published by the presence server, u_i and her contacts are able to compute IDJ_i from her long term identifier ID_i.

In order to be reachable by her contacts, u_i creates a circuit of depth D_p (D_p may or may not be equal to D) to her presence server PS using the heartbeat channels. This presence circuit is built following the same procedure as the one used to construct communication circuits from users to entry points. When the connection is D_p hops long, u_i instructs the last node, E_{P_i}, to send the IDJ_i encrypted with the key of PS to PS. At this point, u_i has an open connection to her presence server, who can list IDJ_i as online.

In Fig. 1(left) we show the heartbeat connections in one epoch. These connections carry *presence circuits* that are unobservable to the attacker. For instance, let us consider that the presence circuit from u_A runs through users u_F and u_E. An adversary can see the bridge between u_E and PS, but cannot distinguish whether this connection comes from u_A (through u_A-u_F-u_E), u_C (through u_C-u_B-u_E or u_C-u_D-u_E), or u_E (through u_E-u_B-u_E, u_E-u_F-u_E, or u_E-u_D-u_E.)

Let us assume u_B wants to communicate with her contact u_A. First, u_B constructs a circuit to PS through the heartbeat channels in a similar way as u_A did to register her presence. We assume that u_A and u_B share a long-term secret key K_{AB}, and that they know each other's long-term IDs (ID_A and ID_B.) User u_B creates a message for PS with the form:

$$E_{PK_{PS}}(IDJ_A, E_{K_{AB}}(E_B, g^{r_B})),$$

where PK_{PS} is the public key of PS, K_{AB} is the shared secret between u_A and u_B, E_B is the entry point of u_B, and r_B is a randomly generated number. PS decrypts the message with its private key, and checks if a user with identifier IDJ_A is connected. If this is the case, then it forwards $E_{K_{AB}}(E_B, g^{r_B})$ through the presence circuit of u_A; otherwise, it ignores u_B's request.

When u_A gets the message from PS, she tries to decrypt it with all her contact keys. When she identifies that the right key is the one corresponding to u_B, she retrieves the entry point E_B of u_B and g^{r_B}. u_A may now decide to communicate with u_B. We note that, if u_A decides to ignore u_B's request for communication, u_B does not know whether or not u_A received the request, or even whether she is online. Should u_A be willing to talk to u_B, she requests her entry E_A to prepare a bridge to E_B for the next epoch. At the beginning of the communication, u_A sends the second part of the Diffie-Hellman key exchange, g^{r_A}, so that the conversation is encrypted with a session key $k_{AB} = g^{r_A r_B}$.

In order to preserve forward secrecy of requests for communications, u_A and u_B update their shared key K_{AB}. In this way, neither of them can be coerced to decrypt an earlier intercepted message. The new key K'_{AB} is computed as: $K'_{AB} = H(k_{AB}, K_{AB})$.

There are some differences between Drac's presence mechanism and Apres [20]. The most important one concerns the way ID's are managed. In Apres, the ID's correspond to relationships (i.e., u_A and u_B share ID_{A+B},) and when u_A connects to the presence server she provides all the ID's she shares with her contacts, plus some extra ones to prevent the server from identifying her by her number of ID's. The main disadvantage of this approach is that, even in the absence of communications, the presence server can see the number of online user relationships. Given a clustered group of contacts who are often online, the presence server may be able to identify the relationships and link the identities between epochs.

3.3   An Epoch in Drac

Figure 1(right) shows the adversary's observation of an epoch in which users $\{u_A, \ldots, u_F\}$ are online in Drac using $D = 2$ (for simplicity, we denote user u_X as X in the reminder of this section.) We omit the connections to the presence server in the figure for the purpose of this example. The communication circuits (represented as - - -) created by the users are the following: A-C-D, B-C-B, C-D-E, D-E-F, E-B-C, and F-E-B. The last node in each circuit is the entry point of the initiator of the circuit, e.g., D is E_A, the entry point of A. Besides, a secure link (represented as ▬) has been created between every pair of nodes that route a circuit. Note that there is no link between A and F, because no circuit is relayed through them. However, the adversary can still observe the heartbeat connection between them (represented as ····.)

In the epoch shown in the figure two communications are taking place. First, F and B are communicating. As both share the same entry point ($E_F = E_B = $B,) no bridge is created and the communication is fully unobservable for the attacker. A and D are having the second conversation, and they have created a bridge between their entry points $E_A = $D and $E_D = $F (represented as ▬.) Although this bridge is distinguishable by the attacker, it is not possible to determine from the observation that A and D are the communication end points. For example, a plausible alternative that would yield the same observation would be that there is only one communication between D and F, and that the circuits are as follows: A-C-D, B-C-D, C-B-C, D-E-F, E-B-E, and F-E-D.

By looking at the circuit connections, the adversary is not able to link users with their entry points because they not only send messages through their own circuit, but also act as "mixes" [6] relaying the traffic of others. Thus, when several circuits traverse a node it is not possible for the adversary to distinguish which input circuit corresponds to which output. As noted in the previous section, all connections must be activated synchronously at the beginning of an epoch. Otherwise, the adversary would see connections ripple down the network when they are created and be able to link users with their entry points. Thus, users must prepare connections in advance during the previous epoch, using the heartbeat channels. For this they have to i) perform key exchanges with all nodes in the circuit to their entry points, ii) find the entry points of the contacts with whom they want to communicate, and iii) instruct their entry point to prepare a bridge to their contact's entry points. We note that this procedure requires users to register their identities for the next epoch when they sign up in the presence server. If two friends want to communicate, they do not need to find their corresponding entry points, but just inform each other through their direct heartbeat connection.

In this paper we restrict our analysis to one epoch, and leave the study of the epoch duration's impact on performance, usability, and security as a subject of future work.

4 Evaluation

4.1 Experimental Setup

In order to perform a preliminary analysis of the anonymity and unobservability properties provided by Drac, we have implemented a software simulator.[1] We have tested three topologies for the network graph that describes how users are connected to their friends: small-world networks [35], scale-free networks [2], and random networks. We note that although these topologies do not necessarily resemble real social networks, they are still of theoretical interest as they allow us to study separately the effects of clustering and power law distributions on the security properties of Drac. Experiments with real social network's graphs should be conducted in order to understand the level of protection offered by a potential deployment of Drac.

The simulator generates networks of N nodes (users) with an average of f edges (friends) selected according to the network topology, and f randomly selected contacts. We simulate a single epoch per experiment. First we simulate the epoch preparation phase, in which each user u_i prepares a communication circuit of depth D hops to her entry node E_i. In addition, users register at the presence server through a heartbeat circuit of depth D_p. We denote the last node in the presence circuit as E_{Pi}. We consider scenarios in which 10% of the

---

[1] The code will be made available by the authors upon request.

N users are communicating with contacts through bridges that connect their respective entry nodes.

Second, we record the observation of the adversary after connections have been activated in the beginning of the epoch. We recall that the adversary observes:

- The heartbeat connections between each pair of users u_i and u_j who share a friendship relationship.
- The connections from the end of the presence circuits (i.e., from the entry nodes E_{Pi}) to the presence server.
- The number of communication circuits routed between each pair of nodes u_i and u_j, which is inferred by looking at the amount of bandwidth used.
- The bridge links B_{ij} that connect the entry nodes E_i and E_j in a communication between two contacts u_i and u_j.

Given the observation of the adversary, in each experiment we randomly select a target user and compute her presence anonymity, communication anonymity, and communication unobservability as described in the next three sections. The results shown in the following sections combine samples from a thousand experiments for each simulation scenario. The baseline simulation scenario is a small-world network of 500 users, with 10 friends and 10 contacts each, and circuit depths D and D_p of three hops. These are the default parameters used in the experiments unless indicated otherwise.

4.2   Anonymity towards the Presence Server

We first examine the anonymity provided by Drac towards the presence server. Let us consider a user u_A who registers at the presence server with pseudonym IDJ_A in a given epoch. The presence server knows that IDJ_A corresponds to a node that is connecting to it through a presence circuit of depth D_p, which is routed over the heartbeat connections. The last node in this circuit is visible to the presence server, and we denote it by E_{PA}.

In addition, we assume that the adversary can see all the heartbeat connections in the network. We recall that, as explained in Sect. 3, heartbeat connections exist between any two users who share a friendship relationship, and that heartbeat traffic is always the same regardless of whether one, several, or no presence circuits are routed over the heartbeat connection.

Given this information, IDJ_A may correspond to any of the users u_i connected to E_{PA} by D_p hops in the network of heartbeat channels. Let $\Pr_i[E_{PA}]$ be the probability that user u_i is u_A. We compute $\Pr_i[E_{PA}]$ by enumerating all possible circuits that start at E_{PA} and lead to u_i after D_p hops, taking into account that nodes may appear several times in the paths. Let $\mathcal{P}_i$ be the total number of such paths leading to u_i, $\Pr_i[E_{PA}]$ is computed as:

$$\Pr_i[E_{PA}] = \frac{\mathcal{P}_i}{\sum_{j=1}^{N} \mathcal{P}_j} \ , \ \ 1 \leq i \leq N$$

We compute the anonymity of u_A towards the presence server as the entropy H_A of the distribution of $\Pr_i[E_{PA}]$ over all users [11,30].

$$H_A = - \sum_{i=1}^{N} \Pr_i[E_{PA}] \log_2 \Pr_i[E_{PA}]$$

Figure 2(left) shows the anonymity of Drac towards the presence server for small-world (SW), scale-free (SF), and random (R) networks of sizes between $N = 100$ and $N = 1000$. The dashed horizontal line indicates the maximum achievable anonymity for a network of size N, which is computed as $\log_2 N$. The 'x' marks the median anonymity for 1000 experiments (each corresponding to an independent target user,) and the vertical line traversing the 'x' indicates the first and third quartiles of the distribution of anonymity results.

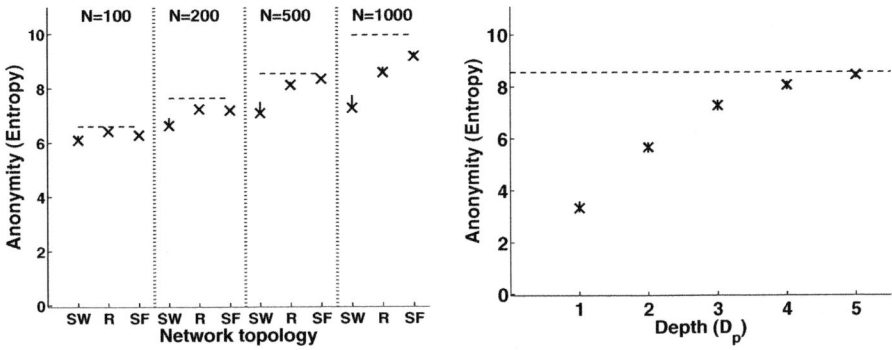

Fig. 2. Anonymity towards the presence server, depending on the network size and topology (left;) and on the depth of the circuits with the baseline parameters (right.)

As we can see in the figure, small-world network topologies provide the lowest anonymity for any network size, and as the network grows their performance becomes worse compared to the other two topologies. This is due to the high degree of clustering of small-world networks, which prevents Drac from taking full advantage of bigger networks: independently of the network size, u_A's connections stay mostly in its own neighborhood. Random networks provide near-optimal anonymity for small network sizes, but as the networks grow the best anonymity performance is shown by scale-free networks. Scale-free networks show a power law degree distribution and grow with preferential attachment. This implies that these networks have some nodes with a very high degree, which grows with the size of the network. High-degree nodes act as mixing hubs that increase anonymity. We choose small-world network topologies in the remaining simulation scenarios in order to test Drac in the least favorable conditions (highly clustered networks) and estimate a lower bound on the anonymity that it offers.

The critical security parameter of the Drac system is the depth of the circuits – which is a system design parameter, as opposed to the network topology or the average number of friends per user. As shown in Figure 2(right) longer presence circuit depths increase the anonymity provided by Drac, at the cost of more communication latency – as the messages need to travel more hops before reaching their destination. In an real-world implementation of Drac, the depth parameter D_p can be tuned to trade bandwidth, latency, and anonymity requirements for any given network, as discussed in Section 5.

4.3   Contact Communication Anonymity

We recall that communications between *friends* are unobservable to the adversary (see Sect. 3.1.) Let us consider that users u_A and u_F are *contacts* who are communicating in a given epoch. We assume that the bridge connection B_{AF} between their respective entries, E_A and E_F, is observable to the adversary (i.e., we assume that E_A and E_F are not friends.) Note that this is a worst-case scenario, as the bridge B_{AF} may not be distinguishable to the adversary if E_A and E_F are friends, and it is fully unobservable when both users share the same entry; i.e., when $E_A = E_F$.

Starting from the fact that an observable bridge B_{AF} evidences that two contacts are communicating, we evaluate the anonymity of each of the two communicating users separately. This is done by analyzing which users may have constructed a communication path ending, respectively, in entries E_A and E_F. Note that this evaluation does not measure end-to-end anonymity. The reason why it is not straightforward to compute end-to-end anonymity is because in Drac the adversary does not have certainty that a given user is communicating, as opposed to systems that do not use dummy traffic [8,14,29]. Information theoretic anonymity metrics [11,30] operate under the assumption that the adversary knows that user u_A is communicating, and then measure the uncertainty of the adversary in identifying the other end of the communication (i.e., *who talks to whom.*) In contrast, Drac provides communication unobservability properties, implying that the adversary is not certain of *who is talking* in the first place. The next section provides a preliminary analysis of unobservability in Drac. In this section, we evaluate the anonymity of user u_A with respect to an adversary that observes the bridge at E_A.

The analysis methodology is similar to the presence anonymity explained in the previous section. The adversary explores all possible circuit paths of depth D and records the frequency with which each user u_i appears as initiator of the candidate circuit that ends in E_A. The main difference with the computation of presence anonymity is that in this case the adversary can see the number of circuits routed between each pair of nodes (by looking at the amount of bandwidth used.)

Figure 3 shows the results of our simulations for the contact communication anonymity provided by Drac in various network conditions. The left-hand side of the figure compares contact communication anonymity for small-world (SW), scale-free (SF), and random networks (R), of $N = 100$ to $N = 1000$ users. We can see that small-world networks provide the lowest anonymity, while scale-free networks provide the best anonymity of the three topologies, for similar reasons as pointed out in the previous section. We note the anonymity sets in this case are smaller than for the presence circuits. The first factor reducing anonymity is that the adversary has additional information with respect to presence – the number of circuits per link. Another factor that reduces communication anonymity with respect to presence anonymity is that communication links are more sparse than heartbeat links. Users route on average $D+1$ communication circuits – regardless of the size of the network and the average number of friends f – and several circuits may be routed to the same friend. Thus, nodes will maintain fewer communication links with friends than heartbeat connections – and at most, the same.

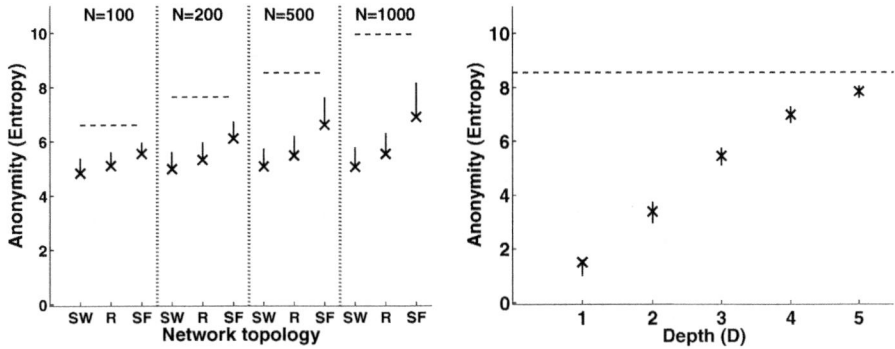

Fig. 3. Anonymity of contact communications towards a global passive adversary, depending on the network size and topology (left;) and on the depth of the circuits with the baseline parameters (right.)

For a constant circuit depth D, Drac provides more anonymity in bigger networks (particularly for scale-free topologies.) We note though that the gap grows between the achieved contact communication anonymity, and the maximum achievable (represented in the figure by dashed horizontal lines) – indicating that longer connection depth would be required to fully take advantage of bigger networks.

In Figure 3(right) we show the variation of anonymity with the security parameter D. As we can see, increasing the depth of the circuits can push the contact communication anonymity of Drac arbitrarily close to the maximum achievable (for a given network size.)

4.4   Contact Communication Unobservability

In this section we provide a preliminary analysis of the unobservability of communications between contacts provided by Drac. In particular, we look at how well the adversary can correctly guess whether or not user u_A is communicating with a contact.

Let C be the total number of contact communications taking place in a given epoch, and let $\mathcal{E}$ be the set of entry nodes routing bridge connections for those communications. If all communications create a bridge connection, then $|\mathcal{E}| = 2C$; if m pairs of communicating contacts share the same entry node, then $|\mathcal{E}| = 2(C - m)$.

We denote by $\Pr_i[E_j]$ the probability that u_i is the user whose entry node is $E_j \in \mathcal{E}$. We compute $\Pr_i[E_j]$ by enumerating all possible circuits that start at E_j and lead to u_i after D hops (note that $\sum_{i=1}^{N} \Pr_i[E_j] = 1$, but that $\sum_{j=1}^{|\mathcal{E}|} \Pr_A[E_j]$ is not necessarily one.) The probability $\Pr[u_A]$ that u_A is one of the $|\mathcal{E}|$ users communicating with a contact through *any* of the entry nodes in $\mathcal{E}$ is computed as:

$$\Pr[u_A] = \frac{\sum_{j=1}^{|\mathcal{E}|} \Pr_A[E_j] \prod_{k=1,k\neq j}^{|\mathcal{E}|} (1 - \Pr_A[E_k])}{\sum_{j=1}^{|\mathcal{E}|} \Pr_A[E_j] \prod_{k=1,k\neq j}^{|\mathcal{E}|} (1 - \Pr_A[E_k]) + \prod_{k=1}^{|\mathcal{E}|} (1 - \Pr_A[E_k])}$$

We assume that the adversary knows the total number of contact communications C, and can correctly identify *all* bridge connections. We construct the following test to compare Drac to an ideal system that provides perfect unobservability – in which the adversary's best guess is to choose at random:

- First, the adversary computes $\Pr[u_i]$ for all users $u_i, 1 \leq i \leq N$.
- The adversary constructs a set $\mathcal{S}$ with the $2C$ users with higher probabilities, and another set $\mathcal{R}$ with $2C$ randomly chosen users. The set $\mathcal{R}$ models the guess of the adversary for the ideal system.
- We randomly select a user u_A who *is* communicating with a contact, and we test if $u_A \in \mathcal{S}$, and if $u_A \in \mathcal{R}$. We repeat this experiment a thousand times and compare the success rate of the Drac adversary with respect to the success rate of ideal system's (random) adversary.

  We perform the same experiment choosing a user u_Z who is *not* communicating, and compare the success rate of the adversaries of Drac and the ideal system by testing the rate with which $u_Z \in \mathcal{S}$, and $u_Z \in \mathcal{R}$.

Figure 4 shows the results of our tests for a small-world network of 500 nodes in which there are $C = 25$ contact communications, each involving two users. The left-hand side of the figure shows the results of our test for a user u_A who is communicating. As we can see, when connections have depth $D = 1$ the adversary is able to correctly guess that u_A is communicating in more than half of the experiments. When the depth increases to $D = 4$, the advantage of the Drac adversary becomes negligible with respect to the adversary of the ideal system (who guesses at random.)

The right-hand side of the Figure 4 shows the results when testing a user u_Z who is not communicating. As in the previous case, the Drac adversary has an advantage for small circuit depths D, but as D increases her success rate becomes no better than random guessing.

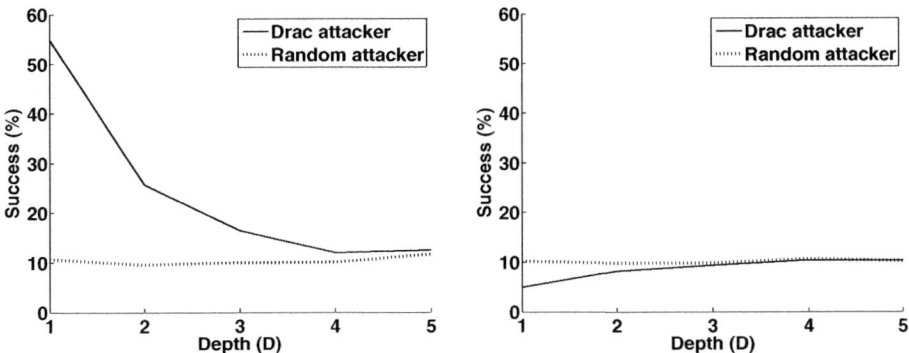

Fig. 4. Comparison of Drac and random adversary success rate in determining that a user is communicating, given that when 10% of the users are communicating. The left-hand side shows the results for a user u_A who *is* communicating, and the right-hand side for a user u_Z who is *not* communicating.

5 Discussion

We have so far provided a high-level description of Drac. In this section we discuss some specifics regarding real world performance, trade-offs, overheads and details of the trust model.

Drac is designed to support real-time, low-volume communications such as IM and controversially VoIP. What makes VoIP different from web-traffic is the extreme predictability of the traffic of a VoIP call, despite the tighter requirements to make it useable. A mouth-to-ear delay of more than 50 ms makes voice reflection annoying and a delay of more than 250 ms makes a two-way conversation difficult. As an indication the free Speex[2] codec allows for a sampling rate of 8 kHz and a bit rate of 2.15 kbps (say 3 kbps to take into account some cryptographic overhead). A compressed sample is generated for every 20 ms of speech, with a look-ahead of 10 ms; i.e., 50 packets a second at a sampling rate of 8 kHz, which corresponds to telephony quality. Each node in Drac needs to establish two such channels (2 kpbs) one for incoming and one for outgoing voice, relayed though multiple nodes. This bandwidth is well within the capabilities of contemporary broadband connections, and a dedicated infrastructure could be cheaply built using off-the-shelf routers to support large number of calls (e.g., for a diplomatic network). Since VoIP is delay sensitive, it is reasonable for nodes to discard packets that have been sitting in a queue for longer than 250 ms, indicating that a UDP based implementation [28] would be preferable for Drac. IM traffic has much less stringent requirements, with a couple of messages a second being necessary, each only a few hundreds of bytes long.

As discussed in the evaluation section the length of the path of each circuit is a key security parameter in Drac. This length is also the key contributor to

---
[2] http://www.speex.org

the overhead of the system: $D + 1$ hops per node would mean that the system would consume $N \cdot (D + 1) \cdot 2 \cdot 3$ kbps at any time, even if there are no calls in progress (each node will be expected to carry $(D + 1) \cdot 2 \cdot 3$ kbps on average.) Research suggests that denial-of-service attacks become more likely when paths are longer [4], but the friend-of-a-friend topology used to route makes it less likely that malicious nodes are present on any hop of short paths. Finally, although in this paper we have assumed that D and D_p are constant for all users, there might be some advantages in allowing users to specify their own circuit lengths, as the adversary has to guess the length as well as the exact sequence of nodes in the circuit.

The trust model used in Drac is one of the most novel, and controversial design choices. We argue that relaying communications over a friend-of-a-friend network provides some security advantages. First, it makes denial-of-service and related attacks [4] less likely, and social defenses against sybil attacks can be readily deployed [10]. Moreover, circuit creation does not require a centralized directory and trust infrastructure, which favors network scalability. Drac also avoids network discovery and random sampling attacks present in other peer-to-peer designs [21]. Users have incentives to route traffic [1] for their friends, and the relative stability of a social graph allows for tit-for-tat strategies to penalise free-loading. Finally, the stability of the social graph also invalidates the models of many traffic analysis attacks that assume anonymity sets to contain a random selection of users alongside the target: filtering out the correlated "noise" from those anonymity sets will be much more difficult under Drac.

On the down side, paths over social graphs need to be longer to achieve good levels of anonymity, and the length depends on the mixing properties of the social graph [7]. Finally, this design choice exposes the long term social network of the user to the adversary: in many cases the purpose of an anonymity network is hiding exactly those relationships. We have taken the view that long term relations are doomed to be exposed through long term attacks [19]. We instead opt to make those visible to better anonymize casual conversations with unusual contacts. Despite the fact that a relation is visible, actual communication events between friends are designed to be unobservable – a stronger guarantee than the usual anonymity. These choices present a novel trust and protection profile in the anonymity design space.

6   Conclusions

Drac is the first system to be designed to withstand a global passive adversary to protect instant messaging or voice-over-IP conversations. The low-volume and regularity of such traffic makes the use of padding practical, compared with padding high variance connections carrying web-traffic. The overhead of Drac is still high, as users relay circuits over each other all the time. We argue that for IM this overhead is still practical, since the original traffic volumes are low to start with. For VoIP a broadband connection should suffice to participate in Drac, following the current "volunteer" model of Tor [14]. For other deployments a dedicated IP infrastructure could also be reasonable – as some high-profile recent communication security failures illustrate, even some well funded state level actors do not currently have a secure traffic analysis resistant diplomatic network [33]. Our design for Drac could perfectly well fulfill that role.

The design of Drac also borrows features from peer-to-peer designs that suppress the distinction between users and infrastructure, with the novel twist of using a friend-of-a-friend network as a communication and trust backbone. This seriously limits the potential for sybil attacks, provides incentives for relaying traffic, and leads to more stable anonymity sets. All these features require a renewed analysis of past attacks to incorporate them, but we are hopeful they will present advantages over the traditional model of routing over a random graph.

Finally, Drac is fundamentally different from other designs regarding the security properties it provides: it reveals the social graph to the adversary, but provides a stronger property – unobservability of communications. Anonymity is provided when pseudonymous contacts have a conversation. This mixture of properties is likely to be useful in different contexts from the traditional anonymity properties that try to hide relationships against a partial adversary. Our analysis of these properties, albeit preliminary, seems promising but many of the definitions, attacks, and analysis frameworks in the literature will have to be adapted to this new context. This work is a first contribution in this direction.

Acknowledgements

The authors would like to thank Josep Balasch for editorial comments that improved the readability of the paper. C. Diaz and C. Troncoso are funded by the Fund for Scientific Research in Flanders (FWO). This work was supported in part by the IAP Programme P6/26 BCRYPT of the Belgian State.

References

1. Acquisti, A., Dingledine, R., Syverson, P.F.: On the Economics of Anonymity. In: Wright, R.N. (ed.) FC 2003. LNCS, vol. 2742, pp. 84–102. Springer, Heidelberg (2003)
2. Barabasi, A.-L., Bonabeau, E.: Scale-free networks. Scientific American 288(5), 60–69 (2003)
3. Bonneau, J., Anderson, J., Danezis, G.: Prying data out of a social network. In: Memon, N., Alhajj, R. (eds.) ASONAM, pp. 249–254. IEEE Computer Society, Los Alamitos (2009)
4. Borisov, N., Danezis, G., Mittal, P., Tabriz, P.: Denial of service or denial of security? In: Ning, P., De Capitani di Vimercati, S., Syverson, P.F. (eds.) ACM Conference on Computer and Communications Security, pp. 92–102. ACM, New York (2007)
5. Borisov, N., Golle, P. (eds.): PET 2007. LNCS, vol. 4776. Springer, Heidelberg (2007)
6. Chaum, D.: Untraceable electronic mail, return addresses, and digital pseudonyms. Communications of the ACM 24(2), 84–88 (1981)

7. Danezis, G.: Mix-networks with restricted routes. In: Dingledine, R. (ed.) PET 2003. LNCS, vol. 2760, pp. 1–17. Springer, Heidelberg (2003)
8. Danezis, G., Dingledine, R., Mathewson, N.: Mixminion: Design of a type III anonymous remailer protocol. In: IEEE Symposium on Security and Privacy, pp. 2–15. IEEE Computer Society, Los Alamitos (2003)
9. Danezis, G., Goldbergp, I.: Sphinx: A compact and provably secure mix format. In: IEEE Symposium on Security and Privacy, pp. 269–282. IEEE Computer Society, Los Alamitos (2009)
10. Danezis, G., Mittal, P.: Sybilinfer: Detecting sybil nodes using social networks. In: NDSS. The Internet Society (2009)
11. Diaz, C., Seys, S., Claessens, J., Preneel, B.: Towards measuring anonymity. In: Dingledine, R., Syverson, P.F. (eds.) PET 2002. LNCS, vol. 2482, pp. 54–68. Springer, Heidelberg (2003)
12. Díaz, C., Troncoso, C., Serjantov, A.: On the impact of social network profiling on anonymity. In: Borisov, N., Goldberg, I. (eds.) PETS 2008. LNCS, vol. 5134, pp. 44–62. Springer, Heidelberg (2008)
13. Dingledine, R., Mathewson, N., Syverson, P.: Tor: The second-generation onion router. In: Proceedings of the 13th USENIX Security Symposium, vol. 2 (2004)
14. Dingledine, R., Mathewson, N., Syverson, P.F.: Tor: The second-generation onion router. In: USENIX Security Symposium, pp. 303–320. USENIX (2004)
15. Feamster, N., Dingledine, R.: Location diversity in anonymity networks. In: Atluri, V., Syverson, P.F., De Capitani di Vimercati, S. (eds.) WPES, pp. 66–76. ACM, New York (2004)
16. Goldberg, I.: On the security of the tor authentication protocol. In: Danezis, G., Golle, P. (eds.) PET 2006. LNCS, vol. 4258, pp. 316–331. Springer, Heidelberg (2006)
17. Johnson, A., Syverson, P.F.: More anonymous onion routing through trust. In: CSF, pp. 3–12. IEEE Computer Society, Los Alamitos (2009)
18. Kate, A., Zaverucha, G.M., Goldberg, I.: Pairing-based onion routing. In: Borisov, Golle (eds.) [5], pp. 95–112
19. Kesdogan, D., Agrawal, D., Pham, D.V., Rautenbach, D.: Fundamental limits on the anonymity provided by the mix technique. In: IEEE Symposium on Security and Privacy, pp. 86–99. IEEE Computer Society, Los Alamitos (2006)
20. Laurie, B.: Apres - a system for anonymous presence. Technical report
21. Mittal, P., Borisov, N.: Information leaks in structured peer-to-peer anonymous communication systems. In: Syverson, P., Jha, S., Zhang, X. (eds.) Proceedings of the 15th ACM Conference on Computer and Communications Security (CCS 2008), Alexandria, Virginia, USA, October 2008, pp. 267–278. ACM Press, New York (2008)
22. Möller, U., Cottrell, L., Palfrader, P., Sassaman, L.: Mixmaster Protocol — Version 2. Draft (July 2003)
23. Murdoch, S.J., Danezis, G.: Low-cost traffic analysis of tor. In: IEEE Symposium on Security and Privacy, pp. 183–195. IEEE Computer Society, Los Alamitos (2005)
24. Murdoch, S.J., Zielinski, P.: Sampled traffic analysis by internet-exchange-level adversaries. In: Borisov, Golle (eds.) [5], pp. 167–183
25. O'Connor, L.: Entropy bounds for traffic confirmation. Technical Report 2008/365, IACR (October 2008)
26. Pfitzmann, A., Pfitzmann, B., Waidner, M.: ISDN-MIXes: Untraceable Communication with Small Bandwidth Overhead. Informatik-Fachberichte, pp. 451–463 (1991)

27. Pfitzmann, A., Köhntopp, M.: Anonymity, unobservability, and pseudonymity - A proposal for terminology. In: Federrath, H. (ed.) PET 2000. LNCS, vol. 2009, pp. 1–9. Springer, Heidelberg (2001)
28. Reardon, J.: Improving Tor using a TCP-over-DTLS tunnel. Master's thesis, University of Waterloo (September 2008)
29. Reiter, M.K., Rubin, A.D.: Anonymous web transactions with crowds. Commun. ACM 42(2), 32–38 (1999)
30. Serjantov, A., Danezis, G.: Towards an information theoretic metric for anonymity. In: Dingledine, R., Syverson, P.F. (eds.) PET 2002. LNCS, vol. 2482, pp. 41–53. Springer, Heidelberg (2003)
31. Syverson, P., Tsudik, G., Reed, M., Landwehr, C.: Towards an analysis of onion routing security. In: Federrath, H. (ed.) PET 2000. LNCS, vol. 2009, pp. 96–114. Springer, Heidelberg (2001)
32. Troncoso, C., Danezis, G.: The bayesian traffic analysis of mix networks. In: Al-Shaer, E., Jha, S., Keromytis, A.D. (eds.) ACM Conference on Computer and Communications Security, pp. 369–379. ACM, New York (2009)
33. Varouhakis, M.: Greek intelligence and the capture of PKK leader abdullah ocalan in 1999. Studies in Intelligence 53(1) (Extracts) (March 2009)
34. Venkitasubramaniam, P., He, T., Tong, L.: Relay secrecy in wireless networks with eavesdroppers. In: Proceedings of the Allerton Conference on Communication, Control and Computing (2006)
35. Watts, D.J., Strogatz, S.H.: Collective dynamics of 'small-world' networks. Nature 393, 440–442 (1998)
36. Wright, C.V., Coull, S.E., Monrose, F.: Traffic morphing: An efficient defense against statistical traffic analysis. In: Proceedings of the Network and Distributed Security Symposium - NDSS 2009, February 2009. IEEE, Los Alamitos (2009)
37. Wright, C.V., Ballard, L., Coull, S.E., Monrose, F., Masson, G.M.: Spot me if you can: Uncovering spoken phrases in encrypted voip conversations. In: IEEE Symposium on Security and Privacy, pp. 35–49. IEEE Computer Society, Los Alamitos (2008)

Private Web Search with Malicious Adversaries*

Yehuda Lindell and Erez Waisbard

Department of Computer Science
Bar-Ilan University, Israel
{lindell,waisbard}@cs.biu.ac.il

Abstract. Web search has become an integral part of our lives and we use it daily for business and pleasure. Unfortunately, however, we unwittingly reveal a huge amount of private information about ourselves when we search the web. A look at a user's search terms over a period of a few months paints a frighteningly clear and detailed picture about the user's life. In this paper, we build on previous work by Castellà-Roca et al. (Computer Communications 2009) and show how to achieve privacy in web searches efficiently and practically without resorting to full-blown anonymous routing. In contrast to previous work, our protocol is secure in the presence of malicious adversaries.

1   Introduction

It is well known that users' search terms to web search engines contain significant amounts of sensitive information and, as such, the aggregation and use of these terms constitutes a severe privacy breach. The only way that a user can protect him or herself from this breach today is to use an anonymous routing system like Tor [7]. However, this can sometimes be an "overkill" measure. This is especially the case since in order to achieve a high level of security, such systems cause a considerable slowdown.

Recently, an interesting model for solving this problem was suggested by [2]. Essentially, their proposal is for a group of users to first *shuffle* their search words amongst themselves. After the shuffle, each user has someone's search word (but doesn't know whose), and the parties then query the search engine with the word obtained. Finally, the parties all broadcast the result to all others. This model is especially attractive because it doesn't involve the overhead of installing a full-blown anonymous routing system, and can be provided as a simple web service.

In [2], the authors present a protocol for private web search in the above model that is secure in the presence of semi-honest adversaries. That is, users' privacy is maintained only if all parties follow the protocol specification exactly. We argue that this level of security is not sufficient, especially due to the fact that the protocol of [2] has the property that a *single* adversarial participant

---

* This research was generously supported by the European Research Council as part of the ERC project "LAST".

M.J. Atallah and N. Hopper (Eds.): PETS 2010, LNCS 6205, pp. 220–235, 2010.

can easily learn the queries of all users, without any malicious behavior being detected. This means that an adversarial entity who is a participant in many searches can learn all of the users' queries without any threat of retribution.

Our results. In this paper we construct a protocol for private web search in the model of [2] that is secure in the presence of *malicious adversaries* that may arbitrarily deviate from the protocol specification in order to attack the system. Our main technical tool is a highly efficient cryptographic protocol for parties to mix their inputs [3] that guarantees privacy in the presence of malicious adversaries. Unlike the usual setting of mix-nets, here the parties themselves carry out the mix. The novelty of our approach is based on the observation that, unlike the setting of voting where mix-nets are usually applied, the guarantee of *correctness* is not necessary for private web search. That is, we allow a malicious participant to carry out a "denial of service" type attack, causing the search to fail. In return, we are able to omit the expensive zero-knowledge proofs of correctness in every stage of the mix.

We stress that simply removing the correctness proofs from a standard mix protocol yields a completely insecure protocol that provides no privacy. For example, we still have to deal with "replacement attacks" where the first party carrying out the mix replaces all of the encrypted search words with terms of its own, except for the *one* ciphertext belonging to the user under attack. In this case, the result of the mix completely reveals the search word of the targeted user (because all other search words belong to the attacker). Our solution to this problem (and others that arise; see Section 3) is based on the following novel idea: instead of inputting search words into the mix, each party inputs an encrypted version of its search word. Then, after all stages of the mix are concluded, each party checks that its encrypted value appears. If yes, it sends true to all parties, and if not it sends false. If all parties send true, they can then proceed to decrypt the search words because this ensures that no honest party's search word was replaced. However, this raises a new challenge regarding how to decrypt the encrypted search word. Namely, a naive solution to the problem fails. For example, if each party encrypted their search word using a one-time symmetric key, then sending this key for decryption reveals the identity of the party whose search word it is. We therefore use a "one-time" threshold encryption scheme based on ElGamal [8] and have the parties encrypt the search words with the combined key. The parties then send their key-part in the case that all parties sent true (a similar idea to this appears in [2] but for a different purpose). We call this a *private shuffle* in order to distinguish it from a standard mix-net. We provide a formal definition of security for a private shuffle and have a rigorous proof of security under this definition.

As we have mentioned, the private shuffle is the main technical tool used for obtaining private web search. However, as is often the case, the cryptographic protocol at its core does not suffice for obtaining a secure *overall solution*. In Section 5 we therefore discuss how a private shuffle primitive can be used to obtain private web search, and in particular how to bypass non-cryptographic attacks that can be fatal. One major issue that arises is how to choose the group of participants, and in particular, how to prevent the case that the adversary controls all but one participant (in which case the adversary will clearly learn the input of the sole honest party). This issue was not addressed in previous solutions.

Related work. A number of different anonymity-preserving techniques can be used in principal for private web search. For example, private information retrieval [4,11] provides the appropriate guarantees. However, it is far too inefficient. A more natural candidate is a to use a mix-net [3]. However, as we have mentioned, considerable expense goes into proving correctness in these protocols. In addition, doing this efficiently and securely turns out to be quite a challenge; see for example [10,6]. For further comparisons of existing techniques to the model that we adopt here, we refer the reader to [2] and the reference within. We remark that our protocol is about twice as expensive as the protocol of [2], and thus the efficiency comparisons between their solution and other existing techniques can be extrapolated to our solution. (For some reason, however, they used ElGamal over $\mathbb{Z}_p^*$ with a large p instead of an Elliptic curve group that would be considerably more efficient.) Our solution has some similarities to that of [2]. However, their protocol suffers from a number of attacks in the case of malicious adversaries, as described below in Section 3.

2   Definitions

In this section we present our definition of security for a private shuffle primitive. The shuffle functionality is simply the n-ary probabilistic function $f(x_1, \ldots, x_n)$ $= (y_1, \ldots, y_n)$, such that for every i, $y_i = x_{\pi(i)}$ where π is a random permutation over $[n]$. Intuitively, a shuffle is *private* if an adversary cannot link between the inputs of the protocol and the outputs of the protocol. Namely, the adversary should not be able to link y_j to an honest party P_i where $j = \pi(i)$. Denoting the number of corrupted parties by t, we have that a random guess regarding a "link" is correct with probability $\frac{1}{n-t}$. Thus, we formalize security by requiring that an adversary controlling t parties can output (i, j) where P_i is honest and $j = \pi(i)$ with probability that is at most negligibly greater than $\frac{1}{n-t}$.

The security experiment. We assume that the parties communicate over an open network with unauthenticated channels. We model this network by having all communication go through an adversary that can listen to all the communication, delete messages and inject messages of its choice. This is formally modeled by providing the adversary with stateful oracles that model the honest parties, as in [1]. The experiment modeling the success of the adversary appears in Figure 1.

Defining security. We are now ready to define security. First, we require non-triviality, meaning that if all parties are honest, then the protocol output is a permuted vector of the inputs. Next, we require that an adversary controlling t out of the n parties can succeed in the experiment ExptShuffle with probability

---

FIGURE 1 (The Security Experiment ExptShuffle$_{\mathcal{A},\pi}^{t,n}(k)$)

1. Invoke the adversary $\mathcal{A}$ with input 1^k and with parameters t and n (k is the security parameter determining the key sizes).
2. Receive from $\mathcal{A}$ a set of t indices $I \subset [n]$ designating the corrupted parties (note that $|I| = t$), and a vector of $n - t$ *distinct* inputs $w_1, \ldots, w_{n-t}$ for the honest parties.
3. Choose a random permutation π over $\{1, \ldots, n - t\}$ and initialize the ith honest-party oracle with input $w_{\pi(i)}$.
4. Execute the shuffle protocol, where $\mathcal{A}$ interacts with the $n - t$ oracles (who each runs the shuffle protocol honestly based on messages received from $\mathcal{A}$).
5. When it concludes, the adversary outputs a pair (i, j) for any i, j of his choice.

We say that the adversary succeeds in the experiment, in which case the output of the experiment ExptShuffle$_{\mathcal{A},\pi}^{t,n}(k)$ equals 1, if and only if $\pi(i) = j$.

---

that is only negligibly greater than $\frac{1}{n-t}$ (where negl is a negligible function if for every polynomial p and all large enough k's it holds that $\mathsf{negl}(k) < 1/p(k)$):

Definition 2. *A protocol* π *is a* private shuffle *if it is non-trivial, and if for every probabilistic polynomial-time algorithm* $\mathcal{A}$, *every integer* $n \in \mathbb{N}$ *and every* $0 < t < n$, *there exists a negligible function* $\mathsf{negl}(\cdot)$ *such that:*

$$\Pr\left[\mathsf{ExptShuffle}_{\mathcal{A},\pi}^{t,n}(k) = 1 \right] \leq \frac{1}{n-t} + \mathsf{negl}(k)$$

3   Constructing a Private Shuffle

In order to motivate our construction, we begin by describing the protocol of [2] that is secure in the presence of semi-honest adversaries. We then describe the difficulties that arise when moving to the malicious model. A basic tool that is used is called *ElGamal remasking*. Intuitively, a remasking operation is a procedure that takes a ciphertext and rerandomizes it so that the result cannot be linked to the original ciphertext. Recall that an ElGamal encryption of a message M with public-key (g, y) is computed by choosing a random $r \in \mathbb{Z}_q^*$ (where the group has order q) and computing $u = g^r$ and $v = y^r \cdot M$; the ciphertext is the pair $c = (u, v)$. The remasking operation is computed as follows:

$$\mathsf{remask}(u, v) = (u \cdot g^{r'}, y^{r'} \cdot v)$$

where $r' \in_R \mathbb{Z}_q^*$. Observe that when $(u, v) = (g^r, y^r \cdot M)$ it follows that $\mathsf{remask}(u, v) = (g^{r+r'}, y^{r+r'} \cdot M)$ and so it is a valid encryption of the same message under the same public key. The fact that $\mathsf{remask}(u, v)$ cannot be linked to (u, v) is due to the fact that r' is random and follows from the decisional Diffie-Hellman (DDH) assumption. An informal description of the protocol of [2] appears in Protocol 3.

Protocol 3 (The protocol of [2] for semi-honest adversaries (overview))

- Parties $P_1, \ldots, P_n$ generate a joint ElGamal public key $y = \prod_{i=1}^{n} g^{x_i}$, where x_i denotes the private key of each party.

- Every party P_j encrypts its search word w_j using the joint public key, obtaining $c_j^0 = (u_j^0, v_j^0)$, and sends it to everyone.

- For every $i = 1, \ldots, n$, party P_i does the following:
  - *Remasks* the ciphertexts $(c_1^{i-1}, \ldots, c_n^{i-1})$ it received from P_{i-1}.
  - Randomly *permutes* the remasked ciphertexts.
  - Sends the shuffled and remasked ciphertexts to P_{i+1}, except for party P_n who broadcasts the result to all the parties.

- Given the shuffled and remasked ciphertexts $(c_1^n, \ldots, c_n^n)$, each party P_i decrypts a single ciphertext $c_i^n = (u_i^n, v_i^n)$. This is carried out as follows:
  - Each party P_j sends each P_i the share $(u_i^n)^{x_j}$ for every $i, j \in \{1, \ldots, n\}$, where x_j is P_j's private key.
  - Given the shares from all parties, each P_i computes $w_i = \dfrac{v_i^n}{\prod_{j=1}^{n}(u_i^n)^{x_j}}$

Although Protocol 3 was defined for the semi-honest model, it is instructive to see what attacks can be carried out by a malicious party:

Stage-skipping attack: A malicious party P_n may remask and permute the initial vector of ciphertexts sent by the parties instead of the vector that it received from P_{n-1}. In this case, when the vector is decrypted P_n will know exactly which party sent which message. Observe that this behavior would not be detected because the remask operation looks identical when applied once or n times.

Input-replacement attack: A malicious party P_1 can learn the input w_j of an honest party P_j by replacing all the ciphertexts in the input vector with individually remasked copies of the *initial* ciphertext (u_j^0, v_j^0). In this case, all of the parties receive w_j; in particular P_1 receives w_j and so knows the search term of P_j.

Targeted public-key attack: A malicious P_n may compute its share of the public key after given all of the g^{x_i} values of the other parties. Specifically, P_n sets its share of the public-key to be $h = g^{x_n}/(\prod_{i=1}^{n-1} g^{x_i})$ for a random x_n. Observe that any encryption under $y = \prod_{i=1}^{n} g^{x_i}$ is actually an encryption under g^{x_n} only because $h \cdot y = g^{x_n}$. Thus, P_n can decrypt the values of all parties and learn who sent what. Once again, this attack would go completely unnoticed.

Private shuffle for malicious adversaries. We now motivate our protocol for private shuffle that achieves security in the presence of malicious adversaries. First, in order to guarantee privacy, we need to ensure that at least one honest user remasks and permutes all of the ciphertext values. This involves ensuring that all parties take part in the shuffle and that the parties shuffle the actual input values (that is, we need to ensure that neither a stage-skipping nor

Protocol 4 (Private Shuffle with Malicious Adversaries)

Input: Each P_j has a search word w_j, and auxiliary input (g, q) as described.

Initialization Stage:

1. Each party P_j chooses random $\alpha_j, \beta_j \in Z_q^*$, sends $g^{\alpha_j}, g^{\beta_j}$ to all the other parties and proves knowledge of α_j, β_j using a zero-knowledge proof of knowledge. P_j signs the message it sends together with the identifier sid using its certified private signing key (from the PKI).
2. Each party verifies the signatures on the messages that it received and aborts unless all are correct.
3. Each party P_j encrypts its input w_j using the public g^{α_i} shares of all the other parties. That is, it chooses a random $\rho_j \in_R Z_q^*$ and computes an encryption $c_j = (g^{\rho_j}, g^{\rho_j \cdot \sum_{i=1}^n \alpha_i} \cdot w_j)$. (The value $g^{\sum_{i=1}^n \alpha_i}$ is computed by multiplying all of the g^{α_i} values received in the previous stage.)
4. Each party P_j re-encrypts its ciphertext c_j using the public g^{β_i} shares:
   (a) The party computes $\Delta_0 = \prod_{i=1}^n g^{\beta_i} = g^{\sum_{i=1}^n \beta_i}$
   (b) It chooses a random value $\rho_j' \in_R Z_q^*$
   (c) It encrypts c_j by computing $(u_j^0, v_j^0) = (g^{\rho_j'}, (\Delta_0)^{\rho_j'} \cdot c_j)$ and sends the result to all the other parties.

The output of this phase is the list of the encrypted c_j's of all the parties, denoted $\mu_0 = \langle (u_1^0, v_1^0), \ldots, (u_n^0, v_n^0) \rangle$.

Shuffle stage: For $j = 1, \ldots, n$, party P_j receives vector μ_{j-1} and computes a shuffled version μ_j as follows:

1. For every (u_i^{j-1}, v_i^{j-1}) in μ_{j-1}, party P_j carries out the following steps:
   (a) **Remask:** it chooses a random $r_j^i \in Z_q^*$ and computes

   $$(u_i', v_i') = (u_i^{j-1} \cdot g^{r_j^i}, v_i^{j-1} \cdot (\Delta_{j-1})^{r_j^i}) \quad \text{where} \quad \Delta_{j-1} = g^{\sum_{i=j}^n \beta_i}$$

   where the computation of Δ_{j-1} can be carried out using the g^{β_i} values sent in the initialization phase.
   (b) **Remove β_j:** it computes $(u_i^j, v_i^j) = (u_i', u_i'^{(-\beta_j)} \cdot v_i')$
2. P_j chooses a random permutation π_j over $\{1, \ldots, n\}$ and applies it to the list of values (u_i^j, v_i^j) computed above; denote the result by μ_j.
3. P_j sends μ_j to P_{j+1}.

The last party P_n sends μ_n to all parties.

Verification stage:

1. Every party P_j checks that its encryption c_j of w_j under public key $\prod_{i=1}^n g^{\alpha_i}$ is in the vector μ_n. If yes it sends (sid, P_j, true), signed with its private signing key, to all the other users. Otherwise it sends (P_j, false).
2. If P_j sent false in the previous step, or did not receive a validly signed message (sid, P_i, true) from all other parties P_i, then it aborts. Otherwise, it proceeds to the next step.

Reveal stage:

1. For every $(u_i, v_i) \stackrel{\text{def}}{=} (u_i^n, v_i^n)$ in μ_n, party P_j removes its α_j from the encryption by sending $s_i^j = u_i^{\alpha_j}$ to P_i (including sending $s_j^j = u_j^{\alpha_j}$ to itself).
2. After receiving all the shares s_j^i, every party P_j computes $w_j = \frac{v_j}{\prod_{i=1}^n s_j^i}$, thereby removing the second layer of encryption and recovering the cleartext word w_j (here j denotes the current index in μ_n and not the index of the party who had input w_j at the beginning of the protocol).

input-replacement attack is carried out). The classic way of achieving this in the mix-net literature [3,10,6] is to have each party P_i prove (at each stage) that the values that it passed onto P_{i+1} are indeed a remasked and permuted version of what P_i received from P_{i-1}. However, this is a costly step that we want to avoid. We therefore provide an alternative solution that is based on a two-stage protocol with double encryption of each input. In the first stage the parties shuffle the inputs without verifying correctness, while gradually removing the outer encryption. Then, at the end of this stage there is a verification step in which all parties check that their input value is still in the shuffled array (under the inner encryption). If all parties acknowledge that their value is present then we are guaranteed that all parties participated in the shuffle and that no inputs were replaced. We can therefore safely proceed to the second stage of the protocol where the inner encryption is privately removed, revealing the shuffled inputs. In addition to the above, we prevent the aforementioned targeted public-key attack by having each party prove that it knows its associated secret key.

We note that in order to prevent a powerful man-in-the-middle adversary from playing the role of all parties except for one, we assume the existence of a PKI for digital signatures; see Section 5 for a discussion of how to achieve this in practice. In addition, we assume that all parties hold a unique *session identifier* sid (e.g., this could be a timestamp), and a generator g and order q of a group for ElGamal.

Remarks on the protocol:

1. For the sake of efficiency, the zero-knowledge proof in the initialization stage can be implemented by applying the Fiat-Shamir heuristic [9] to Schnorr's protocol for discrete log [12]. In order to achieve independence, we also include the sid and the party ID of the prover inside the hash for generating the "verifier query". It is also possible to use the methodology of [5] at the expense of $\log n$ rounds of communication.
2. Observe that each input w_j is encrypted twice under ElGamal. However, the result c_j of the first encryption is actually *two* group elements. Thus, if the same group is used for both layers of encryption, then we need to separately encrypt the two elements in c_j. For the sake of clarity, we present the protocol as if the second encryption under Δ_0 is a larger group in which encryption of both elements is achieved in a single operation.
3. In the first stage of the protocol every party participates in the shuffle. However, as we will see in the proof it suffices to ensure that *one* honest party participated. Thus, if we assume that at most t parties are malicious (for $t < n$), then we can run the shuffle stage for $j = 1$ to $t+1$ only, reducing the number of rounds from n to $t + 1$.

Non-triviality. The non-triviality requirement of a private shuffle is that if all parties are honest then the output is a permutation of the input values $(w_1, \ldots, w_n)$. We prove that this property holds for our protocol by following a single message w_ℓ that goes through the protocol, and showing that all the layers of encryption that are added are properly removed. For clarity, we present this for the case that no permutations are applied (and thus the indices remain the same); this clearly makes no difference.

1. In the initialization phase the message w_ℓ is encrypted first with $g^{\sum_{i=1}^n \alpha_i}$ (using random ρ_ℓ) resulting in c_ℓ, and then c_ℓ is encrypted with $g^{\sum_{i=1}^n \beta_i}$ (using random value ρ'_ℓ) yielding the pair (u_ℓ^0, v_ℓ^0) where $u_\ell^0 = g^{\rho'_\ell}$ and $v_\ell^0 = (\Delta_0)^{\rho'_\ell} \cdot c_\ell = g^{\rho'_\ell \cdot \sum_{i=1}^n \beta_i} \cdot c_\ell$.

2. Assume that before the jth iteration begins, the pair $(u_\ell^{j-1}, v_\ell^{j-1})$ is an encryption of c_ℓ under the ElGamal public key $\Delta_{j-1} = g^{\sum_{i=j}^n \beta_i}$. This clearly holds for $j = 1$ by the way (u_ℓ^0, v_ℓ^0) are generated. We show that this holds after the jth iteration concludes. By the above assumption, before the jth iteration begins, there exists a value $r \in \mathbb{Z}_q^*$ such that $u_\ell^{j-1} = g^r$ and $v_\ell^{j-1} = (\Delta_{j-1})^r \cdot c_\ell$. In the jth iteration of the shuffle stage, party P_j computes $u'_\ell = u_\ell^{j-1} \cdot g^{r_j^\ell} = g^{r+r_j^\ell}$ and $v'_\ell = v_\ell^{j-1} \cdot (\Delta_{j-1})^{r_j^\ell} = (\Delta_{j-1})^r \cdot c_\ell \cdot (\Delta_{j-1})^{r_j^\ell} = (\Delta_{j-1})^{r+r_j^\ell} \cdot c_j$. Thus (u'_ℓ, v'_ℓ) constitute an encryption of c_ℓ under public-key Δ_{j-1}.

   Next P_j computes $u_\ell^j = u'_\ell = g^{r+r_j^\ell}$ and $v_\ell^j = {u'_\ell}^{-\beta_j} \cdot v'_\ell$. It follows that $v_\ell^j = g^{-\beta_j(r+r_j^\ell)} \cdot \Delta_{j-1}^{r+r_j^\ell} \cdot c_\ell = g^{-\beta_j(r+r_j^\ell)} \cdot g^{(r+r_j^\ell)\sum_{i=j}^n \beta_i} \cdot c_\ell = g^{(r+r_j^\ell)\sum_{i=j+1}^n \beta_i} \cdot c_\ell = \Delta_j^{r+r_j^\ell} \cdot c_\ell$. We therefore conclude that after the jth iteration, the result is an encryption of c_ℓ under Δ_j, as required.

3. From the above, we have that after all n iterations are concluded the value c_ℓ is obtained in the clear (observe that $\Delta_n = g^0 = 1$).

4. Next, if all the parties are honest, then they all send true in the verification stage, and all send P_ℓ the values $s_\ell^i = u_\ell^{\alpha_i}$ (for every i). Recall that $c_\ell = (u_\ell, v_\ell)$ where $u_\ell = g^{\rho_\ell}$ and $v_\ell = g^{\rho_\ell \cdot \sum_{i=1}^n \alpha_i} \cdot w_\ell$. Now, $\prod_{i=1}^n s_\ell^i = \prod_{i=1}^n u_\ell^{\alpha_i} = \prod_{i=1}^n g^{\rho_\ell \cdot \alpha_i}$. Thus, $v_\ell = \prod_{i=1}^n s_\ell^i \cdot w_\ell$, implying that $\frac{v_\ell}{\prod_{i=1}^n s_\ell^i} = w_\ell$, as required.

We have proven that the output of the protocol consists of all the original inputs. The shuffle function definition also requires that these be in a randomly permuted order. However, since each party applies a random permutation to the vector of ciphertexts, this immediately follows. We conclude that when all parties are honest, the protocol computes the shuffle functionality as defined.

4   Privacy of Shuffle Protocol

The security of the protocol is based on the decisional Diffie-Hellman (DDH) assumption. Informally, this states that an adversary can distinguish tuples of the type (g, g^a, g^b, g^{ab}) from tuples of the type (g, g^a, g^b, g^c), where a, b, c are random in $\mathbb{Z}_q^*$, with probability that is negligible in k (where k is the bit-length of q). We have the following theorem:

Theorem 5. *Assume that the decisional Diffie-Hellman (DDH) assumption holds in the group of order q generated by g. Then, for every probabilistic polynomial-time algorithm $\mathcal{A}$, every integer $n \in \mathbb{N}$ and every $0 < t < n$, there exists a negligible function $\mathsf{negl}(\cdot)$ such that:*

$$\Pr\left[\mathsf{ExptShuffle}_{\mathcal{A},\pi}^{t,n}(k) = 1\right] \leq \frac{1}{n-t} + \mathsf{negl}(k)$$

We now provide intuition as to why the above theorem holds. The most important point is that as long as at least *one* honest party carries out the shuffle (remask and permute) operation on the vector of inputs, the adversary can succeed in ExptShuffle with probability at most negligibly greater than $1/(n-t)$. This is due to the fact that by the DDH assumption, no polynomial-time adversary can link between an ElGamal encryption (u_i, v_i) and its remasked version (u_i', v_i'), without knowing all β_i values. Thus, after an honest party remasks and permutes the values, the trail from the party who initially sent the relevant encryption is lost. Of course, it is necessary to show that the reveal stage at the end does not de-anonymize the values; however, this is straightforward. In order to show that at least one honest party carried out the shuffle, we show that unless the vector μ_n is the result of *all* parties carrying out the shuffle in turn, the honest parties all abort (except with negligible probability). In order to see this, we first argue that if an adversary carries out an *input-replacement* or *stage-skipping* attack (as described above), then the honest parties all abort except with negligible probability.

1. *Input-replacement attack:* The honest parties all encrypt their inputs w_j under $g^{\prod_{i=1}^{n} \alpha_j}$ and then re-encrypt the result under $g^{\prod_{i=1}^{n} \beta_j}$. Thus the adversary does not know the value of the ciphertext c_j which is the encryption of w_j under $g^{\prod_{i=1}^{n} \alpha_j}$. Since this ciphertext value is of high entropy (even if w_j is not), it follows that if an honest party's input P_j is replaced at any stage of the computation, the correct c_j will not appear in the verification stage. In this case, P_j will send (P_j, false) and all honest parties will abort. Note that since the true confirmation messages are signed, an adversary that controls the communication channels cannot send a true message when the actual P_j sends false.

2. *Stage-skipping attack:* This attack refers to a malicious party P_j remasking and permuting a vector μ_i instead of μ_{j-1}, where $i < j - 1$ and an honest party P_ℓ is between P_i and P_j (note that such an attack is *not* a replacement attack). In order to see why such an attack is detected, recall that the g^{β_j} component of the outer encryption is removed iteratively in each stage. Thus, if P_j takes μ_i it follows that the encryption under g^{β_ℓ} is not removed. In such a case, none of the correct ciphertexts (encrypted under $g^{\prod_{i=1}^{n} \alpha_j}$) will be obtained and all honest parties will send false and abort. (This explains why the β_j components are removed iteratively, and not all together at the end.)

The intuition is completed by observing that if an adversary does not carry out an input-replacement or stage-skipping attack, then it holds that all honest parties participated in the shuffle, as required. The full proof is omitted here due to lack of space in this extended abstract; the full proof will appear in the full version.

5   Private Web Search

In this section we show how to use a *private shuffle* in order to achieve private web search. As we will show below, a system for private web search needs to take into account additional considerations that are not covered by the notion of a private shuffle (or even a fully secure mix-net). In this section we address these considerations, describe the assumptions that we make, and present a general scheme that models real-world threats and is thus implementable in practice.

5.1   Background

As in [2], the basic idea of the scheme is to allow many users who wish to submit a web query to team up in a group, shuffle their queries in a private manner and then have each of them perform one of the queries without knowing who it belongs to. Upon receiving back the query results, each party just sends them to all others in the group so that the original party who sent the query can learn the result. This methodology prevents the search engine from linking between a user and its search query. Furthermore, the users in the group do not know on whose behalf they send a query; all they know is that it belongs to someone within the group. An important question in such a system is how to group users together. One possibility is to do this in a *peer-to-peer* way, so that whenever a user has a query it can notify the peer network in order to find out who else has a query at this time. The parties with queries can then join in an ad-hoc way in order to privately shuffle them before sending them to the search engine. (Note that parties who are currently idle can help by sending dummy queries, if they like.) This is a feasible model, but has significant implementation difficulties. The alternative suggested by [2], and one that we follow for the remainder of this section, is to use a *central server* whom anyone interested in searching can approach. The server then notifies the parties wishing to currently search of each others' identities so that they can form a group in order to carry out a private shuffle. This model is easily implemented by simply having the server be a website offering a "private search" utility.

As we mentioned in the introduction, the problem with the scheme suggested by [2] was that it assumed that all parties are semi-honest. In our view this is highly unrealistic, especially since a single corrupt party can completely break the privacy of the scheme and learn every party's search query. We now show how to achieve private web search in the presence of malicious adversaries. In order to do this, we use the *private shuffle* protocol presented in Section 3 that maintains privacy in the presence of malicious adversaries. We stress that private shuffle within itself does not suffice for obtaining private web search in practice for the following reasons:

1. A malicious central server can choose the group so that it controls all but one user. As we explain below, this completely bypasses the security guarantees of the shuffle.

2. The result of the web search queries must be sent to all parties because we don't know which user sent which query. This means that users learn the search results for all the members in their group, which is much more information than necessary (although the search engine must learn all queries, this is not the case for users).

Below, we will present a system for web search that uses the *private shuffle* protocol, while addressing the above concerns.

5.2   A Private Web Search System

Our solution is comprised of four phases that together enable private web search:

- **Phase 0:** Installation and initialization

- **Phase 1:** Ad-hoc group setup

- **Phase 2:** Private shuffle of the search queries

- **Phase 3:** Query submission and private response retrieval

We remark that an ad-hoc group can be used for many searches, and ideally would be used for a session of a reasonable amount of time. This enables us to reduce the overhead due to running phase 1.

Phase 0 – installation and initialization: Our *private shuffle* protocol requires a PKI and communication with a central server. A natural realization of this would be as an Add-on to a web browser that would supply a functionality which is similar to the search window in the most common web browsers. This Add-on would contain the address of a central server (or a list of servers). Regarding the PKI, since most users do not have a certificate for digital signatures, we have to generate one. The most practical way to do this would be to use a one-time activation of the Add-on after installation, in which a key pair is generated and a digital certificate then downloaded from a CA. Recall that without a PKI, the efficient verification in our *private shuffle* protocol does not guarantee that it was the honest parties in the group that sent true in the verification of the shuffle stage. We stress that a different certificate can be installed on every machine using the Add-on.

Phase 1 – ad-hoc group setup: As mentioned above, users group together with the help of a server S that aggregates the identities of users that wish to currently engage in private web search. Conceptually speaking, in terms of role and trust, the server should be no more than a bulletin board for anonymous users who wish to create an ad-hoc group. In [2], the server was assumed to be a trusted entity who does not collude with any of the users nor with the web search engines. However, the role of grouping users together carries with it a lot of power that can easily be abused. Specifically, consider a server that has $t \geq n$ machines at its disposal (or even a single machine that can pretend to be t different users), where n is the size of the group. Then, the server can always group some single honest user with $n-1$ of the t server-owned users. If an honest user runs a private shuffle in this way, then its privacy is completely lost because the server knows the search queries of all the users except for the honest one. Thus, at the end of the protocol when all queries are revealed, the server knows the exact query made by the honest user. We stress that this holds even if the mix carried out is *perfectly secure*.

In order to prevent the server from grouping the users as it wishes, we have all parties run a type of joint coin tossing protocol so that the t parties controlled by a malicious server are uniformly distributed within all the groups running the shuffle. Let N denote the overall number of parties in the system, let t denote the overall number of parties under the control of the malicious server, and let n be the size of each group running the shuffle. Our coin-tossing protocol uses two random oracles H_1 and H_2. Each party P_i sends $H_1(IP_i, PK_i, r_i)$ to the server to be posted (where r_i is a long random string). Then, the groups are formed by applying H_2 to all the values $H_1(IP_1, PK_1, r_1), \ldots, H_1(IP_N, PK_N, r_N)$. Denote the output of H_2 by $o = (o_1, \ldots, o_N)$ where each o_i is of length $\log N$. Letting o_i be the temporary name of party P_i, we have that the output of H_2 induces an order on the parties by taking the lexicographic ordering of the temporary names. Using this order the users are grouped into groups of size n. Observe that the server can choose the r_j values in $H_1(IP_j, PK_j, r_j)$ after it received all of the honest parties' H_1 values (where P_j is a party under its control). Furthermore, it can do so many times in an attempt to obtain a "bad group" in which all but one party are under its control We therefore need to make sure that the probability that a group is "bad" is very small (e.g., 10^{-40}). This will ensure that the server, after seeing the inputs from the honest users, still cannot find input values that would create a "bad group" in sufficient time. The reason that we use the random oracle H_1 in the process of sending the inputs, instead of just having the parties send (IP_i, PK_i, r_i) is in order to protect the identities of the users. Specifically, the server $\mathcal{S}$ will send the relevant IP addresses only to the relevant group, and so only the server $\mathcal{S}$ providing the service knows the history of which party participated in each group. As we will see below, it is important to prevent this information from being leaked, especially to the web search engine. Otherwise, statistical attacks can be carried out; see below for more details. The group setup appears in Protocol 6.

We now analyze the security of Protocol 6. Recall that in the random oracle model, the output of H_2 is uniformly distributed every time that it is applied to a new value. We begin by analyzing the probability that a bad grouping occurs for a *given* set of values $\{(IP_i, PK_i, r_i)\}_{i=1}^{N}$. (Below we will analyze what this means when the server is malicious.) We call a group "bad" if it consists of $n-1$ malicious parties together with a single honest party. Clearly, this is bad because the server $\mathcal{S}$ then learns the search query of that party. The cases that a group has only a few honest parties is also quite bad, but there is still ambiguity regarding each user's search term. Furthermore, in Section 5.3 we discuss how to further improve this.

Protocol 6 (Group setup protocol)
Let H_1 and H_2 be two random oracles where $H_1 : \{0,1\}^* \rightarrow \{0,1\}^k$ and $H_2 : \{0,1\}^* \rightarrow \{0,1\}^{N \cdot \log N}$. Let n be the size of each group for the shuffle. We set the initial indexing of the parties according to the lexicographical order of their IP addresses.

1. Each P_i chooses a random r_i and sends $H_1(IP_i, PK_i, r_i)$ to the center.
2. After a short predefined time everyone queries the center for the list of parties who have registered.
3. Each party computes $o = H_2(H_1(IP_1, PK_1, r_1), \ldots, H_1(IP_N, PK_N, r_N))$ and divides the result o into chunks of size $\log N$, denoted $o_1, \ldots, o_N$. Party P_i is associated with o_i and the list is sorted according to the o_i values.
4. Grouping is carried out by taking groups of n parties according to the sorting. That is, for $i = 1, \ldots, \lfloor N/n \rfloor$, the ith group G_i is set to be the parties associated with the values $(o_{n \cdot (i-1)+1}, \ldots, o_{n \cdot i})$.
5. The center sends the IP addresses of the group members to the members of each group (i.e. each member gets only the IP addresses of the members in its group).
6. Members of each group send each other their IP address, public key and randomness that were used when registering with the center.
7. Each group member computes $H_1(IP_j, PK_j, r_j)$ for every party P_j in its group and verifies that it matches what was recorded by the center during registration. In addition, it verifies that it received the IP address of all parties that are in its group, by the computation of H_2. If no, then it sends abort to all the parties in its group.

Let bad_i denote the event that the ith group is bad as defined above. We begin by computing the probability that the first group is bad; i.e., that bad_1 occurs. Since the output of H_2 is uniformly distributed, we can compute this by counting the number of ways to choose $n-1$ parties out of t malicious ones times the number of ways to choose a single honest party, divided by the total number of ways to choose a group of size n out of N parties. That is, we have:

$$\Pr[\mathsf{bad}_1] = \frac{\binom{N-t}{1} \cdot \binom{t}{n-1}}{\binom{N}{n}} = \frac{(N-t) \cdot \frac{t!}{(t-n+1)!(n-1)!}}{\frac{N!}{(N-n)!n!}}$$

$$= \frac{\prod_{i=1}^{n-2}(t-i)}{\prod_{j=1}^{n-1}(N-j)} \cdot (N-t) \cdot n$$

$$= \prod_{i=1}^{n-2} \frac{(t-i)}{(N-i)} \cdot \frac{N-t}{N-n+1} \cdot n$$

Noting again that H_2 is a random function, it follows that the above calculation is true for any fixed group. Thus, the above gives the probability of bad_i for every $i = 1, \ldots, \lfloor N/n \rfloor$. As we have mentioned, a grouping is bad if there exists a bad group. Thus, applying the union bound over all $\lfloor N/n \rfloor$ groups we have that:

$$\Pr\left[\exists\ i\ :\ \mathsf{bad}_i\right] \leq \sum_{i=1}^{N/n} \Pr\left[\mathsf{bad}_i\right] = \frac{N}{n}\Pr\left[\mathsf{bad}_1\right] = \prod_{i=1}^{n-2} \frac{(t-i)}{(N-i)} \cdot \frac{N-t}{N-n+1} \cdot N$$

Assuming now that $N >> t$, we have that $\Pr\left[\exists\ i\ \text{s.t. } \mathsf{bad}_i\right]$ is approximately $\left(\frac{t}{N}\right)^{n-2} \cdot N$. Concretely, consider the case of millions of users running this protocol, a malicious server S that controls a few thousand of them, and a group size of about 20. In this case, we have that the probability that there exists a bad group for a given set of H_1 values is smaller than $10^6 \cdot \left(\frac{10^3}{10^6}\right)^{18}$, which is 10^{-48}.

We stress that the above analysis alone is not sufficient. This is due to the fact that, as we have mentioned, it is possible for a malicious server S to modify the H_1 values many times in the aim of obtaining a bad grouping. Specifically, once all honest parties have submitted their values, the server can repeatedly modify the r_j portion of party P_j's input to H_1, where P_j is a malicious user under its control. Since any change to any of the H_1 values results in a completely different ordering of the parties (because H_2 is a random function), we have that the probability of a bad grouping is T times the above, where T equals the number of hashes that the server can compute in the required time interval. With the above example parameters where the probability of a bad grouping is 10^{-48}, the probability that a malicious server achieves a bad grouping within seconds is very small.

Phase 2 – private shuffle of the search queries: Once the users have been grouped together, they run the *private shuffle* protocol of Section 3. However, as we discussed earlier in Section 5.1 (item 2 at the end of the section), we would like to prevent the group members from learning all the search results. This seems problematic because the parties do not know whose query they have and they must therefore broadcast the result to everyone. We overcome this problem by instructing each party to first choose a random symmetric encryption key k_j and then input the pair $wk_j = (w_j, k_j)$ to the shuffle. As we will see next, k_j will be used to encrypt the search result.

Phase 3 – query submission and private response retrieval: After the shuffle protocol is completed, each party holds a pair (w', k'). Each party then submits the search query w' to the search engine and receives back the result. The search result along with the original search term is then encrypted using the key k' with a symmetric encryption scheme (e.g., AES) and broadcast to all group members. Each party attempts to decrypt all search results; the one that decrypts correctly is its own result. In this way, each party only learns its own result and the result of one other random user. Thus, privacy of the queries is better preserved.

5.3   Additional Considerations

We now address some of the issues that concern deployment of our scheme in the real world and discuss the privacy that it provides.

Blending into a crowd: The main idea of our scheme is blending into a crowd. The fact that millions of people from all over the world can participate in the protocol provides a strong sense of privacy, but consideration should be given to the way different populations are grouped together. If 20 people from all over the world are grouped together and all submit the query in their native language, then it is easy to learn the query of each party based on the geographic location of its IP address. When deploying such a system, consideration should be given to these issues and blending into a crowd should actually be blending into a crowd of people with similar characteristics.

The size of a group: Our *private shuffle* protocol provides anonymity with respect to the size of the group; thus the bigger the group the more anonymity one enjoys. Since the size of the group affects both the number of modular operations each party needs to perform and the number of rounds in the *private shuffle* protocol, the size of the group is bounded by the computing power of the users' computers and the acceptable latency. Nevertheless, it is possible to hide in a larger group at the expense of more modular exponentiations but without increasing the number of rounds, as follows. As we have described in remark 3 after Protocol 4, if we can assume that the number of malicious parties within a group is some $t' < n$, then it suffices to run the shuffle stage for $t' + 1$ rounds. Performing a similar analysis to the one above, we have that the probability of having 19 malicious parties within a group of size 50 is actually very close to the probability of having 19 malicious parties within a group of size 20 (when the total number of parties is about a million and the total number of malicious parties is several thousand). Thus, if one can afford the additional number of modular exponentiations that comes with increasing the group size, we can enhance privacy significantly by increasing the size of the group, without paying much more in latency. Observe that in this calculation a group is "bad" if there are $t' + 1$ malicious parties. Thus, if a group is not bad, each honest party's search query is guaranteed to be hidden amongst $n - t'$ other search queries.

Lifetime of a group: Our scheme creates ad-hoc groups that can be changed over time. In terms of efficiency, it is easy to see that remaining within a group for a while saves the cost of running the group selection process. However, users may submit a query to the search engine and logout. In this case the group size would shrink and if it is too small then privacy is compromised. This can be dealt with by starting with a larger group and regrouping once the group becomes too small.

Statistical analysis and changing groups: In terms of privacy, it may seem that the more often people change groups, the more privacy they gain. However, this actually may not always be the case. Consider a central server that colludes with the web search engine. The server S and search engine can then run a statistical analysis to group together queries that are likely to belong to the same user (e.g., by grouping together very low-probability queries). Now, if these queries are carried out in different groups, then the server S can find the (most likely) unique IP address that appears in all of the different groups, and conclude that the queries originated from this address. Thus, changing groups can be problematic. (Of course, without such collusion, this problem does not arise.)

An additional privacy enhancement: The system presented above has the property that each user's search query is revealed to one other *random* group member. However, in some cases a user may prefer to be able to say which user will submit and therefore learn their query (and which users will not learn their query). We can extend our system for private web search to allow this by adding one more layer of encryption to the messages, using the public key of the designated party. Specifically, if a party P_j wishes to have party P_i be the one who submits its query, then it encrypts wk_j along with some redundancy (to verify the correctness when opening) using g^{α_i}. Then P_j executes the private shuffle protocol with the encrypted wk_j. After the messages are shuffled, each party sends the message it received to everyone else, and all parties decrypt the results. In this way, only the designated party P_i is the one that can learn wk_j and it will send the query.

Acknowledgements

We would like to thank Gilad Asharov and Meital Levy for many helpful discussions, and the anonymous referees for helpful comments.

References

1. Bellare, M., Rogaway, P.: Entity Authentication and Key Distribution. In: Stinson, D.R. (ed.) CRYPTO 1993. LNCS, vol. 773, pp. 232–249. Springer, Heidelberg (1994)
2. Castellà-Roca, J., Viejo, A., Herrera-Joancomarti, J.: Preserving User's Privacy in Web Search Engines. Computer Comm. 32(13-14), 1541–1551 (2009)
3. Chaum, D.: Untraceable Electronic Mail, Return Addresses, and Digital Pseudonyms. Communications of the ACM 24(2), 84–88 (1981)
4. Chor, B., Goldreich, O., Kushilevitz, E., Sudan, M.: Private Information Retrieval. Journal of the ACM 45(6), 965–981 (1998)
5. Chor, B., Rabin, M.: Achieving Independence in Logarithmic Number of Rounds. In: 6th PODC, pp. 260–268 (1987)
6. Desmedt, Y., Kurosawa, K.: How to Break a Practical MIX and Design a New One. In: Preneel, B. (ed.) EUROCRYPT 2000. LNCS, vol. 1807, pp. 557–572. Springer, Heidelberg (2000)
7. Dingledine, R., Mathewson, N., Syverson, P.: Tor: The Second-Generation Onion Router. In: Proceedings of the 13th USENIX Security Symposium, pp. 303–320 (2004)
8. ElGamal, T.: A Public Key Cryptosystem and a Signature Scheme Based on Discrete Logarithms. In: Blakely, G.R., Chaum, D. (eds.) CRYPTO 1984. LNCS, vol. 196, pp. 10–18. Springer, Heidelberg (1985)
9. Fiat, A., Shamir, A.: How to Prove Yourself: Practical Solutions to Identification and Signature Problems. In: Odlyzko, A.M. (ed.) CRYPTO 1986. LNCS, vol. 263, pp. 186–194. Springer, Heidelberg (1987)
10. Jakobsson, M.: A Practical MIX. In: Nyberg, K. (ed.) EUROCRYPT 1998. LNCS, vol. 1403, pp. 448–461. Springer, Heidelberg (1998)
11. Ostrovsky, R., Skeith, W.E.: A Survey of Single-Database PIR: Techniques and Applications. In: Okamoto, T., Wang, X. (eds.) PKC 2007. LNCS, vol. 4450, pp. 393–411. Springer, Heidelberg (2007)
12. Schnorr, C.P.: Efficient Identification and Signatures for Smart Cards. In: Brassard, G. (ed.) CRYPTO 1989. LNCS, vol. 435, pp. 239–252. Springer, Heidelberg (1990)

unFriendly: Multi-party Privacy Risks in Social Networks

Kurt Thomas[1], Chris Grier[2], and David M. Nicol[1]

[1] University of Illinois at Urbana-Champaign
{kathoma2,dmnicol}@illinois.edu
[2] University of California, Berkeley
grier@cs.berkeley.edu

Abstract. As the popularity of social networks expands, the information users expose to the public has potentially dangerous implications for individual privacy. While social networks allow users to restrict access to their personal data, there is currently no mechanism to enforce privacy concerns over content uploaded by other users. As group photos and stories are shared by friends and family, personal privacy goes beyond the discretion of what a user uploads about himself and becomes an issue of what every network participant reveals. In this paper, we examine how the lack of joint privacy controls over content can inadvertently reveal sensitive information about a user including preferences, relationships, conversations, and photos. Specifically, we analyze Facebook to identify scenarios where conflicting privacy settings between friends will reveal information that at least one user intended remain private. By aggregating the information exposed in this manner, we demonstrate how a user's private attributes can be inferred from simply being listed as a friend or mentioned in a story. To mitigate this threat, we show how Facebook's privacy model can be adapted to enforce multi-party privacy. We present a proof of concept application built into Facebook that automatically ensures mutually acceptable privacy restrictions are enforced on group content.

1 Introduction

In the last decade the popularity of online social networks has exploded. Today, sites such as Facebook, MySpace, and Twitter combined reach over 500 million users daily [1,2,3]. As the popularity of social networks continues to grow, concerns surrounding sharing information online compound. Users regularly upload personal stories, photos, videos, and lists of friends revealing private details to the public. To protect user data, privacy controls have become a central feature of social networking sites [4,5], but it remains up to users to adopt these features.

The sheer volume of information uploaded to social networks has triggered widespread concern over security and privacy [6,7]. Personal data revealed on social networks has been used by employers for job screening [8] and by local law enforcement for monitoring and implicating students [9]. More sophisticated

M.J. Atallah and N. Hopper (Eds.): PETS 2010, LNCS 6205, pp. 236–252, 2010.

applications of social network data include tracking user behavior [10] and government funded monitoring [11]. Criminals have also capitalized on the trust users place in social networks, exploiting users with phishing attacks and malicious downloads [12,13].

The diverse set of threats posed to users has resulted in a number of refinements to privacy controls [14]. However, one aspect of privacy remains largely unresolved: friends. As photos, stories, and data are shared across the network, conflicting privacy requirements between friends can result in information being unintentionally exposed to the public, eroding personal privacy. While social networks allow users to restrict access to their own data, there is currently no mechanism to enforce privacy concerns over data uploaded by other users. As social network content is made available to search engines [15] and mined for information [16], personal privacy goes beyond what one user uploads about himself; it becomes an issue of what every member on the network says and shares.

In this paper, we examine how the lack of *multi-party privacy* controls for shared content can undermine a user's privacy. We begin by analyzing situations in Facebook where asymmetric privacy requirements between two friends inadvertently weaken one user's privacy. This results in friends, tagged content, and conversations being unintentionally exposed to the public and crawlers. Using our examples as a foundation, we develop a formal definition of *privacy conflicts* to explore both the frequency and risk of information leaked by friends which cannot be prevented with existing privacy controls.

The presence of privacy conflicts between friends results in scattered references about a user appearing to the public, including being mentioned in a story, listed as a friend, or tagged in a photo. While a single conflict may pose a minimal risk to privacy, we show how the aggregate data revealed by conflicts can be analyzed to uncover sensitive information. We develop a classification system that uses publicly disclosed links between friends and the content of leaked conversations to build predictions about a user's gender, religious views, political leaning, and media interests. While predicting personal attributes based on friends has previously been examined [17,18,19,20], we present refinements to these techniques that utilize auxiliary information about mutual friends and the frequency and content of conversations to produce more accurate results. Our techniques highlight how various leaks of seemingly innocuous data can unintentionally expose meaningful private data, eroding personal privacy.

Using a data set of over 80,000 Facebook profiles, we analyze the frequency of asymmetric privacy requirements between friends, uncovering millions of instances where one user may potentially violate another user's privacy. We then process the aggregate information exposed by conflicts with our data analytic techniques, finding we are able to predict a user's personal attributes with up to 84% accuracy by simply using references and conversations exposed by friends.

To mitigate the threat of privacy conflicts, we show how the current Facebook privacy model can be adapted to enforce multi-party privacy. We present two proof of concept applications built into Facebook. One application simulates

Facebook's popular wall functionality, while the other simulates a user's list of friends. The applications automatically determine a mutually acceptable privacy policy between groups of friends, only displaying information that all parties agree upon. Policy arbitration and enforcement is completely transparent to users, removing the risk of privacy conflicts without requiring user intervention.

2   Background and Motivation

Before describing the limitations of privacy in social networks, we present a brief overview of privacy controls currently available to users. While the prospect of friends and family weakening a user's privacy exists in all social networks, we restrict our analysis to Facebook given its status as the largest network with over 400 million users [1].

Facebook provides each user with a profile consisting of a page containing personal information, a list of the user's friends, and a wall where friends can post comments and leave messages, similar to a blog. A typical profile will contain information pertaining to the user's gender, political views, work history, and contact information. Additionally, users can upload stories, photos, and videos and *tag* other Facebook members that appear in the content. Each tag is an unambiguous reference that links to another user's profile, allowing a crawler to easily distinguish between Bob, Alice's friend and Bob, Carol's friend.

Privacy restrictions form a spectrum between public and private data. On the public end, users can allow every Facebook member to view their personal content. On the private end, users can restrict access to a specific set of trusted users. Facebook uses friendship to distinguish between trusted and untrusted parties. Users can allow *friends, friends of friends,* or *everyone* to access their profile data, depending on their personal requirements for privacy.

Despite the spectrum of available privacy settings, users have no control over information appearing outside their immediate profile page. When a user posts a comment to a friend's wall, he cannot restrict who sees the message. Similarly, if a user posts a photo and indicates the name of a friend in the photo, the friend cannot specify which users can view the photo. For both of these cases, Facebook currently lacks a mechanism to satisfy privacy constraints when more than one user is involved. This leads to *privacy conflicts*, where asymmetric privacy requirements result in one user's privacy being violated. Privacy conflicts publicly expose personal information, slowly eroding a user's privacy.

3   Multi-party Privacy

To understand the risks posed by the lack of joint privacy controls in social networks, we construct a formalism for privacy conflicts that defines the situations where a user's privacy can be violated and the extent of information leaked. To develop this formalism, we begin by analyzing scenarios in Facebook where users can unintentionally violate one another's privacy. We then deconstruct these examples into a formalism that captures all potential privacy conflicts.

This formalism plays an important role in Section 4 where we examine how information leaked by privacy conflicts can be analyzed to infer a user's personal attributes and in Section 6 where we show how Facebook can be adapted to enforce multi-party privacy.

3.1   Exploring Privacy Conflicts

Social networks are inherently designed for users to share content and make connections. When two users disagree on whom content should be exposed to, we say a *privacy conflict* occurs. Multiple privacy conflicts can occur between a user and his friends, each revealing a potentially unique sensitive detail. We specifically analyze two scenarios in Facebook — friendship and wall posts — to understand the types of information exposed by conflicts.

Friendship: A central feature of social networks is the ability of users to disclose relationships with other members. Each relationship carries potentially sensitive information that either user may not wish revealed. While Facebook provides a mechanism to conceal a user's list of friends, the user can only control one direction of an inherently bidirectional relationship.

Consider a scenario where a user Alice adopts a policy that conceals all her friends from the public. On the other hand, Bob, one of Alice's friends, adopts a weaker policy that allows any user to view his friends. In this case, Alice's relationship with Bob can still be learned through Bob. We say that a privacy conflict occurs as Alice's privacy is violated by Bob's weaker privacy requirements.

Wall Posts and Tagging: Wall posts and status updates provide users with a built-in mechanism to communicate and share comments with other users. Each post consists of a sender, receiver, and the content to be displayed. Facebook currently allows only the receiver to specify a privacy policy. When Alice leaves a message on Bob's wall, she relinquishes all privacy control over her comments. Similarly, if Alice posts to her own wall, she has sole control over who can view the message, even if she references other users who wish to remain anonymous. By ignoring the privacy concerns of all but one user, information can be exposed that puts other friends at risk.

Consider an example where Alice makes a public comment on her own profile stating *"Skipping work with @Bob and hitting the bars at 9am"*. Bob is unambiguously identified by the message, but cannot specify that the message should not be broadcast to the public per his privacy policy. Alternatively, if Alice posts on Bob's profile about current relationship trouble, she cannot specify that the message should only be visible by her friends, not all of Facebook.

Additional Conflicts: Friendship and wall posts represent only two of numerous situations where Facebook and other social networks lack multi-party privacy. Group membership, fan pages, event attendance, photo tagging, and video tagging are additional situations where multiple parties can be referenced by data, but cannot control its exposure. Each exposure leaks sensitive information about a user even if the strictest privacy controls available are adopted.

3.2   Formalizing Privacy Conflicts

We now formalize multi-party privacy, creating a language to understand how existing privacy controls can still lead to undesired exposures. Consider a single social network user u in the set of all possible users U. We denote the pages owned by u such as the user's wall or friend list as the set G_u. For each page $g \in G_u$, the user u can specify a privacy policy $P_u(g)$ indicating set of users including u who can view the page. For instance, Alice can create a policy stating *everyone* can view her wall page. Here, u is Alice, g is the wall page, and $P_u(g)$ is the set of all of users $u \in U$. We call the policy $P_u(g)$ the *owner policy*, as Alice controls access to the data and can remove it at any time.

Each page $g \in G_u$ contains a grouping of information I which may uniquely reference one or more users represented by the set $S(I)$. Here, Alice tagging Bob and Carol in a wall post i can be represented by $S(i) = \{Bob, Carol\}$. In this case, I is the set of all wall posts on the wall page g.

While the owner u of a page specifies the access restriction $P_u(g)$, each user referenced in the page will have a separate, potentially distinct privacy policy. For instance, while Alice may allow all users to view her wall page, Bob may desire all references of him be visible only to his direct friends. To capture this variation, we say that for each user $w \in S(I)$ there exists an *exposure policy* $V_w(g, I)$ that specifies a set of users permitted by w to view references in I about w on page g. This allows both an owner and exposed user to specify a policy for how data should be accessed, even if their policies are different. The lack of exposure policies in existing social networks is what allows information to be disseminated against a user's will.

We state that a *privacy conflict* occurs between the owner u of a page g and the users $S(I)$ referenced by the page if:

$$\exists i \in I : P_u(g) \nsubseteq \bigcap_{w \in S(i)} V_w(g, i) \tag{1}$$

That is to say, if an owner policy allows any users other than those accepted by *all* exposure policies to view a piece of information $i \in I$, there is at least one exposure policy being violated on page g. Returning to our example, Alice's owner policy $P_u(g) = U$ allows all users to view her wall page. This is in direct conflict with Bob's exposure policy $V_w(g, I) \subset U$ which requires his posts to be accessible only to his friends, not all users. Conversely, if Carol adopts an exposure policy $V_w(g, I) = U$, then Alice and Carol are in agreement on the set of users who can view the the information I on page g and no privacy conflict exists.

An important consequence of Equation 1 is that as the number of users referenced by a piece of information increases, in the absence of mutual friends, the intersection of all exposure policies tends to the empty set. This implies that for photos or wall posts referencing multiple users, it is likely that at least one user is being exposed against their will to undesired parties.

Currently, Facebook and other social networks lack a mechanism to specify an exposure policy. Instead, we can derive these policies based on the owner policy of each user. If Alice allows everyone to view her wall posts, her exposure policy is the same; all references to her in other wall posts should be visible to everyone. By using the formalism of owner policies and exposure policies, we can systematically examine Facebook to identify privacy conflicts and show how these violations can expose sensitive information.

3.3   Formalizing Exposed Data

Using our formalism of privacy conflicts, we can identify the set of all information pertaining to a particular user w that violates w's exposure policy. We denote this set $E(w)$ which contains all Facebook pages including friendships, wall posts, and tags that leak information about w. We define $E(w)$ as:

$$E(w) = \{\forall (u \in U, g \in G, i \in I) : P_u(g) \nsubseteq V_w(g, i)\} \tag{2}$$

The exposure set $E(w)$ represents every piece of information throughout a social network uploaded by other users that contains information about w despite w's intent to keep the information private. While a single leaked friendship or wall post may pose a minimal risk to a user's privacy, we show in Section 4 how the entire exposure set can be used to infer a user's personal attributes.

An important aspect of the exposure set $E(w)$ is distinguishing information visible to the entire social network from information exposed to a limited number of users. Consider a situation where Alice posts a photo and tags Bob. If Alice allows all users $u \in U$ to view her photos and is in conflict with Bob's exposure policy, we say a *global exposure* has occurred. In this case, Bob's information is revealed to Facebook users that have no prior relationship with either Alice or Bob. Conversely, if Alice exposes Bob's information to a set of users that are friends or friends of friends, we say a *local exposure* has occurred. While Bob's information is still being revealed against his will, only users that have some pre-existing relationship with Alice can view the data, not all of Facebook.

4   Inference Techniques

While scattered details about relationships and conversations between users may not pose an obvious threat to privacy, we present two classification systems that utilize the aggregate information exposed by privacy conflicts to infer a user's sensitive attributes. These techniques highlight how seemingly innocuous data leaked by friends can be used to infer meaningful private data, illustrating the necessity of multi-party privacy in social networks. While predicting a user's personal attributes based on friends has been previously examined [17,18,19,20], we present improvements to these techniques that utilize auxiliary information including wall posts, mutual friends, and the frequency of communication between users to further refine predictions.

4.1   Threat Model

The goal of classification is to infer properties about a user based on information either intentionally revealed or unintentionally exposed due to privacy conflicts. We assume that a user restricts access to his list of friends and wall posts and that no *a priori* information about the user exists. Under this scenario, aggregating personal data requires scouring a social network for privacy conflicts that link back to the user. To accomplish this task, we assume the parties involved are marketers, political groups, and monitoring agencies [10,11,16] who have the resources, sophistication, and motivation to glean as much information from social networks as possible. We also assume the interested parties do not form relationships with users or their friends to circumvent privacy controls. When considering the success of gathering privacy conflicts and inferring a user's personal information, we avoid any qualitative analysis of privacy risks such as the damage incurred by a photo being made public. Instead, we attempt to predict eight private attributes from data exposed by privacy conflicts. Four of the attributes target personal information, including a user's gender, political views, religious views, and relationship status. The other four attributes target media interests, including a user's favorite music, movies, television shows, and books.

4.2   Analytic Techniques

In this section, we describe the development of two classifiers that take the set of information exposed about a user throughout Facebook by friends and output predictions about the user's attributes. Currently, we restrict our classifiers to analyzing leaked friend lists and wall posts. A successful prediction using leaked data means that the details exposed by friends contain enough information to further violate a user's privacy, while an unsuccessful prediction means that the leaked data was too limited to draw a meaningful conclusion about a user's attributes. When predicting personal attributes, only one prediction is correct; a user can either be liberal or conservative, but not both. Conversely, media interests represent a multi-label classification problem where users can have multiple favorite books and movies. When predicting media interests, we return up to ten predictions and evaluate whether any one of them is correct.

Baseline Classifier. In order to quantify how access to auxiliary information helps to improve predictions about a user's attributes, we compare the accuracy of each classifier we develop against a baseline classifier. For each attribute, the baseline predicts the most frequent class within our data set. For multi-label attributes such as a user's favorite books where multiple predictions may be correct, the baseline returns the top ten most likely classes.

Friend Classifier. Using links between friends that are publicly exposed by privacy conflicts, the friend classifier attempts to predict a user w's attributes based on other Facebook members w associates with. While a link between two users carries no explicit private data, the friend classifier builds on the assumption that if two users are friends, they likely share correlated interests. The friend

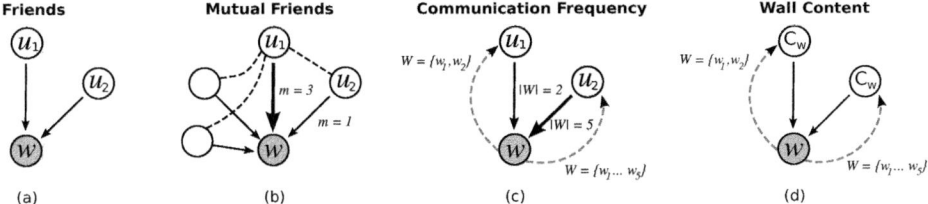

Fig. 1. Classification models for inference. Relationships and wall posts leaked by friends can be used to determine properties about the user w. These values can then be weighted based on the number of mutual friends or the frequency of communication between two friends.

classifier begins by aggregating the publicly accessible features u appearing in all of w's friends' profiles as shown in Figure 1(a). During single-label classification, we limit the set of features aggregated to a friend's gender, political view, religious denomination, and relationship status. Multi-label classification takes a different approach, where to predict a user's musical interests, we only consider the musical interests of his friends; all other features are ignored.

Rather than naively treating each of a user's friends as being equally influential, classification attempts to distinguish between strong and weak relationships and weight features appropriately. Given a relationship (w, f) between a user w and a friend f, each feature u aggregated from f is represented as a tuple (u, m_u, w_u). The weight m_u equals the number of mutual friends shared between (w, f) that are publicly known, as shown in Figure 1(b). The goal of including m_u is to reinforce clique structures which historically share similar interests [21], while removing incidental relationships that are not part of the clique and likely to perturb classification. A similar approach is taken for communication frequency where the weight w_u is set to the number of wall messages that w has sent to f, as shown in Figure 1(c). Including w_u helps to filter out friends that rarely communicate, which was previously identified as a strong indicator of a weak relationship [22].

The resulting list of tuples (u, m_u, w_u) is binned based on distinct features and converted into a feature vector. For single-label classification, a multinomial logistic regression [23] is used to classify every user and segment the feature space into types of friends associated with a user having a specific attribute, such as being male or female. For multi-label classification where the feature space is much larger, a linear regression selects the ten most likely media interests from a user's friends exclusively, ignoring trends identified from classifying other users and their friends. Successful classification for both techniques hinges on users being biased in their selection of friends due to sharing similar interests, while unsuccessful classification would indicate a user selects friends at random.

Wall Content Classifier. The wall content classifier attempts to predict a user w's personal attributes based on text recovered from w's conversations with friends. Classification begins by gathering all the wall posts written by w, but

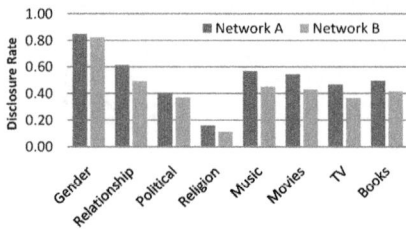

Fig. 2. Profile feature disclosure rates. Users readily supply their gender and media interests, but rarely reveal religious views.

exposed to the public by w's friends. Each post is then concatenated to create a single document containing all of w's discussion that is treated as a bag of words. Using classic document classification techniques, the set of wall posts is converted into a word vector where the associated frequencies of each word are weighted using term frequency–inverse document frequency [24]. The resulting word vectors from every user are classified using a multinomial logistic regression that attempts to segment the feature space into words typically used by women rather then men, or liberals rather than conservatives. Accurate classification hinges on conversations between users differing along attribute boundaries, while inaccurate classification indicates conversations between users are homogeneous despite varying attributes among users.

5   Experimentation

Using the classifiers presented in Section 4, we analyze the accuracy of each technique on two real world Facebook data sets.[1] We begin by providing an overview of our data set and the frequency of potential privacy conflicts, finding that asymmetric privacy settings are common throughout Facebook. We then examine the accuracy of each classifier and whether the intuition behind each technique proved correct. Our results show classification using information gleaned from privacy conflicts consistently outperforms predictions that lack the auxiliary information, proving that conflicts can be analyzed to expose meaningful sensitive information. Further, we find that accuracy is directly related to the number of conflicts between a user and his friends. As more information is unintentionally exposed to the network, we can construct an increasingly accurate image about a user, highlighting the necessity of multi-party privacy.

5.1   Data Set

Our experimental data set consists of over 83,000 real world Facebook user profiles as shown in Table 1. The profiles are drawn from two Facebook subnetworks

---

[1] It is possible – if tedious – to manually or semi-manually gather Facebook profile data without violating Facebook's Terms of Service which prohibits automated crawling.

Table 1. Our data set consists of two geographically distinct subnetworks of Facebook, amounting to over 80,000 profiles used to identify privacy conflicts and infer personal attributes

Statistic	Network A	Network B
Profiles in data set	42,796	40,544
Fraction of Facebook subnetwork	57.70%	52.92%
Number of friends	4,353,669	3,290,740
Number of wall posts	1,898,908	1,364,691
Fraction of profiles public	44%	35%
Fraction of profiles private	56%	65%

distinguished by geographic location, with 43,000 users associating themselves with Network A and another 40,000 users with Network B. In addition to profile pages, our data set contains over 7.5 million links between friends and 3.3 million wall posts. Of the profiles in our data set, 44% of Network A members allow a public user to view their data as opposed to 35% of Network B. This provides us with a subset of over 33,000 profiles with publicly accessible information to analyze for privacy conflicts. The rates which users reveal personal information in their profiles are shown in Figure 2. We find that users readily supply their gender (required when signing up for an account) and media interests, while less than 15% reveal a religious affiliation. After a brief preprocessing phase to correct spelling errors, group semantically similar terms, and prune unlikely labels, we identify 22 labels to describe personal attributes and over a thousand labels for media interests.

5.2   Frequency of Privacy Conflicts

Analyzing our data set, we verify that asymmetric privacy requirements between friends are a common occurrence. Using each profile in our data set, we examine public lists of friends for references to private users. We repeat this same process for wall pages, identifying messages written by private users that are exposed by public pages. The results of our analysis are shown in Table 2. We identify over 1.7 million relationships and roughly 700,000 wall posts referencing private profiles that are publicly exposed by friends due to the lack of multi-party privacy controls. This amounts to approximately 96 references per user in Network A

Table 2. Frequency of privacy conflicts between public and private users. An average private profile in our data set has over 80 references publicly exposed by friends with weaker privacy requirements.

Statistic	Network A	Network B
Number of exposed friends	1,012,280	612,387
Average exposed friends per profile	42.18	23.24
Number of exposed posts	407,278	289,877
Average exposed posts per profile	53.85	43.12

Table 3. Classifier accuracy for profiles with more than 50 privacy conflicts, representing the upper 25% of our data set. Classifiers using leaked private information consistently outperforms the baseline.

Profile Attribute	# of Labels	Baseline	Friend	Wall Content
Gender	2	61.91%	67.08%	**76.29%**
Political Views	6	51.53%	**58.07%**	49.38%
Religious Views	7	75.45%	**83.52%**	53.80%
Relation Status	7	39.45%	**45.68%**	44.24%
Favorite Music	604	30.29%	**43.33%**	-
Favorite Movies	490	44.30%	**51.34%**	-
Favorite TV Shows	205	59.19%	**66.08%**	-
Favorite Books	173	42.23%	**44.23%**	-

and 66 references in Network B. The skew in Network B towards fewer conflicts is a result of fewer publicly accessible pages for the network, as described earlier in Table 1. Analyzing each user's list of friends, we find on average that our data set contains information for only 35% of friends, leaving another 65% of friends with profiles that may leak private information and increase the frequency of conflicts.

5.3   Classifier Accuracy

To test the accuracy of using auxiliary information leaked by friends for predicting private attributes, we run each of the classifiers presented in Section 4 on both networks in our data set. We simulate closed profiles by concealing an open profile's attributes during classification, after which we compare the classifier's results against the true profile values. We measure the predictive success of our classifiers using standard cross-validation techniques; each classifier builds a model using 90% of the profiles in a network and is tested on the remaining 10%. This process is repeated ten times, using a different 10% of the network each round to ensure that every profile is used only once, averaging the results from each run.

The accuracy of each classifier for profiles with over 50 privacy conflicts can be seen in Table 3. We find that the friend classifier consistently outperforms the baseline classifier, predicting profile attributes with up to 84% accuracy. Comparing the results, the wall classifier performs the best at predicting a user's gender, but fails to draw meaningful conclusions about other attributes due to the homogeneity of conversations. Accuracy for both classifiers hinges on having enough auxiliary information leaked by friends to draw meaningful predictions. Plotting accuracy as a function of privacy conflicts, we find that accuracy grows roughly linearly with the amount of exposed information, as shown in Figure 3(a). As our data set contains only 35% of potentially conflicting friends, in practice, classification will be far more accurate given a more complete data set, assuming the trend toward accuracy remains constant. We now examine each of the classifiers in detail, validating the assumptions behind each technique.

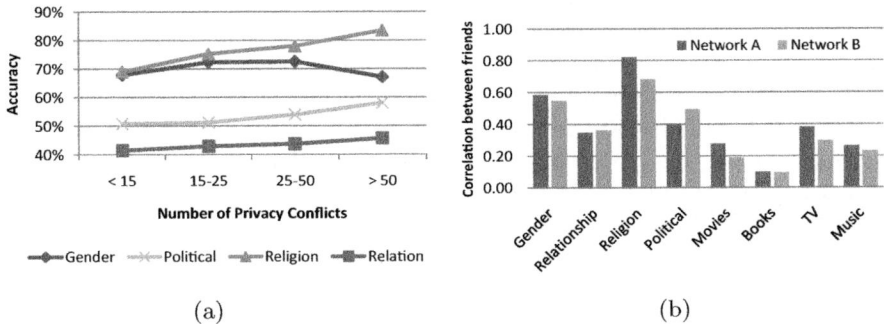

Fig. 3. (a) Accuracy of the friend classifier grows roughly linearly as a function of the number of privacy conflicts. (b) Correlation of attributes between two friends. Our classifiers rely on the assumption that two friends share similar interests. This is largely true with religion, but not for books.

Friend Classifier. The friend classifier operates on the assumption that friends have correlated features, capitalizing on information exposed by a user's friends to infer properties about the user. The friend classifier consistently outperforms the baseline, by up to 13%, for predicting a user's musical interests.

Accuracy of the friend classifier is intrinsically tied to the probability that two friends share the same feature. We measured the rates at which friends share attributes and present the results in Figure 3(b). The friend classifier can predict religion relatively well even for a limited number of samples due to the strong likelihood that two friends will share the same faith when listed. Conversely, predicting a user's gender requires far more samples to overcome the fact that most users are friends with roughly equal numbers of men and women. Surprisingly, the cross-correlation between any pair of attributes is below 20%. This means that using a friend's religion to predict a user's gender is less effective than had the friend's gender been available, but is still useful to include in classification.

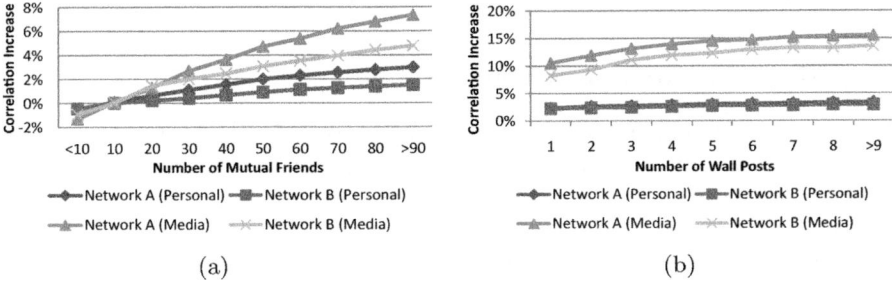

Fig. 4. (a) Analyzing the improvement of feature correlation as a function of mutual friends. Friends with large cliques of mutual friends are more likely to share features, compared to the average. (b) Analyzing the improvement of feature correlation as a function of wall posts. Friends with frequent communication tend to have stronger correlated media interests, compared to the average.

To weight relationships where users are more likely to share correlated interests, the friend classifier includes information about the number of mutual friends and the frequency of communication between two users. To validate the use of both weights, we measured the correlation of attributes between two friends as a function of mutual friends, shown in Figure 4(a), and communication frequency, shown in Figure 4(b). Both figures show a tendency toward shared interests for higher numbers of mutual friends and frequent communication. To understand how these weights improve accuracy, we re-classified our data set using a friend classifier that ignored both mutual friends and wall posts. On average, including the additional weights resulted in 1-2% more accurate predictions.

Wall Classifier. The wall classifier analyzes conversations leaked between friends to determine properties about a user. The results presented in Table 3 show that the classifier performs best when predicting a user's gender, but fails to produce meaningful results for all other attributes. Successful prediction of a user's gender derives from differences between the words used by women and men, while the remaining attributes such as religion or political view show no overwhelming tendency towards discussions that result in different word frequencies. Nevertheless, the appearance of terms such as sports, television shows, and news articles all expose a users's interests and can erode privacy. We leave the application of more sophisticated document classification models for future work.

6   Enforcing Multi-party Privacy

Having explored the extent that privacy conflicts appear throughout social networks and their potential risk, we now present a solution for enforcing multi-party privacy. Using the formalism presented in Section 3, we define a new access control framework for social network data. The framework enforces the mutual privacy requirements of all users referenced by a piece of data to prevent privacy violations, mitigating any risk of aggregating leaked information. We prototype our solution as a Facebook application that transparently enforces multi-party privacy without requiring interaction from users.

6.1   Mutual Privacy Requirements

Privacy conflicts currently arise in social networks because only the owner u of data can specify a privacy policy P_u, regardless of whether multiple users have an interest in keeping the data private. To adopt a mutually acceptable privacy policy for *all* parties, each user w referenced in content must be able to augment the policy set by u. To achieve multi-party privacy, we allow every user w to specify an exposure policy $V_w(g, i)$ for each page g and the information on that page i. The policy V_w's granularity can be page and reference specific, or alternatively, represent a policy for all pages throughout the social network. For example, a user w can specify that only w's friends can view wall posts written by w, encompassing the set of all wall pages, g, and the individual posts

i. Our framework can also accommodate fine-grained policies; for example, a user w can set a policy that allows only friends and not family to view pictures posted by w's friends. In practice, we expect most users to set coarse rather than fine-grained exposure policies that restrict access to all information for a user w.

For each piece of information i on page g, the largest set of users who can view i without violating any user's privacy policy can be represented by the mutual privacy policy $P_m(g, i)$:

$$P_m(g, i) = P_u(g) \bigcap_w V_w(g, i) \qquad (3)$$

P_m represents the set of users that the content owner u and all the associated parties $w \in S(i)$ mutually trust with their personal data. In the absence of mutually trusted friends, P_m tends towards the empty set, resulting in i being hidden from every user. However, the majority of the privacy conflicts we identified involve only two users, such as bidirectional links between friends, reducing the number of policies which must be satisfied. Photos and wall posts that refer to multiple users present a more complex situation where access to content is highly restricted due to multiple exposure policies. The potentially limited size of P_m is a byproduct of satisfying every user's privacy without bias; otherwise, a larger P_m would only violate one user's expectation of privacy.

For social networks that allow a user w to remove references to himself, such as with Facebook photos, multi-party privacy policies represent a stronger alternative. A user removing a reference to himself from a compromising image still leaves the privacy violating content exposed, if only harder to identify. Conversely, multi-party privacy guarantees that every user's privacy requirements are satisfied. This extends to situations where users cannot remove themselves such as with friendships, group membership, and comments, guaranteeing that privacy is always satisfied.

6.2   Prototyping Multi-party Privacy

To demonstrate the feasibility of multi-party privacy, we create two Facebook applications that reproduce the functionality of a friend list and wall page while enforcing mutual privacy policies. These prototypes serve to show how Facebook could implement multi-party privacy; they do not replace the existing friend and wall pages which Facebook prevents from being modified by applications.

Assuming the applications are installed on a fully public profile, the privacy-enhanced friend list conceals the names of friends with exposure policies that prohibit a third party from seeing the relationship. Similarly, the privacy-enhanced wall conceals wall posts if the original sender prohibits a third party's access. Currently, if an exposure policy for a user is not specified, the application places privacy as a priority and automatically conceals references pertaining to the user. For non-public profiles where the owner policy is more restrictive than an exposure policy, the owner policy takes precedent. The result of each of these policies is a system that guarantees a user's wall posts and friends cannot be exposed against his will.

By modifying friend and wall pages to restrict access based on a reader's permissions, we are potentially changing static structures into dynamic documents that must be reprocessed each access. There is already a precedent for implementing tailored pages in Facebook, such as the news feed, which provides each user a distinct set of stories based on their interests and friends that changes as the day goes by. Enforcing multi-party privacy can thus be seen as an extension of news feeds, where the content displayed is based on privacy controls rather than interests. By adopting the enforcement of multi-party privacy, Facebook users gain control over all their private information, even if it is uploaded by another party.

7   Related Work

There is an extensive body of research on protecting and examining privacy in social networks. The most related of these works to our research are attempt to demonstrate flaws in the current privacy controls of social networks. Zheleva et al. [17] examine the risks of revealing group membership and friendships, while He et al. model correlated features between friends as a Bayesian network [18]. Adapting previous approaches to attribute inference, Mislove et al. [20] looked at community structures among friends, finding that tight-knit communities often shared highly correlated features. Our work can be seen as a refinement of their techniques, presenting new ways to identify meaningful friends and filter relationships that are likely to impede inference. We also examine previously unexplored avenues such as wall posts for inference, pointing out that any relationship or tag between two users can potentially violate privacy.

While we limit our discussion to preventing crawling and mining by third parties, other researchers have looked at how to protect information from social network providers and server break-ins. flyByNight [25], NOYB [26], and FaceCloak [27] all use encryption or steganography to protect a user's personal information to prevent a social network operator such as Facebook from reading or mining personal data. Keys are then distributed to trusted friends out of band from the social network operator, allowing friends to decrypt profile information. Despite the potential added privacy from encryption, each of these protection mechanisms rely on the social network to keep track of friends and do not extend to content posted by friends, leaving users exposed to the inference techniques we describe.

Other research in extending social network privacy includes protecting users from third party applications. Social networks such as MySpace and Facebook allow users to install applications such as games or media plugins, in turn granting the application access to all of their personal data. Applications currently lack access control restrictions, allowing programs to offload all of a user's data in addition to that of a user's friends. Felt et al. [28] and Singh et al. [29] both propose new application architectures to restrict personal data available to applications. Because applications are granted access to both the installer's data and the installer's friend's data, application security must address the requirements of multi-party privacy to guarantee users are not put at risk by their friends.

In addition to privacy protections within social networks, data released by network operators to the public also poses a significant challenge to user privacy. De-anonymization efforts [30,31,32,33] have shown that publishing anonymized or restricted social graph information is riddled with complications. These same techniques for de-anonymization can also be used for inferring properties about data leaked by users within social networks, highlighting the need for better privacy controls that suit the range [34,35] of each users privacy expectations.

8   Conclusion

In this paper, we have shown how existing privacy controls in social networks fail to protect a user from personal content leaked by friends. As photos, stories, and data are shared across the network, conflicting privacy requirements between friends can result in information being unintentionally exposed to the public. We formalized multi-party privacy requirements which guarantee that the privacy concerns of all users affected by an image or comment are mutually satisfied. The current lack of multi-party privacy results in scattered references to users throughout social networks that can be collected by adversaries who have the resources, sophistication, and motivation to glean as much information from social networks as possible. We have shown how seemingly innocuous references to users can be aggregated and analyzed to construct meaningful predictions about a user's personal attributes and media interests. This slow erosion of personal privacy can be prevented by the adoption of multi-party privacy controls. We prototyped these controls for Facebook, showing how multi-party privacy can be adopted, returning control over personal data in social networks to users.

References

1. Facebook: Statistics (2009),
   http://www.facebook.com/press/info.php?statistics
2. MySpace: Statistics (2009), http://www.myspace.com/statistics
3. Miller, C.: Twitter makes itself more useful (April 2010),
   http://bits.blogs.nytimes.com/2010/04/14/
   twitter-makes-itself-more-useful/
4. MySpace: Privacy Policy (2008),
   http://www.myspace.com/index.cfm?fuseaction=misc.privacy
5. Facebook: Privacy Policy (2008), http://www.facebook.com/policy.php
6. George, A.: Living online: The end of privacy? New Scientist (September 2006)
7. Sarno, D.: Facebook founder Mark Zuckerberg responds to privacy concerns. Los Angeles Times (2009)
8. CareerBuilder: Forty-five Percent of Employers Use Social Networking Sites to Research Job Candidates, CareerBuilder Survey Finds (2009)
9. Maternowski, K.: Campus police use Facebook. The Badger Herald (January 2006)
10. Greenberg, A.: Mining MySpace. Forbes (2007)
11. Shachtman, N.: Exclusive: U.S. Spies Buy Stake in Firm That Monitors Blogs, Tweets. Wired (2009)
12. Richmond, R.: Phishers Now Hitting Twitter. The New York Times (2008)
13. McMillan, R.: Facebook Worm Refuses to Die. PC World (2008)

14. Room, F.P.: Facebook Announces Privacy Improvements in Response to Recommendations by Canadian Privacy Commissioner (2009)
15. Bradley, T.: Bing Lands Deals with Twitter and Facebook. PC World (2009)
16. Wright, A.: Mining the Web for Feelings, Not Facts. The New York Times (2009)
17. Zheleva, E., Getoor, L.: To join or not to join: The illusion of privacy in social networks with mixed public and private user profiles. In: Proceedings of the 18th international conference on World wide web (2009)
18. He, J., Chu, W., Liu, Z.: Inferring privacy information from social networks. In: Intelligence and Security Informatics (2006)
19. Becker, J., Chen, H.: Measuring Privacy Risk in Online Social Networks. Web 2.0 Security and Privacy (2009)
20. Mislove, A., Viswanath, B., Gummadi, K.P., Druschel, P.: You are who you know: Inferring user profiles in online social networks. In: Proceedings of the 3rd ACM International Conference of Web Search and Data Mining (2010)
21. Jones, E., Gerard, H.: Foundations of social psychology. John Wiley & Sons Inc., Chichester (1967)
22. Gilbert, E., Karahalios, K.: Predicting tie strength with social media. In: Proceedings of the 27th international conference on Human factors in computing systems (2009)
23. Bohning, D.: Multinomial logistic regression algorithm. Annals of the Institute of Statistical Mathematics 44(1), 197–200 (1992)
24. Jones, K., et al.: A statistical interpretation of term specificity and its application in retrieval. Journal of documentation 60, 493–502 (2004)
25. Lucas, M., Borisov, N.: flybynight: Mitigating the privacy risks of social networking. In: Proceedings of the 7th ACM workshop on Privacy in the electronic society, pp. 1–8. ACM, New York (2008)
26. Guha, S., Tang, K., Francis, P.: NOYB: Privacy in online social networks. In: Proceedings of the first workshop on Online social networks, pp. 49–54. ACM, New York (2008)
27. Luo, W., Xie, Q., Hengartner, U.: FaceCloak: An architecture for user privacy on social networking sites. In: Proceedings of the 2009 IEEE International Conference on Privacy, Security, Risk and Trust, PASSAT 2009 (August 2009)
28. Felt, A., Evans, D.: Privacy protection for social networking APIs. In: 2008 Web 2.0 Security and Privacy, W2SP 2008 (2008)
29. Singh, K., Bhola, S., Lee, W.: xBook: Redesigning privacy control in social networking platforms. In: Proceedings of the 18th USENIX Security Symposium (2009)
30. Narayanan, A., Shmatikov, V.: Robust de-anonymization of large sparse datasets. In: IEEE Symposium on Security and Privacy (2008)
31. Narayanan, A., Shmatikov, V.: De-anonymizing social networks. In: Proceedings of the IEEE Symposium on Security & Privacy (2009)
32. Backstrom, L., Dwork, C., Kleinberg, J.: Wherefore art thou r3579x?: Anonymized social networks, hidden patterns, and structural steganography. In: Proceedings of the 16th international conference on World Wide Web (2007)
33. Bonneau, J., Anderson, J., Anderson, R., Stajano, F.: Eight friends are enough: Social graph approximation via public listings. In: Proceedings of the Second ACM EuroSys Workshop on Social Network Systems. ACM, New York (2009)
34. Gross, R., Acquisti, A.: Information revelation and privacy in online social networks. In: Proceedings of WPES 2005, pp. 71–80 (2005)
35. Acquisti, A., Gross, R.: Imagined communities: Awareness, information sharing, and privacy on the Facebook. In: Danezis, G., Golle, P. (eds.) PET 2006. LNCS, vol. 4258, pp. 36–58. Springer, Heidelberg (2006)

The Impact of Unlinkability on Adversarial Community Detection: Effects and Countermeasures

Shishir Nagaraja

University of Illinois at Urbana-Champaign
1308 West Main Street, Urbana, IL 61801, USA
sn275@illinois.edu

Abstract. We consider the threat model of a mobile-adversary drawn from contemporary computer security literature, and explore the dynamics of community detection and hiding in this setting. Using a real-world social network, we examine the extent of network topology information an adversary is required to gather in order to accurately ascertain community membership information. We show that selective surveillance strategies can improve the adversary's efficiency over random wiretapping. We then consider possible privacy preserving defenses; using anonymous communications helps, but not much; however, the use of counter-surveillance techniques can significantly reduce the adversary's ability to learn community membership. Our analysis shows that even when using anonymous communications an adversary placing a selectively chosen 8% of the nodes of this network under surveillance (using key-logger probes) can de-anonymize the community membership of as much as 50% of the network. Uncovering all community information with targeted selection requires probing as much as 75% of the network. Finally, we show that a privacy conscious community can substantially disrupt community detection using only local knowledge even while facing up to the asymmetry of a completely knowledgeable mobile-adversary.

1 Introduction

Anonymous communications are useful in building resistance against a global passive adversary who can subject the targets to traffic analysis. In the context of communication channels, anonymity is described in terms of the channel properties of *unlinkability* and *unobservability*, with many schemes as well as deployed systems [8, 10] focusing their efforts on providing the former property.

While anonymous communications plays an important role in ensuring traffic analysis resistance properties of a communication channel, ensuring user anonymity requires much more work. For instance, traffic data collected by compromising a user's personal computer necessarily impacts the privacy of others in the user's social network. If a small fraction of end-user computers are compromised then how does this impact user anonymity? This is the main question we attempt to answer in this paper.

M.J. Atallah and N. Hopper (Eds.): PETS 2010, LNCS 6205, pp. 253–272, 2010.

It is well known that the practical risk to user privacy increases with the aggregation of personal data. One such instance is that of modern email service providers with huge storage allowances and accessible user interfaces attracting a large number of users. This results in the aggregation of a large amount of social network information within the administrative power of a very small number of people running the service. An attacker who has partial or complete knowledge of the social network can cause significant damage to user privacy.

Analyzing large amounts of social traffic data such as a large corpus of emails is a highly time consuming task. However, if the attacker can also accurately determine community membership then he can massively reduce his work load by reducing only clustering traffic flows one community at a time. Indeed the adversary's capability in detecting community membership brings him significantly closer to significant privacy invasion than the mere discovery of nodes and internode relations (substantiated further in Section 3). Thus the combined use of text analysis methods along with accurate community detection algorithms constitutes an important threat to user privacy. As we shall see, this threat is only slightly mitigated by the use of current anonymous communications technology. To what extent is the risk diminished and what can users do to defend themselves? We develop a graph-theoretic framework to analyse a mobile adversary and apply it to a real-world social network dataset to find out.

The threat model of a mobile adversary is further justified by the increasing popularity of *social-malware attacks* [27]. In their report, Nagaraja and Anderson describe a case of malware-based electronic surveillance of a political organization. By exploiting the social network connecting members within the victim organization, the mobile adversary moved from member to member and managed to copy off entire hard-drives worth of information from most individuals. Subsequently, similar attacks have been reported by hundreds of organizations and individuals in the popular press and in private communications.

The results of this paper only apply to adversarial community detection on **social networks** alone and not to similar sounding applications in very different contexts such as anomaly or misuse detection.

2   Community Detection

The problem of splitting a network into a number of sub-communities is not a new one. The first algorithm for graph partitioning was proposed by Kernighan and Lin [21]. A detailed survey of partitioning algorithms in computer science can be found in [12]. The problem of community detection has also been studied in the context of many graph-theoretic clustering algorithms. In its simplest form, a community may be considered as a group of nodes which are densely connected by edges. For example a variety of node clustering algorithms for graphs with the use of shingling techniques, matrix co-clustering techniques, and tile determination in matrices [5, 16, 17] can be used for community detection in graphs. A related problem is that of local triangle counting [2], which can be leveraged to determine an idea of the unit dense structures (triangles) in the underlying graph. The problem is also related to that of finding dense cliques or dense regions in the underlying graph [1, 31, 38]. These techniques are designed for generic graphs rather than the specific case of social networks. The problem of community detection [7, 22, 24, 35, 36] in social networks has also been widely studied because of the increasing importance of social networking applications. A survey of a number of important algorithms for community detection is provided in [36]. A note on the important statistical properties of web communities is discussed in [24].

3   Motivation and Context

In this paper, we shall study how the topology of the social network of users affects the amount of effort on the attacker's part to uniquely identify the community association of each user, using graph topology information alone. The effectiveness of community detection attacks depends heavily on the topology of the underlying network. If the attacker is not able to detect communities and associate each user with a particular community, then the social network topology is said to be resistant to community detection attacks under the given threat model. Among other things, the threat model specifies how much information is available to the attacker.

The attacker might also employ additional traffic-flow attacks such as capturing and directly clustering network data flows instead of working with the social network topology, we do not consider such attacks here. *Traffic flow analysis* [18, 33] can be used to cluster flows and ultimately classify users into communities using information related to the protocol or mechanism in use. Similar clustering (attack) methods [6, 11, 25, 39] can be applied to human communication in order to de-anonymize the community membership of a social network. However such clustering methods do not scale very well. The reason is simple: the effort expended by an adversary depends on the amount of information processed by the attacker per pair of communicating users Alice and Bob. The community detection attacks we consider here, only use one bit of information: does Alice communicate with Bob, or not? These attack algorithms can be readily extended to also consider the magnitude of communication between Alice and Bob. Such algorithms have two advantages: (a) they are more scalable than traffic flow attack algorithms whilst requiring lesser storage and lesser processing power, and (b) they are robust to variances traffic flow information.

Community detection algorithms are not an end to themselves and they must be used in conjunction with communication traffic flow analysis and/or text classification algorithms for successfully de-anonymizing community membership in a social network. For a standard reference on inductive learning algorithms see Dumais et.al [11].

Applying such algorithms to social network communications is a two stage process. In the first stage, the attacker constructs a (per edge) vector of features from traffic data (say email messages) for every pair of communicating users. In the second stage, he applies a clustering algorithm over the edge vectors.

A popular method from the datamining community is the agglomerative hier-archical clustering [39] which runs in $O(N^{2 \log(N)})$ time and can be applied to cluster edges into communities in a bottom-up manner, where N is the number of vertices in the social network. An alternate approach is the use of stochastic inference techniques [6, 25] that provide extensions to handle classification of document networks and various other features, however these have even higher computational complexity.

While these algorithms have higher computational complexity, they are of much interest in confirming that the communities identified by the membership detection algorithms are actually interesting to the attacker. Instead of running these flow analysis algorithms on the entire communication traffic data, he sim-ply analyzes (the much smaller amount of) traffic flow information corresponding to the identified communities. By reducing the size of the input traffic data, the attacker can not only scale-up traffic flow analysis but also reduce the amount of input noise. This opens up the problem space to sensitive flow-analysis algo-rithms that might otherwise be unusable in the presence of noisy data.

4   Analytical Framework for Hidden Communities

4.1   Modularity

We consider social networks comprising of people and relations. The social net-work is represented by a graph $G(V, E)$, where people are represented as nodes, while relationships between people are represented as edges. Sets V and E are the set of all nodes and and the set of all edges, respectively. Each edge is associ-ated with an integer weight which is an indicator of the quantity of information exchanged between the two end-points.

In this paper, we will study the problem of adversarial community detection in large-scale networks. As discussed earlier, we would like to determine naturally forming communities in the network. We note that such properties are naturally satisfied by utilizing the concept of *modularity* of vertex sets which previously been used with some success. Before discussing the definition of communities, we will first define some notations and definitions, and explain the concept of modularity in an intuitive way.

Modularity is a notion of community structure where communities are not defined by dense clusters of vertices connected by a small number of edges (*small cuts*). Rather, communities are defined by vertex sets that have either less than *expected* number of edges across each other. Informally, a module is a subgraph whose nodes are more likely to be connected to one another than to the nodes outside the subgraph.

We assume that the *entire network* from which the communities are defined is denoted by $G = (V, E)$, where V is the universal set of nodes, and E is the set of edges defined on V. For ease in explanation, we assume that edges are undirected, although the technique can also be generalized to the directed case. Modularity is defined on a vertex set with respect to *only the subgraph induced by a particular set of nodes.* Therefore, let us first define the concept of an induced edges and induced subgraph for a vertex subset.

Definition 1 (Induced Edges). *Let $G = (V, E)$ be a given graph with node set V and undirected edge set E. Let $S \subseteq V$ be a subset of vertices from G. Then, the induced edge set $L(S, E)$ for the vertex set V is defined as all the edges $R \subseteq E$, such that both ends of any edge in R lie in S in the original graph G. The set R is denoted by $L(S, E)$.*

Thus, the induced edge set uses only the edges for which both edges lie within a given vertex subset. All other edges are ignored. The induced edges can be immediately used to define the induced graph $I(G, V)$.

Definition 2 (Induced Graph). *Let $G = (V, E)$ be a given graph with node set V and undirected edge set E. Let $S \subseteq V$ be a subset of vertices from G. Then the induced graph $I(G, S)$ for the vertex set S is defined as the subgraph including only the vertex set S and all induced edges on this vertex set, which have both ends within S. Thus, the induced graph $I(G, S)$ essentially corresponds to the graph $(S, L(S, E))$ with vertex set S and induced edge set $L(S, E)$.*

A given network might have several embedded subgraphs with a range of connectivity characteristics. In general, we would like to determine the embedded networks, which have high level of information flow, but whose edges are a result of local emergent processes rather than defined by a globally agreed blueprint to achieve such a flow. Therefore, we define the concept of *modularity* of a set of nodes S, with respect to the *induced graph* for vertex set V.

Using previously defined terms, consider graph $G = (V, E)$ where V is the universal set of nodes, and E is the set of edges defined on V, consider the induced graph $I(G, S)$ for a vertex set S. Let d_i^G be the sum of edges incident on vertex i in graph G. Given G, we define a graph G_{random} with the same number of vertices, but where every possible edge is created with probability $d_i d_j / 2|V|$. That is, the endpoints are randomly selected.

Definition 3 ((S, V)-modularity). *The (S, V)-modularity of a set of vertices $S \subseteq V$ in G is the difference between the number of edges whose endpoints lie entirely in S computed over* **induced graph** *$I(G, S)$ and the* expected *number of edges whose endpoints lie in S computed over induced graph $I(G_{random}, V)$. Therefore, if $a(S)$ be the sum of degrees of vertices S in the induced graph $I(G, S)$, and $r(S)$ be the expected sum of degrees of vertices S in induced graph $I(G_{random}, S)$ then the (S, V)-modularity is defined as follows:*

$$Q(S, V) = \frac{a(S) - r(S)}{\sum_{i \in S} d_i^G} \tag{1}$$

We note that a high value of $Q(S, V)$ implies that most of the edges are used in *mixing* information within S rather than between S and $V - S$. A low value of $Q(S, V)$ implies that S is a rather poor choice for a community of nodes. Formally, we can now define the problem of determining all the vertex subsets which are relatively sparse and have modularity above a certain user-defined threshold. We define the (α, β)-hidden community as follows:

Definition 4 $((\alpha, \beta)$-hidden community). *Consider a graph $G = (V, E)$. We define the (α, β)-hidden community as a subset S of vertices, which satisfies the following properties:*

- *The set S is a subset of the universal set of vertices V.*
- *The total number of edges in the induced graph $I(G, S)$ is at most $\alpha \cdot |V|$.*
- *The induced graph $I(G, S)$ has modularity at least β. In other words, we have $Q(S, V) \geq \beta$.*

We note that the above definition is focussed on determining an *edge structure* in the community which is focussed on high amount of information flow, in the presence of edge formation based on social communication; i.e. no DHTs or random-graph topologies. Clearly, the level of information flow implies the presence of a community, but the relatively sparse presence of edges (compared to highly dense graphs) ensures that such a community is hidden to methods which work purely with techniques such as the clustering coefficient. The definition above can then be used to create a problem definition on determining hidden communities with respect to the parameters α and β.

Problem 1 (Hidden Community Detection). Consider a network $G = (V, E)$. We wish to determine *all the vertex subsets $S = \{S_1 \ldots S_r\}$* which satisfy the following properties:

- Each vertex subset S_i is an (α, β)-hidden community with respect to the graph G with $\alpha = 0.25$ and $\beta = .10$.
- Each vertex set S_i is *maximal* with respect to S. In other words, there is no other vertex set $T \in S$, such that $T \supset S_i$.

The principle of maximality is useful in reducing the size of the output, and ensuring that redundant subsets are not unnecessarily reported.

The choice of β is based on empirical observation that most detected communities have $\beta > .25$ (a complete graph has a modularity of 1).

Finally, we note that the above model of hidden communities is **not designed to take covert networks into account**, but rather members of the general public whose privacy is easily compromised due to the network externalities of electronic surveillance programs [9]. We seek to understand and address the latter category of risks.

4.2   Threat Model – Mobile Passive Adversary

Our threat model is based on the mobile adversary model first proposed by Ostrovsky and Yung [30]. The attacker is a malicious global passive adversary whose goal is to detect (α, β)-hidden communities in the network. Our model is inspired by an ISP level adversary that wishes to detect hidden communities. Our study deals with two scenarios, the case of the fully knowledgeable adversary and the partially knowledgeable adversary.

Adversary with full knowledge: Since the attacker is global, he is aware of the existence of people (vertices) in the social network graph. When communicating parties make no attempt at anonymizing communication, the attacker is also aware of the social relations (interconnecting edges) between them.

Adversary with partial knowledge: If anonymous channels [8, 10, 32] guaranteeing unlinkability[1] are used, then the attacker is only aware of all the vertices of the graph but does not have any information about the edges. To successfully detect hidden communities the attacker must uncover as much information about edge relationships as possible. He does so by placing **probes** on vertices of the graph. This might be achieved by a strategically placed keylogger on a victim's computing device as in the case of the Tibetan attacks [27], for example. Further, the attacker has finite probing capability and cannot simultaneously probe everyone. In any time interval t, the attacker can only probe a fraction of people on the social network to uncover topology information.

Additionally, our attacker is **mobile**, which means he can remove a probe from one vertex and place it on a different vertex of the attacker's choice at time $t' > t$. The number of probes ϵ is finite, hence the attacker can only compromise a fraction of vertices at any point in time. However as the attacker is mobile, he can progressively learn about the entire network over an extended period of time. Each time interval corresponds to a *round*.

Definition 5 (mobile ϵ-attacker:). *Consider a graph $G = (U, A)$ and $0 < \epsilon \leq 1$, the ϵ-attacker is a global passive adversary who can **probe**(observe all communications originating from) a set of vertices $f_t \subseteq U$ upper bounded at $|f_t| = \epsilon|U|$ at round $t > 0$.*

In other words an attacker is allowed to place probes over a constant fraction of vertices, and also, move the probes from vertex to vertex at the beginning of a new round.

Definition 6 ((ϵ, t)-view:). *Consider graph $G = (U, A)$ and an ϵ-attacker. The (ϵ, t)-view is defined as the graph $I(G, V)$ induced by vertex set V, where $V = \{f_0 \cup f_1 \cdots \cup f_t\}$ is the set of all vertices probed by the attacker by round t.*

Finally, an attack involves the use of two types of strategies. In every round, a *surveillance strategy* drives probe placement while a *community detection strategy* processes the information gathered by the attacker. At each round t, the surveillance strategy (is an algorithm) that accepts an (ϵ, t)-graph and outputs the set of vertices T that shall be probed in round $t+1$. Similarly, the community detection strategy (a different algorithm) accepts an (ϵ, t)-graph and outputs a set of (α, β)-hidden communities. Essentially, the attacker builds a graph using all the edge and vertex knowledge gained in previous rounds and then analyzes it using a community detection algorithm to discover any hidden communities.

---

[1] When nodes of a network communicate via anonymous channels that offer unlinkability, an attacker monitoring network traffic cannot identify communication endpoints but knows traffic volume information. When unobservable channels are used the attacker cannot distinguish between communicating and non-communicating users.

4.3   Measuring Anonymity

Measuring anonymity in the context of this paper, is the measurement of the efficiency of community detection – the fraction of hidden-community detected.

As described in previous sections, the attacker combines various surveillance and community detection strategies to discover the community structure of a social network. Privacy sensitive users might wish to keep their community membership anonymous. However network topology inherently contains information about community memberships, and a mobile ϵ-adversary can gain access to this information. On the other hand privacy conscious members of a social network might wish not to be identified as belonging to a certain community or club even as they participate in it.

There are several ways in which one can express the anonymity a system provides. The notion of anonymity within Crowds [34] is close to the notion of anonymity we consider here – instead of being identified as a member of a specific community, the anonymity seeking user would wish to be identified as being part of a significantly larger community of users. However instead of a qualitative metric we measure anonymity quantitatively.

The adversary is said to have successfully de-anonymized the social network membership if he can accurately uncover vertex sets corresponding to one or more embedded communities. The *false negative rate FN* is defined as the fraction of (α, β)-community nodes being misclassified as being part of the larger community of vertices $V - S$.

Definition 7 (Community anonymity). *Invoking the concept of anonymity sets, the anonymity of a (α, β)-hidden community under a specific community detection strategy Ω is defined as follows:*

$$A((\alpha, \beta), \Omega) = \frac{V - FN * S}{|V - S|} \qquad (2)$$

We shall also refer to A using the term **miss-ratio**.

5   Newman's Community Detection Algorithm

As we have explained previously, a modularity based community detection method can be used to de-anonymize community membership in a social network by identifying vertex subsets corresponding to high modularity *scores*. Modularity based methods are fairly accurate among the scalable methods of community detection. They have been well tested and studied in a variety of social and biological networks within the complex networks community [14, 28].

Modularity reflects the extent, relative to a random network, to which edges are formed within communities rather than across them. By using modularity as a metric, we can assess the quality of any assignment of nodes to the same community (Eqn. 1). Hence, identifying community membership becomes a modularity maximization problem. Accordingly, Newman [28] proposed a community detection algorithm that optimizes the selection of S by calculating the second eigenvector over a matrix of modularity scores for each edge in $G(V, E)$. Let $N = |V|$ and we assume each vertex has $\log(N)$ edges as a rough approximation in a social network, Newman's algorithm computes scales as $O(N^2 + N \log(N))$.

Due to shortage of space, we refer the interested reader to the full description of Newman's algorithm in the original paper [28].

5.1 Alternate Algorithms and Approaches to Community Detection

Apart from Newman's modularity algorithm, we did consider *edge importance* based community structure detection approaches as well. In these approaches, the attacker iteratively removes the edges with the highest *importance*, which can be defined in different ways. Girvan and Newman [29] defined edge importance by its shortest path betweenness. The idea is that the edge with higher betweenness is typically responsible for connecting nodes from different communities. The fastest algorithm to calculate betweenness centrality is credited to Brandes [4], it has a computational complexity of $O(N^2 \log(N))$.

Fortunato [13] proposed *information centrality* to measure edge importance, defined as the relative *network efficiency* [23] drop caused by the removal of an edge. The time complexity of his algorithm is $O((N \log(N))^3 \times N)$. As the time complexity of betweenness and information centrality algorithms is not acceptable for community detection in massive networks, we removed these from our evaluation.

Further, preliminary experiments we conducted showed that when communities in G are separated by a *small-cut*, Newman's community detection algorithm performed fairly well in the presence of random errors (edges and nodes randomly added/removed across the cut) in the input topology – a linear increase in random noise in the network topology results in a linear increase in number of false positives, as opposed to an exponential increase of false positive rate we observed in the case of min-cut based methods.

Conductance based techniques such as SybilInfer [37] and SybilGuard [37] are interesting approaches that can be used for community detection based on the metric of graph conductance [20]. While these approaches are good for analyzing structured tightly knit communities that are separated by small cuts (such as DHTs and Sybil networks), their applicability in our context needs further study. One possible hurdle might be that conductance of the cut separating the hidden community (see section 5.2) and the rest of the graph is 0.0998. The SybilInfer work used a cutoff threshold of 0.10 to identify a cut between a Sybil community and the rest of the graph, while other cuts in the social network tended to have conductance in excess of 0.9.

5.2 Email Communication Network

Our network dataset [19] comprises of a social network harvested from email exchanges within a mid sized university of 1700 researchers, graduate students and staff. Each email address was mapped to a person. We discarded all email messages where either the sender or the receiver email address was not a university email address. This means we have left out relationships where two persons at the university might be connected via an outsider, and this could impact our results. We disregarded unidirectional email messages which removed bulk email messages as well as most spam. We added an edge between every two nodes that had sent at least one message in each direction. The weight of the edge was set as the sum total of messages exchanged between two nodes.

Next, we extracted the largest connected component or giant component consisting of 1133 people and 10903 relation. The data we obtained contained emails from two different departments, and this was correctly detected by the modularity community detection algorithm. We shall consider the smaller of the two partitions as the "hidden" community (in the sense that community members desire privacy) as far as our experiments are concerned, and the larger one as the "main" network into which the nodes of the hidden community will attempt to blend into. The giant component consists of two partitions: partition G_M with 831 nodes and 6807 edges shall be our main network and G_C, will be our (α, β)-hidden community of 302 nodes and 2574 edges.

6   Efficiency of Community Membership De-anonymization

In our model, the adversary's goal is to accurately determine the membership of each community in the network. Our first experiment attempts to measure the efficiency of community detection by different surveillance strategies. The ϵ-mobile adversary is limited by the number of probes (ϵ), which in turn limits his rate of gathering topology information. This in turn affects the success of

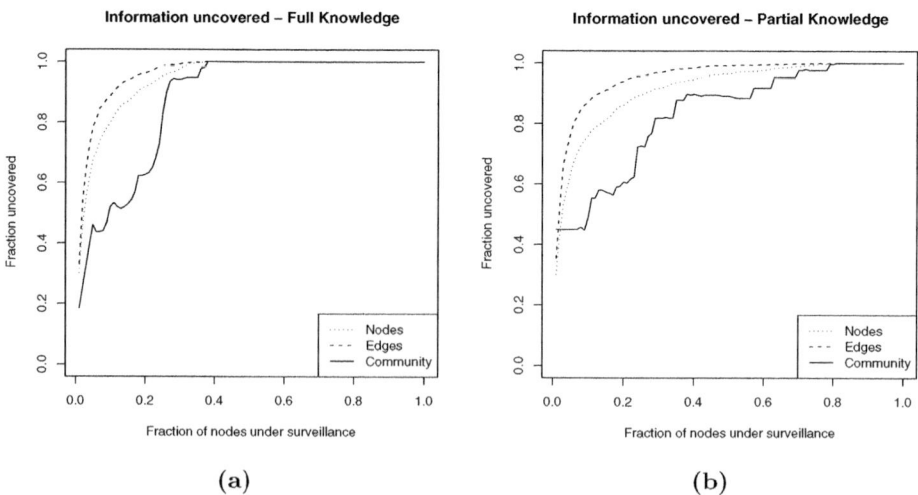

Fig. 1. De-anonymization efficiency

community de-anonymization goals, and we wish to measure how the adversary's success varies as the fraction of the network being directly probed increases.

We wish to determine the minimum ϵ value at which the ϵ-mobile adversary can fully determine community membership. To do so, we first establish the upper bound of attacker efficiency. For this purpose we consider the ϵ-mobile adversary in the context of full knowledge, as discussed in section 4.2. This might seem like a trivial exercise since the fully knowledgeable adversary learns little by probing. However full knowledge allows the attacker to compute the optimal probing sequence. Therefore this represents the best possible performance (upper bound) an ϵ bounded adversary might possibly come up with. We plot the fraction of nodes and edges discovered by the fully-knowledgeable adversary **using the probes alone**, in figure- 1.a, to show the upper bound of attacker efficiency. We also plot the fraction of the hidden-community detected (this is simply $1 - missratio$) using the graph uncovered by probing. Later in the section we will compare these with the efficiency of the *epsilon*-mobile adversary in the case of partial knowledge in figure- 1.b.

Of the many possible centrality measures that could be used to generate the optimal probing sequence, the most appropriate from the perspective of information flow is the flow betweenness centrality measure devised by Freeman [15]. The betweenness centrality C_b^v of a node v is defined as the number of all pairs shortest paths that pass through v:

$$C_B^v = \sum_{x \in V} \sum_{y \neq x \in V} \frac{\sigma_{xy}(v)}{\sigma_{xy}} \qquad (3)$$

Where σ_{xy} is the number of shortest paths between nodes x and y.

The upper bound of de-anonymizing community membership using this strategy is shown in figure- 1.a. After probing 8% of the nodes in the decreasing order of betweenness centrality, the adversary is aware of the existence of 76% of the nodes and 85% of the edges. This partially confirms one of the results of an earlier study by Danezis and Wittneben [9].

Interestingly, our study reveals that the community membership of only 50% of the nodes is correctly identified. The adversary then makes further progress as shown in table 1.

Table 1. Knowledge gained by attacker using optimal probing strategy

$\%probed = t\epsilon|V|$	% nodes	% edges	%Community uncovered
8	76	85	48
28	96	99	95
38	100	100	100

We now measure the adversary's accuracy in discovering community membership under the case of partial information. The ϵ-adversary with partial knowledge performs surveillance with a (non-optimal) probing sequence generated using traffic volume information. The adversary sorts the nodes in descending

Table 2. Knowledge gained by attacker using probe placement based on traffic volumes

$\%probed = t\epsilon|V|$	% nodes	% edges	%Community uncovered
8	73	84	45
28	96	90	58
38	97	91	86

order of traffic volumes and places a constant fraction of nodes under surveillance in successive rounds.

Figure- 1.b, shows the fruits of the adversary's efforts. The lack of full topology knowledge particularly dents the adversary's ability to effectively spy on the network as summarized in table 2: When 8% of the nodes are spied upon, 45% of the hidden community nodes are correctly identified whilst uncovering 73% of nodes and 84% of edges. However, while 90% of the nodes and 96% of the edges are known to the adversary by putting 28% of the nodes under surveillance, the only 58% of the hidden community known.

In terms of pure numbers the adversary is able to acquire a significant amount of topology knowledge by putting 28% of the network under surveillance in both threat models. However, hidden-community discovery is much harder. In the partial case, it requires the adversary to put almost 80% of the nodes under direct surveillance to enable him to accurately localize 99% of the hidden community nodes. This is in stark contrast to the upper bound provided by the case of the fully knowledgeable adversary who only needs to place 37% of the nodes under surveillance to gain the same amount of membership information.

6.1 Discussion

Does this mean that the use of anonymous communications increases the work load of the adversary by almost 100%? No, this is true only when the adversary needs to uncover the membership information of all nodes within the network. Our results show that in both the adversary models, placing 8% of the nodes under direct surveillance compromises the community membership of almost 50% of the nodes.

Since close to 80% of the population must be monitored to detect all the communities, it means that in the short run, government surveillance budgets are more likely to cause harm to privacy than to uncover hardened cells. On the other hand, it also means the social malware will be significantly successful even if only a small fraction of the user base is infected.

We are therefore interested in the privacy preserving countermeasures for **larger user communities** rather than for **covert communities** which will be invisible anyway. Being larger they are associated with higher detection rates, and are more difficult to hide. This is the reasoning behind the choice of community sizes for our experiments in section 5.2.

We note that the adversary's efficiency in community membership assignment in the case of partial knowledge is not only markedly lower than that of full topology knowledge, but has a slower growth rate. This is not surprising given the relatively complex structural characteristics of the information the adversary is trying to uncover.

7   The Efficiency of Counter-Detection Measures

We shall now consider defense responses to the ϵ-mobile community detecting adversary. To do so, we allow the (α, β)-hidden community to rewire itself in order to disrupt community detection.

We adopt the following defense model with multiple rounds: members of the hidden community can employ one of a number of counter-detection strategies involving topological rewiring, limited by a counter-detection budget at the beginning of every round. The adversary then runs community detection algorithms to deduce membership in every round.

Several topological manipulation options are open to the (α, β)-hidden community. Since the community is defined by vertex sets we do not explore counter-detection strategies based on removing vertices from the community. We also discount edge removal as a countermeasure since that would also disrupt information flow. Therefore, we shall focus our analysis on various strategies of *edge-addition* alone. The strategy of edge-addition can be also be understood as a method of selectively adding *cover traffic* to the network. Note that depending on the context of the social network this may not be a feasible defense in all contexts.

7.1   Counter-Detection Strategies Based on Edge Addition

The application of any counter-detection strategy consists of adding C additional edges (defense budget) whose end-points are chosen as follows.

Each end point is chosen according to a vertex centrality metric. We have previously discussed flow betweenness centrality, see Eqn. 3. We shall consider two more vertex centrality metrics: eigenvector centrality and degree centrality. A fourth option is to treat vertex centrality as a random value.

Degree centrality of a vertex i, d_i^G, is the sum of edges incident on vertex i in graph G.

Eigenvector centrality score [3] of a vertex corresponds to the values of the first eigenvector of the graph adjacency matrix; these scores may, in turn, be interpreted as arising from a reciprocal process in which the centrality of each vertex is proportional to the sum of the centralities of those vertices with whom he or she shares an edge.

Let $W = \{HB, HE, HD, RAND\}$ be a set of centrality measure functions. Let c be the set of hidden community nodes, and m be the set of main network nodes, corresponding to the entire vertex set of graphs G_C and G_M from Section 5.2. Each strategy involves adding an edge (i, j) with edge endpoints i and j chosen either from sequence $R_{X \in M}(c)$ the sequence of nodes in decreasing order of centrality measure X from the hidden-community vertex set, or similarly from $R_{X \in W}(m)$ the sequence of nodes drawn from the main network vertex set in decreasing order of centrality measure X. Also, each edge has one end-point in G_C and another in G_M.

For instance, $R_{HB}(c)$ defines a sequence of ordered vertices over c with decreasing of high-betweenness centrality values. Similarly, we have sequences $R_{HD}(c)$, $R_{HE}(c)$, $R_{RND}(c)$, $R_{HD}(m)$, $R_{HE}(m)$, and $R_{RND}(m)$.

An edge addition strategy is denoted as $Xx - Yy$ where $X, Y \in W$ and $x, y \in c, m$. Counter-detection strategy **HBc-HBm** involves adding an edge with an endpoint in $R_{HB}(c)$ and the other in $R_{HB}(m)$. Counter-detection strategies **HDc-HDm, HEc-HEm, RNDc-RNDm**, and hybrid measures, **RNDc-HBm, RNDDc-HDm, RNDc-HEm, HBc-RNDm, HDc-RNDm, HEc-RNDm** are similarly defined.

The effect of countermeasures on the anonymity of community membership is shown in figure 2. Each graph is averaged over 50 iterations. We note here that some of the graphs in figure 2 exhibit high kurtosis with the result that they appear to have abrupt rises and falls. While we could have removed those values to make the graphs smoother, without changing the conclusions we have drawn from our results, we have chosen to retain them in order to better understand the reason for high kurtosis.

7.2   Evaluating Counter-Detection Defense Measures

Let us first consider the case of the adversary with full topology knowledge and an unlimited surveillance budget, which will provide us with an upper bound in our results.

The first strategy we analyzed for hiding G_C was the naive RNDc-RNDm strategy: edge addition with random end points selected from either G_C or G_M. Figure 2 shows the privacy gains brought by this strategy, indicated by the blue line with an 'x' motif. This curve shows the resilience of the modularity detection algorithm to the presence of random errors – a linear increase in random error leads to a linear increase of injected faults. Therefore it makes for a poor defense strategy and is the worst performer among the strategies we considered; the addition of a 1000 random edges (50% of hidden community edge budget) results in a miss-ratio of only 20%.

Having learnt that the naive strategy is of little use in hiding the hidden community in a real world network, we proceeded to apply the next set of techniques, namely the purely centrality based strategies. The betweenness centrality strategy HBc-HBm (black line with circle motif) and HDc-HDm (red line with triangle motif) are average performers, with a peak miss-ratio of 50%, for additional edges of 10% of the hidden community. In addition, HDc-HDm also requires relatively larger amount of resources before delivering a miss-ratio above 30%.

Finally we look at the four hybrid strategies of edge addition, combining random node selection in one community with strategic selection in the other. Of the three strategies involving strategic selection in the main partition (requiring knowledge of popular nodes), RNDc-HBm (blue line with a diamond) and RNDc-HDm (pink line and triangle motif) perform equally well, with 78% of the hidden

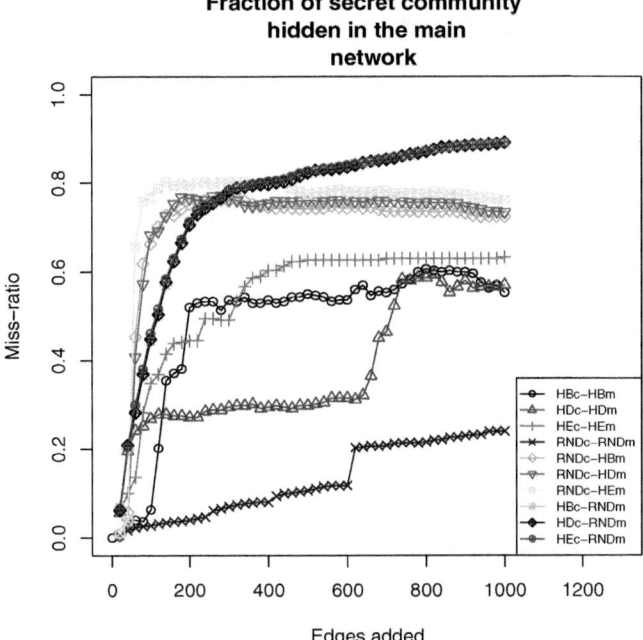

Fig. 2. Anonymity of hidden community under modularity based community detection

community nodes hidden from detection with only an additional edge budget of 1% of the hidden community.

The final three hybrid strategies involve local topology knowledge: HBc-RNDm indicated by the '*' motif and HDc-RNDm indicated by solid diamond. They work almost as well as the previous hybrid strategies on this network, however they require almost twice as many edges to offer the same level of protection. Even more interestingly, these strategies offer a high anonymity with 93% of the hidden community being wrongly classified as being part of the larger community. This indicates that strategies with local knowledge can be as efficient at countering community detection as strategies dependent on global topology information which bodes well for increased privacy.

Our counter-detection defense measures show that, if the defenders have full topology knowledge, then at a cost of 3 additional communication links per hidden community node, the modularity of the graph can be rewired leading to increasing the miss-ratio up to 90%, in the adversary's membership calculations. In both cases, of partial and full topology knowledge, the defenders can drive up the miss-ratio to 80%, with a investment of only 0.01 edges per hidden community node or approximately 1% of existing hidden community edge resources.

Figure 3 shows the efficiency of surveillance when counter-detection tactics are deployed by hidden communities. Strikingly, while people and relations are discovered rapidly, the percentage of community membership information available to the attacker remains limited to 12% in the best performing counter-detection

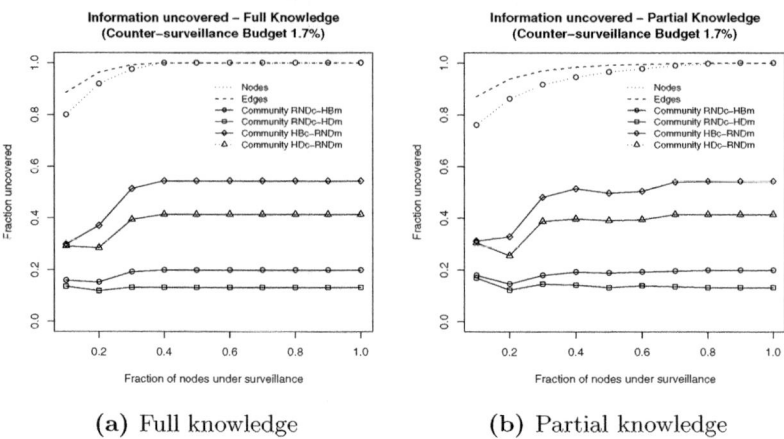

(a) Full knowledge   (b) Partial knowledge

Fig. 3. Effects of counter-detection measures on adversarial community detection

tactic. The RNDc-HDm strategy, where random members in the hidden community connect with hub nodes in the larger community, is attractive as a counter strategy in several ways. First, hub nodes with high degrees of connectivity are well known; and second, since hidden community members bearing responsibility for implementing the strategy do so in a decentralized manner and are easily replaceable if removed [26].

Further, we observe that the use of current anonymous communications technology by the hidden community does not change their privacy gains against community detection. As such, mere unlinkability falls short of the required level of security, and full unobservability is required to prevent the adversary's success. Since current anonymous communication networks do not provide unobservability, the best defenses lie in modifications at the fundamental level of network topology.

It is worth noting that as the size of the network increases, modularity based community detection can meet with a lower degree of success [14]. This is because as the network grows, it reaches a point where the expected number of edges between communities drops below 1. Past this point, modularity based detection does not give good results. Therefore while the small network of thousand or so nodes worked out well in our study, the results (of counter-surveillance) may not directly apply to larger social networks.

Why do these countermeasures work? So far, we have avoided all discussion of how the countermeasures work from a theoretical viewpoint. We now address this aspect. Going back to the definition of modularity in Eqn. 1, we can see that community boundaries are delineated on the basis of where there are fewer edges than expected. Edges between high centrality nodes are expected with a lower probability than those between nodes with lower centrality scores. When the number of edges connecting high-centrality nodes (or even random nodes) with other high-centrality nodes increases the number of actual edges becomes closer to the "expected" number of edges as per eqn. 1. This is the theory behind the successful countermeasures we have considered.

It is interesting to note that, in Fig. 2, community detection sometimes drops before increasing again. It appears that additional topology knowledge can sometimes be detrimental to community detection. We see similar non-linear behavior in Fig. 3, where extra defense edges can sometimes cause a decrease in community anonymity. We have no explanation for this phenomena.

8   Related Work

Past work by Danezis and Wittneben [9] highlighted the privacy compromising network externalities involved in computer insecurity when police execute wiretapping warrants. Their work considered the risk of privacy invasion due to indirect surveillance concluding that the privacy of a large fraction of users would be compromised once unlinkability was broken.

We take a markedly different approach by extending the definition of user privacy to include information about community memberships in a social network. We show the close link between the use of anonymous communications and its impact on the success of a community detecting adversary. Additionally, we also consider countermeasures and empirically demonstrate their effectiveness in enhancing user privacy.

9   Discussion and Conclusions

We have presented a model of surveillance and privacy preservation based on the detection of community structure in social networks. We have studied the network externalities of privacy compromise from a new angle, the detection of community structure and membership. In this paper, we have analyzed the interplay between detection and counter-detection strategies. We have some concrete results to present. We have shown that while structural elements of a network such as nodes and edges are easily discovered when small fractions of the network are placed under surveillance, discovering community structure information requires the adversary to invest in a significantly higher surveillance budget.

We have also shown that, regardless of whether network members communicate through an anonymous communications channel, placing 8% of the network under selective surveillance based on traffic volume is enough to compromise the community membership information of at least 45% of the nodes in the network. Our results also show that where the adversary is interested in understanding the community membership information of a far higher fraction of the nodes, the use of anonymous communication networks can increase the adversary's cost by almost 100% (80% of nodes under surveillance to uncover 99% community membership information).

Further, we have analyzed the dynamics of community hiding. First, we have shown that naive strategies of edge addition between randomly selected pairs of nodes from either partition have limited community hiding capability.

Hybrid strategies involving a combination of random and high centrality endpoints work best – edges are added between randomly chosen community nodes and a high centrality nodes in the main network allowing thus requiring only local knowledge on the part of the hidden community. Specifically, up 80% of the hidden community went undetected with a counter-detection budget of only 1% of total hidden community network edge resources. A variant strategy that associates high centrality hidden community nodes to randomly chosen nodes in the main delivers a more striking result: Up to 93% of the hidden community remained hidden with 10% additional edge resources (too expensive) while 80% could be hidden with a mere 2% additional edges (reasonable).

Our results show that membership de-anonymization attacks based on exploiting partial link knowledge as well as full link knowledge can be successfully repelled if the hidden community carries out selective topological rewiring. Counter-detection mechanisms merely require local knowledge and can bring clear privacy gains even when faced by an adversary with global knowledge.

Acknowledgements

The paper greatly benefited from discussions with Prateek Mittal and encouragement from George Danezis. The author would like to thank Aaron Johnson for agreeing to shepherd the paper. The author also expresses his thanks for feedback from Himanshu Khurana and the detailed comments from anonymous reviewers.

References

1. Abello, J., Resende, M.G., Sudarsky, S.: Massive quasi-clique detection. In: Rajsbaum, S. (ed.) LATIN 2002. LNCS, vol. 2286, p. 598. Springer, Heidelberg (2002)
2. Becchetti, L., Boldi, P., Castillo, C., Gionis, A.: Efficient semi-streaming algorithms for local triangle counting in massive graphs. In: KDD (2008)
3. Bonacich, P.: Power and centrality: A family of measures. The American Journal of Sociology 92(5), 1170–1182 (1987)
4. Brandes, U.: A faster algorithm for betweenness centrality. Journal of Mathematical Sociology 25(2), 163–177 (2001)
5. Chakrabarti, D., Papadimitriou, S., Modha, D., Faloutsos, C.: Fully automatic cross-associations. In: KDD (2004)
6. Chang, J., Blei, D.M.: Hierarchical relational models for document networks (2009)
7. Clauset, A., Newman, M.E.J., Moore, C.: Finding community structure in very large networks (August 2004)
8. Danezis, G., Dingledine, R., Mathewson, N.: Mixminion: Design of a type iii anonymous remailer protocol. In: IEEE Symposium on Security and Privacy, pp. 2–15 (2003)
9. Danezis, G., Wittneben, B.: The economics of mass surveillance and the questionable value of anonymous communications. In: Anderson, R. (ed.) Proceedings of the Fifth Workshop on the Economics of Information Security (WEIS 2006), Cambridge, UK (June 2006)

10. Dingledine, R., Mathewson, N., Syverson, P.: Tor: The second-generation onion router. In: Proceedings of the 13th USENIX Security Symposium (August 2004)
11. Dumais, S., Platt, J., Heckerman, D., Sahami, M.: Inductive learning algorithms and representations for text categorization. In: CIKM 1998: Proceedings of the seventh international conference on Information and knowledge management, pp. 148–155. ACM, New York (1998)
12. Elsner, U.: Graph partitioning - a survey. MONARCH - Dokumenten- und Publikationsservice (2005),
    http://archiv.tu-chemnitz.de/cgi-bin/interfaces/oai/oai2.pl (German)
13. Fortunato, S., Latora, V., Marchiori, M.: Method to find community structures based on information centrality. Physical Review E 70(5) (2004)
14. Fortunato, S.: Community detection in graphs. arxiv eprint 0906.0612 (January 2010), http://arxiv.org/abs/0906.0612
15. Freeman, L.C.: Centrality in social networks: Conceptual clarification. Social Networks 1, 215–239 (1978)
16. Gibson, D., Kumar, R., Tomkins, A.: Discovering large dense subgraphs in massive graphs. In: VLDB (2005)
17. Gionis, A., Mannila, H., Seppänen, J.K.: Geometric and combinatorial tiles in 0–1 data. In: Boulicaut, J.-F., Esposito, F., Giannotti, F., Pedreschi, D. (eds.) PKDD 2004. LNCS (LNAI), vol. 3202, pp. 173–184. Springer, Heidelberg (2004)
18. Gu, G., Perdisci, R., Zhang, J., Lee, W.: BotMiner: Clustering analysis of network traffic for protocol- and structure-independent botnet detection. In: Proceedings of the 17th USENIX Security Symposium, Security 2008 (2008)
19. Guimerà, R., Danon, L., Díaz-Guilera, A., Giralt, F., Arenas, A.: Self-similar community structure in a network of human interactions. Phys. Rev. E 68(6), 065103 (2003)
20. Kannan, R., Vempala, S., Vetta, A.: On clusterings: Good, bad and spectral. J. ACM 51(3), 497–515 (2004)
21. Kernighan, B.W., Lin, S.: An efficient heuristic procedure for partitioning graphs. Bell Systems Technology J. 49(2), 292–370 (1970)
22. Kumar, R., Raghavan, P., Rajagopalan, S., Tomkins, A.: Trawling the web for emerging cyber-communities. In: WWW (1999)
23. Latora, V., Marchiori, M.: Economic small-world behavior in weighted networks. The European Physical Journal B - Condensed Matter 32(2) (2002)
24. Leskovec, J., Lang, K.J., Dasgupta, A., Mahoney, M.W.: Statistical properties of community structure in large social and information networks. In: WWW (2008)
25. McCallum, A.K.: Mallet: A machine learning for language toolkit (2002), http://mallet.cs.umass.edu
26. Nagaraja, S., Anderson, R.: The topology of covert conflict. In: Moore, T. (ed.) Pre-Proceedings of The Fifth Workshop on the Economics of Information Security (June 2006)
27. Nagaraja, S., Anderson, R.: The snooping dragon: social-malware surveillance of the tibetan movement. Technical Report UCAM-CL-TR-746, University of Cambridge (March 2009)
28. Newman, M.: Modularity and community structure in networks. PNAS 103(23), 8577–8582 (2006)
29. Newman, M., Girvan, M.: Finding and evaluating community structure in networks. Physical Review E (Statistical, Nonlinear, and Soft Matter Physics) 69(2) (2004)

30. Ostrovsky, R., Yung, M.: How to withstand mobile virus attacks (extended abstract). In: PODC 1991: Proceedings of the tenth annual ACM symposium on Principles of distributed computing, pp. 51–59. ACM, New York (1991)
31. Pei, J., Jiang, D., Zhang, A.: On mining cross-graph quasi-cliques. In: ACM KDD Conference (2005)
32. Pfitzmann, A., Hansen, M.: Anonymity, unobservability, and pseudonymity: A consolidated proposal for terminology. Draft (July 2000)
33. Reed, M.G., Syverson, P.F., Goldschlag, D.M.: Anonymous connections and onion routing. IEEE Journal on Selected Areas in Communications 16(4) (1998)
34. Reiter, M.K., Rubin, A.D.: Crowds: anonymity for web transactions. ACM Trans. Inf. Syst. Secur. 1(1), 66–92 (1998)
35. Satulouri, V., Parthasarathy, S.: Scalable graph clustering using stochastic flows: Applications to community discovery. In: KDD Conference (2009)
36. Tang, W., Liu, H.: Graph mining applications to social network analysis. In: Aggarwal, C., Wang, H. (eds.) Managing and Mining Graph Data (2010)
37. Yu, H., Kaminsky, M., Gibbons, P., Flaxman, A.: Sybilguard: Defending against sybil attacks via social networks. In: SIGCOMM (2006)
38. Zeng, Z., Wang, J., Zhou, L., Karypis, G.: Out-of-core coherent closed quasi-clique mining from large dense graph databases. ACM Transactions on Database Systems 31(2) (2007)
39. Zhao, Y., Karypis, G., Fayyad, U.: Hierarchical clustering algorithms for document datasets. Data Min. Knowl. Discov. 10(2), 141–168 (2005)

How to Share Your Favourite Search Results while Preserving Privacy and Quality

George Danezis[1], Tuomas Aura[2], Shuo Chen[1], and Emre Kıcıman[1]

[1] Microsoft Research,
One Microsoft Way, Redmond, WA 98052-6399, U.S.
{gdane,shuochen,emrek}@microsoft.com
[2] Helsinki University of Technology,
P.O. Box 5400, FI-02015 TKK, Finland
tuomas.aura@tkk.fi

Abstract. Personalised social search is a promising avenue to increase the relevance of search engine results by making use of recommendations made by friends in a social network. More generally a whole class of systems take user preferences, aggregate and process them, before providing a view of the result to others in a social network. Yet, those systems present privacy risks, and could be used by spammers to propagate their malicious preferences. We present a general framework to preserve privacy while maximizing the benefit of sharing information in a social network, as well as a concrete proposal making use of cohesive social group concepts from social network analysis. We show that privacy can be guaranteed in a k-anonymity manner, and disruption through spam is kept to a minimum in a real world social network.

1   Introduction

A fundamental problem contemporary web-based information retrieval (IR) face is *ranking*. Given a user query, the IR system has to produce a ranked subset of documents that are most likely to satisfy the user's information needs. To achieve this, techniques beyond simple indexing are required and there are benefits in taking into account social structure when searching for information [15]. Recent research [20] suggests that users' information needs are correlated: it is likely that a document that has been accessed by Alice will also be relevant to her friend or colleague Bob. If only Alice and Bob were able to make use of this information, their search results could be improved.

Two key security problems have to be addressed to enable the sharing of *preferences* about search results and documents in a social network, namely *privacy* and *quality*.

Privacy is necessary to ensure that users do not learn about each others' exact search patterns or retrieved documents. It is unacceptable to allow particular query items or documents to be linked with certainty to a user by third parties. In this work we consider privacy guarantees against both adversarial sybil nodes that infiltrate the network, as well as curious coalitions of the users' friends.

M.J. Atallah and N. Hopper (Eds.): PETS 2010, LNCS 6205, pp. 273–290, 2010.

Quality in the context of security means that the ranking system should not be overly influenced by nodes that maliciously inject information to manipulate the ranking of certain resources. Search engine spamming is a serious problem, and any sharing of information has the potential to provide the spammers with an additional tool. The key goal of our scheme is to limit the influence of spammers to mostly those nodes that consider them as 'friends' and limit any further spread of their poisoned preferences.

Our approach to solving this problem involves propagating the user's useful search results—more generally we call this the user's *preferences*—within a random subgroup of the user's social network. We create those subgroups carefully to ensure they are *cohesive*, i.e., with very high density of links between all nodes. The subgroups form a core anonymity set, and are infiltration resistant to prevent spammers from being able to send their preferences to everyone. We present a general model that can be instantiated in many ways depending on the choice of cohesive subgroup – our concrete solution uses the *k-plex* definition [24].

We note that the problem of anonymously propagating information with a social network is far from unique. Similar systems are required for viral marketing, where products are recommended to users according to whether someone socially related to them bought them. Restaurant or movie recommendations are another example of systems that benefit from users socially sharing their preferences, without leaking specifics about what they see or where they are. Generally our solution applies to any system that (a) collects user preferences, (b) aggregates them centrally or locally on a social graph, (c) does some processing operation on the aggregate, (d) and returns the result, or influences the output to users. We will use the concrete example of personalised social search throughout this work, while engineering our solution to be general to the full class of problems.

After reviewing the literature on personalised social search in Section 2, we define an abstract model of our problem and the families of solutions we consider in Section 3. Then in Section 4 we propose a concrete strategy for sharing information in personalised search using cohesive social sub-groups and study the extent to which it satisfies our goals. In the final section we discuss some nuances of such system and offer conclusions.

2   Related Work

Personalized search, that tailors web search results based on preferences of users, is already widely deployed by major search engines [27,30]. Personalized social search goes a step further and determines the ranking of documents based on the preferences within the social network of users. It is already piloted by smaller online search engines, like Eurekster [29]. Google is currently piloting a mechanism that allows users to re-rank results [16]. The re-rankings are not directly shared but used centrally to increase the quality of the overall results. The Microsoft Research U Rank prototype [18] allows users to re-rank their results, and share them with their direct friends, without any further provision for privacy.

Many studies have looked into the privacy preferences of users, in relation to information they share over social networks [21,1]. They conclude that search preferences are considered sensitive, and the controversy surrounding AOL search data leak confirms this[1].

Eurekster [29] allows users to designate search mates, with whom they share their search preferences. Effectively any query and subsequent information is shared within this group of friends. Some primitive privacy features are provided through the ability to perform private searches, as well as the ability to delete past searches from being visible to others. Our approach, on the other hand, allows users to share, to some degree, their preferred search results, without compromising their privacy. Additional privacy controls, based on opt-outs like in Eurekster, are orthogonal to our scheme and can be applied independently.

Social networking site, like Facebook,[2] have also tried to share user preferences amongst friends, but for the purposes of viral marketing. The "Facebook Beacon" system caused controversy by sharing user's preferences, often generated outside of the Facebook site, with their network of friends. The initial privacy strategy of an opt-out mechanism was turned into an opt-in mechanism after some pressure [10].

We use the naive sharing strategy of simply broadcasting preferences to the sets of friends or friends-of-friends of a node as a benchmark to assess the security benefits of our proposal. Without better privacy and quality preserving techniques, this naive scheme is the one most likely to be deployed, as has been the case in Facebook Beacon and Eurekster.

A serious body of scientific work is concerned with preserving privacy in online services. Our schemes borrow privacy notions like k-anonymity from the literature on data sanitation and anonymization [23,2]. The basic premise of those schemes is that any inference drawn by an observer should be attributable to at least k participants, effectively forming an anonymity set. To our knowledge, this is the first time that k-anonymity is used in the context of data mining on social networks.

The adversary model we consider—an attacker is assumed to control a very large number of nodes in the network—was first introduced in the context of peer-to-peer systems by Douceur as the Sybil attack [13]. Our approach is centralised, and admission control [3] as well as intrusion detection methods could be used to keep the number of corrupt nodes down. Despite this, we aim to resist attacks without such measures, keeping the cost of running the system down and relying on distributed trust decisions for security. These two approaches are complementary and can be combined.

Our security assumptions to combat sybil attacks aiming to degrade privacy and quality are based on the tradition of SybilGuard [33], SybilLimit [32] and SybilInfer [7]. They assume that honest nodes form a connected social graph, and only few misguided nodes introduce an unbounded number of adversary

---

[1] CNN money included AOL releasing search data as #57 of its "101 Dumbest Moments in Business" for the year 2007.

[2] http://facebook.com

nodes. This small number of nodes or links to bad nodes can be used as a 'choke point' to limit the impact of the adversary on the running of the system. The idea of using the social structure itself to fend systems against those attacks was first proposed in [6] and [19].

For privacy we also consider a more traditional threat model, in which a coalition of a user's friends is curious to find out her preferences. The assumption of a limited fraction of dishonest or misguided nodes in a set goes back to work on secret sharing [26], threshold cryptography [28] and double entry book keeping in banking [22].

3   Model of Anonymity in Preference Sharing

Preference sharing has often been implemented with little regard to privacy. In this section we cast the problem of sharing preferences privately against an adversary (sections 3.1 and 3.2). We discuss how to correctly measure anonymity (section 3.3), as well as a generic framework that achieves privacy and utility for preference sharing (section 3.4). Finally, we discuss how quality is preserved in our model (section 3.5).

3.1   Preference Sharing

The most basic concepts in our model are the universe of users U and the universe of preferences P. We say that a user $u \in U$ may *set a preference* $p \in P$. The system then *propagates* the preference from the *source* u to a set of users $T \subseteq U$, which is called the *target group*. We also say that the source user has an *initial preference* and the target users have *propagated preferences*.

We assume that users submit their preferences to a trusted centralised system, that is in charge of performing the search and ranking of results, as current search engines are. The target group for the propagated preferences is chosen by the system from *possible target groups* $\mathsf{Groups}(u, p) \subseteq \mathbf{P}(\mathbf{P}(U))$ (a set of sets of users). We also assume that each preference is set by only one user at a time, which simplifies the model greatly, as we will see, without loss of generality.

Note that the source user itself does not decide the possible target groups or the actual target group. The system chooses the target group based on a *propagation policy*, which is partly specified by the function Groups. The goal of this paper is to find a propagation policy that meets several sometimes conflicting criteria:

1. First, the policy should preserve privacy.
2. Second, the policy should take into account social relations between the users to increase the relevance of propagated policies to the target users.
3. Third, the policy should be easy to implement.

The selection of the target group may be deterministic or nondeterministic. With deterministic target selection, $|\mathsf{Groups}(u, p)| = 1$ for all u and p. With nondeterministic selection, there can be multiple possible target groups and the actual target group is chosen randomly from them. (For the time being, let's assume uniform random selection.) An interesting case is one where the target group is selected from multiple possibilities based on a pseudorandom function and a secret key. In that case, the selection process is similar to a random oracle: the target group T is chosen randomly from $\mathsf{Groups}(u, p)$ for each new u, p pair but, if the selection is repeated for the same parameters, the target group will not change.

3.2   Anonymity and the Adversary Model

After the preference setting and propagation, each user has a set of initial preferences, which remains secret to that user, and propagated preferences, which are considered public[3]. The adversary is a coalition of users that observe the propagated preferences and try to determine which user initially sets each preference. We base our analysis on a rather strong adversary that knows the function Groups and can observe all the propagated preferences. Real-world systems can of course make it difficult for the adversary to observe all preferences through access control, network security and cryptography.

The assumption that each preference is set by at most one user at a time, is explained by the following: we assume that the attacker can observe the target group for each instance of setting the preference, rather than observing only the end result of multiple users setting the preference. This is a kind of worst-case scenario, but also corresponds with the fact that users are unlikely to set their preferences at exactly the same time and each act of setting may affect the propagated preferences for other users.

After observing a preference p propagated to a target group T, the adversary can narrow down the identity of the source to the following set:

$$U_{\mathsf{anon}} = \{u' \in U \mid T \in \mathsf{Groups}(u', p)\} \tag{1}$$

This set is called the *anonymity group*. The adversary knows that one member of the anonymity group initially set the preference. The size of the anonymity group $|U_{\mathsf{anon}}|$ can be used as a measure of anonymity. This is similar to k-anonymity in computer-security literature [4]. Note that here U_{anon} and k depend on u and p. We say that a preference propagation policy *preserves k-anonymity* if $k \leq |U_{\mathsf{anon}}|$ for all u and p.

The relation between the members of the anonymity group must be *symmetric* in the sense that, for a given preference and target group, if u' is in the anonymity group when the real source is u, then u is in the anonymity group when the real source is u'. This is natural because an anonymity group arises from the fact that any one of them could be the real source.

The adversary defined above corresponds to an outsider who can require all users to reveal their propagated preferences but does not have access to anyone's initial preferences. This could, for example, be someone who demands that users show their current search results, which are influenced by propagated preferences.

---

[3] This is a modeling assumption, and real world systems may further limit their visibility.

We are also interested in an adversary that has, additionally, access to the initial preferences of some colluding users. These could, for example, be a set of friends who try to figure out the source of a preference propagated to them. For an adversary with the combined knowledge of a coalition of users U_{bad}, the anonymity set is reduced to $U_{\mathsf{anon}} \setminus U_{\mathsf{bad}}$. In practical situations, however, we expect the size of the coalition to be small, often just a single user. This is because the members of the coalition need to trust each other to tell the truth about their initial preferences, and because sybil attacks will be prevented by the user of social networks (see section 3.4).

From equation 1, we make the important observation that privacy does not depend on the random selection of the target group T. A deterministic algorithm could be just as anonymity-preserving, as long as it picks the same target group for several users. Randomized selection does not guarantee anonymity either: it needs to be carefully designed to produce anonymity sets of sufficient size. This is why we consider both deterministic and nondeterministic propagation algorithms.

Finally, we make a couple of further observations. First, the target groups cannot be selected independently for each source user because they need to coincide, or otherwise the anonymity sets will be small. This has implications to the extent that the target group selection can be distributed. Second, the possible target groups for each preference can be selected independently of other preferences. The parameter p is carried in the notation as a reminder of this fact. Third, if privacy is the only goal, we could just as well select the empty target group (no preference sharing) or the all-users group U (share with everyone). This is in fact the current practice of recommender systems (such as Amazon or Netflix). The reasons for selecting something in between, which will be discussed in section 3.4, are unrelated to privacy, but crucial for adding value to search while preventing spam.

3.3 Probabilistic Anonymity Model

Above, we have not considered the probability distribution between different choices of target groups. This lead to using k-anonymity as the measure of privacy: the anonymity group includes everyone who might be the source, no matter how unlikely it is. Now, we extend the model to take into account probabilities. Given a source u and a preference p, the probability distribution of target groups is denoted by $P(u, p, T)$. The function Groups can now be defined as

$$\mathsf{Groups}(u, p) = \{T \subseteq U \mid P(u, p, T) > 0\}$$

As established in the literature [25,11], anonymity in the probabilistic model is measured by entropy, i.e., the adversary's uncertainly about the identity of the source. Entropy is measured in bits, i.e., how many more bits of information would the adversary need to be certain of the source identity. We assume that all users are initially equally likely to be the source (equal a-prior probabilities), and that only one at a time sets the preference. When the adversary observes a preference p propagated to a target group T, the entropy for the source can be calculated as follows.

$$H(u|p, T) = \sum_{u \in U_{\text{anon}}} (\frac{P(u, p, T)}{S}) \cdot (-\log_2(\frac{P(u, p, T)}{S})) \text{ where } S = \sum_{u \in U_{\text{anon}}} P(u, p, T)$$

What can we learn from this? Obviously, the larger the anonymity set, the higher the entropy. Analogous to our earlier comparison of deterministic and nondeterministic propagation policies, we also note that it makes no difference how many different choices $|\text{Groups}(u, p)|$ there are for T. The most important lesson from the above formula is that, given a fixed-size anonymity set, the entropy is maximized when all members of the anonymity set are equally likely to choose the specific target group. It does not matter how or whether this probability is large or small, as long as it is uniform across the possible sources.

3.4   Preference Sharing in a Social Network

The privacy model above does not explain why we want to propagate the preferences in the first place. Our aim is to select a target group that is by some measure *close* to the source, so that the propagated preferences are relevant to the group. This will not only result in more effective use of the preference information but also in *spam resistance*. It is important to note, however, that there is no simple right way for defining closeness between users. Before considering possible definitions, we will consider some general factors in propagation policies that are based on the concept.

Since the preferences set by a user are naturally closest to its own needs, we only consider propagation policies that are *reflexive* in the sense that each user is in all of its own propagation targets:

$$T \in \text{Groups}(u, p) \text{ implies } u \in T. \tag{2}$$

In a reflexive propagation policy, the anonymity group is always a subset of the target group.

For a given target group T, we denote $U_{\text{ext}} = T \setminus U_{\text{anon}}$. Thus, the target group is the disjoint union of the anonymity group and an *extended group*: $T = U_{\text{anon}} \dot\cup U_{\text{ext}}$.

The discussion so far gives one possible outline for constructing propagation algorithms. The algorithm can be executed independently for each preference p, or the same groups can be used for many preferences:

1. Select anonymity groups in such a way that they cover all users U. Members of the anonymity set should be close to each other, based on some arbitrary social metric.
2. For each anonymity set, decide on the extended groups. The members of the extended groups should be close to the members of the anonymity set, but not necessarily to each other.

It makes sense to start by fixing the anonymity groups because that is an easy way to guarantee k-anonymity. If we instead expected anonymity to arise prob- abilistically, it would be difficult to guarantee that they all will be sufficiently large. The members of each anonymity group need to be all close to each other because any one of them could be the source. The members of the extended group, on the other hand, are targets and need to be close to potential sources.

A simpler model would be one where $U_{ext} = \emptyset$ and $T = T_{anon}$. In this restricted model, preferences are shared mutually among a sets of users who are close to each other, such as the members of a club or a clique of users who all know each other. An advantage of the more general model, especially when $|T| \ll |U_{anon}|$, is that the preferences can be propagated to a larger number of target users without any reduction in anonymity. In practical social networks, we are looking at anonymity sets of around ten users and target groups that are one order of magnitude larger (as studied is section 4.3).

We are particularly interested in social networks that are based on a *friendship graph* $G \subseteq U \times U$. The friendship relations in this kind of graph are typically symmetric, which means that any metric of closeness between members will be symmetric as well. In the above outline for propagation algorithms, the first step is to select anonymity sets in such a way that all their members are close to each other.

3.5   Spam Resistance

For the purposes of modeling spam resistance, we categorise nodes in the system as being in one of three categories: *honest nodes* genuinely share their preferences, and *dishonest nodes* try to propagate to honest nodes spam preferences. We consider that a class of honest nodes are *misguided* in that they have created friendship links with dishonest nodes.

We can use this intuition to build anonymity sets U_{anon} and broadcast groups U_{ext} that are *infiltration resistant*. This means that once a number of honest nodes are part of a group they are unlikely to form links with dishonest nodes, thus disallowing them from broadcasting their preferences within the group. Part of our security analysis is concerned with validating this property in a real-world social network.

4   Outline of Solution

We propose a concrete nondeterministic propagation strategy that is based on broadcasting users' preferences within socially cohesive subgroups. The sub- groups can be overlapping, and are formed by k-plexes of some s-minimal size. A k-plex is a sub-graph of size $g_s \geq s$ of the social network in which all nodes link to at least $g_s - k$ other nodes in the sub-graph. It is an established relaxation of cliques (which are a special case for $k = 1$) that defines robust and cohesive subgroups, extensively used in social network analysis [24].

The properties of s-minimal size k-plexes make them a very good fit for sup- porting our security and functional properties. The parameters k, defining how many links can be missing within a subgroup, as well as s, the minimal size of the subgroup, are naturally related to quality and privacy.

First, k-plexes of a minimum size s are *infiltration resistant*. For a single node of a coalition of c nodes to be part of a k-plex they need to form a large number of links l_c:

$$l_c = \max(s - k, [(s - k) - (c - 1)] \cdot c) \geq s - k \tag{3}$$

This has a direct security implication for quality since a small number of misguided nodes in a k-plex forming links with adversary nodes, will not allow those nodes to infiltrate the k-plex, containing other honest nodes. (Although misguided nodes can be conned into joining k-plexes dominated by corrupt nodes.) Therefore limiting broadcast of preferences within those sub-groups curbs the potential for abuse and spam – an adversary will have to invest a lot of effort to infiltrate them, and a few vigilant members of each group will be able to thwart such actions.

While a set of k-plexes form the anonymity groups U_{anon} each of them is augmented by a set of additional nodes i.e., the extended broadcast group U_{ext}. Membership of nodes to the extended broadcast group is parameterized by a threshold T on the number of friends a node has that belong to the anonymity group U_{anon}. If a node has T or more friends in U_{anon} then it belongs to the extended broadcast group U_{ext}.

4.1 The *Preference-Sharing* Algorithm

The preference sharing algorithm works in two phases. First a pre-computation extracts cohesive sub-groups that are used to form anonymity sets U_{anon}, and their corresponding extended broadcast groups U_{ext}. Only the structure of the social network is required to perform group extraction. In a second phase preferences are continuously set by users and are propagated to other users through the extracted groups. Only propagated preferences are collected to compute the ranking of resources for each user, and the initial preferences can even be forgotten.

The parameters of the *preference-sharing* algorithm are:

- k, the parameters of the k-plexes we use.
- s_a, the size of the anonymity set required.
- T, a threshold that defines the extended broadcast groups membership.

We require $s_a > 2k$ and $T > 1$ (in our analysis we use $k = 2$, $s_a = 8$ and $T = 2$). These conditions ensure that the diameter of the sub-groups extracted is at most 2 [31]. This in turn enforces strong locality and makes the extraction of the cohesive subgroups faster.

Sub-group extraction. First the anonymity sets are extracted. Given the social graph G a set of k-plexes of size s_a is extracted and associated with each user. These are the sets U_{anon} that form the core anonymity sets providing privacy for preference propagation. Second the extended broadcast groups for each

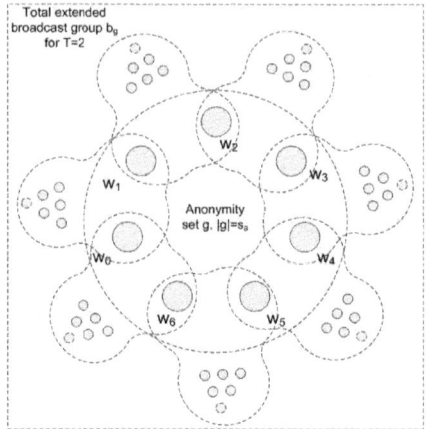

Fig. 1. An illustration the anonymity groups and the broadcast groups selected to propagate a single preference

anonymity set are extracted. For each cohesive subgroup U_{anon} we define a broadcast set U_{ext} containing all nodes that are friends with at least T members of the cohesive subgroup. This defines a 'wider circle' of people around each subgroup to which preferences will also be broadcast.

Sub-group extraction is not necessarily real-time and can be performed periodically depending on how often the social graph changes. The anonymity sets for each user contained in U_{anon} as well as their broadcast groups U_{ext} can be reused for propagating multiple preferences. Sub-group extraction does not need to be exhaustive either. In this work we chose to extract the set of k-plexes for each user that contain at least all neighbours of each node which share a k-plex with the user. This strategy ensures that all the friends that share a cohesive subgroup with a node could possibly be receiving the user's preferences.

Preference-propagation. At some point in time, a user u sets a preference for a p. Our system chooses at random a k-plex containing the user $g \in_R \{U_{\text{anon}}\}$ to act as the anonymity set for this preference. If there is no such k-plex no propagation of results takes place, and the algorithm ends. Otherwise, the preference of node u is broadcast to all nodes in $U_{\text{anon}} \cup U_{\text{ext}}$, i.e., the anonymity set and the extended broadcast group corresponding to the selected anonymity set U_{anon}.

Each node $v \in b_g$ aggregates all preferences broadcast in a multiset of preference P_{vi} relating to a resource i. Each broadcast updates the multiset with the received preference $P'_{vi} = \{f(i, u)\} \uplus P_{vi}$. A simple function can then be applied to this multi-set of preferences to determine the final preference of this each node relating to each resource $g(i, v)$.

4.2   Privacy Analysis

Our first task is to evaluate the privacy offered by the preference-sharing algorithm, against two types of adversaries. The first is a very powerful global adversary, that can see the preferences output by the preference sharing algorithm for every single node in the network. Yet this adversary is passive in that it does not know the private inputs to the algorithm and tries to infer them. The second threat we consider is a curious coalition of a user's friends, that wants to infer what her preferences are.

Global passive adversary. We assume that an eavesdropper can see all the propagated preferences. Through those they can extract the sub-group g (of size s_a) that formed the core of the anonymity set used to propagate a particular preference $f(i, u)$.

Any of the members of g *could* have been the originators of the preference. This already ensures some plausible deniability and privacy to the real originator. To be more specific one has to calculate the probability a user set a preference given that it was broadcast in sub-group g, that we will denote as $\Pr[u|g]$. By applying Bayes theorem we can express it in terms of known quantities:

$$\Pr[u|g] = \frac{\Pr[g \in_R G_u] \Pr[u]}{\sum_{w \in g} \Pr[g \in_R G_w] \Pr[w]} \tag{4}$$

$\Pr[g \in_R G_u]$ is the probability that a user u chooses group g and $\Pr[u]$ is the a-prior probability we assign to user u being the originator of a preference i. If we assume that the a-prior probability over all users is uniform, and that they all choose the sub-groups $g \in_R G_u$ uniformly out of the sets G_u we get:

$$\Pr[u|g] = \frac{1}{|G_u| \sum_{w \in g} \frac{1}{|G_w|}} \tag{5}$$

In case all users chose amongst a set of fixed size $|G_u| = c$, this expression simplifies, and the sought probability becomes: $\Pr[u|g] = 1/s_a$. This related nicely the parameter s_a of the algorithm with the privacy provided. The larger s_a the larger the anonymity provided, when measured information theoretically.

Yet there is likely to be an imbalance between the sizes of the sets G_u for different users. We try to establish what the worse case scenario is, assuming that we have some maximal size of $\max |G_u| = c_{max}$ as well as some minimal size $\min |G_u| = c_{min}$. In those cases we still have that:

$$\Pr[u|g] < \frac{c_{max}}{c_{min}(s_a - 1) + c_{max}} \tag{6}$$

This expression makes it possible to compute the probability a preference is associated with a user. A system can either try to keep it low by choosing carefully sub-groups to guarantee $c_{min} \leq |G_w| \leq c_{max}$, or simply not propagate preferences in case this probability is higher than a threshold.

The adversary model assumed is extremely conservative, assuming that most information in the system is available to pinpoint g. It is most likely that coalitions of dishonest nodes will receive much less information. In particular a single node in the system will not be able to distinguish which of the nodes in its set b_u was the originator of a preference.

Yet an important concern is the possibility that nodes in the anonymity set g are in fact corrupt. We assume this is very difficult since k-plexes are infiltration resistant. Sharing a k-plex of size s_a with s_a dishonest nodes, requires a misguided node to make $s_a - k + 1$ bad friends. In any case such an attack would only affect misguided nodes in the system, which we assume are in a minority.

Honest nodes (with mostly honest friends) will never find themselves in a k-plex dominated by dishonest nodes. Even a misguided node with fewer than $s_a - k + 1$ dishonest friends will never have their privacy totally compromised through infiltration.

Coalition of curious friends. The second key threat to the privacy to users are their very own friends. A collection of a user's friends may exchange information about their private preferences in an attempt to infer the preferences of a user.

First we note a very strong privacy property against such attacks. In any case coalitions of fewer than $s_a - 1$ users will fail to attribute a preference with certainty to a single user. This is a very strong result that sets a lower bound on the size of the conspiracy.

At least $s_a - 1$ nodes are necessary to fully de-anonymize a preference, but this condition is not sufficient to perform an actual attack. It is also necessary that the coalition of node coincides exactly with the members of the cohesive sub-group used as an anonymity set to broadcast the preference. This places additional restrictions and difficulties in creating such a malevolent coalition.

Through simulations we try to estimate the quality of anonymity remaining after such an attack. For those we use about 100000 user profiles downloaded through the `livejournal` public interfaces using snowball sampling. Only symmetric links were kept to form a social graph. We assume that a fraction f of all users collude to deanonymize users. These users are curious but make no special effort to place themselves in the social graph to maximise the information they receive (they are not as such sybil nodes – just curious friends.) Therefore we assume they are randomly distributed across the network.

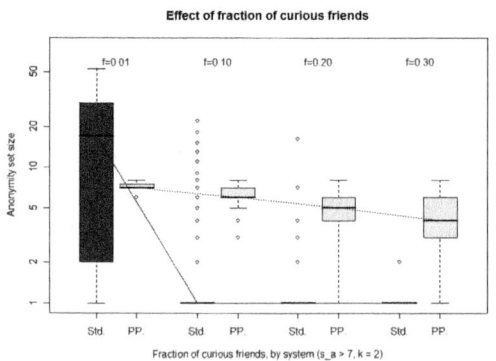

Fig. 2. The sizes of the anonymity sets remaining after a colluding coalition of friends tries to de-anonymize a preference. The fraction f represents the probability a friend is participating in the adversary coalition.

Figure 2 summarises the results of attack simulations on a real-world social network. The Preference Propagation (PP.) algorithm (yellow, right hand size columns) is compared with the naive strategy (Std.) of broadcasting preferences to all friends (red, left hand side columns.) When a very low number of nodes collude to infer a user's preference ($f = 1\%$) the naive scheme provides good anonymity, since on average a corrupt users cannot narrow down the originator of a preference beyond his full circle of friends. Yet as the fraction of curious nodes grows ($f = 10\%, 20\%, 30\%$) the anonymity sets for the standard strategy shrink to zero aside from some exceptional cases. On the other hand the anonymity sets of the Preference Propagation algorithm remain large with high probability. Their reduction is only due to the fraction of curious nodes actually being in the anonymity set of the propagated preference.

4.3   Quality Analysis

The second security objective of the proposed preference propagation algorithm is to limit the potential for the propagation of spam. Our objective is to limit the propagation of preferences from dishonest nodes mostly to the misguided nodes, but to make it difficult for such preferences to travel any further in the social graph.

The simple minded 1-hop propagation algorithm, in which users only broadcast their preferences to their neighbours, by definition achieves this property. Its down side is that the number of nodes that could benefit from the shared preference is limited to the number of friends. The simple extension of this scheme to a 2-hop broadcast extends the reach of the shared preferences but also makes it very likely that nodes are the recipients of some spam. Figure 3 (right) plots the number of nodes that are affected by users with different degrees in each mechanism. As expected the preference propagation algorithm affects a wider circle per node than the simple 1-hop propagation. At the same time the number of nodes included in a extended broadcast group is smaller than the reach of the 2-hop naive propagation.

Despite the order of magnitude increase in the nodes affected by the preference propagation algorithm compared with the 1-hop scheme, quality is to a large extent maintained, even for larger fractions of misguided nodes all connected to collaborating dishonest nodes. Figure 3 (left) illustrates the probability that a node receives spam for all systems, as the fraction of misguided nodes grows, in a real social network. In the 2-hop scheme receiving spam becomes quasi-certain even when a small minority of users are misguided ($f = 1\% - 10\%$). For the preference propagation scheme on the other hand the probability of receiving spam remains low even for large fractions of misguided nodes. It is in fact closely tracking the probability of being misguided for low rates of infiltration ($f = 1\% - 10\%$). For higher rates of infiltration ($f = 10\% - 30\%$) the probability non-misguided honest nodes receive spam increases slowly (marked at "PP. (Non Misg.)" on the illustration.)

There is a further fine, but important, difference between the proposed preference propagation algorithm and the traditional 1-hop or 2-hop schemes. In our approach the dishonest nodes, connected to the misguided honest nodes, must

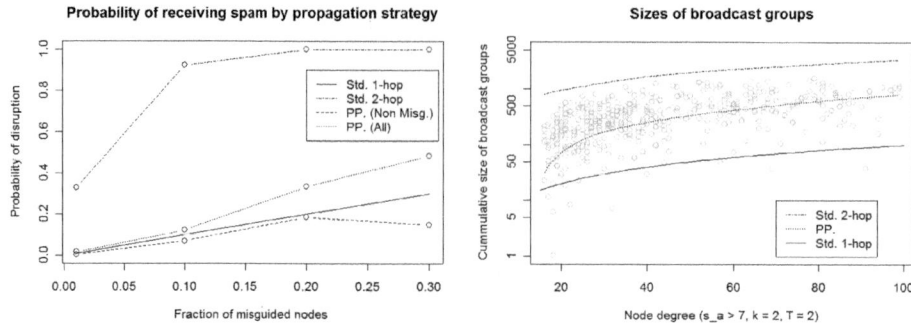

Fig. 3. The probability of honest nodes receiving malicious preferences, depending on the fraction of malicious nodes in the system (Left). The size of the naturally occurring broadcast groups as a function of node degree, compared with the 1-hop and 2-hop neighborhood (right).

all be acting in a coordinated way to spam the system. They need to form cohesive subgroups between themselves and the users to broadcast their preferences. In effect it means that *a single adversary* must be connected to a fraction f of the honest nodes, unless they start applying social engineering to target related nodes to form cohesive subgroups.

The standard 1-hop and 2-hop propagation on the other hand does not require adversaries to coordinate in any way to spam. This means that the total fraction of misguided nodes, connecting to even unrelated adversaries, needs to be f for the probability of attack illustrated in figure 3 (left) to hold. It is much more likely that the total number of misguided nodes reaches a fraction f, than the number of misguided nodes connected to a single adversary's nodes reaches the same fraction. Unless there is a conspiracy at a massive scale it is difficult to imagine a single adversary connecting sybils to more than 10% of honest nodes in a larger network, at which point purpose built sybil attack defenses based on social networks should be employed [7].

Even in the absence of other sybil defenses the proposed system offers excellent guarantees against spam, as 10% of misguided nodes would lead to barely more than 10% of nodes being spammed (Figure 3 (left)). At the same time our strategy affords honest preferences a wide reach, of an order of magnitude above simply propagating preferences to friends (Figure 3 (right)).

4.4   Future Work: Adversarial Profiling

As preferences are propagated in groups it might be possible for adversaries to modify established disclosure attacks [17,8] to try to de-anonymize or profile users. For example if a user keeps receiving preferences about rare comic books, or another relatively rare subject, from many anonymity sets they might assume a single user is the originator and try to intersect the anonymity sets to de-anonymize them. The general attack considers users on one side, each with some abstract interests, and propagated preferences on the other side. Every time a preference is propagated to a broadcast group, this is modeled as a communication though a mix with the same anonymity set. Then the statistical disclosure attacks can be applied to extract user profiles in the long term.

The effectiveness of this attack in this new context is not clear, as the adversary has to ascribe preferences to categories – a fuzzy step that was not previously necessary. Subgroups are also likely to be coherent in their preferences which creates dependencies in the anonymity sets not previously considered by disclosure attacks. Adapting those traffic analysis techniques to extract preference profiles could be a valuable contribution to the literature. Bayesian models of such attacks are likely to be the most amenable to this setting [9].

5   Conclusions

We presented a general framework for anonymously sharing information in a social network. Our framework guarantees some k-anonymity, maintains high value by allowing information to be shared based on social proximity, and increases the cost of spamming the network. Our approach, extracting special cohesive social structures to protect users, adds to a body of work that uses social network information for security, as SybilInfer does for sybil defenses [7], and other proposals for automatically extracting privacy policies in social networks [5]. In the absence of a top-down trust structure we believe that the hints the users provide as to who they know and trust are the only way to bootstrap such policies, even though they might not be as bullet proof as traditional mandatory access control systems. Notions of differential privacy [14] can also be used to show that a published statistic leaks no identifiable information, and the application of this framework to our problem would be an interesting avenue for future work.

The framework we provide can be extended through alternative definitions of broadcast groups, that may provide a different anonymity, quality and spam-resistance trade-offs. Some structures could make use of explicit user hints of groups and communities, or even try to route preferences to groups that would most benefit from those (i.e., preferences about technical searches staying within technical communities). A further open question remains: how can traditional long term traffic analysis attacks be adapted, from inferring patterns of communications, to inferring users profiles despite the anonymization?

Acknowledgments. Dogan Kesdogan was the first to relate to the authors the idea that anonymity and privacy really comes down to "anonymity set engineering", which this work contributes to.

References

1. Acquisti, A., Gross, R.: Imagined communities: Awareness, information sharing, and privacy on the facebook. In: Danezis, G., Golle, P. (eds.) PET 2006. LNCS, vol. 4258, pp. 36–58. Springer, Heidelberg (2006)

2. Byun, J.-W., Kamra, A., Bertino, E., Li, N.: Efficient k-anonymization using clustering techniques. In: Kotagiri, R., Radha Krishna, P., Mohania, M. K., Nantajeewarawat, E. (eds.) DASFAA 2007. LNCS, vol. 4443, pp. 188–200. Springer, Heidelberg (2007)

3. Castro, M., Druschel, P., Ganesh, A.J., Rowstron, A.I.T., Wallach, D.S.: Secure routing for structured peer-to-peer overlay networks. In: OSDI (2002)

4. Ciriani, V., De Capitani di Vimercati, S., Foresti, S., Samarati, P.: -Anonymity. In: Yu, T., Jajodia, S. (eds.) Secure Data Management in Decentralized Systems. Advances in Information Security, vol. 33, pp. 323–353. Springer, Heidelberg (2007)

5. Danezis, G.: Inferring privacy policies for social networking services. In: Balfanz, D., Staddon, J. (eds.) AISec, pp. 5–10. ACM, New York (2009)

6. Danezis, G., Lesniewski-Laas, C., Frans Kaashoek, M., Anderson, R.J.: Sybilresistant dht routing. In: De Capitani di Vimercati, S., Syverson, P.F., Gollmann, D. (eds.) ESORICS 2005. LNCS, vol. 3679, pp. 305–318. Springer, Heidelberg (2005)

7. Danezis, G., Mittal, P.: Sybilinfer: Detecting sybil nodes using social networks. In: NDSS. The Internet Society (2009)

8. Danezis, G., Serjantov, A.: Statistical disclosure or intersection attacks on anonymity systems. In: Fridrich, J. J. (ed.) IH 2004. LNCS, vol. 3200, pp. 293–308. Springer, Heidelberg (2004)

9. Danezis, G., Troncoso, C.: Vida: How to use bayesian inference to de-anonymize persistent communications. In: Goldberg, I., Atallah, M.J. (eds.) Privacy Enhancing Technologies. LNCS, vol. 5672, pp. 56–72. Springer, Heidelberg (2009)

10. Davis, W.: Facebook hit with privacy complaint. The Online Media Post, June 2 (2008)

11. Díaz, C., Seys, S., Claessens, J., Preneel, B.: Towards measuring anonymity. In: Dingledine, Syverson (eds.) [12], pp. 54–68

12. Dingledine, R., Syverson, P.F. (eds.): PET 2002. LNCS, vol. 2482. Springer, Heidelberg (2003)

13. Douceur, J.R.: The sybil attack. In: Druschel, P., Frans Kaashoek, M., Rowstron, A.I.T. (eds.) IPTPS 2002. LNCS, vol. 2429, pp. 251–260. Springer, Heidelberg (2002)

14. Dwork, C.: Differential privacy: A survey of results. In: Agrawal, M., Du, D.-Z., Duan, Z., Li, A. (eds.) TAMC 2008. LNCS, vol. 4978, pp. 1–19. Springer, Heidelberg (2008)

15. Evans, B.M., Chi, E.H.: Towards a model of understanding social search. In: CSCW 2008: Proceedings of the 2008 ACM conference on Computer supported cooperative work, pp. 485–494. ACM, New York (2008)

16. Horling, B., Kulick, M.: Personalized search for everyone. The Official Google Blog, December 4 (2009)

17. Kesdogan, D., Agrawal, D., Pham, D.V., Rautenbach, D.: Fundamental limits on the anonymity provided by the mix technique. In: IEEE Symposium on Security and Privacy, pp. 86–99. IEEE Computer Society, Los Alamitos (2006)

18. Kiciman, E., Wang, C.-K., Chen, S., Mertsalov, K.: U rank (2008) Project webpage, http://research.microsoft.com/en-us/projects/urank/

19. Levien, R.: Attack resistant trust metrics (2003) Draft Available at, http://www.levien.com/thesis/compact.pdf

20. Mislove, A., Gummadi, K.P., Druschel, P.: Exploiting social networks for internet search. In: Proceedings of the 5th ACM Workshop on Hot Topics in Networks (HotNets), Irvine, CA, November 2006, ACM, New York (2006)

21. Olson, J.S., Grudin, J., Horvitz, E.: A study of preferences for sharing and privacy. In: van der Veer, G.C., Gale, C. (eds.) CHI Extended Abstracts, pp. 1985–1988. ACM, New York (2005)
22. Pacioli, L.: Summa de arithmetica, geometrica, proportioni et proportionalita. Manuscript circulated in Venice (1494)
23. Samarati, P., Sweeney, L.: Generalizing data to provide anonymity when disclosing information (abstract). In: PODS, p. 188. ACM Press, New York (1998)
24. Scott, J.: Social network analysis. Sociology 22(1), 109 (1988)
25. Serjantov, A., Danezis, G.: Towards an information theoretic metric for anonymity. In: Dingledine, Syverson (eds.) [12], pp. 41–53
26. Shamir, A.: How to share a secret. Commun. ACM 22(11), 612–613 (1979)
27. Sherman, C.: Yahoo bolsters personal search. Search Engine Watch Blog, April 26 (2005)
28. Shoup, V., Gennaro, R.: Securing threshold cryptosystems against chosen ciphertext attack. J. Cryptology 15(2), 75–96 (2002)
29. Sullivan, D.: Eurekster launches personalized social search. Search Engine Watch Blog, January 21 (2004)
30. Sullivan, D.: Google relaunches personal search - this time, it really is personal. Search Engine Watch Blog, June 28 (2005)
31. Wasserman, S., Faust, K.: Social network analysis: Methods and applications. Cambridge Univ. Pr., Cambridge (1994)
32. Yu, H., Gibbons, P.B., Kaminsky, M., Xiao, F.: Sybillimit: A near-optimal social network defense against sybil attacks. In: IEEE Symposium on Security and Privacy, pp. 3–17. IEEE Computer Society, Los Alamitos (2008)
33. Yu, H., Kaminsky, M., Gibbons, P.B., Flaxman, A.: Sybilguard: defending against sybil attacks via social networks. In: Rizzo, L., Anderson, T.E., McKeown, N. (eds.) SIGCOMM, pp. 267–278. ACM, New York (2006)

A   Measuring k-Plexes in the Wild

The privacy offered by our scheme against passive adversaries as well as dishonest nodes is closely related to the minimal size of the cohesive subgroups defining our anonymity sets, namely s_a. This parameter is not up to the designer of the system to tune, and is heavily dependant on the natural sizes of cohesive subgroups appearing within real-world social networks. Choosing s_a to be too large means that few nodes can broadcast their preferences, but choosing it to be too small results in lower degrees of anonymity for preferences.

To better understand the range of possible subgroup sizes s_a we measure the number of nodes reachable through a k-plex with parameters $k = 2$, $s_a > 4$ and $s_a > 7$. We use the Live Journal (LJ) data set[4], where edges represent the mutual consent of two LJ users to read each others' private journal entries. Figure 4 illustrates the number of users reachable for these two parameters. It is clear that the number of nodes sharing cohesive subgroups with a user grows roughly linearly with the degree of the node. As expected the a higher s_a leads to fewer nodes being in cohesive subgroups of that size. We use $s_a > 7$ throughout all our experiments, since it seems to offer a good trade-off between privacy and reachability.

The natural emergence of social structures that are large and cohesive could be of great importance for other security designs. Traditional threshold cryptosystems, or secret sharing schemes, assume that their processes are distributed across a number of participants out of whom some are honest. Yet there has been little research in measuring the natural sizes of subgroups in a social network over which such functions could be distributed. Our work is the first to inform the debate with such figures.

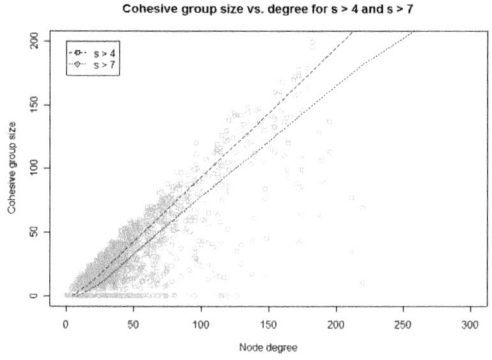

Fig. 4. Reach of cohesive groups per node degree and s_a value

---

[4] http://www.livejournal.com/

Erratum to: Privacy Enhancing Technologies

Mikhail J. Atallah[1] and Nicholas J. Hopper[2]

[1] Purdue University, Department of Computer Science,
West Lafayette, IN 47907-2107, USA
mja@cs.purdue.edu
[2] University of Minnesota, Department of Computer Science & Engineering,
Minneapolis, MN 55455, USA
hopper@cs.umn.edu

Erratum to:
M.J. Atallah and N. Hopper (Eds.)
Privacy Enhancing Technologies
DOI: 10.1007/978-3-642-14527-8

The book was inadvertently published with an incorrect name of the copyright holder. The name of the copyright holder for this book is: © Springer-Verlag Berlin Heidelberg. The book has been updated with the changes.

The updated original online version for this book can be found at
DOI: 10.1007/978-3-642-14527-8

M.J. Atallah and N. Hopper (Eds.): PETS 2010, LNCS 6205, p. E1, 2010.

Author Index

GPSR Compliance

*The European Union's (EU) General Product Safety Regulation (GPSR)
is a set of rules that requires consumer products to be safe and our
obligations to ensure this.*

*If you have any concerns about our products, you can contact us on
ProductSafety@springernature.com*

In case Publisher is established outside the EU, the EU authorized
representative is:

Springer Nature Customer Service Center GmbH
Europaplatz 3
69115 Heidelberg, Germany

Batch number: 09490872

Printed by Printforce, the Netherlands